Speaking Clearly

Speaking Clearly:
Improving Voice and Diction

Sixth Edition

Jeffrey C. Hahner
Pace University

Martin A. Sokoloff
Pace University

Sandra L. Salisch
Pace University

Boston   Burr Ridge, IL   Dubuque, IA   Madison, WI   New York   San Francisco   St. Louis
Bangkok   Bogotá   Caracas   Kuala Lumpur   Lisbon   London   Madrid   Mexico City
Milan   Montreal   New Delhi   Santiago   Seoul   Singapore   Sydney   Taipei   Toronto

McGraw-Hill

A Division of The **McGraw·Hill** Companies

SPEAKING CLEARLY: IMPROVING VOICE AND DICTION
Published by McGraw-Hill, an imprint of The McGraw-Hill Companies, Inc. 1221 Avenue of the
Americas, New York, NY, 10020. Copyright © 2002, 1997, 1993, 1990, 1983, by The McGraw-Hill
Companies, Inc. All rights reserved. No part of this publication may be reproduced or distributed
in any form or by any means, or stored in a data base or retrieval system, without the prior
written consent of The McGraw-Hill Companies, Inc., including, but not limited to, in any
network or other electronic storage or transmission, or broadcast for distance learning.
Some ancillaries, including electronic and print components, may not be available to customers
outside the United States.

This book is printed on acid-free paper.

6 7 8 9 0 DOC/DOC 0 9 8 7 6

ISBN-13: 978-0-07-239726-0
ISBN-10: 0-07-239726-8

Editorial director: *Phillip A. Butcher*
Senior sponsoring editor: *Nanette Kauffman*
Developmental editor II: *Jennie Katsaros*
Marketing manager: *Kelly M. May*
Associate project manager: *Destiny Rynne*
Production associate: *Gina Hangos*
Coordinator of freelance design: *Mary Kazak*
Cover design: *Sarah Studnicki*
Senior supplement coordinator: *Rose M. Range*
Media producer: *Lance Gerhart*
Compositor: *Carlisle Communications, Ltd.*
Typeface: *10/12 Bookman Light*
Printer: *R. R. Donnelley & Sons Company*

Library of Congress Cataloging-in-Publication Data
Hahner, Jeffrey C.
    Speaking clearly : improving voice and diction / Jeffrey C. Hahner, Martin A. Sokoloff,
  Sandra L. Salisch.—6th ed.
      p. cm.
    Includes bibliographical references and index.
    ISBN 0-07-239726-8
      1. Public speaking. 2. Voice culture. 3. English language—Diction. 4. English language—
Phonetics. I. Sokoloff, Martin A. II. Salisch, Sandra L. III. Title.

PN4121 H17 2002
808.5—dc21   2001030373

www.mhhe.com

Contents

Chapter Three
The Speech Process   23

Chapter Four
The Sounds of American English   43

AFFRICATES

Chapter Nine
The Vowels and Diphthongs   213

Chapter Eleven
Vocal Expressiveness   303

contents

To the Instructor

"Taking (and teaching) a college course in voice and diction can often be a real challenge."

That statement began the preface to the first edition of *Speaking Clearly* in 1983, and it's still valid today. Students are trying to learn new speech behaviors, or change old ones, under conditions that are usually far from ideal. Many students who enroll in speech improvement courses are looking for a quick fix of voice and diction in order to solve a current personal or career problem. They often discover that either they can't accomplish the improvements they seek or the improvements they do make are temporary. Time is still one of the main stumbling blocks; it's extremely difficult to change voice and diction patterns that have existed since early childhood in just one short semester, or in one even shorter summer session. The setting continues to be an additional stumbling block; students are usually operating on a time-sharing basis in the classroom, not in a one-to-one setting with an instructor. It's also difficult to concentrate intensively on speech improvement outside of class when life's pressures are competing more than ever for students' time and attention: other classes, jobs, family, social activities, and so on. Finally, it seems that students will always believe they risk embarrassment when they try to use what they're learning in class in real-life communication situations. So if taking (and teaching) a course in voice and diction is *still* a challenge, it's because conditions are *still* far from ideal.

That's why we originally wrote this book. And, our experience with 17 years of previous editions has shown us that *Speaking Clearly* eliminates some of the obstacles to success in taking (and teaching) a voice and diction course and increases students' chances to achieve significant and lasting changes in voice and diction.

Approach of the Book

This book reflects our experience of 35 years of teaching voice and diction courses to thousands of college students. Over the years, we've identified many of the factors that we believe spell success in speech improvement. We've pooled our knowledge, our experience, and the materials that we've developed to provide a book that capitalizes on the success factors. In this book we bring you the things we do that *work:* specific materials and approaches we use that have proven themselves effective in the classroom.

The approaches we use reflect our background and experience in speech pathology, and as such, are based on sound principles. One such approach is the use of voice and diction drills in increasing order of difficulty. These drills distinguish between the less and more difficult productions of a given sound and prevent students not only from trying to progress too rapidly, but from starting at levels inappropriate for beginners. These drills give early successes and rewards, minimize discouraging failures, and help students to develop a healthy, positive attitude. Sentences in most drills are designed to present the target sounds at a frequency close to that of normal conversation. Words are familiar and can be phased into students' everyday conversations.

Our experience in speech pathology has left us with a difficult decision regarding a popular, commonly used tool: the tongue twister. On the plus side, tongue twisters are fun. On the down side, we've found that they tend to contribute to more failures than successes in the production of any given sound. One reason is that tongue twisters are so loaded with a particular sound that they are *designed* for failure. Often, students give up when tongue twisters prove too difficult; then all improvement on the desired sounds stops. Keeping these pros and cons in mind, we do use some tongue twisters for fun, but they are only in drills at the highest level of difficulty. By the time students reach the tongue twisters they should be proficient at lower levels.

We have also kept in mind the fact that students sometimes find it awkward or embarrassing to drill aloud on materials that, while providing ample practice on target sounds, may not make sense as far as content is concerned. Since students tend to resist using practice materials that sound too "silly," we've made every effort to create materials that students can feel comfortable practicing, either alone or as part of a classroom group.

As voice and diction instructors and speech pathologists, we've found it extremely helpful to use ear-training techniques to help our students develop accurate auditory pictures of the correct production of target sounds. In this way, students can learn to monitor and correct their own productions of the sounds as well as learn to produce the sounds more easily. We have provided, in Chapter 5, a step-by-step training process that can be applied in the classroom by the instructor or individually by the students as an out-of-class assignment. It is also possible to use the ear-training steps as a means of assessing each student's ability to discriminate between his or her own standard and non-standard productions of target sounds.

The organization of this book reflects the order in which we teach voice and diction, and the one we found to be the most widely used: diction covered before voice. We believe that we're more successful when we deal with diction first because it takes more time to achieve lasting change in diction than in voice or vocal expression. This is not to say that there is only one way to approach voice and diction improvement. Instructors can choose any organization they're comfortable with; the chapters can be used in any order.

About the Sixth Edition

We've continued listening to our readers and to the instructors who review or use our text. As a result, the sixth edition has been significantly improved and reorganized. Here is a summary of some changes, followed by descriptions of the chapters.

- **Format**   The first, and perhaps most noticeable change is the larger format of the book. Although the second through fifth editions were a larger format than the first edition, we still heard complaints that the book was difficult to hold when reading aloud, and often forced page-turning when selections continued overleaf. By going to a larger format, we hope we have eliminated many of the frustrating aspects of a small format. We have modified the layout to make the book more attractive and, we hope, easier to use.
- **Pronunciation List**   It's back! When the fifth edition grew too big, and we had to cut something, a few adopters suggested we cut the list of frequently mispronounced words. We didn't anticipate the furor that would erupt! So at the request of many adopters and reviewers, the list is back in Appendix A, where it belongs.
- **Readings**   We have changed a number of readings. We dropped some that students just didn't read, some that didn't work, and some that seemed dated. We've replaced those readings and added new ones that we think students will enjoy and use effectively. We've also increased the number of "challenge" readings throughout.
- **Audio CD Program**   The audio program that was formerly available on cassettes at additional cost has been replaced with an audio CD that is bundled gratis with the book. This valuable program, which provides drill materials for diction, voice and vocal expression, is now available to all students and instructors. The recording is of professional quality, and it can easily be used in language labs, computers, and personal CD players. By bundling the CD with the book, instructors can assign voice and diction drills to all students with confidence.
- **Instructor's Manual**   The instructor's manual has been further expanded and improved. There are more suggestions and ideas for implementing the procedures and materials provided in the text. There are sample course outlines, quizzes, homework assignments, out-of-

class projects, classroom exercises, advice on grading, and sources for additional materials and information to augment instruction.

Chapter by Chapter

Chapter 1: Introduction

This chapter now focuses exclusively on the speech communication process and contains an expanded treatment of communication along with a communication model. The "How to Use This Book" section has been moved to the Student and Instructor Prefaces, where it was more appropriate.

Chapter 2: Dealing with Nervousness

Significant numbers of beginning students in voice and diction have a high degree of apprehension about the course in general, and about its "performance" aspects in particular. As a result, they suffer varying degrees of stage fright when asked to read or speak aloud in the classroom. Chapter 2 gives students information about the nature and causes of stage fright and provides them with concrete ways to manage stage fright successfully. Formerly this information was in an appendix, but many instructors felt that students tended to read it too late in the course for the information and exercises to be useful. Therefore, we now cover the topic in one of the earliest chapters in the book.

Chapter 3: The Speech Process

This chapter examines speech sounds and the way we make them. As such, it provides a necessary foundation for voice and diction improvement. We recognize that too much technical information may stall students, so we have rewritten and simplified large portions of this chapter, and revised and improved much of the artwork. As a result, we believe that the basics of the speech process as presented in this chapter are now much easier to understand and remember.

Chapter 4: The Sounds of American English

This chapter presents theory and practical applications of the International Phonetic Alphabet as a tool to teach the component sounds of English. With the exception of providing more examples of phonemes in words and eliminating inconsistencies in transcription, we have kept this chapter virtually unchanged.

Chapter 5: Improving Diction: The Basics

This chapter provides an overview of the steps to improving voice and diction, along with specific instructions and exercises, and remains unchanged.

Chapters 6, 7, 8, and 9: Consonants, Vowels, and Diphthongs

These chapters present theory and drills on all the component sounds of American English. They are the heart of the book and are the chapters where many students will spend most of their time. Although we had reorganized many of the specific consonant and vowel sections in the fourth and fifth editions, user suggestions resulted in more improvements in this edition. One major change is immediately noticeable. Many adopters told us they would like to see the consonant sounds covered in more than one chapter, so we have organized them into four separate chapters. To reduce some confusion over diphthongs, we now cover diphthongs along with their associated initial vowel.

Chapters 10 and 11: Voice Production and Vocal Expressiveness

In Chapters 10 and 11, guided activities for voice analysis and improvement are alternated with theory about effective voice characteristics. Chapter 10 is a basic how-to presentation of the various aspects of voice production: breathing for speech, loudness, pitch, relaxation, and various vocal qualities. We have expanded coverage of vocal fry, an increasingly frequent problem. Chapter 11 analyzes the paralinguistic elements involved in vocal expressiveness, such as rate, duration, pausing, stress, and pitch variations. We have replaced and updated many readings, and added new readings that we think will be of more interest to a diverse group of students.

Appendix A: Pronunciation Guide

Appendix A provides an extensive list of frequently mispronounced common words, organized according to type of mispronunciation. The lists show standard and nonstandard pronunciations for each word, and with a little practice your students should be able to pronounce them correctly.

Appendix B: Guide to Foreign Accents

Appendix B covers foreign accents—the many ways in which American English may be spoken by speakers who have learned English as a second language. This updated appendix lists the features of a number of accents and provides a guide to practice materials for the sounds affected.

Appendix C: Diagnostic Materials and Speech Checklists

Appendix C consists of lists of sentences and connected speech passages containing all the sounds of American English in a variety of phonetic contexts. You can use these passages in objectively evaluating your students' speech for nonstandard sounds. At the end of Appendix C we have provided the Speech Evaluation Checklist we use when we evaluate our own students. You may reproduce the checklist as often as you like.

Glossary

We've defined most of the important terms used in this book and placed a list of them in one convenient spot.

Acknowledgments

In its seventeenth year, this sixth edition of *Speaking Clearly* reflects the continuing, invaluable assistance of many colleagues, friends, and students at Pace University and other institutions. We have received extraordinary support from all our colleagues at Pace University, especially Carol Alpern, Bill Page, Mary Ann Murphy, Silvana Bogin, Harry Weinstein, Elizabeth Maysilles, and Mary Stambaugh. They are our own testing lab, helping us weed out practice materials that don't work as well as we intended, and replacing them with materials that prove to be effective. To our editors, Nanette Kauffman and Jennie Katsaros, we express our appreciation for their skill, understanding, and a job well done.

Finally, a special acknowledgement, in love, respect, and sadness for our late colleague Jerry M. Goldberg. A fine teacher and an effective and respected department chairman, Jerry was one of the most enthusiastic users of our book. He continually provided us with suggestions and materials that we gladly incorporated in *Speaking Clearly*. Thanks, Jerry, for being with us. We'll miss you.

Feedback

We've tried to bring you the best book we could that would help you teach the principles of voice and diction and to enable your students to put those principles into practice as quickly and effectively as possible. Please contact us and let us know how the book worked for you, and if you have suggestions as to how we can improve the book. You can write to us at the Department of Communication Studies, Pace University, Pace Plaza, New York, NY 10038-1502. We'd like to hear from you.

To the Student

Taking a college course in voice and diction can often be a real challenge. You're trying to learn new speech behaviors, or change old ones, under conditions that are usually far from ideal. First, behavioral changes don't happen overnight, and most of us want quick rewards. Second, to change behaviors successfully you must fit your practice sessions in with all the other demands on your time—other classes, jobs, family, social activities, and so on. Third, most speech instruction usually takes place in the classroom with other students, not on a one-to-one basis with an instructor. Not only might you receive less time than you think you need, there's always the worry about feeling embarrassed in front of other students. Finally, it takes a while to feel comfortable trying out new behaviors in day-to-day communication situations.

That's why we wrote this book. And, our experience with 17 years of previous editions has shown us that *Speaking Clearly* eliminates some of the obstacles to success in taking a voice and diction course and increases your chances to achieve significant and lasting changes in voice and diction.

A Guide to Speaking Clearly

This book contains a wide variety of materials related to improving voice and diction. You'll save yourself time and effort later on if you spend a while now familiarizing yourself with the book. First, browse through the entire book. See how it's laid out, what's covered in each chapter and appendix, how the index is organized, and so on. Once you know how it works, you'll be able to find the materials you want more quickly, and you can use the book more effectively.

Chapter by Chapter

Each chapter is a complete unit in itself and can be used separately. This means your instructor can assign chapter readings in whatever order he or she prefers. Each chapter begins with a statement of objectives that you should be able to achieve through reading the chapter and participating in related work in class. Important terms you should know are listed in a glossary at the back of the book.

Chapter 1 provides an introduction to the basics of communication and explains why a course in voice and diction is important and how it can help you increase the value of one of your most important assets. The chapter discusses how other people may react to speakers' communication styles. It also covers the elements of the communication process including the effects of "noise" (external, listener-generated, and speaker-generated) on the communicative process.

The thought of speaking aloud in class or before a group makes many people uncomfortable. If you feel that way, we strongly recommend that you read and re-read Chapter 2, which deals with stage fright and anxiety. Try the practice activities according to your own needs or as your instructor assigns them. We're sure that you'll feel much more at ease and be more confident after you read this chapter.

Chapter 3 examines the speech sounds we make and the ways in which we make them. The chapter begins with a description of sound, then examines its physical and psychological characteristics; it continues with descriptions of the anatomy and physiology of the structures we use in order to articulate and to produce voice. There are technical terms, but we've tried to keep them to a minimum. By understanding the speech process and structures of speech you'll be able to more efficiently learn and change speech behaviors.

Chapter 4 presents theory and practical applications of the International Phonetic Alphabet (IPA) for the purpose of teaching you the component sounds of American English. The chapter first discusses the differences between speech and writing and examines the nature of alphabets. Next, it describes and presents the IPA as a tool to help you learn the phonemes used in American English. The chapter goes on to describe the authors' definition of such concepts as dialect and standard and nonstandard speech. It concludes by describing some of the systems for classifying sounds. The exercises in phonetics in Chapter 4 will help you master the dual skills of transcribing in IPA and reading orally from IPA symbols, and will sensitize you to the auditory aspects of language. Chapter 4 also provides the framework for Chapters 6 through 9.

Chapter 5 is very short but extremely important. This is a how-to chapter that shows you the steps to improving voice and diction. It's similar to a set of instructions that helps you assemble a bicycle: if you don't read the instructions in advance, you might assemble the bike incorrectly. In any case, it will probably take you longer to get it right. Chapter 5 has a section with the strange title of "Ear Training," designed to help you to improve your auditory discrimination. Read this section thoroughly and be certain to do the exercises. You'll find them effective in teaching you the differences between the standard and nonstandard sounds of our language. Finally, Chapter 5 has a set of warm-up exercises that will help you make your practice sessions more effective.

Chapters 6 through 9 present theory and drills on all the component sounds of American English. Wherever possible, we have arranged the drills according to level of difficulty. This allows you to practice with less or more difficult materials, depending on your level of skill at producing the particular sound.

We have tried to design our practice sentences so that they are close to what people might say in normal conversation. Except for certain challenge materials, we have made every effort to avoid loading each sentence with words containing the sound being practiced. Even though tongue twisters can be fun to attempt, our experience has shown us that often they are not particularly useful in helping you correct misarticulated sounds. They can be useful in fine-tuning, so you'll find some tongue twisters in the challenge materials for certain sounds.

In Chapters 10 and 11, guided activities for voice analysis and improvement are alternated with theory about effective voice characteristics. We have divided instructions for carrying out vocal exercises and activities according to the level of difficulty for practice that you direct yourself.

Chapter 10 is a basic how-to presentation of the various aspects of voice production, covering breathing for speech; loudness, pitch, relaxation; and various vocal qualities. Chapter 11 analyzes the paralinguistic elements involved in vocal expressiveness, such as rate, duration, pausing, stress, and pitch variations. It's here that we provide many readings for you to practice what you've learned in the previous chapters.

At the back of the book are three appendixes and a glossary. Appendix A provides an extensive list of frequently mispronounced common words, organized according to type of mispronunciation. The lists show standard and nonstandard pronunciations for each word. With a little practice you should be able to pronounce them correctly.

Appendix B covers foreign accents—the many ways in which American English may be spoken by speakers who have learned English as a second language. This appendix lists the features of a number of accents and provides a guide to practice materials for the sounds affected. By understanding the difference between a foreign accent and American English, you may reduce the time it takes to achieve significant accent reduction.

Appendix C consists of lists of sentences and connected speech passages containing all the sounds of American English in a variety of phonetic contexts. You and your instructor can use these passages in evaluating your speech for nonstandard sounds. We suggest you use the Speech Evaluation Checklist at the end of Appendix C to make a record of your evaluation. You may reproduce this checklist as often as you like to record your own evaluations as well as evaluations you may make of the speech of others.

The glossary lists most of the important terms used in this book. Use the glossary whenever you're unsure of a term or you need to refresh your memory.

Speaking Clearly: The Speech Lab

The Speech Lab (which is the audio CD that comes with this book) is a complete set of practice drills and reading materials for diction, voice, and vocal expression. The materials have been professionally recorded in language-lab style so that you can repeat what you hear after the speaker says it. Your instructor may assign exercises along with the text, or you may use the CD on your own. If you use your usual portable CD player with headphones, no one will even know that you're doing your speech homework.

Feedback

We've tried to bring you the best book we could that would help you learn the principles of voice and diction and put those principles into practice as quickly and effectively as possible. Please contact us and let us know how the book worked for you, and if you have suggestions as to how we can improve the book. You can write to us at the Department of Communication Studies, Pace University, Pace Plaza, New York, NY 10038-1502. We'd like to hear from you.

part one

introduction to speech communication

Why do you communicate? How do you do it? Why do some people communicate more effectively than others? How can I gain more self-confidence? How can I become a more effective speaker?

These are typical of the questions asked by people like you who are about to start working on voice and diction. Part I of this book will answer these and other questions you may have and start you on the way to speaking clearly.

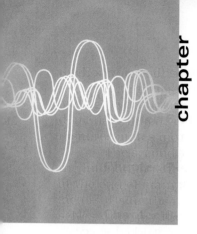

introduction

Objectives

After reading this chapter you should be able to:

- Explain why you may want or need to improve your voice and diction behaviors
- Explain clearly the communication process and the role played by voice and diction in that process
- Discuss some of the reasons people respond positively or negatively to others' voice and diction patterns
- Describe the concept of communication noise and how noise affects communication

Some time ago a series of employment interviews was held on our campus. Several male seniors who were considered to be likely candidates for jobs with highly rated accounting firms appeared for their interviews. They were all shined and polished, and they had learned all they needed to know to make favorable impressions on the interviewers. Their academic credentials were highly suitable; they were all set. What happened? You guessed it! They failed the interviews.

Why? The interviewers told the director of our Career Planning Center that the speech patterns of the students were more appropriate for manual laborers than professional accountants and that these particular students would not be considered for employment.

Consider this case: One of our students in a voice and diction class, a rather petite young woman, made her first tape recording. This woman was also a student teacher, and during the conference that followed the recording session, she complained that she was having trouble maintaining discipline in her student teaching assignment. She said that she was assigned to teach several high school English classes and that most of the students towered over her physically. They paid little attention to her instructions, and she was feeling increasingly frustrated. She had never heard herself on tape before, and when she did, she realized that her voice was quite high-pitched and weak. She said, "I sound just like a little girl." After some voice retraining she returned to class.

She found that with her "new" voice she was able to get her students' attention and really get down to the business of teaching.

Here's another example. In the class of one of the authors, there was a young woman whose habitually high-pitched voice and very harsh resonance usually resulted in expressions of discomfort on the part of other students; it was as though someone had scraped chalk across a blackboard. The young woman was unaware of the other students' reactions, which occurred almost every time she spoke in class—and in all likelihood, in other situations outside of class. Her message was frequently lost because of the way she voiced it. After hearing herself on tape and receiving feedback from other students, she worked successfully to improve her voice quality.

One final example: One of the authors worked part-time for a telecommunications company during his college years. One of his supervisors was nicknamed "Double-Work Mike," not because Mike worked twice as hard but the jobs he assigned frequently had to be done over again because his instructions were hard to understand. The author remembers with embarrassment one instance where he spent an entire morning searching for a particular "curl" of wire. Had the author known that Mike pronounced the word *oil* as if it were *Earl*, he would have realized that what Mike wanted was an ordinary *coil* and not an unusual *curl*.

These incidents, and many others like them, are familiar to anyone who is trained to observe the way people speak. As you think over some of your own communication history, you can probably remember several times when you made snap judgments about people solely on the basis of how they presented themselves through speaking. In other words, *how* a person says something, rather than *what* that person says, forms a lasting impression. We form these impressions because we have come to believe that a person's personality is reflected in the way he or she speaks. What if our first impression is wrong? If our relationship with that individual continues, it may take a long time for us to change our opinion.

Communication patterns usually tell us a lot about a person. We often make judgments about someone by the way he pronounces words; the loudness, quality, and inflection of his voice; the way he uses gestures; the way he stands; what he does with his eyes and face. We make these judgments unconsciously, but we make them just the same.

Most of us, in truth, have not one but several styles of communicating. For example, when we're speaking with our friends we usually talk quite differently from the way we talk when we're being interviewed for a job. In any of these situations, chances are we're trying to make a good impression and get the other person to respond to us in a favorable way.

"But," you may say, "I've been talking all my life, and I haven't had any trouble. Why should I study speech? What will it do for me?" The answers to these questions—the reasons for studying speech—will, of course, vary from student to student. For one student the reason might be a desire to communicate effectively. You may have no difficulty communicating in the specific geographic and social environment called home, but in a different environment, your present speech patterns might be so different from those around you that people pay more attention to the *way* you speak than to *what* you have to say. For another student the reason might be a wish to make a good impression. It may be that your present speech patterns could, at one time or another, prevent you from getting the job you're after, the promotion you deserve, the date with that person who is so special to you.

Perhaps it is the way you pronounce certain words or how loudly you speak or the quality of your voice or some other aspect of your speech that, in some way, prevents your communication from being as effective as you would like. The result is you may not be successful in getting the desired response from those with whom you are communicating.

Once they've thought about these reasons, most of our students say, "Okay, you've convinced me. But I *can't* change the way I speak; I'm too old! I'd just be wasting my time." We don't agree! First, you don't have to learn to speak all over again. You only have to add another speaking style to those you already possess, to be used when it's appropriate for the particular speaker, listener, or occasion. Second, the ability to learn new speech patterns doesn't depend on your age but on your motivation. It's simply a matter of learning new muscle habits and developing dormant listening skills. If you want to do it, you can! How long it takes you to improve your speech depends on how badly you want to do it and the amount of time you're willing to spend on practice.

The Communication Process

Now is a good time to talk about communication: what it is, how it operates, and what influence your speech has on your communication and its effectiveness.

Communication is the symbolic process of sharing meanings. Someone who has a certain idea, thought, or feeling uses this process in such a way that a similar idea, thought, or feeling arises in the mind of another person. For example, say you just met someone and you want to convey the message "I like you, and I would like a chance to get to know you better."

The first step in the process would be for your brain to reach back into its file of experiences and dig out the words that would best express the idea. To come up with the appropriate words, your brain would probably review a number of different ways to express the same idea and, based on your attitudes, values, and past experiences, select those words you think would result in the most effective, least risky way of conveying your message.

The next step would be for your brain to regulate the various structures and muscles your body uses to produce speech so that you could transmit the words of your message. These words, when spoken, exist in the form of sounds or vibrations of the air molecules surrounding you. When these vibrations reach the ear of another person (such as the person you intended should hear them), the vibrations change into nerve impulses that travel to the brain, where they are translated into ideas.

At this point, you have directed a message toward a person you'd like to get to know better, and you hope that person understands you and shares your feeling. You're probably fairly confident that if you chose the right words, your message was received and understood correctly. But then you get a response that's very different from the one you were hoping for. Why might this have happened?

Chances are you were a victim of communication noise.

Noise

In an ideal situation, the message created in the brain of the other person would be exactly the same as the one that originated in yours. Most of the time this doesn't happen, though, because of a number of factors that operate in almost all communication situations. These factors are frequently called barriers to communication, or simply noise. Noise exists in human speech communication because, at this time, we have no way to link the speaker's brain directly to the listener's. In a way, we could compare you and your listener to a television station and a TV set; they're miles apart, but an attempt is made to have a picture appear on the TV set that is the same as the one in the studio. When the picture is different, it's because of noise. The noise could be generated at the source ("Please stand by. . ."), by something between your set and the studio (an electrical storm), or by something wrong inside your TV set (crossed wires). Similarly, three kinds of noise exists in speech communication: external, listener-generated, and speaker-generated.

Figure 1–1 is a model of the communication process with two participants. Notice that both participants are involved in speaking and listening activities simultaneously, and that the process is not a one-way process. Let's examine the types of noise and the potential of each to interfere with every step in the communication process.

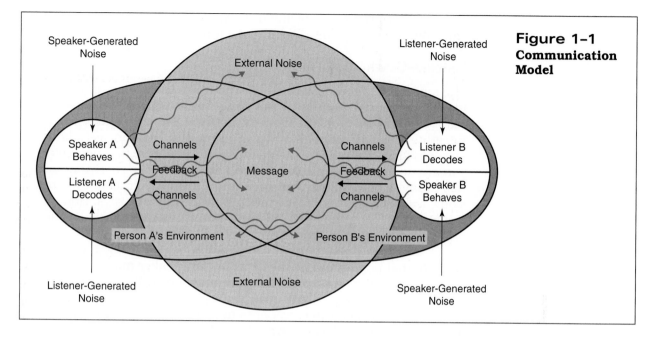

**Figure 1–1
Communication
Model**

EXTERNAL NOISE

Just as a TV signal can be distorted while it's traveling between the studio and your set at home, so can your communication be subjected to distortion from noise between you and your listener.

The noise may be *acoustic,* that is, other sounds (not generated by speaker or listener) that block out speech or make hearing difficult. It is hard to understand conversations at a loud party, for example. For the same reason, people who live near busy airports learn to lip-read every time a jet takes off. The effect of acoustic noise on speech is that if you hear the words at all, you still can't be sure you heard them correctly.

There are *visual* noises, too. Have you ever sat in a classroom trying to pay attention to a lecture or discussion while your eyes and mind keep straying to the window to something happening outside? That something outside is a visual noise. (We also use the visual sense to help us understand speech; there's less chance of error when you can see the speaker's lips.)

Even something as simple as temperature can introduce noise in the communication process. When one of our classroom buildings was brand-new, there was a problem with the heating system that occurred in the middle of a very cold winter. Everyone sat bundled up in hats and coats in the classrooms, and faculty tried to conduct classes while students shivered and made vain efforts to keep warm. As you might guess, the instructors' messages didn't get through very effectively.

These are just a few illustrations of how external factors can disrupt communication, or at least make it more difficult.

LISTENER-GENERATED NOISE

The receiver of the communication, though, can also be at fault. Think for a moment about all the factors you bring to each communication situation and how they might affect the way you listen to, understand, and integrate what someone is saying to you. How do you feel about the speaker, for instance? Do you like, respect, or admire that person? If so, you are much more likely to be open and receptive to what that person has to say. If you dislike, fear, or distrust the speaker, chances are you won't accept or agree with very much of what he or she says. How do you feel about the way the other person talks? Does that particular accent or way of pronouncing words turn you off?

A speaker may remind you of someone you dislike, so you may listen to that person with some bias. Or the speaker may remind you of someone you like, in which case your reaction to that person's words may be very positive.

Another factor to consider is how you feel about the subject you are talking about. Do you have a lot of fixed ideas, attitudes, or values about the subject? Is it something that you feel very strongly about? It's likely that if your answers to the last two questions are yes, your mind will be fairly closed to ideas or attitudes that differ from yours.

Do you react emotionally to certain words or phrases that have strong associations for you? How would you feel, for instance, if someone called you or your ideas dumb, communistic, or reactionary? How willing would you be to listen objectively to that person?

These are all examples of factors existing within the listener that may increase or diminish the likelihood of effective communication taking place.

SPEAKER-GENERATED NOISE

Not all our communication takes place as a result solely of the language (words) we choose to utter. We also convey meaning in a number of other ways: the loudness level of our voice, how rapidly or slowly we speak, the way we use silence, the range of vocal pitches we use, and our vocal qualities. We refer to these elements of spoken communication as *Paralinguistics*. We also express a great deal of meaning by the ways in which we move, stand, gesture, and position our bodies. We call these visible aspects of communication *kinesics*, or body language. Other aspects of nonverbal communication include the clothing we wear and the way we use time and space, which also affect the way in which our message is received. All in all, nonverbal communication provides the accompaniments of spoken language that help make our meanings complete—helping to transmit the whole sense of what we want to say.

Speakers can create noise that interferes with accurate message transmission through a number of different types of behaviors. Disturbing *linguistic behaviors* can constitute "noise" experienced as faulty grammar or syntax, incorrect word choices, or faulty production of any of the sounds that make up the words. Disturbing *paralinguistic behaviors* might include such interferences as uneven loudness, rate, or rhythm; inappropriate pitch or stress patterns; and unusual or abnormal voice qualities. *Nonverbal behaviors* can also cause problems; your gestures or facial expressions might not be appropriate for your message. All these behaviors can take the attention of your listener away from what is being said and focus it on how it is being said.

In this text, we deal primarily with the behaviors that constitute speaker-generated noise: those parts of your speech pattern that may call attention to themselves or in some way make your message hard to understand or cause your listener to misinterpret your message. We'll present both theory and practical exercises to help you eliminate such noise and make your spoken communication more effective.

Summary

Communication is the symbolic process of sharing meanings using both verbal and nonverbal channels. First impressions are largely based on nonverbal factors, such as pronunciation, speech patterns, vocal attributes, gestures, posture, face, and eyes. There are a number of barriers to effective communication, collectively termed noise. The three types of communication noise are external, speaker-generated, and listener-generated.

Suggested Readings

Adler, R. B., and Towne, N. *Looking Out, Looking In.* 9th ed. Fort. Worth, TX: Harcourt Brace, 1999.

Littlejohn, S. W. *Theories of Human Communication.* 5th ed. Belmont, CA: Wadsworth, 1996.

Lucas, S. E. *The Art of Public Speaking,* 7th ed. New York: McGraw-Hill, 2001.

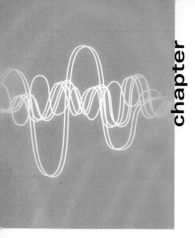

dealing with nervousness

Objectives

After reading this chapter and practicing the activities presented, you should be able to:

- Explain the commonly held misconceptions about stage fright
- Describe the causes and physical symptoms of stage fright
- Manage stage fright through long-term and short-term treatments
- Have increased your self-confidence and reduced your stage fright

When you first started reading this book, you probably thought about the future: you, making an oral presentation, in front of an audience. You also may have thought back to the time you made a presentation in another class or appeared in a school play. As you thought about those occasions, chances are strange things began to happen to you. Your mouth may have begun to feel dry, your stomach got a bit shaky, and your hands became slightly sweaty and cold. What was happening? You were feeling some symptoms of stage fright.

Stage fright goes by a number of names: presentation anxiety, speech anxiety, and just plain nervousness. Whatever we call it, the fact remains that it is the single biggest problem students face in speech classes. Every year in our freshman speech courses we meet graduating seniors who have delayed taking the course for four whole years simply because of their stage fright. Each student, you see, is usually convinced that he or she is the only one with stage fright and is, therefore, abnormal. Since most people believe that stage fright indicates some kind of flaw in a person's personality, a devastating cycle begins: people become *afraid of their stage fright.* Each time they must speak in front of an audience, they get nervous; their nervousness causes them to make the mistakes they were afraid of making, which causes them to be at least as nervous the next time they must speak to an audience.

One reason stage fright is such a problem is that people avoid talking about it; no one wants to admit that he or she has stage fright. We've learned a lot about stage fright over the years, and we would like to share some of what we've learned with you. Let's start by separating fact from fiction.

Fiction:	Stage fright is abnormal.
Fact:	Stage fright is normal; almost everyone has it.

Other than those related to health and safety, what's the number one fear in the nation? That's right: stage fright! Numerous surveys of inexperienced speakers show that, on the average, 75 percent admit to having stage fright and more than 35 percent think it's a serious problem. Surprisingly, stage fright is also considered to be a problem by about 76 percent of experienced speakers—lecturers, politicians, and business people. Those who perform for a living also have stage fright. In a recent *TV Guide* article, Olivia Newton-John told how her stage fright leaves her shaking and crying before a performance. And Jane Fonda has admitted to having "tremendous fear," a sentiment echoed by Sir Laurence Olivier and many others.

The point we're trying to make is that *stage fright is perfectly normal!* It's so normal, in fact, many speech experts feel that the person who does not have stage fright should be considered abnormal.

Fiction:	Stage fright is always harmful.
Fact:	Stage fright can be helpful.

You may be surprised to learn that stage fright can actually help you give a better performance. It's true! When you feel the symptoms of stage fright, you become more alert and alive, and you may be better able to listen and adjust to the situation. You are also more "up" and may appear more eager and involved in getting your message across to your listeners. If you don't have stage fright, you run the risk of putting your audience to sleep.

Fiction:	Stage fright should be eliminated.
Fact:	You should understand, expect, accept, control, and use stage fright to make yourself a more effective speaker.

Before we can tell you how to deal effectively with your stage fright, we should see what stage fright is, what causes it, and how it works.

Stage Fright Defined

Stage fright is a normal state of anxiety and arousal; a combination of fear and excitement. Stage fright usually occurs when you are facing a speaking situation that has an unpredictable outcome. Naturally, the situation that comes to mind is presenting to an audience, but there are other situations in which you may experience stage fright. It's quite common in job interviews, telephone calls, business meetings, classroom reports, club announcements, even meeting your prospective in-laws. What is the ratio of anxiety to arousal in the stage fright you experience at a given moment? It will vary depending on you, the particular situation, and a number of other factors that we will explain in the balance of the chapter.

What Causes Stage Fright?

Stage fright is a speaker's response to a "fight or flight" situation. Here's an example of such a situation. You're taking a walk in the woods on a pleasant autumn afternoon. As you stroll around the base of a huge tree, you get the shock of your life! Suddenly, unexpectedly, you come face to face with a giant, hungry, growling grizzly bear! What are you going to do? Whatever you do, you probably won't stop to think about it because at this point your body goes on "automatic pilot." It reacts automatically to prepare itself either to fight the bear or to run away as far as is humanly possible. A number of things happen very quickly: your muscles tense; your heartbeat and breathing speed up; glands in your body begin to secrete essential fluids.

Bodily functions that are usually controlled voluntarily are now running on pure emotion. You act now, think later. And you may not become aware of your actions until *after* they have occurred. The mother of one of the authors surprised a burglar in her home in the middle of the night. She bodily threw him out of the house and then sat trembling by the phone for two hours before she could control herself enough to call the police.

The same kind of situation can occur in speech. You may face an audience and experience fear for any number of reasons. Your body interprets the feelings of fear to mean you are facing a real physical threat, such as the bear in the forest or the burglar in the house. As a result, your automatic pilot prepares your body either to fight the audience or to run away from it, and your mind no longer controls what your body does.

Physical Symptoms of Stage Fright

The symptoms of stage fright are easily explained, once you understand what causes it. They all relate to the fact that your body is ready to run or fight. Not everyone experiences all the symptoms, and the symptoms may vary from situation to situation. Which stage fright symptoms in the following list have you experienced?

Butterflies in the stomach. This is one of the first symptoms. Energy in your body needs to be pumped to those parts that are going to get it out of danger. Since the process of digestion requires a lot of energy, that process halts and energy is diverted to the arms and legs. The food you've eaten just sits in your stomach, undigested, until the danger is past.

Dry mouth. The process of digestion begins in the mouth with the secretion of saliva. Since saliva production has also been halted, your mouth becomes very dry. And it does not matter how much water you drink; your mouth stays dry.

Rapid breathing. Increased energy demands mean an increased need for oxygen, so your breathing speeds up accordingly.

Rapid heart rate. The heart must circulate the blood through the body more quickly in order to distribute oxygen to the skeletal muscles you'll use in running or fighting.

Trembling hands, weak knees, unsteady voice. Almost all your skeletal muscles are under tension. As a result, they begin to tremble. Voice production is controlled by skeletal muscles, and you can hear the results of the excess tension.

Perspiration. Even though your mouth becomes dry, your body becomes increasingly wet with perspiration. This is simply an attempt to control body temperature. Because there is more blood circulating near the surface of the body, there is more body heat. Your body sends perspiration to the surface, and as the perspiration evaporates, it cools your body.

These symptoms are the ones most commonly experienced in stage fright. We're sure you can add some of your own to the list.

What Can You Do about Stage Fright?

For most people, the symptoms of stage fright can be quite unnerving. Think back to the first time you can remember experiencing stage fright. What frightened you more, the speaking itself or the strange, terrible things your body was doing to you?

The point is this: If you don't understand what's happening to you, more fear can develop. In other words, *stage fright can be fear of fear!*

Let's repeat what we said earlier. You shouldn't try to eliminate stage fright. Instead, you should *understand it, expect it, accept it, control it,* and *use it* to make you a more effective speaker. Don't expect that your fear is going to magically vanish once you learn its secrets. If you think you can be totally free from stage fright, you're probably setting yourself up for failure.

Dealing with stage fright involves three treatment stages: long-term, short-term, and what we call "first aid."

Long-Term Treatments

Understand Your Stage Fright

By learning about the causes and symptoms of stage fright, you take away the fear of the unknown. When you realize that stage fright is perfectly normal, you remove a lot of unnecessary doubt about your sanity.

Talk about Stage Fright

Think about times you've had stage fright. Discuss those times with someone who is close to you. You'll find that talking it over clears up some of the mystery about it. You'll also find that the person with whom you're talking will want to share similar experiences with you.

Be Realistic about the Situation

Remember that your audience is nothing like the imaginary bear you faced in the woods. The audience can't cause you any physical harm. In fact, most audiences and listeners are genuinely interested in what you have to say, and they want you to do well. That's especially true in speech classes, where your fellow students would rather listen to you than think about their own cases of stage fright.

Develop a Communication Orientation

The reason you're facing your listeners and making a presentation is to communicate, not to perform. If you think of what you're doing as performing you will probably also be thinking of the "reviews" you expect you will receive. This evaluation orientation will undoubtably increase your anxiety about the outcome; "Will they like me? Will I make mistakes? How harshly will they judge me?"

It's much more productive to concentrate on achieving your communication objectives. Sure, there are *some* important performance aspects about communication in front of an audience, but your main purpose is to have certain ideas, thoughts, and feelings arise in the minds of the listeners. And that's what your listeners are most interested in—*what* you're saying. They expect you to make mistakes, perhaps lose your place, and have some long pauses, because that's normal.

PUT THINGS IN PERSPECTIVE

One way to put things in perspective is to play the game we call "What's the worst that can happen?" Here's what we mean. Imagine that when you get up to read in front of the class today, you're going to make a mistake. The professor is going to flunk you, your grade average will drop below 2.00, and you'll be dismissed from college. You probably won't be able to get a job without a college degree and you won't be eligible to collect unemployment. Your parents will throw you out of the house, and then you'll be forced to beg for food in the streets. All because of this one speech assignment.

When playing this game, let your imagination run wild. The result will make your fears seem kind of silly. Once you are able to poke fun at your fears, they will no longer seem more important than they really are.

DEVELOP REALISTIC EXPECTATIONS

The reasons we have heard over the years as to why people are "nervous" about speaking in front of a class tend to fall into two categories: *realistic* and *unrealistic.* Those that are realistic ("I won't be adequately prepared," is a popular one) can be dealt with in realistic ways and are usually not major problems. The unrealistic fears, strangely enough, cause most of the problems and cause people to anticipate speaking situations with dread. One such common fear has to do with using notes: "If I have to stop speaking for a moment to collect my thoughts or look at my notes, those one or two seconds of silence will be fatal." The truth of the matter is that, though a few seconds may feel like an eternity to you, they will go largely unnoticed by your listeners. In fact, your listeners may appreciate the opportunity to digest what you're saying or may think that you've paused for dramatic effect.

Another unrealistic fear has to do with setting standards: "People will be judging me and therefore I can't make any mistakes." Unfortunately, for years most of us have received the message that the only acceptable behavior in an educational setting is perfection. While this may be an appropriate expectation in subject areas where we deal with factual, concrete bits of information, it is not appropriate in areas that deal with human behavior. We believe it is quite unreasonable, even impossible, to expect perfection in any skill. If you were to listen to any number of educated people talk, even professional presenters, you would hear all kinds of behaviors that could be labeled as *nonfluencies:* repeating all or parts of words, hesitating, interjecting such sounds as "um," "er," and "like," and even distorting some speech sounds. Although you wouldn't deliberately go out of your way to use them, these are all *normal* aspects of speech behavior. To help yourself recognize and deal with unrealistic fears about speaking, try the activities below.

Activities

1. Pick a few people you believe to be effective speakers. Listen to their speech. We're sure you can find some of the nonfluencies we described above. Are these behaviors disruptive to the speakers' communication? Probably not. Under most circumstances, you wouldn't even notice most of them.

2. While you are having a conversation with a friend or classmate, deliberately pause for a couple of seconds between phrases or sentences. See if the other person is aware of anything different. If not, lengthen the pauses until the other person notices. You'll be surprised how long a "normal" pause can be.

3. Imagine that you are explaining something to one person. That wouldn't produce too much anxiety, would it? Now imagine explaining the same thing to two people. That probably wouldn't be any more stressful than with one person. Now explain to three people. Then four people, then five, and so on. Continue until you reach the number at which you would feel that the situation is becoming stressful. What is that number? Ask yourself why that number of people would be stressful when one person less would not. Can you come up with any acceptable reason?

Now ask yourself, please, to allow into the group just one more person without getting uptight. Imagine yourself talking to that number of people. Is it getting easier? Repeat this exercise, adding just one more person each time until you reach your absolute limit.

Gain as Much Experience as Possible

Try to speak before an audience as often as you can, in as many different types of situations as you can. There are many opportunities for you to make brief presentations, to "get the feel" of talking to a group. For example, you could make an oral report in one of your classes, introduce a speaker at a seminar, participate in a debate, or speak up at a board of education meeting or some other form of public hearing. Each time you speak, you'll feel a little more confident. Experience is really the best teacher.

Learn to Relax

We're sure that, at one time or another, someone has said to you "Relax!" We're also sure that you found it to be easier said than done. You may not be surprised to learn that many people have difficulty deliberately relaxing in stressful situations, but you may be surprised to know that you can *learn* to relax. You can break through much of the tension related to stage fright by regularly practicing a few relaxation exercises.

Because these exercises are also useful when working on breathing for speech, we've placed them in Chapter 10:

Progressive relaxation	page 291
Fantasy	page 291
Head rolling	page 292
Sighing	page 292
Yawning	page 293

After some consistent practice, you should be able to spend a few minutes getting yourself quickly into a relaxed physical and mental state. Then you'll be able to present yourself and your material in a more confident and effective way.

Visualize Your Presentation

Athletes routinely use the technique of *visualization* not only to help them feel more confident but to actually improve performance. You don't need the type of training that a sports psychologist would administer to use visualization to reduce your nervousness about speaking; the technique is simple.

With your eyes closed, picture yourself getting up to speak and walking to the lectern, podium, or table where your notes will be. Then imagine yourself making your presentation, step by step, point by point, making eye contact with your listeners, gesturing, and moving your body. Imagine that you can hear your voice: loud, strong, and confident. Then imagine the end of the presentation (with applause or congratulations, if appropriate), walking back to your seat, and sitting down.

You can vary your visualizations to fit the specific situation and setting, but the result won't change: your visualization of success will make you feel more confident.

Short-Term Treatments

Be Prepared

Know what you're doing, and you'll feel much more confident and more at ease. Don't worry about how you look or sound; you'll find that your memory seems better and that ideas and words flow more smoothly.

Practice, Practice, Practice!

By "practice" we don't mean a silent reading; we mean saying the words out loud! If you don't practice out loud, you won't have much confidence in yourself. How many times should you practice? There's no magic number; just practice as much as you feel you need. Try to practice in front of another person to get the feeling of saying the words to someone other than yourself. Pick someone who can be objective. We don't recommend brothers or sisters for this because they usually delight in making you feel even worse (if that's possible). If no one is available, use a mirror. And don't forget your trusty tape recorder; it doesn't lie.

Don't practice on the day of your presentation. Chances are you'll be more nervous than usual that day. Nervousness causes errors that cause more nervousness, causing even more errors, causing even more nervousness, causing . . . and so on, reducing you to a mass of quivering jelly. We recommend that your last practice session be on the night before you're due to talk. Last-minute preparations really don't help at all.

Talk about What's Happening Now

Explain to yourself, or to others, what's happening to your body. For example, when you feel the first symptoms of stage fright, you might say, "Oh-oh, my mouth is starting to feel dry, and my tongue is like a big ball of cotton. I guess that means my digestion is starting to slow down. Yup, I must be right; I can feel some butterflies starting to fly. I wish I hadn't eaten that pepperoni pizza for lunch. Now my hands are beginning to sweat, and I can feel a slight trembling in my knees. I guess I'm caught in an approach-avoidance conflict. Let's see, what's going to come next? I should start to feel my heart pounding." When you talk about what's happening to you in such an objective way, the physical feelings seem less frightening and almost become welcome signs of normality. You have removed some of the mystery, and you feel more in control.

Check Out the Room

Look over the room before you speak; it won't feel so strange later on. Make sure everything is set up and works. Do you need a desk or lectern, does the mike work, is the tape recorder plugged in, and so on? If you look over the room before your presentation, things become a little less uncertain.

Burn Up Excess Energy

Remember, your body begins to go on automatic pilot quite a while before you actually have to speak, and tension builds up in your muscles. There are some things you can do that will help you feel more relaxed:

jog around the building, but don't overdo it; get off the bus or subway a few stops early and walk the rest of the way; take the stairs instead of the elevator, and so forth. Engaging in mild forms of exercise will help you get rid of excess energy. Just make sure you don't exhaust yourself.

Relaxation exercises will also help you now. Try the techniques we presented under "Long-Term Treatments."

GET ENOUGH SLEEP THE NIGHT BEFORE

If you're well rested, you'll feel more sure of yourself and be more in control of your muscles and their movements.

First-Aid (On-the-Spot) Treatments

THINK ABOUT OTHER THINGS

Look at what's going on in the room around you. Listen carefully to what another speaker has to say. Read a magazine while you're waiting for that job interview. Think about *anything* except your presentation. Whatever you do, *don't* engage in any last-minute practice sessions.

PAUSE BEFORE YOU SPEAK

You can use that time to expend a little energy and to gather your thoughts. Stand, if possible; it's a lot easier to produce a loud, clear voice while you're standing up than while you're confined to a chair. Standing also uses more energy than sitting.

Take some time to arrange your notes. Move things so that they're to your liking. Each little task uses energy and helps you to shake the jitters.

Make sure you have an adequate supply of air before you start talking. That way you won't rush into your presentation with a low air supply and run out of steam almost immediately.

USE ENERGY WHILE YOU TALK

Use gestures and move your body naturally. If you don't overdo it, you'll look lively, and you'll also be getting rid of useless energy at the same time. Plan some gestures in your practice sessions. You'll feel more comfortable when you use them during the actual presentation.

LOOK FOR FRIENDLY FACES

The audience is not made up of grizzly bears. You'll see smiles of encouragement that will make you feel much better about being there.

Summary

Stage fright is the response experienced by most speakers to a "fight or flight" situation. There are many commonly held misconceptions about stage fright and its physical symptoms. Dealing with stage fright involves three treatment stages: long-term, short-term, and "first aid."

Try the things we've suggested, but don't expect instant success. Understanding stage fright means learning to understand yourself, and that takes time. Even we, the authors of this book, have never lost our own cases of stage fright completely; nevertheless, we feel pretty confident about speaking in front of an audience. We're sure that, in time, you will too.

Suggested Readings

Allen, S. *How to Make a Speech.* New York: McGraw Hill, 1986.

Adler, R. B., and Towne, N. *Looking Out, Looking In.* 9th ed. Fort Worth, TX: Harcourt Brace, 1999.

Garner, A. *Conversationally Speaking.* New York: McGraw Hill, 1981.

Phillips, G. M. *Help for Shy People.* Englewood Cliffs, NJ: Prentice-Hall, 1981.

Zimbardo, P. G. *Shyness: What It Is, What to Do About It.* Reading, MA: Addison-Wesley, 1977.

chapter

3

the speech process

Objectives

After reading this chapter you should be able to:

- Describe what sound is, how it is produced, and how it travels
- Describe the objective and subjective characteristics of sound
- Identify and explain the structures, steps, and processes involved in speech production
- Explain the relationship between sound and speech

In this chapter we will examine speech sounds and the ways in which we make them. We will also take a brief look at the bodily structures, organs, and systems we use to produce those sounds. We believe that if you have a basic understanding of the speech process you will be able to learn the sounds of American English more easily (Chapter 4), practice them more efficiently (Chapters 5 to 9), develop more effective voice production (Chapter 10), and read aloud more expressively (Chapter 11). In our opinion, if you know *how* something works, you can use and control it more accurately.

The Nature of Sound

What Sound Is

When we talk about sound, we're *not* talking about hearing. Hearing is something that happens within your body (outer ear, middle ear, inner ear, nervous system, brain) as a result of sound. Sound is an actual physical event in which acoustic energy is generated. Hearing is the way you receive that acoustic energy from the air and eventually change it to meaningful nerve impulses in your brain.

The physical event that we call sound consists of vibratory energy that travels through the molecules of the air in ever-widening circles away from the source of the sound. To produce sound you need three things: a *vibrator*, a *force* to set the vibrator in motion, and a *medium* through which vibrations will travel. Here's how the process works. When we apply some force to a body that is capable of vibration, such as a guitar string, a bell, or a drum, the vibrator applies some of its energy to the molecules of air surrounding it. The molecules vibrate in a way that alternates squeezing together (compressions) and spreading apart (rarefactions). The alternating compressions and rarefactions spread out in waves traveling in all directions from the vibrating source and are perceived by the ear as sound (see Figure 3–1).

We all know that sounds don't travel forever. Each molecule of air sends along some of its energy to the molecules next to it; these molecules send along some of their energy to the molecules next to

Figure 3–1
A Force Sets an Object into Vibration. The Resulting Sound Waves Travel in All Directions Away From the Source.

them, and so on. Each molecule transmits some of the energy, and the process continues until there's no energy, and no sound, remaining.

Characteristics of Sound

Although you can't see sound, you can observe, measure, and describe its characteristics objectively, and you can also interpret and describe its characteristics subjectively. (We'll explain the differences between "objective" and "subjective" when we describe the individual characteristics of sound.) Three of the objective characteristics of sound are important for you to understand. They are *frequency, intensity,* and *complexity.* Their subjective counterparts are *pitch, loudness,* and *quality.*

FREQUENCY AND PITCH

Frequency means the number of vibrations that occur in a given period of time. The frequencies of sounds vary because some vibrating objects vibrate more rapidly than others and, in turn, cause the molecules of air to vibrate at the same rate. Frequency is measured in Hertz (Hz) where 1 Hz equals 1 vibration per second. Humans can hear sounds that range from frequencies as low as 20 Hz to the upper limit of hearing of about 20,000 Hz.

How rapidly an object vibrates depends basically on three factors: the object's *mass, tension,* and *length.* In general, small, short, highly tense objects vibrate more rapidly than large, long, low-tension objects (see Figure 3–2).

While frequency is an objective (physically measurable) characteristic of sound, *pitch* is subjective. That is, pitch is determined by the listener's judgment; it occurs within you. Pitch is what we call the

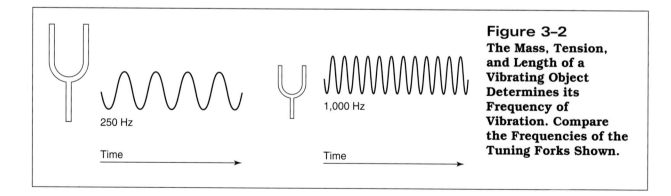

Figure 3–2
The Mass, Tension, and Length of a Vibrating Object Determines its Frequency of Vibration. Compare the Frequencies of the Tuning Forks Shown.

250 Hz

Time

1,000 Hz

Time

highness or lowness of a sound. The relationship is direct; the higher the frequency, the higher the pitch we hear; the lower the frequency, the lower the pitch.

INTENSITY AND LOUDNESS

Intensity is the objective measurement of the amount of energy a sound has. If you apply a greater force to the vibrating object, it will transfer more energy to the air around it. As a result, each molecule of air shoves the next one a little harder, so more energy means higher intensity. A not too pleasant analogy would be a series of chain-reaction collisions in a line of cars at a toll booth. There's much more energy transmitted in a 25-mph collision than in one at 5 mph. And, as with sound, the greater the energy, the farther the sound travels.

Just as pitch is the subjective interpretation of frequency, *loudness* is the subjective interpretation of intensity. We perceive high-intensity sounds as being louder than low-intensity sounds.

COMPLEXITY AND QUALITY

Figure 3–1 shows the way waves of sound travel through the medium (air) away from the source. If we graphically display the movement of one molecule in any one of the waves around a vibrating tuning fork, the resulting waveform is a simple sine curve.

That's because a tuning fork is designed and built very precisely to produce a very simple kind of sound that we call a pure tone. By simple we don't mean easy; we mean that it's not complex. A pure tone is a very clear, musical tone with the same movement of the molecules repeating over and over again.

Our bodies, as well as most other sound-producing objects, don't produce just one simple pure tone. Instead, we produce very complex tones that are made up of many pure tones. The term *complexity* refers to the overall composition of the relative intensities and frequencies of the pure tones that make up a complex wave. Figure 3–3 shows the composition of three complex sounds. Compare these with the pure tones shown in Figure 3–2.

The subjective interpretation of complexity is called *quality*. As you know, sounds differ in ways other than loudness and pitch. Each complex sound is unique: there's some intangible *quality* that makes every voice different. Listen to two singers singing the same note or the same note played by two different musical instruments. You can hear the differences; there are two distinguishable voices and instruments.

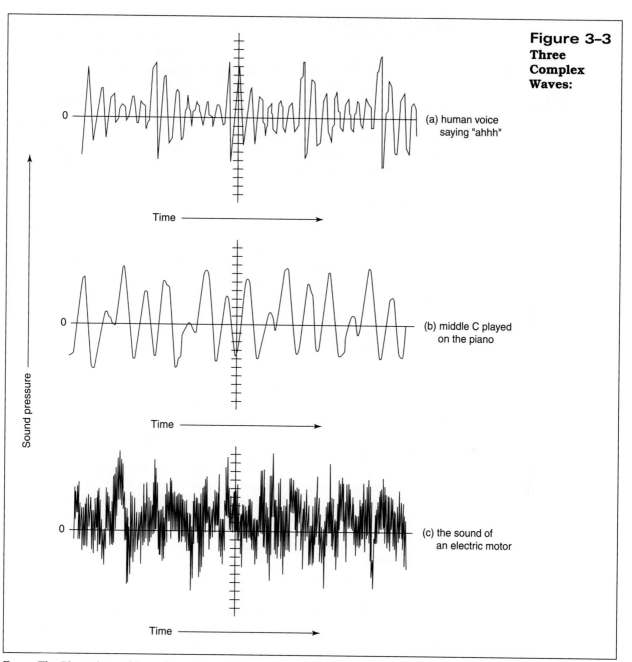

**Figure 3–3
Three
Complex
Waves:**

(a) human voice saying "ahhh"

(b) middle C played on the piano

(c) the sound of an electric motor

From: The Physiology of Speech and Hearing: An Introduction. Raymond Daniloff, Gordon Schuckers, Lawrence Feth (Englewood Cliffs, N.J.: Prentice-Hall, 1980), p. 87.

The Speech Process

Now we're ready to talk about a particular type of sound: the sound of human speech. First, let's look at how humans produce speech sounds. You'll remember that you need three things to produce sound: a force, a vibrator, and a medium. The human body has all the necessary equipment to fill these needs and is an excellent sound producer. There are five distinct processes in producing speech sounds: *innervation, breathing, phonation, resonance,* and *articulation.* Because this is not an advanced text in human anatomy, we'll cover these processes as lightly as possible.

Innervation

There is a highly complex pattern of nerve impulses traveling from the brain to the parts of the body that work together to produce speech. These parts include the muscles of the abdomen and chest, which control breathing; the muscles of the larynx, which are involved in the original production of voice; the structures of the pharynx, larynx, and mouth, which resonate the voice sounds; and, finally, the muscles that control the tongue, palate, and lips to produce the vowels and consonants, the process we call articulation.

To understand the need for precision and accuracy in all these movements, let us examine the articulatory movements of the tongue in a short speech sample. The first words of Lincoln's Gettysburg Address, "Four score and seven years ago," involve an average of four tongue movements per word. At a very slow rate of 120 words per minute we would be required to perform 480 tongue movements for each minute of speech. In addition, if we were to miss the exact place of articulation of each sound by a fraction of a millimeter, the sound produced would probably come out as a completely different sound. Such precise and accurate movements are possible only because of the incredibly rapid and complex patterns of nerve impulses to and from the brain.

Breathing

We use breathing for our first requirement: a force to move the vibrator. Breathing is the process of bringing air into the lungs and forcing it out again. While the air is on its way out, you can use it to set the vocal folds vibrating and thereby produce voice. You can use the mouth to block or impede the breath stream in some way to produce consonant sounds. The way we breathe, that is, actually bring air in and out of the lungs, is quite a simple process. The way we initiate nerve impulses and muscle contractions to control the process is far from simple, so we're not going deeply into that. Nevertheless, you should understand how the mechanism for breathing is constructed.

The Mechanism

Your breathing mechanism is illustrated in Figure 3–4. It consists of the following elements: the *nasal and oral cavities,* which provide openings in your body that reach to the *pharynx,* or throat. The pharynx leads to the *larynx,* which is the uppermost portion of the *trachea,* or windpipe. The trachea then divides into smaller and smaller tubes that compose the *lungs.* Surrounding the lungs is a structural framework of bone, cartilage, and muscle (see Figure 3–5).

The ultimate objective of breathing is to deliver fresh air to the lungs, to exchange oxygen for waste products (carbon dioxide), and to remove air after it has been used. We do this by increasing and decreasing the size of our lungs, taking advantage of a basic law of physics: air flows from high pressure to low pressure.

The lungs can't increase their size by themselves; they have no muscles. Instead, during inhalation, the muscles of the chest elevate

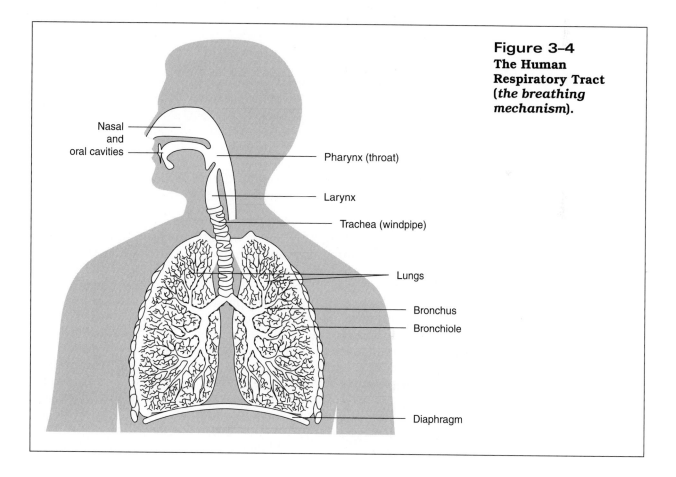

**Figure 3–4
The Human
Respiratory Tract
(*the breathing
mechanism*).**

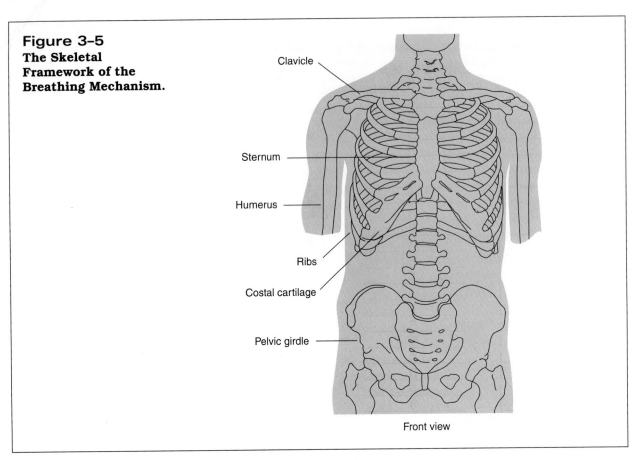

Figure 3-5
The Skeletal Framework of the Breathing Mechanism.

Clavicle

Sternum

Humerus

Ribs

Costal cartilage

Pelvic girdle

Front view

and expand the chest walls, while the *diaphragm* contracts and flattens out. Look at Figure 3–6. This is a schematic diagram of the breathing mechanism during inhalation and exhalation. It shows how the vertical and horizontal dimensions of the chest increase during inhalation. You can verify this yourself. Place one hand lightly on your chest and the other on your abdomen. Breathe deeply in and out. You should feel expansion of both your chest and abdomen as air enters.

Why does the air come into your lungs? The answer is fairly simple. When you increase the dimensions around your lungs, you increase the volume of air the lungs can take in; at the same time, you are lowering the air pressure in your lungs to slightly below the pressure of the air outside your body. Because there is an open passageway from your lungs to the outside (through your nose and mouth), air rushes in as a result of the lowered pressure in your lungs. The air will continue to enter the lungs until the pressure inside equals the pressure outside.

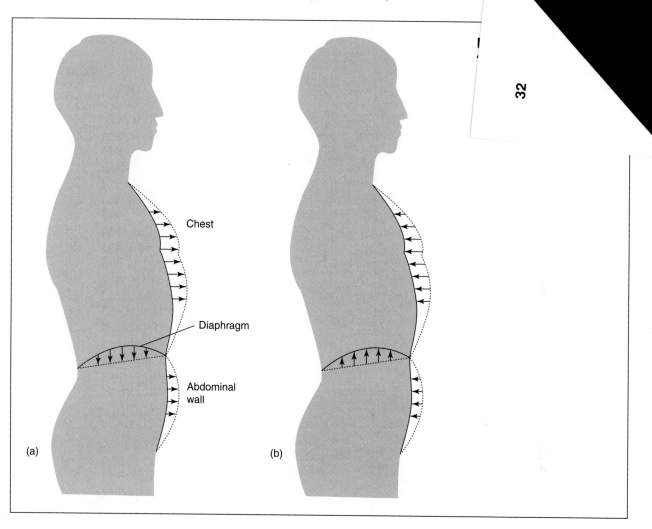

Chest

Diaphragm

Abdominal
wall

(a)　　　　　(b)

A difference in pressure is also the reason air leaves your lungs. When you compress your chest, the air pressure in your lungs becomes slightly higher than that outside your body. So once again, air goes from an area of high pressure to an area of low pressure.

Let's review the process. Muscles of the chest lift and expand the chest walls. The diaphragm contracts, lowering the floor of the chest cavity. The lungs expand along with the chest walls, and their volume increases. As volume increases, pressure lowers, and air comes into the lungs. Now the chest walls contract, the diaphragm is pushed back up, and pressure in the lungs increases, causing air to leave. That's one complete cycle of breathing.

BREATHING FOR SPEECH

Quiet-rest breathing is a low-energy process of a regular nature. Few muscles are involved; the diaphragm does most of the work of inhalation, and muscle relaxation helps exhalation. Each cycle of breathing takes roughly as long as the next, and inhalation and exhalation time frames are also equal. Breathing for speech, however, is quite different. For that you take in the amount of air you need for the number of words you plan to say, and you take it in as quickly as possible. Then you try to be a miser with that air, using it as slowly and efficiently as possible, so that you don't run out of air while you're speaking. So when you're breathing for speech, you depend on short inhalations and long, controlled exhalations (see Figure 3–7). We use slow, sustained contractions of the abdominal muscles for the major portion of breath control. (We'll talk more about speech and breath control in Chapter 10.)

We all know that the wind can move things. We also know that its energy can be harnessed to drive mechanical devices such as windmills. Well, that's what we do in speech; we harness the wind, in this case the breath stream, and set it to work in producing voice and speech sounds. We'll see how that happens when we discuss the next two processes.

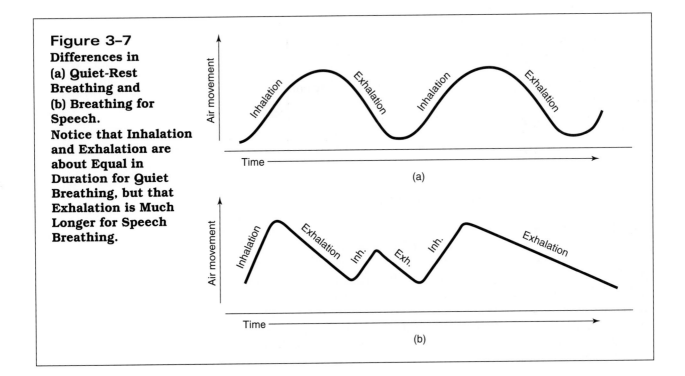

Figure 3–7
Differences in (a) Quiet-Rest Breathing and (b) Breathing for Speech.
Notice that Inhalation and Exhalation are about Equal in Duration for Quiet Breathing, but that Exhalation is Much Longer for Speech Breathing.

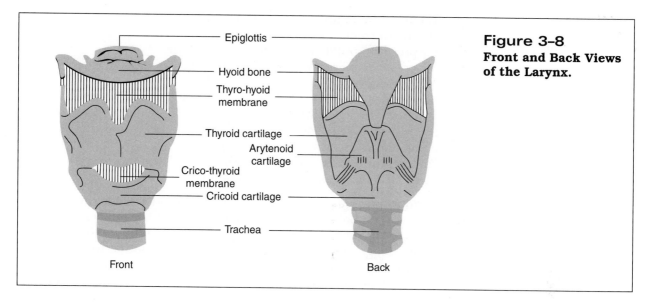

Figure 3–8
Front and Back Views of the Larynx.

Phonation

Very simply defined, phonation is the production of sound using the larynx. First, locate the larynx. Figure 3–8 shows the front and back views of the larynx. Now take the thumb and forefinger of one hand, and very gently pinch your "Adam's apple" (thyroid cartilage). With your forefinger, trace the outline of your thyroid cartilage. This cartilage forms the outside wall of the larynx.

The larynx functions very nicely as a valve. By contracting muscles within the larynx, you're able to move the vocal folds so that they come together, entirely closing off the larynx. Why would you want to do this? Primarily to keep food and other substances out of your lungs, but also to build up air pressure for coughing, to hold your breath, to exert strength such as in heavy lifting, and so on. Look at Figure 3–9a. It shows you an overhead view of the vocal folds during phonation. Figure 3–9b shows the same view, but during quiet breathing.

SOUND PRODUCTION

We said earlier that a vibrating object and a force are needed to produce sound. Well, we've got both elements here; the breath stream provides the force, and the vocal folds become the vibrating object. Here's how the process works:

1. Air is inhaled.
2. The vocal folds meet, completely closing the larynx and stopping the airflow.

3. The diaphragm and chest muscles relax; the abdominal muscles slowly contract.
4. Air pressure builds up below the vocal folds.
5. Air pressure increases until it overcomes the muscular forces holding the vocal folds closed.
6. Air escapes in very rapid bursts, creating waves of sound in the air above the vocal folds. After each burst, the air pressure decreases and the vocal folds close, causing the pressure to build up again. In this way, the cycle repeats.
7. You continue to hold the vocal folds closed and force air between them for as long as you want to phonate.

You can demonstrate this type of sound production in other ways. Blow up a balloon, then stretch the lips of the balloon tightly by pulling the sides of the tube away from each other. You should be able to produce a high-pitched buzz or whistle. Here's another way. Stick out your tongue, lay it on your lower lip, and hold it down with your upper lip. Now, blow air beneath your tongue! You've created what's known as a "raspberry." Both it and the balloon whistle were created aerodynamically in the same way you create voice.

PITCH

We said earlier that the mass, length, and tension of a vibrating object determine the frequency of vibration. These same factors determine how rapidly your vocal folds vibrate, too.

First, let's consider the normal, usual pitch of your voice. That's determined primarily by the length of your vocal folds; the longer the vocal folds, the lower the pitch of your voice. That, along with the size and shape of the resonating cavities, accounts for people having differently

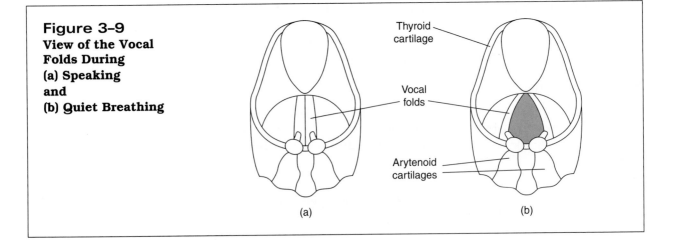

Figure 3–9
View of the Vocal Folds During
(a) Speaking and
(b) Quiet Breathing

Thyroid cartilage

Vocal folds

Arytenoid cartilages

(a)   (b)

pitched voices. It's also the reason why, in general, women's voices are higher than men's. Since you have no control over how long your vocal folds grow to be or over the basic size of your resonating cavities, you don't have much control over the frequency at which your vocal mechanism resonates most efficiently.

The second thing to consider is how you vary pitch to give speech the intonation patterns so necessary for meaning, as in the rising pitch at the end of many questions. Again, mass, length, and tension are the factors. Using the muscles of the larynx, including the vocal folds themselves, you vary the mass, length, and tension of the folds, and thereby change their frequency of vibration.

Resonance

A third way we vary pitch is through resonance. If you could listen to the sound of your voice *in* your larynx, you wouldn't recognize it as voice at all because, in the larynx, voice is only a buzzing noise. Something else has to happen to make that buzzing noise into recognizable voice. That something is resonance.

Resonance is the amplification and modification of sound by the cavities of the vocal tract. Those cavities are the larynx, pharynx, sinuses, oral cavity, and nasal cavity (see Figure 3–10). First, we will explain

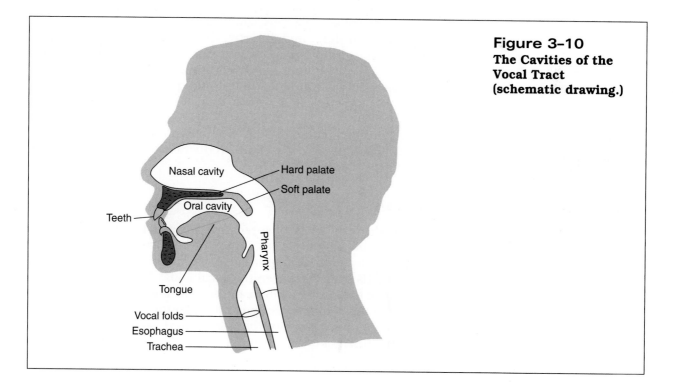

Figure 3–10
The Cavities of the Vocal Tract (schematic drawing.)

resonance in general, then resonance in the vocal tract. We'll also spend time on resonance in Chapter 10 when we discuss vocal quality.

Take an empty soda bottle. Blow across and into the neck so as to produce a low-pitched sound like a foghorn. Think for a minute about what happened; you got more sound out of that bottle than you put into it! That's right. All you did was send some air into the bottle (at just the right angle), and you got a deep, rich sound. You actually set the air inside the bottle vibrating, and the foghorn sound was produced, richer and louder than the sound you put in.

Now fill the bottle about a third of the way. Blow into it again. The sound you produce this time should be higher-pitched. That's because the water takes up space and reduces the volume of air that can resonate. And, if you'll remember, smaller vibrating bodies usually vibrate more rapidly than larger ones. So the pitch of the sound you hear from the bottle varies with the amount of air in the bottle. Try it. Either add some water or take some out; the pitch of the sound will rise or fall. Incidentally, the shape of the resonator also affects the way it operates. As you change the volume of air in the bottle, you're also changing the shape of the resonating cavity. So the important thing about a resonator is its size and shape.

RESONANCE IN THE VOCAL TRACT

The cavities in your head and neck are resonators; they're open chambers filled with air. They're actually very sophisticated resonators, for you can change their size and shape and, thereby, change the tones they resonate.

We use the vocal resonators to transform the buzz of the vocal folds into voice. The resonators selectively amplify the buzz and not only make your voice louder but also give it its unique quality. You're using your resonators as though they were a series of bottles of various sizes and shapes.

We also use resonance in the production of the different consonant and vowel sounds. Most of that production occurs in the mouth and is called articulation.

Articulation

Articulation is the production of speech sounds as a result of movement of the structures of the vocal tract. Figure 3–11 shows the articulators. They are the tongue, teeth, lips, gum ridge, hard palate, soft palate, lower jaw, and the glottis (space between the vocal folds). We use the articulators to (1) change the size and shape of the mouth for resonating vowels and (2) produce the consonants by creating sounds. You'll learn more about consonants and vowels in Chapters 6, to 9, so we'll discuss their production only briefly here.

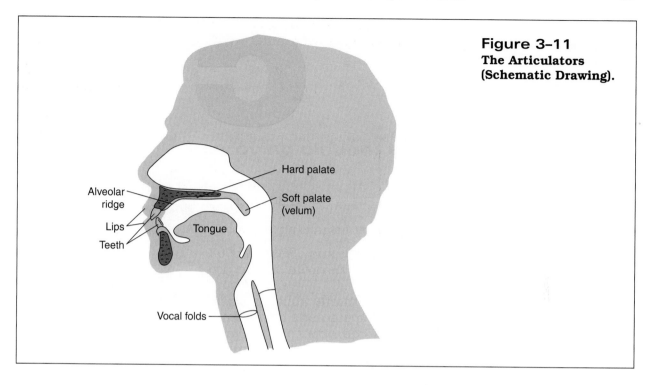

Figure 3–11
The Articulators (Schematic Drawing).

Hard palate

Alveolar ridge

Soft palate (velum)

Lips

Tongue

Teeth

Vocal folds

When you produce vowels, you take the vocal buzz and put it into a differently sized and shaped "bottle" for each vowel. Try this: say *hee-haw*. You should be able to feel your mouth, which was almost closed for *hee*, opening wide for *haw*. By opening wider, you changed from a small resonating cavity to a large one. Figures 3–12, 3–13, and 3–14 show three vowels: [i] as in *tea*, [u] as in *too*, and [ɑ] as in *calm*. Note how you vary your mouth's size and shape to produce these three distinctly different vowel sounds.

Consonants are an entirely different matter. Say the word *kick*. At the beginning and the end, you should feel your tongue pressing up to the soft palate, then exploding air to produce the consonant [k] as shown in Figure 3–15. Now, try the word *tea*. With this word, you create the explosion by pressing the tongue to the gum ridge. Figure 3–16 shows the production of [t]. Figure 3–17 shows the production of a voiceless fricative, [s] as in *see*. The arrow in Figure 3–17 shows that the airflow is constricted, not totally blocked, between the tongue, gum ridge, and teeth. Finally, Figure 3–18 shows production of the nasal continuant, [m] as in *me*. You can see that the mouth is closed at the lips and the soft palate is lowered to allow air to leave through the nose.

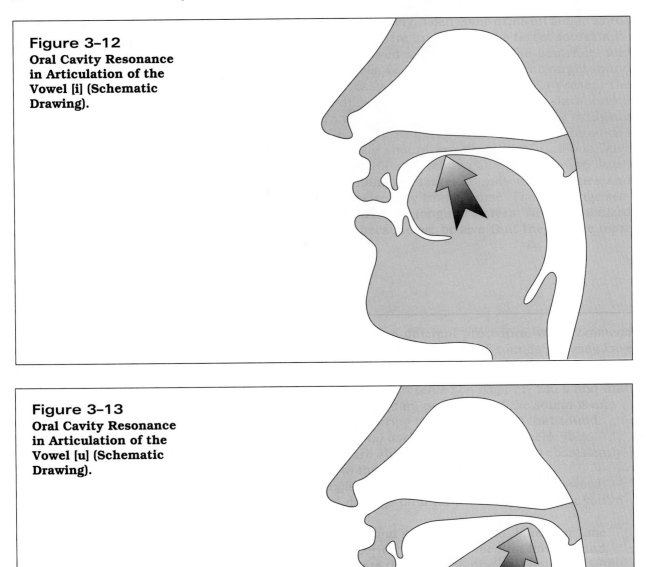

Figure 3–12
Oral Cavity Resonance in Articulation of the Vowel [i] (Schematic Drawing).

Figure 3–13
Oral Cavity Resonance in Articulation of the Vowel [u] (Schematic Drawing).

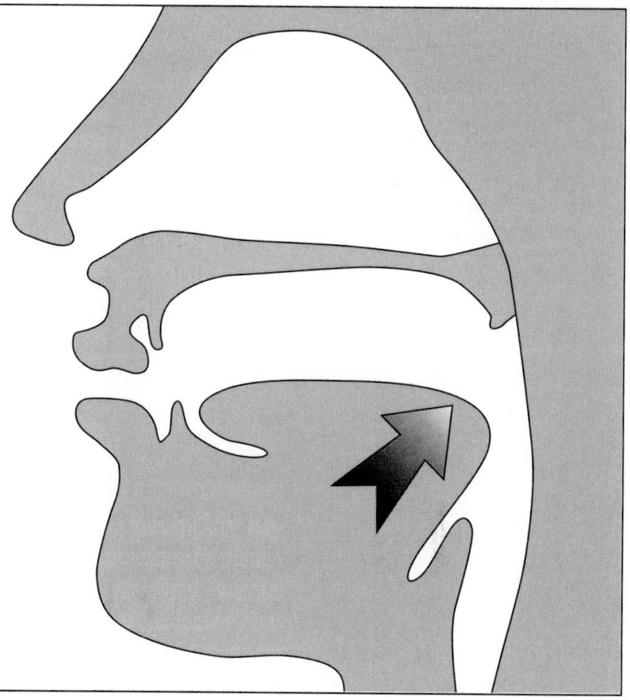

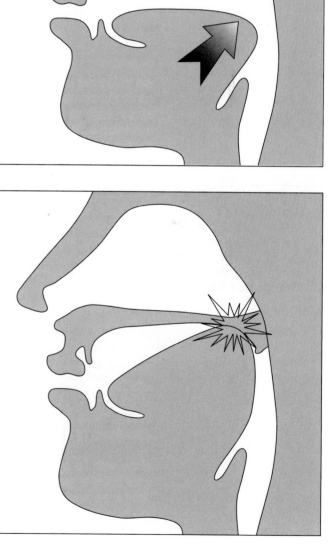

Figure 3–14
Oral Cavity Resonance
in Articulation of the
Vowel [ɑ] (Schematic
Drawing).

Figure 3–15
Articulation of the
Consonant [k]
(Schematic Drawing).
The place of production
is between the tongue
and the soft palate.

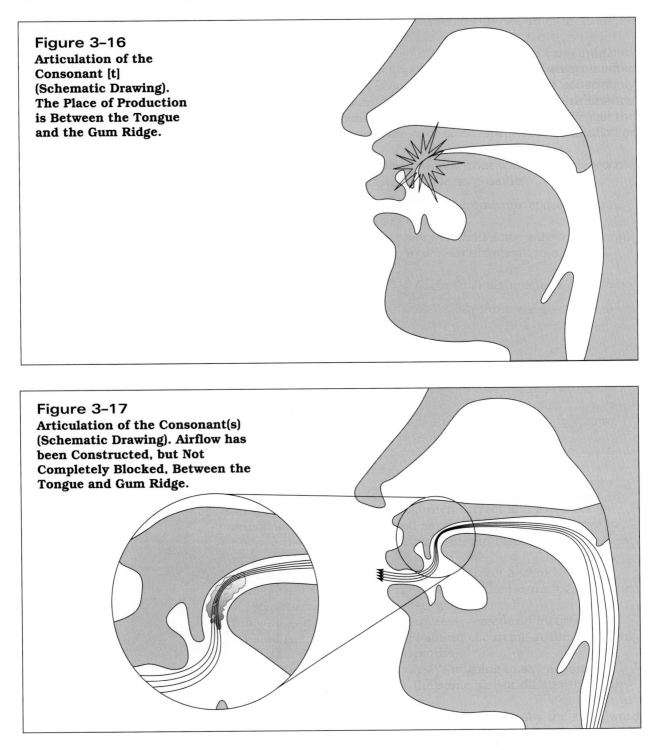

Figure 3–16
Articulation of the
Consonant [t]
(Schematic Drawing).
The Place of Production
is Between the Tongue
and the Gum Ridge.

Figure 3–17
Articulation of the Consonant(s)
(Schematic Drawing). Airflow has
been Constructed, but Not
Completely Blocked, Between the
Tongue and Gum Ridge.

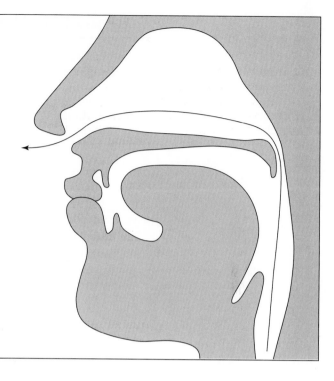

Figure 3–18
Articulation of the
Consonant [m]
(Schematic Drawing).
The mouth is closed at
the lips, and air is
emitted through the
nose.

Articulation is an amazing process. You make an incredible number of complicated movements just to produce a simple sentence. And what's more amazing, you're able to duplicate the movements, returning time and time again to exactly the right spot.

Summary

We use six processes in producing speech sounds: audition, innervation, breathing, phonation, resonance, and articulation. Audition is the process of hearing. Innervation is the neural control of the speech and breathing mechanism. Breathing is the inhalation and exhalation of air and provides the force for sound production. Phonation is the production of vocal sound by the vocal folds. Resonance is the amplification and modification of sound using the cavities of the vocal tract. Articulation is the movement of the vocal tract structures to produce speech sounds.

Suggested Readings

Culbertson, W. R., and Tanner, D. C. *Introductory Speech and Hearing Anatomy and Physiology Workbook.* Boston: Allyn & Bacon, 1997.

Daniloff, R., Schuckers, G., and Feth, L. *The Physiology of Speech and Hearing: An Introduction.* Englewood Cliffs, NJ: Prentice-Hall, 1980.

Palmer, J. *Anatomy for Speech and Hearing.* 4th ed. Baltimore: Williams & Wilkins, 1993.

Perkins, W. H., and Kent, R. D. *Functional Anatomy of Speech, Language, and Hearing: A Primer.* Englewood Cliffs, NJ: Prentice-Hall, 1991.

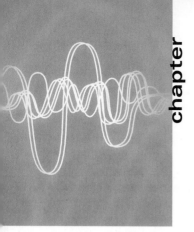

4

the sounds of American English

Objectives

After reading this chapter and participating in related classroom work, you should be able to:

- Explain the reasons for the differences between English speech and English spelling
- Describe the theoretical bases of the International Phonetic Alphabet (IPA)
- Relate the symbols of the IPA to the phonemes we use in speech
- Explain the difference between phonemic and phonetic variations in sounds
- Demonstrate confidence and competence in the use of the IPA
- Begin to discriminate differences between various productions of the phonemes

Speech Comes First

Each of you now reading this book has been given a great and wondrous gift. It's a gift that has been given to only a very small fraction of all the people who have ever lived on this planet. In fact, only two-thirds of the people alive today have it. What is this gift? Literacy—the ability to read and write.

Literate people are fortunate in many ways, but when they begin to study speech, they are often placed at a disadvantage. They have been given, as Marshall McCluhan said, "an eye for an ear." In other words, literate people frequently confuse speech with writing. Illiterate people, on the other hand, know something that few literate people are aware of: *language is speech, and writing is only its reflection.*

Writing attempts to do what the tape recorder does, to capture and make available something that has been said (or thought) in another place and at another time. Of course, the tape recorder does a much better job.

Imagine that instead of reading the sentences on this page, you were listening to a tape recording of the authors speaking these sentences. You would hear many things that can't be put in print, things that make up the total spoken content of our words. You would hear qualities of voice as well as rate and emphasis. You could make fairly accurate guesses as to the age of the authors and their emotional states at the time. Certainly you would know whether the voice belonged to a male or female. But what do you know about the authors as a result of *reading* the words? Unless the words describe him or her, what can you know of an author's age or gender from reading? Nothing! We strip speech of its qualities when we reduce talk to the medium of writing. Communication that began as something designed for our ears is, finally, transmitted to our eyes.

Sounds, Not Letters

There's a lot of confusion about writing and speech. Most people don't seem to be aware that letters and sounds are different in fundamental and important ways.

Speech and Writing Confusion

Most of us are unable to deal with words other than in writing, and it's hard to understand why. You probably wouldn't say that you had heard a picture or that you had seen music. Nor would you claim to smell a flavor or taste an aroma. But this confusion of the senses—it's called *synesthesia*—affects most people in their beliefs about language. Somehow, they find it hard to grasp the fact that *speech consists of sounds that come out of your face and writing is marks you make with your hand.* It's because of this mix-up between visual and auditory reflections of language that many people believe speech consists of "saying letters." For example, if you say *thinkin'* or *goin'* in place of *thinking* or *going,* you are said to be "dropping the *g*." But you also know that the *l* of *almond,* the *t* of *listen,* and the *ch* of *yacht* are all "silent letters," so although you're not producing them, you're not dropping them, either. Or perhaps you've heard a person pronounce his name and later, seeing it spelled, you've wondered, "Why would he pronounce it *that* way when he spells it *this* way?" We really do depend on our eyes to translate what we hear with our ears.

Why do we have these mix-ups between the auditory and the visual? Mainly because the system that educated us supports the belief that talking is subordinate to writing. The reason for that belief is inherent in the long, arduous, and formal process by which we learn to write as compared to the casual, easy, and seemingly automatic way we learn to speak. Think about it. Someone had to teach you how to write; years and years of study, great feats of memorization, hours upon hours of practice, and most of this occurring within the atmosphere of the classroom. Did anyone teach you how to speak your native language? Or did your speech develop without the classroom, without books, without exams, without conscious learning? That's why you use the written word as the point of reference for the spoken; you have been taught to depend on letters instead of sounds.

The Problem with Letters

The difference between sounds and letters is a fundamental one and is really indispensable to you if you want to understand spoken language. Writing is a passive medium. It reflects what we say in a subtle and mysterious way. The written word *cat* is a good example of this. It is composed of a series of marks—*c, a,* and *t*—that allow us to recapture the utterance *cat.* But the marks are not the same as the utterance. When we say aloud the word *cat,* we produce speech sounds by movements of structures within the head, throat, and chest. Our spelling of the word *cat* cannot reflect those movements with any great degree of direct correspondence.

English Spelling and English Speech

The alphabet we use today was first used about 1,300 years ago. When it was new, it accurately reflected the patterns of speech because it adhered to the underlying principle of all alphabets. This principle has two conditions: (1) each written symbol will represent one spoken sound; (2) no spoken sound shall be represented by more than one symbol. In other words, *there should be one, and only one, symbol for every sound in the language.*

   Today the situation is, to put it mildly, not quite what it was. English spelling no longer accurately reflects English speech sounds. The reason is, speech is dynamic, personal, and transitory while writing is static, institutionalized, and permanent. Language changes over time, but writing is frozen. The written language you learned was going out of date 1,000 years ago!

   How many English languages are there? If you're talking about *written* languages, the answer is one. With the exception of a few minor spelling differences—*color/colour,* for example—every English writer uses exactly the same symbols in exactly the same way. If you're talking about spoken English languages, the answer is thousands! Does an English speaker from Boston speak the same way as someone from New York City? Does someone from Atlanta sound the same as someone from San Francisco? On hearing them, would you mistake the words of a native of Trinidad for the words of someone born and raised in Quebec? Speakers all over the world write English in essentially the same way, but the letters they write would give you no clue to the way they sound.

At this point, English has strayed so far from the alphabet principle that it's a miracle we can pronounce from spelling at all. For example, take George Bernard Shaw's often quoted spelling of "fish" as *ghoti*, with the *f* from enou*gh*, the *i* from w*o*men, and the *sh* from na*ti*on. Or how about this: take the *mn* from autu*mn*, the *ai* from pl*ai*d, and the *c* from *c*ello and you can write *mnaic* for "match." Try another. Take the *k* of *k*iss, the *a* sound of mer*i*ngue, and the *t* sound of de*bt* for an unusual spelling of "cat": *kibt*.

We could give you many more examples, but we've made our point. There is enough duplication and overlap in our spelling to allow any word to have more than one "logical" pronunciation. And that gives us, in this speech class, a problem.

You're going to be spending a lot of time talking about speech sounds. But because of the inadequacies of English spelling, you don't have any accurate means of taking notes in such a way that your notes can tell you about sounds. Here's an example: the vowel sound in the word *do* is also in all the following spellings: *ewe, beauty, crew, shoe, cool, group, rude, fruit, true, rheumatism,* and *Sioux!* At the same time, the letter *e* has all of the following pronunciations: *pet, few, sew, eye, women, mete, serve, sergeant,* and *Jones!* You may know what you mean at the time you write your notes, but what about hours later? Do you think you'll remember which sound you meant when you wrote, "Work on *e* tonight?"

IPA

Fortunately, we do have a tool that will help us out of our dilemma: the International Phonetic Alphabet (IPA). This alphabet (*not* a language) was designed about 100 years ago for the purpose of writing down the sounds of a language. IPA is international, meaning it can be applied to any language; it is phonetic, meaning it is based on observed speech sounds; it is an alphabet, meaning it adheres without exception to the alphabetic principle of one sound per symbol. Although you may not have heard of IPA until now, it is in widespread use today by people who wish to accurately record spoken language. IPA is used extensively by actors, radio and TV announcers, speech pathologists, teachers, and anthropologists, as well as by linguists.

IPA can be very useful to you as you learn more about speech. First, by learning the IPA symbols, you will be learning to distinguish all the sounds of spoken English. In other words, we'll use IPA as an ear-training tool. Second, as you become familiar with IPA, you'll begin to associate the symbols with actual movements of the speech mechanism, which will reinforce the sounds as you learn them. Third, IPA solves the problems created by English spelling; it provides us with a common framework for understanding speech sound variations.

IPA Transcription

When you write something in IPA you *transcribe* it. If you are new to IPA, you may be tempted to regard transcription as merely being a weird version of English spelling, and you may spend your time trying to find equivalents between written English spelling and this new, unfamiliar alphabet. If you do that, you're trying to move from one written form to another without the intervening awareness of the *sounds* of speech. This practice will only slow down your learning of IPA. Remember, you use IPA symbols only to record speech; it is not for writing.

To help distinguish between IPA transcription and traditional English spelling, IPA symbols are always enclosed in brackets. For example, *k* is the eleventh letter of the English alphabet, but [k] is the IPA symbol used in transcribing the first sound in the English words *king, queen, cool,* and *choir* and the last sound in *rock* and *antique.*

In the main, IPA uses the familiar symbols derived from the Latin-origin alphabets, including English, in use in western European languages. But even if the symbols look familiar to you, don't confuse them with the English letters whose names you've known for years.

IPA does have symbols for the phonemes of most languages spoken today. In order to avoid confusion, we'll concentrate only on the symbols representing the phonemes of American English.

The list of symbols shown in Table 4–1, given with key words and dictionary symbols, is completely adequate to transcribe just about any utterance spoken in American English and show accurately the phonetic (sound) content of that utterance. You'll also find practice materials at the end of this chapter that will help you learn phonetic transcription.

Table 4–1
The Phonemes of American English (IPA Alphabet)

Phonetic symbol	Dictionary symbol	Key words	Description
p	p	pat-pen-tap	voiceless bilabial plosive
b	b	boat-bad-lab	voiced bilabial plosive
t	t	top-tea-cat	voiceless lingua-alveolar plosive
d	d	dog-day-mad	voiced lingua-alveolar plosive
k	k	key-kick-cake	voiceless lingua-velar plosive
g	g	go-game-egg	voiced lingua-velar plosive
f	f	four-feel-off	voiceless labio-dental fricative
v	v	very-vine-love	voiced labio-dental fricative
θ	th	thin-thick-bath	voiceless lingua-dental fricative
ð	t͞h, <u>th</u>	the-those-bathe	voiced lingua-dental fricative
s	s	snake-see-face	voiceless lingua-alveolar fricative
z	z	zoo-zap-buzz	voiced lingua-alveolar fricative

(continued)

Table 4–1
(*Continued*)

Phonetic symbol	Dictionary symbol	Key words	Description
ʃ	sh	she-shoe-ash	voiceless lingua-palatal fricative
ʒ	zh	beige-pleasure	voiced lingua-palatal fricative
h	h	hot-hat-head	voicless glottal fricative
ʍ	hw	where-which-why	voiceless bilabial glide
w	w	watch-wear-weather	voiced bilabial glide
r	r	red-roses-right	voiced lingua-alveolar glide
j	y	yes-yellow-onion	voiced lingua-palatal glide
l	l	left-loose-ball	voiced lingua-alveolar lateral
m	m	man-me-aim	voiced bilabial nasal
n	n	no-knee-can	voiced lingua-alveolar nasal
ŋ	ng	sing-hang-king	voiced lingua-velar nasal
tʃ	ch	chair-cheat-each	voiceless lingua-alveolo/palatal affricate
dʒ	j	judge-Jane-wage	voiced lingua-alveolo/palatal affricate
i	ē	see-east-free	high front tense vowel
ɪ	ĭ	sit-in-pit	high front lax vowel
e	ā	ate-pay-able	mid-front tense vowel
ɛ	ĕ	bet-bed-end	mid-front lax vowel
æ	ă	pat-flat-Adam	low front tense vowel
a	ã	dance (Boston "a")	low front lax vowel
ɑ	a	calm-honest-car	low back lax vowel
ɒ	a	hot (British "a")	low back tense vowel
ɔ	ô	awful-often-all	mid-back lax vowel
o	ō	so-open-hotel	mid-back tense vowel
ʊ	oo	book-push-wood	high back lax vowel
u	oo	too-pool-food	high back tense vowel
ʌ	ŭ	up-uncle-usher	low central stressed vowel
ə	ə	banana-sofa-about	mid-central unstressed vowel
ɝ(ɜ)	ur	early-urn-pearl	mid-central stressed vowel with retroflexion
ɚ	ər	father-perhaps	mid-central unstressed vowel with retroflexion
ɑɪ	i	ice-light-time	diphthong—low front to high front
ɑʊ	ou	how-out-ouch	diphthong—low front to high back
ɔɪ	oi	coin-boy-oyster	diphthong—low back to high front
eɪ	ā	game-daze-rain	diphthong—mid-front to high front
oʊ	ō	road-home-doze	dipthong—mid-back to high back
iɚ-iə	ēr	ear-here-peer	diphthong—high front to low mid-central unstressed with or without retroflexion
ɛɚ-ɛə	âr	air-pare-where	diphthong—mid-front to low mid-central unstressed with or without retroflexion
ɑɚ-ɑə	är	are-car-barn	diphthong—low back to low mid-central unstressed with or without retroflexion
ɔɚ-ɔə	ôr	or-door-shore	diphthong—mid-back to low mid-central unstressed with or without retroflexion
uɚ-ɔə	o͝or	tour-poor-sure	diphthong—high back to low mid-central unstressed with or without retroflexion

The Phoneme

Each IPA symbol represents one *phoneme* of American English. A phoneme, though, is not exactly one sound. Instead, it is better described as a *sound family.* Let's look at it this way: the word *dog* refers to a type of animal that includes many different subtypes ranging from great danes to chihuahuas with all sorts of dogs in between. The word *dog*, though it doesn't tell you exactly what kind of dog, fits any type in the dog family. Well, we have sound families, too. Take the phoneme [k], for example. It doesn't sound exactly the same in *kit* as it does in *skit*, but it's still in the family of [k].

The Allophone

Say the following sentence aloud: "I can open a can of beans." Now say it again, and this time listen to the two utterances of the word *can*. The vowel seems to change slightly, doesn't it? Now reverse the *cans*, saying the noun as if it were the verb. It may sound strange to you, but it doesn't change the meaning. That's because both those sounds are allophones of the phoneme [æ]. An *allophone* is a (*variation of a phoneme.*) You can hear that it's slightly different, but not different enough to call it another phoneme. So remember, even though we say we're using one sound per symbol, each IPA symbol really represents a family of sounds that are so similar, it's hard to hear the differences among them.

Phonetics and Phonemics

The difference between phonetics and phonemics is like the difference between a musical performance and its underlying musical score. A composition may be played by a string quartet or by a 60-piece orchestra, or it may be whistled by one person. Take the case of one composition performed in two ways: first, played by the Beatles, and second, delivered to your captive ears as elevator music. You know that these performances share a specific and precise pattern (the melody), but you also know that they are very different as physical events.

Similarly, with speech, the sounds we utter (phonetics) are realizations of underlying sound categories (phonemics) that exist in the minds of speakers and listeners who share a common language.

We use a modified phonemic approach in this text. That is, we emphasize phonemic distinctions and look at phonetic differences wherever we think a closer examination of articulatory events would be helpful.

Dialects and Standard Speech

Up to now we've been talking as though there were but one spoken American English. But you know from your own experience that there are varieties, or *dialects*, spoken across the nation.

DIALECTS

A dialect is a variation of a language; it is spoken by a subgroup of speakers. This subgroup differs geographically or socially or ethnically from the rest of the speakers of the language. The dialect can differ in pronunciation, vocabulary, and grammar. For example, how do you say *Florida?* Do you use the vowel in *oar* or the vowel in *are?* Do you call the paper container you use for groceries a *sack* or a *bag?* Do you say "I be going" or "I am going"? These are just a few examples of dialectical differences.

REGIONAL DIALECTS

Linguists generally identify four large geographical areas within the United States that have definable regional dialects. These regional dialects are Eastern, New England, Southern, and General American. In addition, many linguists recognize a major dialect within the Eastern region: New York Metropolitan. Within each dialect area, however, there are likely to be wide variations, so don't expect all speakers within a region to sound alike.

STANDARD SPEECH

Is there any one standard way to speak American English? Any one standard dialect that doesn't vary across the country? Is any one regional dialect preferable to another? We don't think so. When the authors speak of "standard," we refer to the speech of one of the major regional dialects that we listed above. Within that region, we view the standard as the following: Standard speech describes the language of the majority of the educated people in the region. You can find a listing of the significant phonetic features of the major regional dialects on pages (59–60) at the end of this chapter.

NONSTANDARD SPEECH

If you live in Massachusetts and say the word *greasy* so that it rhymes with *fleecy*, your production would be considered standard. Should you use the same pronunciation in North Carolina, your production would be nonstandard. Why? Because in North Carolina, most people say *greasy* so that it rhymes with *breezy*. What's standard in one place may not be standard in another. And what's standard for one social subgroup may be nonstandard in another.

Notice that when we say "nonstandard," we simply mean "different." We don't believe that any region has a "better" dialect than another region. Is there any advantage to speaking "standard" for an area? We think so. It has to do with the way listeners may judge you simply by the way you speak. The standard of an area usually carries more prestige for the speaker simply because it reflects the way the well-educated speak. It also provides a more formal way of speaking that is probably more versatile than the way you speak with your family and friends.

FOREIGN ACCENTS

If you've learned a second language, chances are you learned to speak it not like a native but, rather, with an accent that reflected your first language. For example, if your first language is American English, you learned to speak Spanish, say, with an American accent. Conversely, if your first language is Spanish, you probably speak English in a way that indicates that fact to your listeners. Why do these accents exist? They come about as a result of the phonemic differences between languages. Let's use English and Spanish as examples. In English, the words *seat* and *sit* are pronounced with two very distinct phonemes [i] and [ɪ]—very distinct, that is, to someone whose native language contains those sounds. Since Spanish does *not* have the [ɪ] of *sit,* the native Spanish speaker doesn't hear that there are two separate sounds produced, and he says, "I will seat down on the seat." *Sit* and *seat* probably sound the same to him; the difference must be taught.

If you are having difficulty recognizing the differences between your first language and American English, see Appendix B, "Guide to Foreign Accents," and talk to your instructor for guidance.

Classification of Sounds

The phonemes of our language are placed in three general categories: consonants, vowels, and diphthongs. Each category differs from the others in the way its sounds are produced, particularly in the way the articulators modify the breath stream. Let's examine them individually.

Consonants

The consonant sounds are produced when the articulators obstruct the breath stream either completely or partially. Make the first sound in the word *kiss.* You produce it by holding the back of the tongue firmly against the soft palate, which shuts off the breath stream completely. Then you build up air pressure and suddenly explode the air past the point of obstruction. The last sound in *kiss,* though, only needs a partial obstruction. You force the breath stream through the narrow opening between your tongue and teeth, making a hissing sound.

The consonant sounds are classified according to three factors: voicing, place of articulation, and method of articulation (see Table 4–2).

Table 4–2
Consonants: Method of Articulation

Place of articulation	Plosives		Fricatives		Nasals		Glides		Lateral		Affricates	
	VS	V	VS	V	VS	V	VS	V	VS	V	VS	V
Bilabial (both lips)	p	b				m	ʍ	w				
Labio-dental (lip-teeth)			f	v								
Lingua-dental (tongue-teeth)			θ	ð								
Lingua-alveolar (tongue-gum ridge)	t	d	s	z		n		r		l		
Lingua-alveolo/ palatal (tongue-gum ridge/palate)											tʃ	ʤ
Lingua-palatal (tongue-palate)			ʃ	ʒ				j				
Lingua-velar (tongue-soft palate)	k	g				ŋ						
Glottal (vocal folds)			h									

VOICING

If you produce voice at the same time that you produce a consonant sound, the consonant is said to be *voiced*. If there is no voice with the consonant, it is *voiceless*. The difference is usually fairly easy to hear, but if you have trouble telling if a consonant is voiced or voiceless, try this: Gently rest your fingers on either side of your thyroid cartilage (Adam's apple) and hum. You should be able to feel vibrations with your fingertips. Now say the first sound in the word *vat*. Again, there should be vibrations. Now say the first sound in the word *fat*. You shouldn't feel vibrations because the word *fat* begins with a voiceless sound.

Look at Table 4–2. You'll see that a number of the consonant sounds are in pairs on the chart. We call these pairs *cognates*. Cognate sounds are sounds produced in the same place, in the same way, using the same articulators: the only difference is one sound is voiced, the other is voiceless.

PLACE OF ARTICULATION

The point at which we obstruct the breath stream is an important factor in consonant classification. To identify the physical place of articulation, we use the names of the articulators involved. Look again at Table 4–2. The places of articulation of the various consonants are listed down the left side of the chart. The listings are (1) bilabial (both lips); (2) labiodental (lip-teeth); (3) lingua-dental (tongue-teeth); (4) lingua-alveolar (tongue-gum ridge); (5) lingua-alveolo/palatal (tongue-gum ridge/palate); (6) lingua-palatal (tongue-palate); (7) lingua-velar (tongue-soft palate); (8) glottal (the space between the vocal folds). The first sound in the word *pet*, for example, is a bilabial sound—you make it with both lips.

METHOD OF ARTICULATION

Method of articulation means the physical process used to produce the sound. The various methods of articulation are listed from left to right in Table 4–2. Let's take the time now to explain each method briefly.

1. *Plosives* are sounds you make by blocking off the breath stream entirely for a very short period of time, just long enough to build up some air pressure behind your articulators. You then suddenly "explode" this air to produce the sound. The first sound in *pet* is a plosive.
2. *Fricatives* differ from plosives in that you don't have to block off the breath stream as completely. All you need is a very narrow opening through which you can squeeze some air. The first sound in the word *see* is a fricative.
3. *Nasals* are just as the name suggests. You produce the nasals by lowering the soft palate and blocking the oral cavity with the lips or the tongue. You then let the air go out the nostrils. The first and last sounds in the word *man* are nasals.
4. *Glides* are consonant sounds you make while you're moving your articulators from one position to another. You can hear and feel the motion. The first sound in the word *yes* is a glide. Say it slowly to feel the gliding motion.
5. *Lateral sounds* (English has only one) are produced by dropping the sides of the tongue and allowing the air to leave by the sides of the mouth. The first and last sounds in the word *lull* are laterals.
6. *Affricates* are really consonant combinations. The two English affricates are formed by joining together a voiceless plosive with a voiceless fricative, and a voiced plosive with a voiced fricative. The first and last sounds in the word *charge* are affricates.

You'll learn the method of articulation in more detail when you read Chapters 6 through 9 on consonants and vowels.

Vowels

What are the vowels of spoken English? Your first impulse is probably to say that the vowels are "a, e, i, o, u, and sometimes y." Wrong! Those are, unfortunately, the vowels of *written* English. We don't name the vowels of spoken English to separate them from the consonants; instead, we define them by how they are produced. The vowels of spoken English are *speech sounds produced without obstruction of the breath stream* by the articulators. Here's an example: Open wide and say *ahhh.* You'll notice that the breath stream is not blocked at all.

Classification of Vowels

We use three factors to classify the vowels. They are height of the tongue, place of production, and muscle tension. Let's briefly explain each one, and you can look at the vowel chart (Figure 4–1) as we go along.

HEIGHT OF THE TONGUE

You raise your tongue to different heights to create different vowel sounds. Say the words *see* and *saw.* You should be able to feel your mouth opening for the word *saw.* That's because *saw* has a lower tongue position than *see.*

PLACE OF PRODUCTION

"Place" really refers to the part of the tongue primarily responsible for producing a particular vowel—the front, middle, or back. The vowel in

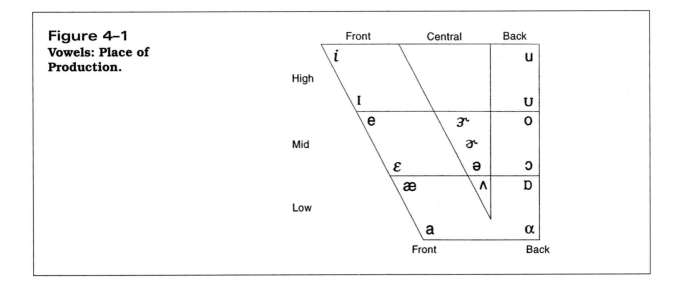

Figure 4–1
Vowels: Place of Production.

see is made with the front of the tongue; the vowel in *saw* is produced with the back of the tongue.

Muscle Tension

The tension of the tongue muscles also affects vowel production. Try this: Place the thumb and forefinger of one hand lightly on your neck above the larynx. Swallow. You should be able to feel muscle contractions. Keeping your fingers in the same place, say the words *see* and *sit*. The vowel in *see* is tense, so you can probably feel the tongue muscles contracting. The vowel in *sit* is lax (no tension) so you won't feel the muscles contracting as much.

Diphthongs

A diphthong is a *vowel blend;* two vowels are blended together and said in such a way that the sound begins with one vowel and ends with the other. You use a smooth, gliding motion, and although two vowels are used, the resulting diphthong is perceived as one sound. The sound that follows the initial consonant in the word *time* is an example of a diphthong.

Phonetic Transcription Practice

Now it's time for you to begin practicing phonetic transcription. It will take a while for you to train yourself to stop thinking of sounds as being letters and to train yourself to hear fine differences between sounds. At the start, you'll frequently feel frustrated, but after all, you've probably never had to do this type of listening before.

The following transcription exercise will quickly help you increase your skill level. The exercise is divided into four levels of difficulty. The first level contains single-syllable words, the second and third contain multi-syllable words, and the fourth, simple phrases. You'll notice that there are three columns; work across the columns, one word at a time. In the left column are the words to transcribe. In the center column write the number of *sounds* (not syllables) in each word. Don't be concerned with the number of letters in the words; count how many sounds you hear when the words and phrases are said out loud. In the right column, transcribe the word using IPA symbols.

If you can, have someone read the words aloud to you, or listen to a tape recording. Transcribe what you actually hear, not what you think *should* be said. Don't write what you hear in English spelling; you'll only confuse the visual and auditory inputs. When you've completed the first-level words, go on to the second level and then to the third. After you've completed the entire exercise, you're ready to move on to complex sentences and longer utterances on your own.

Words for Phonetic Transcription Practice: Level 1

Transcribe the following words in IPA. The answers are at the end of this chapter beginning on page 60. We've filled in the correct answers for the first word as an example. Diphthongs count as one sound.

	Word	*Number of Sounds*	*IPA Transcription*
1.	pat	3	[pæt]
2.	boat		[ ]
3.	flat		[ ]
4.	rope		[ ]
5.	two		[ ]
6.	east		[ ]
7.	room		[ ]
8.	dog*		[ ]
9.	fed		[ ]
10.	snake		[ ]
11.	grass		[ ]
12.	phone		[ ]
13.	thought*		[ ]
14.	this		[ ]
15.	think		[ ]
16.	awful*		[ ]
17.	raise		[ ]
18.	book		[ ]
19.	cheap		[ ]
20.	lunch		[ ]
21.	plane		[ ]
22.	roll		[ ]
23.	sell		[ ]
24.	easy		[ ]
25.	table		[ ]

*See notes on regional occurrence of [ɔ], page 60.

Words for Phonetic Transcription Practice: Level 2

Transcribe the following words in IPA. The answers are at the end of this chapter on pages 61 and 62. Diphthongs count as one sound.

	Word	*Number of Sounds*	*IPA Transcription*
26.	judge		[ ]
27.	bother		[ ]
28.	wheel		[ ]
29.	embassy		[ ]
30.	yellow		[ ]

31. tire _____ [_____]
32. laughing _____ [_____]
33. friend _____ [_____]
34. thumb _____ [_____]
35. pens _____ [_____]
36. cage _____ [_____]
37. vision _____ [_____]
38. beige _____ [_____]
39. cruise _____ [_____]
40. prank _____ [_____]
41. shops _____ [_____]
42. street _____ [_____]
43. pains _____ [_____]
44. cute _____ [_____]
45. broad* _____ [_____]
46. track _____ [_____]
47. painting _____ [_____]
48. fools _____ [_____]
49. desks _____ [_____]
50. strong* _____ [_____]

*See notes on regional occurrence of [ɔ], page 60.

Words for Phonetic Transcription Practice: Level 3

Transcribe the following words in IPA. The answers are at the end of this chapter on page 62. Diphthongs count as one sound.

Word	Number of Sounds	IPA Transcription
51. machines	_____	[_____]
52. shouted	_____	[_____]
53. relative	_____	[_____]
54. Chicago	_____	[_____]
55. oyster*	_____	[_____]
56. boiler*	_____	[_____]
57. English	_____	[_____]
58. laundry*	_____	[_____]
59. downtown	_____	[_____]
60. calm	_____	[_____]
61. burgers	_____	[_____]
62. early	_____	[_____]
63. arrive	_____	[_____]
64. rather	_____	[_____]
65. under	_____	[_____]
66. church	_____	[_____]

67.	jumbo jet	_____	[_____]
68.	exit	_____	[_____]
69.	wages	_____	[_____]
70.	crime	_____	[_____]
71.	prizes	_____	[_____]
72.	computer	_____	[_____]
73.	magazines	_____	[_____]
74.	carwax	_____	[_____]
75.	flounders	_____	[_____]

*See notes on regional occurrence of [ɔ], page 60.

Phrases for Phonetic Transcription Practice: Level 4

Transcribe the following words in IPA. The answers are at the end of this chapter on pages 62 and 63. Diphthongs count as one sound.

Phrase		Number of Sounds	IPA Transcription
76.	passed over	_____	[_____]
77.	bunch of bananas	_____	[_____]
78.	took vitamin pills	_____	[_____]
79.	greased lightning	_____	[_____]
80.	electrical engineer	_____	[_____]
81.	extra dirty shoes	_____	[_____]
82.	fire hydrant	_____	[_____]
83.	common goals	_____	[_____]
84.	hockey game	_____	[_____]
85.	gold nuggets	_____	[_____]
86.	collect call*	_____	[_____]
87.	live at five	_____	[_____]
88.	threw the book	_____	[_____]
89.	basic black dress	_____	[_____]
90.	the last straw*	_____	[_____]
91.	buzzing bees	_____	[_____]
92.	beach house	_____	[_____]
93.	shipping chickens	_____	[_____]
94.	gale wind watch	_____	[_____]
95.	air pollution	_____	[_____]
96.	curve ball	_____	[_____]
97.	jet juice	_____	[_____]
98.	garlic bread	_____	[_____]
99.	star wars*	_____	[_____]
100.	wooden spoon	_____	[_____]

*See notes on regional occurrence of [ɔ], page 60.

Regional Dialects

The following charts show how each of the regional dialects tends to differ from General American on certain sounds. As we said earlier, there are wide variations within each dialect area so all speakers within a particular region won't sound exactly alike.

Southern Regional Dialect

Sound	Word	General American	Southern
[ɛ]	pen	[pɛn]	[pɪn]
[ɛ]	red	[rɛd]	[rɛəd]
[ɛ]	yes	[jɛs]	[jɛjəs]
[ɛɚ]	Mary	[mɛɚɪ]	[meɪrɪ]
[ɪ]	hid	[hɪd]	[hɪjəd]
[ɪɚ]	dear	[dɪɚ]	[dɪjə]
[æ]	pass	[pæs]	[pæjəs]
[ɔɚ]	store	[stɔɚ]	[stowə]
[u]	Tuesday	[tuzdeɪ]	[tjuzdeɪ]
[ɑɪ]	time	[tɑɪm]	[tɑ:m]
[ɑɪ]	tired	[tɑɪɚd]	[tɑ:d]
[ɑɚ]	car	[kɑɚ]	[kɑ:]

Note: Elongation of a vowel is indicated by [:].

Eastern Regional Dialect

Sound	Word	General American	Eastern
[æ]	ask	[æsk]	[ɑsk]
[ɑ]	hot	[hɑt]	[hɒt]
[ɚ]	word	[wɚd]	[wɜ:d]
[ɚ]	father	[fɑðɚ]	[fɑðə]
[au]	now	[nau]	[nɛau]
[ɪɚ]	here	[hɪɚ]	[hɪə]
[ɛɚ]	pair	[pɛɚ]	[pɛə]
[ɑɚ]	car	[kɑɚ]	[kɑə]
[ɔɚ]	floor	[flɔɚ]	[flɔə]
[uɚ]	poor	[puɚ]	[puə]

Note: Elongation of a vowel is indicated by [:].

The New York regional dialect usually includes the features of the Eastern dialect plus the following:

New York Regional Dialect

Sound	Word	General American	New York
[æ]	can't	[kænt]	[kɛənt]
[ɔ]	tall	[tɔl]	[tɔəl]
[ɔ]	Florida	[flɔrɪdə]	[flɑrɪdə]
[ɝ]	hurry	[hɝɪ]	[hʌrɪ]
[aɪ]	time	[taɪm]	[təɪm]a

Note: [ɔ] as in *tall* is diphthongized and has a significant degree of lip-rounding.

New England Regional Dialect

Sound	Word	General American	New England
[æ]	ask	[æsk]	[ask]
[æ]	ask	[æsk]	[ɑsk]
[u]	Tuesday	[tuzdeɪ]	[tjuzdeɪ]
[ɑ]	hot	[hɑt]	[hɒt]
[ɝ]	third	[θɝːd]	[θɜːd]
[ɚ]	father	[fɑðɚ]	[fɑðə]
[ɪɚ]	fear	[fɪɚ]	[fɪə]
[ɛɚ]	hair	[hɛɚ]	[hɛə]
[ɑɚ]	car	[kɑɚ]	[kɑə]
[ɔɚ]	floor	[flɔɚ]	[flɔə]
[uɚ]	poor	[puɚ]	[puə]

Notes: The New England [a] as in *ask* is frequently called the "broad a." [ː] indicates elongation of a vowel.

Phonetic Transcription Practice Answers

Answers for Phonetic Transcription Practice: Level 1 Words

W+ord	Number of Sounds	IPA Transcription
1. pat	3	[pæt]
2. boat	3	[bot]
3. flat	4	[flæt]
4. rope	3	[rop]
5. two	2	[tu]
6. east	3	[ist]
7. room	3	[rum]
8. dog*	3	[dɔg]
9. fed	3	[fɛd]
10. snake	4	[snek]
11. grass	4	[græs]
12. phone	3	[fon]

13.	thought*	3	[θɔt]
14.	this	3	[ðɪs]
15.	think	4	[θĩŋk]
16.	awful*	4	[ɔfəl]
17.	raise	3	[rez]
18.	book	3	[bʊk]
19.	cheap	3	[tʃip]
20.	lunch	4	[lʌntʃ]
21.	plane	4	[plen]
22.	roll	3	[rol]
23.	sell	4	[sɛl]
24.	easy	3	[izi]
25.	table	4	[tebl]

*See notes on regional occurrence of [ɔ], page 60.

Answers for Phonetic Transcription Practice: Level 2 Words

	Word	*Number of Sounds*	*IPA Transcription*
26.	judge	3	[dʒʌdʒ]
27.	bother	4	[bɑðɚ]
28.	wheel	3	[ʍil]
29.	embassy	6	[ɛmbəsi]
30.	yellow	4	[jɛlo]
31.	tire	3	[tɑɪɚ]
32.	laughing	5	[læfɪŋ]
33.	friend	5	[frɛnd]
34.	thumb	3	[θʌm]
35.	pens	4	[pɛnz]
36.	cage	3	[keɪdʒ]
37.	vision	4	[vɪʒn]
38.	beige	3	[beɪʒ]
39.	cruise	4	[kruz]
40.	prank	5	[præŋk]
41.	shops	4	[ʃɑps]
42.	street	5	[strit]
43.	pains	4	[peɪnz]
44.	cute	4	[kjut]
45.	broad*	4	[brɔd]
46.	track	4	[træk]
47.	painting	6	[peɪntɪŋ]
48.	fools	4	[fulz]
49.	desks	5	[dɛsks]
50.	strong*	5	[strɔŋ]

*See notes on regional occurrence of [ɔ], page 60.

Answers for Phonetic Transcription Practice: *Level 3 Words*

Word	Number of Sounds	IPA Transcription
51. machines	6	[məʃinz]
52. shouted	5	[ʃaʊtəd]
53. relative	7	[rɛlətɪv]
54. Chicago	6	[ʃɪkɑgo]
55. oyster*	4	[ɔɪstɚ]
56. boiler*	4	[bɔɪlɚ]
57. English	6	[ĩŋglɪʃ]
58. laundry*	6	[lɔndri]
59. downtown	6	[dɑʊntɑʊn]
60. calm	3	[kɑm]
61. burgers	5	[bɝgɚz]
62. early	3	[ɝli]
63. arrive	4	[ərɑɪv]
64. rather	4	[ræðɚ]
65. under	4	[ʌndɚ]
66. church	3	[tʃɝtʃ]
67. jumbo jet	8	[dʒʌmbo dʒɛt]
68. exit	5	[ɛksɪt]
69. wages	6	[weɪdʒəz]
70. crime	4	[krɑɪm]
71. prizes	6	[prɑɪzəz]
72. computer	8	[kəmpjutɚ]
73. magazines	8	[mægəzinz]
74. carwax	7	[kɑrwæks]
75. flounders	7	[flɑʊndɚz]

*See notes on regional occurrence of [ɔ], page 60.

Answers for Phonetic Transcription Practice:
Level 4 Phrases

Phrase		Number of Sounds	IPA Transcription
76.	passed over	7	[pæst ouvɚ]
77.	bunch of bananas	13	[bʌntʃ əv bənænəz]
78.	took vitamin pills	14	[tuk vaɪtəmɪn pɪlz]
79.	greased lightning	11	[grist laɪtnɪŋ]
80.	electrical engineer	15	[ɪlɛtrɪkəl ɛnʤənɪɚ]
81.	extra dirty shoes	13	[ɛkstrə dɝti ʃuz]
82.	fire hydrant	10	[faɪɚ haɪdrənt]
83.	common goals	9	[kɑmən goulz]
84.	hockey game	7	[hɑki geɪm]
85.	gold nuggets	10	[gould nʌgəts]
86.	collect call*	9	[kəlɛkt kɔl]
87.	live at five	8	[laɪv æt faɪv]
88.	threw the book	8	[θru ðə bʊk]
89.	basic black dress	13	[besɪk blæk drɛs]
90.	the last straw*	10	[ðə læst strɔ]
91.	buzzing bees	8	[bʌzɪŋ biz]
92.	beach house	7	[bitʃ haʊs]
93.	shipping chickens	11	[ʃɪpɪŋ tʃɪkənz]
94.	gale wind watch	10	[gɛəl wɪnd wɑtʃ]
95.	air pollution	9	[ɛɚ pʌluʃən]
96.	curve ball	6	[kɝv bɔl]
97.	jet juice	6	[ʤɛt ʤus]
98.	garlic bread	10	[gɑrlɪk brɛd]
99.	star wars*	6	[stɑɚ wɔɚz]
100.	wooden spoon	8	[wʊdn spun]

*See notes on regional occurrence of [ɔ], page 60

part two

diction

Objectives

After completing the work in Part II, you should be able to:

- Identify the various consonantal and vowel phonemes and the production problems associated with each
- Identify your target phonemes, that is, the specific phonemes you misarticulate and the nature of each misarticulation
- Distinguish regional variations of target phonemes
- Be able to produce, at the instructor's request, each target phoneme correctly, in isolation, words, and phrases
- Identify others' misarticulations, and feed that information back in a helpful, nonjudgmental way

65

In this extremely important section, you get a chance to put theory into practice in your own speech. Chapter 5 gives an explanation of our general approach and a set of instructions for improving diction. It is short, but it is one of the most important chapters in the book. It covers material that will save you time and effort as well as increase your chances of success. The first part of the chapter outlines a routine you can follow. The second part will help you distinguish between accurate and inaccurate productions of sounds. The third part gives you a set of warmup exercises to follow before you practice. You'll make faster progress if you take the time to read this chapter and try the warmups before working on any of the sounds in Chapters 6 to 9.

Chapters 6 through 9 deal with the individual consonantal and vowel phonemes of American English. Each chapter consists mainly of drill materials for correcting and improving production of specific consonant, vowel, and diphthong sounds. The specific exercises for each sound are organized in ascending order of difficulty; that is, they become increasingly difficult. As you begin a particular phoneme you start with words, phrases, and sentences that are easy to articulate; then the material becomes increasingly difficult as you progress. Finally, when you are very near to mastering the phoneme, you'll find material that is more challenging and, in many cases, more interesting. Work on the drills in that order so that you can be more successful in accomplishing your goals.

Each consonant and vowel chapter is listed below along with the page at which coverage of the individual sounds begins.

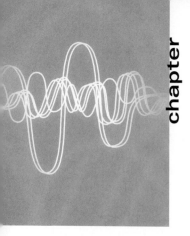

improving diction: the basics

Objectives

After reading this chapter, you should be able to:

- Follow specific procedures in order to discriminate between correct and incorrect productions of your target sounds or vocal productions
- Plan and follow effective procedures for working to replace your targets with alternate productions
- Demonstrate motivation for working actively in the improvement process

We've all seen televised competitions in which world-class skaters, gymnasts, or divers perform incredibly complicated and dangerous routines. Have you ever wondered how they are able to perform the same exact sequence of moves, time after time, with almost no variation? Sure, they make mistakes, but few and far between. Have you also ever wondered what goes into perfecting such routines? One thing is certain: athletes don't start with the finished product. They build their routines move by move, starting with the simplest. After they master simple moves, they add more complex and difficult moves, while still practicing the first. By the time athletes are ready for serious competition, their routines are second-nature to them.

To a certain extent, improving diction is a little like learning a complicated gymnastic routine. When you are successful, you have mastered a complicated routine, one that requires fine auditory discrimination and precise muscular control, and you perform it spontaneously. You achieve success in much the same way as the gymnast. First you master the simplest moves, and then you increase the level of difficulty and complexity until you have mastered your target sound.

That's the way, too, that we present exercises on the individual sounds of American English in Chapters 6 through 9: by level of difficulty. Each section starts with a sample sentence, typical spellings, a description of the sound, and, in many cases, drills to help you to produce the sound accurately. Then come drills on single words under headings that indicate where in the word the target sound is located. The word level is followed by the phrase, the sentence, and longer connected speech levels. Level 1 drills contain the target sound in contexts that are fairly easy to produce; level 2 drills present the sound in slightly more difficult sound contexts. Don't start level 2 drills until you are sure you have mastered level 1. Level 3 drills are more difficult, usually dealing with troublesome sound combinations and contrasts. You absolutely should not try level 3 until you have mastered level 2. The most difficult level we call the "challenge" level. At this level, exercises contain the target sounds in quantities and combinations that may be extremely troublesome. The challenge sections are the only places you'll find tongue twisters. We've minimized the use of tongue twisters because we believe that they cause more people to fail than to succeed.

How to Do It

Unless your instructor specifies a different procedure, we recommend that you use the following routine for working on sounds you may have difficulty articulating correctly.

1. *Follow the ear-training guide presented on page 71.* You'll find that having a clear, accurate auditory perception of the sound is an essential first step in mastering the production of that sound.
2. *Try producing the sound by itself.* Have someone check your production. Once you are able to produce the sound consistently and correctly, go on to the drill words.
3. *Try the sound in single words.* Take your time with each word. Listen carefully, and don't go on until you're satisfied that you've said the word correctly.
4. *Try the sound in phrases and sentences.* Again, take your time. You're not trying to be perfectly accurate the first time around. And it's okay to exaggerate the sound in practice; not all of what you do in practice will come out in conversational speech.
5. *Become aware of the position and movements of your articulators.* As you are working on step 2, try to experience the feeling of what is happening to your tongue, your lips, your hard and soft palates. This can be helpful in stabilizing the correct production of the sound. You'll probably find it helpful to monitor yourself visually with the aid of a mirror, particularly when you're working on the sounds produced at the front of the mouth. You may want to buy a small compact or shaving mirror to use in practice and to take to class with you.

6. *Don't be discouraged.* Remember, you may be trying to change habits of long standing, so there's a good chance that your first efforts won't be immediately successful. Frequent practice is often necessary to achieve the results you're after.

7. *Practice for a short period every day.* Twenty minutes a day, *every day.* You won't tire as easily, and you won't forget as much between practice sessions.

8. *Gather your own practice materials.* Make word lists from the words *you* use every day. Read articles from newspapers and magazines or dialogues from plays. The idea is to become proficient in contexts that are usable to you.

Special Speech Problems

Now that you've studied all the sounds of the language, you probably realize that some of the phonemes are harder to produce accurately than others. Because they are difficult, it's fairly common to find some phonemes misarticulated by children, and it's not unusual to hear the same misarticulations by teenagers and adults. Possibly your speech instructor, or someone else, has told you that you misarticulate one or more of these phonemes: [s] and [z], [ʃ] and [ʒ], [l], [r], and for some people [θ] and [ð].

By *misarticulation* we mean omissions, substitutions, and distortions. Misarticulation of these particular phonemes can often be difficult and time-consuming to correct and may require more time than is available to you in class. If this is the case, we suggest you ask your instructor for evaluation and assistance. If you're working on these sounds on your own, arrange for an evaluation at a speech clinic or speech and hearing center at your school or in your community.

Ear Training

Speech pathologists tell the apocryphal story of the mother who was trying to correct her child's pronunciation of the word *soap.* It seems that the child was saying *thoap.* The mother said to the child, "The word is *soap*, not *thoap.* Now say *ssss.*" And the child did. "Say it again," said the mother, "say *ssss-ssss-ssss.*" Of course the child said it, perfectly. "Now say *soap.*" And the child said *thoap.*

Like that child, you and I have an auditory image of how each word we say should sound. And when you customarily say a word and misarticulate a sound or sounds in that word, you hear your own pronunciation as being correct. The way you pronounce your words and articulate your sounds becomes the comfortable, familiar, and "right" way.

You may not notice that your production of a sound is different from the way others pronounce that sound.

When you change the way you articulate a sound from an incorrect to a correct production, it is important to monitor the way you make that sound until you are able to make it correctly without consciously trying. It is therefore important that you master auditory discrimination of your accurate and inaccurate productions of that sound. We call the process of learning to discriminate accurately *speech discrimination* or *ear training*.

Here are a few simple rules to follow that will make the process of ear training as effective and worthwhile as possible:

1. *Work with someone,* possibly a partner from your speech class, who pronounces your sounds correctly.
2. *Have your partner cover his or her mouth* in some way so you won't be getting visual clues. (The partner should speak in a normal voice.)
3. *Always go from an easier performance task to a more difficult task.*

Ear-training performance tasks range from easy to difficult in the following categories:

RECOGNITION

1. Train your ear to recognize whether the target sound occurs in a word spoken by the partner.
2. Train your ear to recognize *where* the target sound is in a word (beginning, middle, end) when spoken by the partner.

DISCRIMINATION

1. Train your ear to distinguish between correct and incorrect productions of the target sound as produced by your partner in random order, and be able to point out and distinguish the correct from the incorrect version.
2. Train your ear to distinguish between correct and incorrect productions, but with the target sound at the beginning, then the end, then the middle of nonsense syllables.
3. Train your ear to distinguish between correct and incorrect productions, but with the target sound occurring at the beginning, end, and then middle of actual words.
   Example A: Your partner says, "I'm going to say a word two times. Tell me whether I say it the same way or differently: *soap-thoap.*" **Answer:** "Differently."
   Example B: Your partner says, "I'm going to say the same word twice, but the [s] sound will be correct in one production and

incorrect in the other. Tell me which is correct, the first word or the second word: *soap—thoap."* **Answer:** "The first word."

4. Train your ear to distinguish between correct and incorrect productions, but with the target sound in words, phrases, then sentences.

Perform tasks 1 through 4 using a tape recorder to record your sound production. Then listen to the tape with your partner and identify your own correct and incorrect productions of the target sound. Then repeat tasks 1 through 4 without the tape recorder.

When you practice ear training, you'll do better if you make sure you're performing each task at a satisfactory level before you advance to the next. If you follow this procedure, by the time you've repeated the tasks, you probably will be able to accurately monitor your own productions of the target sound. Then you should repeat the tasks each time you practice your target sound or sounds.

Warm-ups

Now you're almost ready to start working on the sounds of American English. To help you progress more rapidly, we suggest you try some warm-up exercises before each practice session (even though you may feel slightly ridiculous).

This sensitizing exercise should help you become more aware of your articulators and how you use them in speaking.

1. Place the top of your tongue between your upper lip and the upper tooth farthest back in your mouth on the right side. Now, slowly slide your tongue tip forward to the front teeth, then all the way back on the left side. Now, reverse the movement; first forward to the front teeth, then back to the teeth on the right side. Repeat, placing the tongue tip between the lower lip and the lower teeth.
2. Touch the inside of the upper front teeth with the tongue tip. Slowly slide the tip upward. The first soft tissue you feel is the gum. Next, you will feel a bump extending backward inside your mouth. This is the gum ridge, or alveolar ridge. Several consonant sounds are produced with the tongue tip touching this ridge.

   Now, drop the tip of the tongue to the floor of your mouth, open your mouth, and alternately raise the tongue tip, touch the alveolar ridge, and drop the tongue again.
3. Starting with the tip of your tongue at the gum ridge, slowly curl the tip upward and backward along the roof of your mouth. You should encounter a concave area. This is the hard palate. In case you have difficulty locating it, it's the place where peanut butter always gets stuck.

Now drop your tongue. Raise it so that the front third is touching the hard palate. With your mouth open, alternately raise the tongue to the hard palate and lower it. Do this a few times as rapidly as you can.

4. Hold a mirror in front of your mouth so that you can see the back of your mouth. With your mouth wide open, say *ga-ga-ga.* You should be able to see the back of your tongue rising up and the back part of the roof of your mouth dropping down to meet it. This part of the roof is called the soft palate or velum. Alternate raising and lowering the tongue and soft palate, first by repeating *ga-ga-ga,* then by performing the sound movement but without making any sound.

Now you're ready to start on the sounds of American English.

the consonants: plosives

[p]   [b]   [t]   [d]   [k]   [g]

Objectives

After completing the work in this chapter, you should be able to:

- Recognize the consonantal plosives and the production problems associated with each
- Identify your own misarticulations of the consonantal plosives (if any), and the nature of each misarticulation
- Distinguish regional and foreign variations of the consonantal plosives
- Produce the consonantal plosives correctly, at the instructor's request, in isolation, words, and phrases
- Help others to identify their misarticulations of the consonantal plosives in a nonjudgmental way

General Instructions

This chapter consists mainly of drill materials for correcting and improving production of the consonantal plosives. The exercises are organized in ascending order of difficulty, that is, they become increasingly difficult. As you begin a particular phoneme you start with words, phrases, and sentences which are easy to articulate, then the material becomes increasingly difficult as you progress. Finally, when you are very near to mastering the phoneme, you'll find material that is more challenging and, in many cases, more interesting. So that you can be more successful in accomplishing your goals, it's important that you work on the drills in that order. If you haven't already, we suggest that you read Chapter 5 in which the basics of improving diction are outlined.

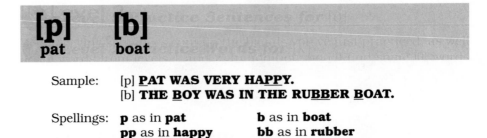

[p]   **[b]**
pat   boat

Sample: [p] **PAT WAS VERY HAPPY.**
            [b] **THE BOY WAS IN THE RUBBER BOAT.**

Spellings: **p** as in **pat**   **b** as in **boat**
            pp as in **happy**   **bb** as in **rubber**
            gh as in **hiccough**   **pb** as in **cupboard**

Description

[p] and [b] are cognate sounds; [p] is a voiceless bilabial plosive, [b] is voiced. You produce them by stopping the airstream with your lips, building up pressure, and suddenly releasing the air.

Production: [p]

1. Put your lips together; press them fairly firmly closed.
2. Build up air pressure in your mouth; don't let any air escape through your nose. Keep your teeth slightly apart.
3. Allow the air pressure to force your lips apart making an audible explosion of air.

Production: [b]

1. Follow all the steps for [p], but start to produce voice at the same time that your lips close.

2. Don't press the lips as firmly or hold them together as long as you did for [p].

COGNATE CONFUSION

People whose first language is Arabic or Chinese (or another Asian language) frequently find it difficult to distinguish between voiced and voiceless plosives. They may voice the voiceless sound, and vice versa, which turns the [p] into a [b] and the [b] into a [p]. Speakers of Romance languages (French, Italian, Spanish) sometimes weaken the articulation of voiceless plosives so that plosives such as [p] sound voiced. Check your production by trying the following contrast drill.

Contrast Drill for [p] *and* [b]

Say the words in the following lists aloud. First read down the list of [p] words, making sure you don't feel or hear voice. Then read down the list of [b] words, this time listening and feeling for voice. For the last step, read across, contrasting pairs of words—the first word voiceless, the second voiced.

[p]	[b]		[p]	[b]
pat	— bat		lap	— lab
pet	— bet		rope	— robe
pie	— by		rip	— rib
pen	— Ben		staple	— stable
pond	— bond		rapid	— rabid
cap	— cab		napped	— nabbed

[p] **Level 1**

[p] and [b] are sounds you learned to produce with very little difficulty. The problems that exist with these sounds are usually minor and are corrected quite easily.

PROBLEM: FRICATIVE [p]

If you don't press your lips together firmly enough [p] loses its explosive quality and sounds rather like an [f]. To avoid this, make sure your lips touch each other firmly and completely, leaving no gaps that can let air escape. Also, don't let the air out until you've built up sufficient pressure to make a strong, sudden sound. As you read the level 1 drills, feel for lip pressure and closure.

Level 1 Practice Words for [p]

Say the words in the following lists slowly and clearly. Listen carefully, and also feel for the right degree of lip pressure. Don't voice the [p]; there are no [b] words in this list. The words in the *Middle* list column all have a strong [p]. Don't overdo the final [p].

Beginning	*End*	*Middle*
pea	seep	Japan
peak	keep	append
piece	peep	unpaid
peck	jeep	upon
pin	tip	Muppet
pig	cheap	mopping
pick	dip	napkin
picnic	deep	happy
pen	teacup	teapot
pie	ape	tepee

(continued)

	Beginning	End	Middle
	penny	cape	apply
	pendant	gape	upwind
	pay	tap	caper
	pain	step	opposed
	page	stop	apology
	pace	gap	upper
	pot	cup	taping
	pant	cope	suppose
	pack	top	impact
	put	mop	appoint
	pawn	hoop	opponent
	poke	hope	opinion

 ### *Level 1 Practice Phrases for* [p]

Say the following phrases slowly:

stew pot	pay day	unpaid penny
step up	stop gap	pick up
tea cup	ping-pong	cheap jeep
pink napkin	cupcake pan	deep teacup

Level 1 Practice Sentences for [p]

Say the following sentences slowly but easily. Don't overdo it. Read them a number of times, and, if you can, have someone listen to you.

1. They were like two <u>peas</u> in a <u>pod</u>.
2. I <u>hope</u> you'd like a <u>piece</u> of <u>pie</u>.
3. The <u>pencil</u> <u>point</u> shattered on <u>impact</u>.
4. <u>Stop</u> <u>taping</u> after the first <u>page</u>.
5. <u>Step</u> <u>up</u> the <u>pace</u> on the way to the <u>peak</u>.
6. My <u>opponent</u> <u>apologized</u> for <u>pushing</u> me.
7. Do you <u>keep</u> the <u>penny</u>-saver <u>coupons</u>?
8. The <u>jeep</u> drove <u>uphill</u> through the <u>pit</u>.
9. <u>Pat</u> knocked over the <u>paint</u> after the <u>picnic.</u>
10. I <u>put</u> my money in the <u>pick-up</u> truck on <u>pay</u> day.
11. She found a <u>penny</u> under the <u>napkin</u> near the <u>cupcake.</u>
12. The <u>Ping-Pong</u> match had a <u>happy</u> ending.
13. <u>Pay</u> the <u>pawn</u> ticket for the <u>Japanese</u> <u>teapot.</u>
14. They <u>pushed</u> and <u>panted</u> until the <u>pig</u> was <u>pinned.</u>
15. <u>Opinion</u> was divided over the <u>unpaid</u> <u>appointment.</u>

[p] **Level 2**

PROBLEM: STRESS

When [p] and [b] are followed by stressed vowels, as in *apart* and *above*, you must make a strong plosive sound. You should feel the air on your hand if you hold it about two inches in front of your mouth and say *pie*. But when an unstressed vowel follows, the [p] and [b] won't be as strong. They are also weaker when they are followed by [l], [r], [s], and [t].

The words at this level are slightly more difficult to say because of the other consonants appearing in them. Say the words slowly and clearly. Listen carefully, and feel for the right degree of lip pressure. There are no [b] words in the list, so—as in level 1—try not to voice the [p].

 ### *Level 2 Practice Words for* [p]

Beginning	End	Middle
pearl	creep	apart
Peter	reap	repay
peal	sleep	appear
pushed	slope	repair
pooled	strip	vapor
peach	skip	superior
parlor	chip	repel
pelt	gripe	dripping
pelvis	clap	space
person	grape	special
parole	strap	responsive
pension	chop	slipper
punch	shop	zipper
pier	scoop	compel
paddle	snip	hopping

 ### *Level 2 Practice Phrases for* [p]

Say the following phrases slowly,

stop sign	slipping zipper	grape pop
repair shop	superior straps	responsive person
sip of punch	paddle in the pool	slipper strap

Level 2 Practice Sentences for [p]

Read the following sentences slowly and clearly. Don't overemphasize. Read them a number of times. If you can, have someone listen to you.

1. In my opinion, pearls come from superior oysters.
2. Vapor curled up from the ship's swimming pool.
3. Responsible persons repair their own paddles.
4. They were compelled to push the grapes up the slope.
5. We pooled our personal funds to pay for repairs.
6. The stop sign appeared to be sloping.
7. The pealing chimes rang from the shipping pier.
8. The grape pop really packed a punch.
9. A scoop of peach ice cream melted in the parlor.
10. I was hopping mad when they pelted me with wood chips.

[p] Level 3

At this level you'll find words that are slightly more difficult to say, usually because they are blends of [pl], [pr], or [pt]. Make sure to produce the [p], but be aware that the stress will vary; emphasize the [p] only slightly in [pl] and [pr], and don't give any emphasis to the [p] in [pt]. Notice that when *ed* follows *p*, it's pronounced [pt]. For example, *wrapped* is pronounced the same as *rapt*.

 Level 3 Practice Words

Try saying the words in the following lists slowly and clearly.

[pl] *All Positions*	[pr] *Beginning and Middle*	[pt] *Middle and End*
please	priest	crept
place	praise	except
pleasant	press	slept
plastic	prank	rapt
plow	proud	wrapped

[pl] *All Positions*	[pr] *Beginning and Middle*	[pt] *Middle and End*
hopeless	progress	concept
explicit	repressed	hoped
staple	represent	popped
apply	appropriate	leaped
ample	opera	topped
plume	prince	soaped
applause	prize	optical
aplomb	probe	cryptic
plum	prune	mapped
plank	appraise	septic
pliers	pretty	peptic

[p]
[b]

 ## Level 3 Practice Phrases for [p]

plastic wrapper	explicit promise
prune plums	pleasant place
cryptic concept	slept at the opera
accept applause	hopelessly repressed
proud priest	

 ## Level 3 Practice Sentences for [p]

Follow the directions given for level 2 sentences.

1. I was pleased to represent the opera company.
2. We planted plastic tulips in the spring.
3. You must display your pool pass.
4. There was an ample supply of press cards.
5. He plowed the pea patch under this spring.
6. It was hopeless to try to repair the stapler.
7. Practical jokes are not appropriate in this place.
8. The patient dropped his toothpaste in the water pitcher.
9. The zookeepers opposed the sheepshearing.
10. He unwrapped all the presents except Paul's.

[b] **Level 1**

 Level 1 Practice Words for [b]

Say the words in the following lists slowly and carefully. Listen closely and correct your production until you are sure you have a clear and correct sound. Remember that the [b] should have slightly less pressure than the [p]. Remember, too, that [b] is a voiced sound.

Beginning	End	Middle
beam	fib	about
bean	jib	abound
beet	cab	above
beef	tab	abeam
bed	nab	abbey
bend	ebb	hobby
bake	lab	maybe
book	hub	nobody
because	dub	hobo
bait	tub	cabinet
bucket	tube	Cuba
bad	job	fibbing
back	fob	webbing
bind	mob	obey
bond	stab	abate
boat	web	ebony
Boston	swab	abacus
banana	scab	obedient
bank	snob	ebbing

 Level 1 Practice Phrases for [b]

Say the following phrases slowly.

bunch of bananas	bean bag	big hot tub
bank job	bind books	ebony abacus
bad back	bait bucket	hobby cabinet

 Level 1 Practice Sentences for [b]

Read the following sentences slowly and clearly. Don't overdo it. Read them a number of times, and if you can, have someone listen to you.

1. The <u>hobo</u> left the train in <u>Boston</u>.
2. <u>Bob</u> rented a <u>cabin</u> with a <u>beamed</u> ceiling.

  3. The <u>bait</u> was sold <u>by</u> the <u>bucket</u>.
  4. She stayed in <u>bed</u> due to a <u>bad</u> <u>back</u>.
  5. The <u>ebony</u> <u>cabinet</u> was full of <u>Cuban</u> cigars.
  6. I wouldn't give that <u>bag</u> of <u>books</u> to <u>anybody</u>.
  7. There is a <u>bundle</u> of <u>beanbags</u> <u>above</u> the <u>tub</u>.
  8. <u>Maybe</u> we left the <u>abacus</u> in the <u>abbey</u>.
  9. The <u>banana</u> <u>boat</u> was <u>abeam</u> when the tide was <u>ebbing</u>.
10. The <u>cookbook</u> showed a <u>tub</u> full of <u>bacon</u> and <u>beef</u>.

[b] Level 2

PROBLEM: FRICATIVE [b]

This problem occurs most often in American English when a person's first language is Spanish. Then, the pronunciation of *berry* may sound like *very*. This happens because the native Spanish speaker substitutes a Spanish phoneme, a bilabial fricative, that sounds rather like [v] to English speakers. If you make this substitution, maintain firm lip pressure when you read the practice words.

Level 2 Practice Words for [b]

The words in the following lists are slightly more difficult to produce because of the other consonants present. Say the words slowly and distinctly.

Beginning	*End*	*Middle*
beach	glib	abyss
bear	slab	caboose
Bill	slob	saber
best	rib	Robert
bell	rob	ribbon
Bette	rub	labor
bird	lobe	October
birch	strobe	harbor
bail	scribe	subway
bizarre	globe	ruby
buzzer	tribe	rabbit
burned	grab	urban
bull	club	auburn
bashful	crab	eyeball
bias	drab	throbbing

[p]
[b]

🔘 *Level 2 Practice Phrases for* [b]

Say the following phrases slowly.

throbbing earlobe	bashful bull	urban subway robber
best rubies	labor in October	birds in the birches
burning ribbons	global tribes	bell and buzzer

🔘 *Level 2 Practice Sentences for* [b]

Read the following sentences slowly and clearly. Read them a number of times. If you can, have someone listen to you.

1. Bette was too bashful to join the club.
2. After Bill planted a birch tree, he baled hay.
3. The ruby-red hummingbird flew near the harbor.
4. Robert's bull was judged best in the October show.
5. They tried to grab the bear near the caboose.
6. You can get an urban sunburn on Tar Beach.
7. The bells and buzzers gave me a throbbing headache.
8. The rabbit tried to rub his rib like a bird.
9. He labored to inscribe his name on the globe.
10. The tribe threw the saber into the abyss.

[b] Level 3

🔘 *Level 3 Practice Words for* [b]

The [b] words in the following lists contain various blends and combinations. Also, some of the words will have [p] for contrast. Try the words, saying them slowly and clearly.

[bl]	[br]	[bd]
bleed	breathe	mobbed
blip	bridge	rubbed
blade	abrade	blabbed
blend	bread	knobbed
black	brand	stubbed
block	brown	fibbed
Casablanca	cobra	barbed
blimp	umbrella	probed
oblong	abroad	abdicate
able	abracadabra	snubbed

Level 3 Practice Phrases for [b]

Say the following phrases slowly and clearly.

scrub the curb	collectible blimps
Casablanca bridge	bland probes
brand-new broom	raspberry pablum
billion pebbles	brown icecubes
combat drumbeat	black umbrella

Level 3 Practice Sentences for [b]

Now you can try sentences that combine difficult blends and also offer [p] and [b] for contrast.

1. They made a billion balloons in December.
2. The view from the bridge was pretty bleak.
3. The party at Pebble Beach disturbed the neighbors.
4. We had crabcakes and boiled lobster at the clambake.
5. The parrot would only say, "Pretty boy, pretty boy."
6. Over all, the Labor party asked probing questions.
7. They probably had icecubes in the cooler at the curb.
8. In September, I saw Bogart in *Casablanca*.
9. I fed raspberry pablum to my baby brother.
10. The brand-new lightbulbs burned out.

Challenge Sentences for [p] *and* [b]

The following sentences contain [p] and [b] in difficult blends and combinations; scan them silently before you read them out loud.

1. The puppy bumped his paws and stopped abruptly.
2. The purple bubble burst its bonds and popped up.
3. The bouncy baby bubbled and babbled happily after its bottle.
4. Barbary pirates were a positive threat to the prosperity of European companies before the growth of large populations.
5. Do people prefer bright baubles or pretty peonies and poppies?
6. Special spirits inspired Spencer not to do his job in dribs and drabs.
7. The proper production of breakwaters can prevent broad-beamed boats from broaching.
8. The blushing bride breathed happily after the priest blessed the bridal breakfast.

(continued)

9. The imbibing of Burgundy and Beaujolais was practiced during every bountiful repast.
10. Every prospective producer should practice punctuating pages of prompt books before buying scripts.
11. Bobbie misbehaved badly, imbibing barrels of malted milkshakes.
12. Many people pay an appropriately high price protecting their private property.
13. Peter Piper protested at being labeled a pepper pickler.
14. Begorrah, breathed the Hibernian bridegroom, blushing happily.
15. Robber barons should beware of the possibility of abandoning their supposed nobility.

Challenge Materials for [p] *and* [b]

1. A facile play-by-play announcer can generally find abundant work in local markets, although this work will generally be on a part-time basis. In small and medium markets, newspeople, staff announcers, and even sales personnel add to their income by broadcasting local sports. This is a difficult assignment, however, requiring good on-air skills and an extensive knowledge of the sport. . . .

Baseball games have many periods of little or no activity, so the play-by-play person must be able to fill with talk of interest to the audience. This ability will become particularly apparent in rain-delay situations.

Baseball play-by-play also entails the ability to follow action quite a distance away. Good vision, or the ability to compensate for poor vision by an in-depth knowledge of the game is essential.

Lewis B. O'Donnell, Carl Hausman, Philip Benoit,
Announcing: Broadcast Communicating Today

2. *Barber's Laws of Backpacking*
(1) The integral of the gravitational potential taken around any loop trail you choose to hike always comes out positive. (2) Any stone in your boot always migrates against the pressure gradient to exactly the point of most pressure. (3) The weight of your pack increases in direct proportion to the amount of food you consume from it. If you run out of food, the pack weight goes on increasing anyway. (4) The number of stones in your boot is directly proportional to the number of hours you have been on the trail. (5) The difficulty of finding any given trail marker is directly proportional to the importance of the consequences of failing to find it. (6) The size of each of the stones in your boot is directly proportional to the number of hours you have been on the trail. (7) The remaining distance to your chosen campsite remains constant as twilight approaches. (8) The net weight of your boots is proportional to the cube of the number of hours you have been on the trail. (9) When you arrive at your campsite, it is full. (10) If you take your boots off, you'll never get them back on again. (11) The local density of mosquitoes is inversely proportional to your remaining repellent.

Milt Barber, *The Official Rules*

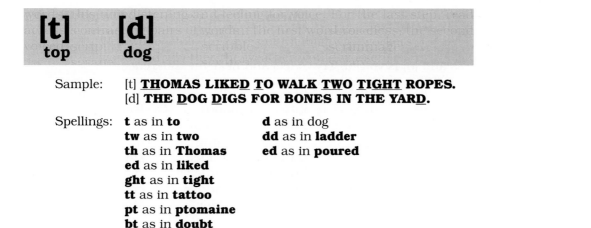

Sample: [t] **THOMAS LIKED TO WALK TWO TIGHT ROPES.**
[d] **THE DOG DIGS FOR BONES IN THE YARD.**

Spellings: **t** as in **to**   **d** as in dog
tw as in **two**   **dd** as in **ladder**
th as in **Thomas**   **ed** as in **poured**
ed as in **liked**
ght as in **tight**
tt as in **tattoo**
pt as in **ptomaine**
bt as in **doubt**

Description

[t] and [d] are cognate sounds. [t] is a voiceless lingua-alveolar plosive. You produce it by blocking the airstream with the tongue and upper gum ridge, building up air pressure and suddenly releasing it. [d] is produced in the same way. Just add voice as you produce it.

Production: [t]

1. Narrow the tongue and place it against your upper gum ridge. Make sure the sides of the tongue touch the sides of the upper molars. Lower your jaw slightly, keeping your teeth apart.
2. Hold your tongue firmly in place against the gum ridge. Force some air from your lungs and allow pressure to build up behind your tongue.
3. Let the air pressure overcome your tongue and force it away from the gum ridge. This way, the air escapes quickly and goes over the dropped tongue and between the teeth.

Production: [d]

Follow steps 1 and 2, and start step 3. As the air pressure begins to force your tongue away from the gum ridge, add voice. Try to time your voicing so that it begins at exactly the same time that your tongue starts to leave the gum ridge.

Cognate Confusion of [t] and [d]

Some nonnative speakers may confuse these cognates, especially at the end of a word. This is particularly true when a speaker's first language is German.

🔘 *Contrast Drill for* [t] *and* [d]

Slowly read the following pairs of words aloud. Remember, [t] is voiceless and [d] is voiced. Try to feel and hear the difference.

[t]	[d]	[t]	[d]	[t]	[d]
tea — dee		kitty — kiddy		feet — feed	
tip — dip		rated — raided		hit — hid	
ten — den		writing — riding		let — led	
tan — dan		butted — budded		sat — sad	
tie — die		knotted — nodded		right — ride	
tuck — duck		matter — madder		cot — cod	
toe — doe		otter — odder		shoot — shooed	

[t] Level 1

PROBLEM: DENTALIZATION

[t] and [d] are tongue-gum ridge sounds. Some people, including those whose first language is Spanish or Italian, tend to dentalize the sounds; that is, they make the sounds on the back of the upper front teeth. Look closely at your mouth in the mirror while you say the word *tea.* If you can see the sides of your tongue peeking around your upper incisors, you're probably dentalizing. You can hear a difference, too. A dentalized [t] sounds hissy and slightly "wet."

Place the tip of your tongue lightly on the upper gum ridge. (The exact spot is where you burn yourself when you bite into a piece of steaming hot pizza.) Don't press too hard; if you do, the tongue spreads out and overlaps onto the teeth. Now say the following words aloud, reading *across* the page. Alternate saying the words, first dentally and then non-dentally. (Say the words in parentheses dentally.)

(tea)	tea	(tea)	tea	(tea)	tea	(tea)	tea	(tea)	tea
(tap)	tap	(tap)	tap	(tap)	tap	(tap)	tap	(tap)	tap
(top)	top	(top)	top	(top)	top	(top)	top	(top)	top
(toe)	toe	(toe)	toe	(toe)	toe	(toe)	toe	(toe)	toe
(too)	too	(too)	too	(too)	too	(too)	too	(too)	too
(die)	die	(die)	die	(die)	die	(die)	die	(die)	die
(day)	day	(day)	day	(day)	day	(day)	day	(day)	day
(do)	do	(do)	do	(do)	do	(do)	do	(do)	do
(dog)	dog	(dog)	dog	(dog)	dog	(dog)	dog	(dog)	dog

Use a light touch with your tongue, and return it precisely to the same place each time. Listen carefully as you say the words. Try to eliminate the "wetness."

Level 1 Practice Words for [t]

Say the words in the following lists slowly and distinctly, reading down each column. Start with the *Beginning* words. These have short, precise sounds; don't hold them longer than necessary. Listen carefully, and adjust your production until you are satisfied that the sound is clear and correct.

Beginning	*End*	*Middle*
tea	eat	attack
team	meet	vantage
teen	neat	autumn
tip	pit	atone
Tim	mitt	intend
tin	knit	voted
take	fate	vitamin
tape	bait	eaten
Ted	bet	enter
ten	net	guitar
tag	at	entire
tan	fat	banter
time	cat	center
Tom	cot	attire
top	pot	cuter
tub	but	computer
tong	caught	outer
toss	fought	item
toe	coat	fighter
tone	note	data
took	put	attend
too	cute	meter

Now read the *End* column again, and try not to *over*correct the [t]. When this sound is the last sound in a word, it usually is not aspirated; that is, you should not make it with a puff of air.

 ## *Level 1 Practice Phrases for* [t]

Say the following phrases slowly.

top ten	two-tone	tea time
tag team	fat cat	cute note
toe tapping	tan boot	tomtom
computer center	after autumn	took vitamins
tank full of bait	took his coat	meet the voters
enter data	attend the fight	tick tock

Level 1 Practice Sentences for [t]

Say the following sentences slowly but naturally. Don't overdo it. Read them a number of times and, if you can, have someone listen to you.

1. A tan cat was asleep on his coat.
2. It was fate that we met.
3. Enter the data into the computer.
4. Ten cars were towed from the parking meter.
5. He was caught only ten miles from the attack.
6. Take the note from under the tea pot.
7. Tim saw the team taking vitamins.
8. Was Tom fixing the motor at ten?
9. She bought a tank-top swimsuit.
10. He put the tape across the gate of the tomb.
11. Tom is the tense boy who plays the guitar.
12. Night is a good time to meet in autumn.
13. It was too cute to put on top.
14. The attack was fought near the mine pit.
15. I put the tip of my toe in the center of the tub.

[t] Level 2

PROBLEM 1. OMISSION OF [t] IN THE MIDDLE AND END OF WORDS

This problem is most common when you must produce another consonant immediately before [t]. For example, the word *past* [pæst] becomes pass [pæs]. This generally occurs simply because you *underarticulate;* that is, you don't raise your tongue up quite high enough to produce the [t]. Your mind, however, fills in the missing [t] because of context (*He went pass the end of the street*) and so you don't notice the omission. The following contrast drill will help you listen for the omission.

Contrast Drill for Omission of [t]

Read the following pairs of words slowly and carefully. Take extra effort to produce the [t]. You should be able to hear her [t] clearly in the second word of each pair.

pass	— past	lease	— least
guess	— guest	roof	— roofed
chess	— chest	miss	— mist
stay	— state	ten	— tent
row	— wrote	star	— start
mass	— mast	tess	— test

PROBLEM 2: CONFUSION OF [t] AND [d] IN THE END OF WORDS

Words that end in *ed* such as *raced, banned,* and *feasted* can sometimes cause confusion as to whether the last sound should be a [t] or a [d] and whether it should be part of a separate syllable or just added to the previous one. Here are some general rules that may help:

1. If the sound preceding *ed* is voiceless, pronounce the *d* as a [t]. **Example:** *wrapped* [ræpt]
2. If the sound preceding *ed* is voiced, pronounce the *d* as [d]. **Example:** *banned* [bænd]
3. If the sound preceding *ed* is a [d] or a [t], the *ed* is pronounced as a separate syllable, [əd]. **Example:** *patted* [pætəd]

 ## *Level 2 Practice Words for* [t]

Say the words in the following columns slowly and clearly, reading down the columns starting with *Beginning.* These words have slightly more difficult combinations to produce; also, you'll have to remember the rules about "ed." This drill continues on the next page.

Beginning	*End*	*Middle*
teach	feast	feasted
tease	greased	cheated
teeth	leased	eastern
till	grit	sister
tiller	slit	misty
table	slate	later
tale	debate	visitor
telephone	blessed	invested
terrain	west	lettuce
tax	flat	faster
tally	passed	pastor
touch	just	router
tunnel	dust	rusted
tardy	smart	charted
taco	forest	lasting
toddler	thought	loiter
torch	lost	daughter
toil	brought	oyster
told	wrote	hotel
toad	scout	rotor
Toledo	ghost	poster
tooth	roofed	sooty
tour	goofed	rooster

(continued)

[t]
[d]

Beginning and End	Beginning and Middle	Middle and End
tint	telltale	rotate
taunt	tested	extort
toast	toasted	intent
taste	tasting	state
toot	tooted	attest
tent	talented	start
tensed	tilted	stunt
tilt	titanic	attempt

 Level 2 Practice Phrases for [t]

attempted to start	western forest	late visitors
telephone table	greased lightning	great debate
state taxes	brought the note	visitor's tent
toddler teaser	pastor's daughter	smart thoughts
talented sister	telephone talk	tasted lettuce

 Level 2 Practice Sentences for [t]

Say the following sentences slowly and distinctly, but don't exaggerate the [t].

1. Sometimes the tongue is faster than the eye.
2. Which is the most expensive hotel in Toledo?
3. The pastor arrived ten minutes later than his sister.
4. The tangle of wires rested against the telephone pole.
5. The stunt car brushed against the sides of the tunnel.
6. The rooster was faster than greased lightning.
7. I saw *The Best of the West* last night.
8. The forester passed through the dusty terrain.
9. I can attest to the quality of the teaching.
10. Her daughter lost the slate-colored poster on the tour.
11. He leased the torch to the tardy visitors.
12. The scout faced ten wagons to the east at sunset.
13. The best man's toast to the newlyweds was outstanding.
14. They attempted to extort ten dollars each from the teachers.
15. The smart patient sought help from the first doctor.

[t] Level 3

PROBLEM 1: SUBSTITUTION OF [d] FOR [t]

The most common problem with [t] is the tendency for people to voice it when it is not in the syllable receiving the primary stress, as in the words *batter, butter, bitter, sitting,* and *party.* The result is a substitution of [d] for [t]. To avoid this, use a light touch of your tongue on the gum ridge, and be sure to stop voicing for the brief instant that it takes for you to produce the [t]. Try the following:

[t]
[d]

 ### Production Drill

Read the words in the following lists, reading across the page. Gradually shorten the pause between the syllables, and reduce the amount of [h].

bat . . . her	bat . . her	bat . her	bat her	batter
but . . . her	but . . her	but . her	but her	butter
bit . . . her	bit . . her	bit . her	bit her	bitter
kit . . . he	kit . . he	kit . he	kit he	kitty
let . . . her	let . . her	let . her	let her	letter

 ### Contrast Drill for [d] *and* [t]

Say the following pairs of words slowly. Try to feel and hear the difference between the [d] and [t].

[d]	[t]	[d]	[t]
badder	— batter	bidder	— bitter
leader	— liter	padding	— patting
seeding	— seating	pudding	— putting
wading	— waiting	faded	— fated
riding	— writing	wedding	— wetting
raiding	— rating	heeding	— heating
shudder	— shutter	ladder	— latter

 ### Practice Words for [d] *for* [t] Substitution

batter	bitter	butter
writing	rating	wetting
shutter	latter	heating
sitting	pretty	city
letter	suited	pity
twenty	thirty	forty
fifty	sixty	seventy
patted	petting	kitty
sooty	smarter	litter

Now take the words above and others you can find to practice with, and make up short, simple sentences. Ask your instructor or a member of your class to listen to you and to be especially aware if you are overcorrecting.

PROBLEM 2: [t] FOLLOWED BY [n] OR [l]

This is an especially difficult combination of sounds to deal with because it occurs so frequently. There's no mystery about it, though, and it's not hard to correct. Typical words are *little, bottle, kitten.*

The trick is this: don't let your tongue move away from the gum ridge after making the [t]. When it's followed by an [l], you simply hold up the tip and let the sides drop, exploding the air laterally. When it's followed by an [n], drop the soft palate and let the air come out the nose. Be careful not to substitute [d] for [t]. Here are some practice words:

[tl]	[tn]
battle	button
petal	mountain
little	cotton
glottal	bitten
bottle	certain
total	kitten
metal	fountain
cattle	mitten
settle	mutton
accidental	rotten
oriental	au gratin
parental	forgotten
continental	batten

Make sure you're not producing a *glottal stop* instead of a [t]. A glottal stop is not really a sound at all. You make it simply by stopping the air flow momentarily with the vocal folds. Try it with the word *little.* Leave out the [t] in the middle and say "li/le." That's a glottal stop. It's not a [t] but our minds perceive it as one.

 ### PROBLEM 3: [tθ] OR [tð] COMBINATIONS

There is a time when the standard way to produce the [t] is on the teeth instead of the gum ridge. That's when it's followed by [θ] or [ð], as in *hit the ball* or *at the game.* You anticipate the placement of the tongue on the teeth for the [t], and you get it there a little early. It requires a little extra effort to produce the [ð] or [θ] after the [t]. Try these phrases:

hit the ball	at the game	at third
bright thought	put out the light	sent that
went through	eight-thirty	sit there

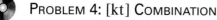

 PROBLEM 4: [kt] COMBINATION

When the [kt] combination occurs at the end of a word, we sometimes tend to omit the [t]. Try the following words. Make sure to say the [t].

act	fact	tact	duct
knocked	peeked	faked	locked
checked	rocked	soaked	trucked
impact	exact	infect	obstruct
correct	precinct	suspect	respect

 PROBLEM 5: [tr] BLEND

If you let your tongue slide back off the gum ridge on its way to making the [r], it sounds as though you're adding [tʃ], and making the plosive [t] into a fricative. Say the following words slowly and carefully. Do you hear a [tr] or a [tʃ]?

treat	trip	true	trap	train
trust	trout	trial	truck	trawl

Production Drill

Read the words in the following lists aloud, from left to right. Gradually close the gap between the syllables as you go.

tuh . . . rue	tuh . . rue	tuh . rue	tuhrue	true
tuh . . . rip	tuh . . rip	tuh . rip	tuhrip	trip
tuh . . . rap	tuh . . rap	tuh . rap	tuhrap	trap

 Practice Words for [tr]

Beginning	*Beginning*	*Middle*	*Middle*
true	transistor	entrust	theatrical
trip	tractor	detract	partridge
trap	trial	entrap	Patrick
treat	truce	entreat	contrived
troop	trowel	entropy	Amtrak
track	trouble	actress	attribute
train		electric	

Practice Sentences for [tr]

1. The electric train went off the track.
2. Patricia was a true actress.
3. It was a treat to make the trip on Amtrak.
4. We had nothing but trouble with the new tractor.
5. He contrived to trick the contractor.

[t]
[d]

[t]
[d]

PROBLEM 6: AFFRICATED [t]

When you make the [t], don't press your tongue too tightly against the gum ridge. Sometimes this may result in the normally plosive [t] sounding like a fricative or, more accurately, like a combination plosive and fricative. For example, the word *too* [tu] might sound like [tsu]. So when you make the sound [t], make sure there is a clean, sharp break that you can feel as your tongue leaves the gum ridge.

The same problem occurs when [t] and [d] are blended with [r], as in *drew* and *true*.

PROBLEM 7: [sts] CLUSTER

Sometimes the combination of [t] plus [s] or the [sts] combination can be difficult. If you have problems with these, see [s], level 3, page 146.

 ### *Level 3 Practice Sentences for* [t]

1. The lieutenant tried to calm the victim.
2. The troop train tripped the electronic switches.
3. It's a fact that cattle stay away from electric fences.
4. Take the trail to the right, then turn left.
5. Gilbert was the most treacherous tropical storm of this century.
6. The call went to the precinct at eight-thirty.
7. The little kitten liked to drink milk from the bottle.
8. The tea kettle was made of bright metal.
9. I thought I saw a fountain in the courtyard.
10. The first baseman tossed the ball to the shortstop.
11. The satellite tracking system operated infrequently.
12. The crates of buttons were incorrectly packed.
13. Frequent typhoons twisted the trees on the mountains.
14. His shorts were made from fifty percent cotton twill.
15. I asked him to close the shutters and put out the lights.

Challenge Sentences for [t]

1. Twenty teachers of Latin trusted their students not to start trouble.
2. Tommy Tune tapped his way to stardom with twinkle toes.
3. The detective was tricked into betraying his secret to the beautiful temptress.
4. The dentist dropped his button into the fountain and bit his metal fountain pen abruptly.
5. If Patrick trusts his mother's sister mistakenly in a distracted instant, is he liable to be sued for "Auntie trust?"

Challenge Materials for [t]

1. Betty Botter bought some butter.
   But, she said, the butter's bitter.
   If I put it in my batter,
   It will make my batter bitter.
   But a bit of better butter
   Will make my batter better.
   So she bought a bit of butter
   And put it in her batter.
   And it made her batter worse.

2. At exactly twelve midnight on New Year's Eve, a celebrant stood on top of the Times Building and dumped a big vat of Italian food on all the revelers.

His friend looked up at him and screamed, "I told you confetti, you fool, not spaghetti!"

Joey Adams, *Strictly for Laughs*

3. There's only one place to find all the largest known specimens of native and naturalized trees in the United States - The National Register of Big Trees! American Forests has been keeping the Register since 1940 when a forester named Joseph Stearns issued his rallying cry: "Let every tree lover, every forester, every lumberman rally . . . to fight for the preservation of our biggest tree specimens." Since then, the Register has become an institution with big tree coordinators in all 50 states and a cadre of big tree hunters always on the lookout for new champion trees.

American Forests
http://www.americanforests.org/garden/big_trees/big_trees_subhome.html

[t]
[d]

[d] **Level 1**

Almost all the misarticulations that can happen with [t] can also happen with [d]. This might be a good time, then, to review the [t] problems covered earlier, and to do the Contrast Drill on p. 88 and the drill for dentalization on p. 88.

     Here are level 1 practice words. Take your time with them; say them slowly and clearly. Listen carefully and correct your production until you are satisfied that you are producing the correct sound. These are short, precise sounds; don't hold them too long.

 Level 1 Practice Words for [d]

Beginning	*End*	*Middle*
deep	seed	wedding
deem	bead	feeding
dip	kid	India
dim	bid	bidding
day	aid	wading
date	made	shady
den	fed	shedding
damp	said	bedding
Dan	add	candy
dash	sad	handy
Don	odd	body
dock	nod	hot dog
dive	wide	shoddy
duck	bud	cider
dust	mud	muddy
dog	sawed	under
dawn	pawed	undo
dough	mowed	odor
doze	code	soda
dew	hood	pudding
duke	food	moody

Level 1 Practice Phrases for [d]

dusty dog	wedding day	dive under
made in the shade	feeding at dawn	sad kid
odd candy	in debt to	dashing Dan

 Level 1 Practice Sentences for [d]

1. The grass was <u>damp</u> with <u>dew</u> at <u>dawn.</u>
2. They <u>had</u> <u>soda</u> on their <u>wedding</u> <u>day.</u>
3. Her hair was <u>damp</u> <u>under</u> her <u>hood.</u>
4. It was <u>dumb</u> to <u>dive</u> <u>under</u> the <u>dock.</u>
5. They broke the <u>code</u> by <u>adding</u> the <u>dates.</u>
6. <u>Cider</u> from <u>India</u> has an <u>odd</u> <u>odor.</u>
7. <u>Don</u> feels <u>moody</u> in <u>bad</u> weather.
8. The furious <u>bidding</u> was <u>led</u> by the <u>doctor.</u>
9. We went <u>wading</u> in the <u>deep</u> <u>shady</u> pool.
10. He <u>sawed</u> logs and <u>mowed</u> the lawn in the <u>dim</u> light.

[d] **Level 2**

PROBLEM: OMISSION OF [d] IN THE MIDDLE AND END OF WORDS

Sometimes it's easier to simply skip [d] than to take the extra effort to produce it. This usually happens when [d] is preceded by other consonants, such as in the words *sounds, buzzed,* and *called.* Correcting this problem is not quite as easy as you would think, so don't start on it until you have completed level 1 drills.

When you read the following lists of words aloud, make sure you put a [d] every place it should be. Be especially careful at the end of words; make an extra effort to voice the sound so you don't substitute [t] for it, but at the same time, don't overcorrect it.

Some of the words in the following list have [t] in them, and in some [d] occurs more than once. There are also other consonants in the words that may make the accurate production of [d] more difficult.

[t]
[d]

 Level 2 Practice Words for [d]

Beginning	End	All Positions
diesel	plead	heeded
deer	reared	speeded
ditto	filmed	building
discreet	skilled	did
data	famed	raided
dateline	skated	razed
desk	ranged	amazed
dentist	hemmed	added
desert	sled	decided
Dallas	clad	divided
dunk	blood	detained
dirty	word	dented
dot	bird	doubled
doll	plod	darted
dart	guard	dandy
dory	toward	dangled
doily	void	dirtied
doting	sewed	padded
duty	brood	bedded
duel	stewed	deducted

 Level 2 Practice Phrases for [d]

dangled in the void	amazed the guard	padded sled
dirty doilies	dented the desk	double dipped
hemmed and hawed	decided to divide	doting dentist

Level 2 Practice Sentences for [d]

1. He avoided the dirty extra duty.
2. The datelines ranged from Dallas to Desert City.
3. I decided to find some diesel fuel after daybreak.
4. Dawn poured oil in the dirty old pan.
5. We plodded toward the dentist's building.
6. The guard was detained after the building was razed.
7. He dunked the ball discreetly.
8. The deer reared up and ran around the sled.
9. Did you drop the dividers from the bill?
10. The padded doilies were soiled.

[d] **Level 3**

PROBLEM 1: OMISSION OF [d] BEFORE [z]

 Level 3 Practice Words for [dz]

Say the words below carefully. Try to produce one sound that combines [d] and [z] together.

hands	bands	stands	sands
reeds	heeds	beads	weeds

Notice that these words all end in [z]. Make sure you're saying the [d] firmly and pronouncing the [z]. Let's try some more.

seeds	feeds	leads	needs
bids	kids	lids	rids
raids	maids	fades	shades
lends	bends	sends	tends
lands	strands	grands	brands
binds	finds	grinds	blinds
pounds	sounds	mounds	grounds

PROBLEM 2: [dr] BLEND

This problem is similar to the affricated [tr]. When you let your tongue slide back off the gum ridge on the way to producing the [r], it sounds as if you're adding [dʒ] and making the plosive [t] into the fricative [ʒ].

Level 3 Production Drill for [dr]

Use the same technique you used for the [tr] blend. Slowly read the syllables below aloud from left to right, pausing between the syllables, gradually forming the word at the end of each row. Make a clean break between the tongue and the gum ridge. Don't slide the tongue along the palate. As you read, gradually shorten the pause between the syllables.

duh . . . rue	duh . . rue	duh . rue	duhrue	drew
duh . . . rip	duh . . rip	duh . rip	duhrip	drip
duh . . . raw	duh . . raw	duh . raw	duhraw	draw

 Level 3 Practice Words for [dr]

dream	adrift	draw	hundred
drip	adroit	drain	droop
drape	hydrant	drop	drag
overdrawn	adrenaline	hydrogen	cathedral
drink	dressing	driver	Padre Island

[t]
[d]

PROBLEM 3: [d] FOLLOWED BY [n] OR [l]

Another problem occurs frequently when [n] follows [d]. Use the same technique you used for [tn], and leave your tongue tip touching the gum ridge for [n]. This technique also works for [d] followed by [l].

Level 3 Practice Words for [dn] and [dl]

hidden	madden	riddle	middle
sudden	ridden	idle	paddle
widen	sadden	poodle	padlock
rodent	shouldn't	redlight	dwindle
student	redness	waddle	meddle

Level 3 Practice Sentences for [d]

1. The students chase rodents in the dorms.
2. It saddens me to see dwindling woods.
3. One hundred paddles were hidden in the woods.
4. The hydrant drained into the middle of the road.
5. Feed the birds sunflower seeds.
6. The dory was suddenly set adrift.
7. You shouldn't let your hands be idle.
8. I drew a cash advance for five hundred dollars.
9. I hadn't ridden since I was a kid.
10. He lends me dozens of books of riddles.

Challenge Sentences for [d]

1. It's difficult to detect defective transistors.
2. Stetson's wrist festered after he treated the rust with fast-acting detergent.
3. Dierdre didn't deserve the treatment she received at the hands of the dirty dozen.
4. I'd bet dollars to doughnuts that the director didn't traumatize the actress directly.
5. Discreet diplomats don't state matters categorically under duress in difficult situations.

Challenge Sentences for [d] and [t]

1. Tatiana retorted to Trudy's taunts with truly appropriate distaste.
2. Teachers are always trusting of students' honesty during midterm testing times.

3. Little laddies in kindergarten develop diverse dependencies on their daddies' dollars.
4. Totally mad instructors tell terrible tales of their student days.
5. Latent traumas too frequently come to roost in the form of trials and tribulations.
6. "Attempt this item," this tutor told the reluctant teenager.
7. "Tillie the Toiler" was a cartoon character in the forgotten days of the past.
8. Lots of ladies left their hats on the table during the day's activities.
9. Picture yourself getting to sit at the left side of the senator's freestanding lectern.
10. Didn't Audrey defer discussion due to the mad nature of the afternoon debate?

Challenge Materials for [d] and [t]

1. Following the trail with the sureness of a bloodhound came General Zaroff. Nothing escaped those searching black eyes, no crushed blade of grass, no bent twig, no mark, no matter how faint, in the moss. So intent was the Cossack on his stalking that he was upon the thing Rainsford had made before he saw it. His feet touched the protruding bough that was the trigger. Even as he touched it, the general sensed his danger and leaped back with the agility of an ape. But he was not quite quick enough; the dead tree, delicately adjusted to rest on the cut living one, crashed down and struck the general a glancing blow on the shoulder as it fell; but for his alertness, he must have been smashed beneath it. He staggered, but he did not fall; nor did he drop his revolver. He stood there, hugging his injured shoulder, and Rainsford, with fear again gripping his heart, heard the general's mocking laugh ring through the jungle.

Richard Connell, *The Most Dangerous Game*

2. *Welcome to the U.S. Coast Guard*
Founded in the 1790's as part of the Department of Treasury, the United States Coast Guard is now part of the Department of Transportation, protecting U.S. interests at home and around the world. In peacetime and during war, the Coast Guard is at work around the clock, 365 days a year, patrolling shores, saving lives, protecting property and enhancing the flow of commerce. From helping the victims of floods and storms, to keeping millions of dollars worth of illegal drugs from flooding American communities, to teaching boating safety and cleaning up oil spills, the Coast Guard is, like its motto, Semper Paratus, Always Ready.

Admiral James M. Loy, Commandant, USCG,
http://www.uscg.mil/hello.html

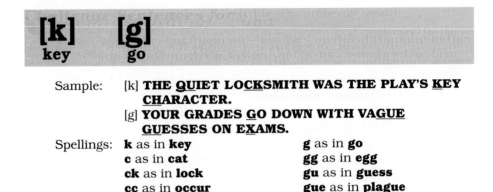

Sample: [k] **THE QUIET LOCKSMITH WAS THE PLAY'S KEY CHARACTER.**
[g] **YOUR GRADES GO DOWN WITH VAGUE GUESSES ON EXAMS.**

Spellings:
k as in **key**
c as in **cat**
ck as in **lock**
cc as in **occur**
ch as in **echo**
qu as in **queen** (with [**w**])
que as in **plaque**
cqu as in **lacquer**
kh as in **khan**
x as in **lax** (with [**s**])

g as in **go**
gg as in **egg**
gu as in **guess**
gue as in **plague**
x as in **exam** (with [**z**])
gh as in **ghost**

Description

[k] and [g] are cognate lingua-velar sounds; [k] is voiceless, but [g] is voiced. They are plosives that you produce by blocking the breath stream with the back of the tongue and soft palate, building up the pressure, and suddenly releasing it.

Production: [k]

1. Open your mouth slightly.
2. Raise the back of your tongue and press it against the soft palate.
3. Build up air pressure behind the tongue. Don't let any air escape through your nose.
4. Let the air pressure force your tongue away from the palate. Make sure the release is sudden—an explosion.

Production: [g]

Follow the same steps as for [k]. Produce voice as the tongue begins to block the airstream.

Production Drill

These two sounds require a firm and complete closure between the back of the tongue and the soft palate. If you don't have complete closure, you produce a weak or almost fricative sound. In a similar problem, people sometimes allow air to enter the nasal passages, nasalizing the sound. If you have either of these problems, try the drill below.

Say the following sounds, reading across. Say them forcefully. Try to get as much air out on [k] and [g] as you do on [p] and [t].

[p . . . t . . . k . . . g]
[p . . . t . . . k . . . g]
[p . . . t . . . k . . . g]

Now try the following. Say [k] three times as strongly as you can, then say the word that follows.

[k k k] cat   [k k k] cat   [k k k] cat
[k k k] cap   [k k k] cap   [k k k] cap

Now try the same thing with [g].

[g g g] gap   [g g g] gap   [g g g] gap
[g g g] gab   [g g g] gab   [g g g] gab

COGNATE CONFUSION OF [k] AND [g]

This is really a problem in voicing. It usually occurs as a simple error of pronunciation, or it could be due to failure to voice the [g]. The following contrast drill should help you distinguish between [k] and [g].

 ### Contrast Drill for [k] and [g]

First read down the column of [k] words. Then read down the column of [g] words. The last step is to read pairs of words across. Read slowly and carefully, and make sure to hear and feel the difference between voiceless [k] and voiced [g].

[k]	[g]	[k]	[g]
Kate — gate		sacking — sagging	
came — game		lacking — lagging	
cape — gape		lock — log	
cap — gap		tuck — tug	
cash — gash		pick — pig	
cut — gut		duck — dug	
coast — ghost		rick — rig	
coat — goat		chuck — chug	

[k] **Level 1**

PROBLEM 1: PRONUNCIATION OF THE LETTER [x]

Many people become confused about how to pronounce *x;* whether it's a [ks] or a [gz]. Usually they fail to voice the [gz]. This won't happen if you know a couple of simple rules.

1. When *x* is followed by a vowel in a stressed syllable, it's almost always pronounced [gz]. **Example:** *exam* [egzæm]. There are a few exceptions to this rule, such as *oxalic acid,* in which the *x* is followed by a stressed syllable and is pronounced [ɑksælɪk].
2. When *x* is followed by a pronounced consonant or an unstressed vowel, it's pronounced [ks]. **Examples:** *extra* [ɛkstrə], *exceed* [ɛksid], and oxen [æksən].
3. When the word ends in *x,* it's pronounced [ks]. **Example:** *wax* [wæks].
4. When the letter *x* stands alone, it's pronounced [ɛks]. **Example:** *x-axis* [ɛksæksɪs].
5. When a word begins with *x,* it's pronounced [z]. **Example:** *xerox* [zɪɝɑks].

In other words, the only time you pronounce *x* as [gz] is when it's followed by a stressed syllable. Here are some words in which the *x* is a [gz]:

exact	examine	example	exhibit
exist	exert	exempt	exotic
executive	exuberant	exhaust	exaggerate

Here are some words in which the *x* is a [ks]:

ax	exit	except	excuse
mix	experiment	explain	Dixie
box	exciting	excellent	exposed

PROBLEM 2: OMISSION OF [k] IN THE *cc* AND *ex* SPELLING

Don't omit [k] in words such as *accept.* Although *cc* can be pronounced [k], as in *occur,* in words like *accept* the *cc* indicates a [k] followed by an [s]. Try these words:

accept	accident	access	vaccination
accessory	accent	accelerate	successive
except	excited	expect	extract
excavate	expose	experiment	experience

Level 1 Practice Words for [k]

[k]
[g]

Say the words in the following lists slowly and carefully. Correct your production until you are satisfied that you are producing a firm, clear sound. Start with the *Beginning* words.

Beginning	*End*	*Middle*
key	beak	because
keep	peek	peeking
kit	pick	picking
kid	stick	sticking
cape	fake	aching
cane	bake	making
chemistry	neck	beckon
Kevin	check	echo
can	pack	backhand
cab	tack	sacking
cup	buck	duckpins
come	stuck	lacquer
common	stock	backhoe
calm	dock	doctor
cause	chalk	walking
cough	walk	hockey
coat	joke	backer
comb	smoke	checkup
cushion	took	joker
cookie	book	picky
coop	spook	okay

 Level 1 Practice Phrases for [k]

common cause	back ache	Cape Cod
echo echo echo	a buck a book	neck check
cup of cookies	making cushions	hockey stick

 Level 1 Practice Sentences for [k]

1. Put on your <u>backpack</u> and <u>take</u> a <u>walk</u> to the <u>dock.</u>
2. I bought <u>duck</u> <u>decoys</u> on <u>Cape</u> <u>Cod.</u>
3. He had a <u>neck</u> <u>ache</u> from playing <u>hockey.</u>
4. I left my <u>hiking</u> <u>stick</u> in the <u>pickup.</u>
5. <u>Kevin</u> wrote the <u>book</u> on <u>sticking</u> <u>keys.</u>
6. The <u>key</u> to the <u>chemistry</u> <u>cabinet</u> is in the <u>lock.</u>
7. The engine's <u>knock</u> was <u>caused</u> by low <u>octane</u> fuel.
8. <u>Doctors</u> advise <u>making</u> time for <u>checkups.</u>
9. The <u>backhoe</u> <u>stuck</u> in the <u>chalky</u> soil.
10. <u>Cookies</u> <u>commonly</u> find their way under <u>cushions.</u>

[k] **Level 2**

 Level 2 Practice Words for [k]

The words at this level generally have slightly more difficult sound combinations. In addition, some words have more than one [k] and may have [g] for contrast. Say the following words carefully and slowly. Make sure you don't omit the [k] at the end position, but don't overemphasize it.

Beginning	*End*	*Middle*
keel	streak	working
kilowatt	bleak	liquor
king	trick	locker
cute	drink	flicker
cumulus	shrink	looking
curious	flick	turkey
cable	milk	raccoon
keg	desk	silky
kelp	drank	lucky
catch	thank	Alaska
kangaroo	task	tracking
carry	park	drinking
courtesy	work	shrinking
culprit	jerk	parking
curb	hulk	sticking
cargo	fork	anchor
cold	historic	gasket
course	prank	flunking
cool	blank	thanking

All Positions		
skunk	kicking	chemical
Antarctic	practical	casket
electric	blackjack	kink

 Level 2 Practice Phrases for [k]

drink of milk	bleak streak	historic prank
kangaroo court	curious looking	sticking anchor
cute king	catch a skunk	practical work

 Level 2 Practice Sentences for [k]

1. The kangaroo is a curious kind of animal.
2. It was hard work catching King Kong.
3. He went to Alaska tracking the culprits.
4. The anchor went into the locker with a loud clank.
5. He was elected Kilowatt King by the electric company.
6. The cashier shook with fear after he caught the raccoon.

7. We had a continental breakfast in the park before work.
8. There's a lot of work for marketing consultants.
9. It wasn't practical to be carrying cargo.
10. I had a lucky streak at the casino.

[k] **Level 3**

Many people have problems with [k] when it is blended with certain other consonants such as [l], [r], [s], and [w]. When you read the following words, try to produce the [k] blends as one sound; mesh them together, don't separate them.

 Level 3 Practice Words for [k]

[kl]	[kr]	[ks]	[kw]
claim	crisp	hoax	quiet
clasp	crew	Cokes	quit
clash	crush	jokes	quilt
cloth	cross	fix	queen
incline	concrete	Bronx	quest
enclose	recruit	excellent	quack
inclement	Democrat	fixture	qualify
buckle	sacrifice	mixture	inquest
sickle	incredible	expand	conquest
ankle	increase	express	acquaint
circle	microfilm	axiom	acquit
icicle	incriminate	excuse	inquire
bicycle	accrue	exercise	acquire

 Level 3 Practice Sentences for [k]

1. Excuse me, is this the express train to the Bronx?
2. He broke his bike when it didn't clear the curb.
3. His insurance rates increased after he filed his claims.
4. A cycle of breathing consists of one inhalation and one exhalation.
5. He hid the incriminating microfilm in the camera.
6. I couldn't close the clasp on the buckle.
7. Biking is an excellent form of exercise.
8. The new recruits made incredible sacrifices.
9. They cleared a circle on the incline.
10. The mixture expanded and spilled on the cloth.
11. I couldn't break through the crowd to the box seats.
12. He fixed the clock so that it worked fairly accurately.
13. He flexed his muscles as he picked up the ax.
14. He quit so quietly I thought it was a hoax.
15. The quilt was acquired by the queen.

Challenge Sentences for [k]

1. Chris couldn't skate or ski until he fixed the broken clasp on his exercise jacket.
2. Clarence declared that Clarissa should quit her quest and become quiet.
3. Speak succinctly and quickly, or the wicked queen will lock up your Cokes.
4. Buckle the package to your bicycle to decrease the constant destruction of its cordage.
5. Clancy declaimed "Casey at the Bat" at the Coroner's Convention across the causeway from Connecticut.
6. I bought a box of biscuits, a box of mixed biscuits, and a biscuit mixer.
7. I requested a cup of proper coffee in a copper coffee cup.
8. "Y'all come back," called the colorful and loquacious Chesapeake Bay skipjack skipper.
9. Rebecca was crowned college Homecoming Queen because she was so cute.
10. If a conductor can carry electricity, how come he can also direct an orchestra?

Challenge Materials for [k]

1. The Curriculum is a large creature but little understood. It is so long that it stretches almost from one end of the Catalog to the other, leaving room only for the Calendar, the Faculty and Administration, and the Index, which are squeezed in before and after the lengthy and complicated Curriculum.

The size of the Curriculum is accounted for by its being full of Fields, Disciplines, Departments, Requirements, Concentrations, and Prerequisites. At the heart of the Curriculum are the Courses, which are themselves full of esoteric little symbols, meaningful only to Academians, such as 112a,b, MWF, and TTH. There may also be such cryptic words and expressions as "arranged," "half-course," and "May be repeated for credit."

Richard Armour, *The Academic Bestiary*

2. *Quill:* Type of feather material attached to a hook shank to imitate the look of an insect's segmented body. How it is that, say, a trout, which has extremely acute eyesight, can mistake a crude clump of duck feathers and deer fur for some insect it sees every day is a complete mystery, but it certainly undermines the concept of fish as "brain food."

Fishing: An Angler's Dictionary

[g] Level 1

 Level 1 Practice Words for [g]

Say the words in the following lists slowly and distinctly. Listen closely and adjust your production until you are satisfied that the sound is clear and strong enough, but don't overdo it. Start with the *Beginning* words.

Beginning	*End*	*Middle*
geese	fatigue	ego
give	big	agony
gift	wig	began
gate	vague	dignify
gave	egg	misguided
game	beg	again
get	nutmeg	engage
guess	peg	begin
gab	sag	wagon

Beginning	*End*	*Middle*
gadget	bag	navigate
gun	bug	magnet
gum	Doug	agate
gush	tug	disgust
gown	jug	bagpipe
guide	bog	August
gone	hog	yoga
gaudy	fog	toga
go	dog	dugout
gopher	vogue	Uganda
good	dug	megaton
gooey	hug	foghorn
goof	mug	negotiate

 Level 1 Practice Phrases for [g]

begin again	dog days	get a guide
engagement gift	gaudy wagon	gooey gum
big foghorn	gushing jug	jog in the bog

Level 1 Practice Sentences for [g]

1. The <u>fog</u> made it hard to <u>navigate</u> the <u>big</u> <u>tug</u>.
2. The <u>geese</u> <u>began</u> to push <u>against</u> the <u>gate</u>.
3. I had to <u>beg</u> <u>Doug</u> to <u>go</u> to the <u>game</u>.
4. The <u>guide</u> used <u>magnetic</u> <u>gadgets</u> to find the <u>geese</u>.
5. I <u>guess</u> I left the <u>bag</u> of <u>nutmeg</u> in the station <u>wagon</u>.
6. It's <u>good</u> for your <u>ego</u> to <u>jog</u> with your <u>dog</u>.
7. He <u>gave</u> toy <u>bagpipes</u> as <u>gifts</u> <u>again</u>.
8. The <u>gophers</u> <u>dug</u> <u>big</u> tunnels in the peat <u>bog</u>.
9. The <u>dog</u> <u>days</u> of <u>August</u> are <u>disgustingly</u> hot.
10. We <u>negotiated</u> with the <u>dignified</u> man from <u>Uganda</u>.

[g] **Level 2**

 Level 2 Practice Words for [g]

Words at this level have sound combinations that make it more difficult to produce a distinct [g]. In addition, the [g] may appear more than once in a word, and some words may have [k] for contrast.

Say the words in the following lists carefully and slowly. Make sure to produce the [g] in each word. Be careful not to overemphasize the [g] in the end position.

Beginning	*End*	*Middle*
gear	league	beguile
guilt	intrigue	figure
guild	twig	forget
gaze	plague	elongate
gainful	leg	nugget
gale	flag	smoggy
gallon	snag	trigger
gamble	brag	buggy
gang	cog	hugging
gasket	clog	luggage
garden	frog	organ
garage	analog	regard
garlic	dialogue	regular
gull	plug	sugar
girth	rug	signature
girl	bulldog	cigarette
gall	slug	vigorous
gauze	monologue	elegant
going	colleague	fragment
gold	rag	foggy

Level 2 Practice Phrases for [g]

forget dialogue	gold nuggets	gauze fragment
elegant luggage	hugging the rug	gang of girls
intriguing bulldog	going, going, gone	regular sugar

 Level 2 Practice Sentences for [g]

1. The vague statement of guilt had no legal standing.
2. He gambled that he wouldn't hit the trigger guard.
3. The garden was full of elegant forget-me-nots.
4. The fragments of garlic were covered with gauze.
5. The luggage and baggage carts were guarded closely.
6. It was going to be difficult to shift gears.
7. It was too buggy and foggy to go frog hunting.
8. Regular coffee is served with milk and sugar.
9. I felt guilty after forgetting the monologue.
10. The girl's signature was vague and elongated.

[g] Level 3

Here are practice words for the blends [gl], [gr], [gz], and [gd]. Say them slowly as blends, not separating consonants. In other words, there should be no pause between the consonants of the blend, nor should any vowel be inserted. Say the following words distinctly, reading down the columns, listening for both consonants in each blend.

Level 3 Practice Words for [gl], [gr], [gz], ***and*** [..gd]

[gl]	[gr]	[gz]	[gd]
gleam	grease	eggs	bagged
glitter	green	pigs	fatigued
glimpse	grip	twigs	wagged
glare	grin	begs	lagged
glad	graduate	tugs	gagged
glance	grant	rigs	tagged
glass	grass	clogs	shrugged
glottis	gross	bugs	bugged
gloves	grunt	bags	logged
glucose	groom	wags	zagged
aglow	agree	exact	zigged
angler	aground	exist	lugged

(*continued*)

[k]
[g]

[gl]	[gr]	[gz]	[gd]
igloo	angry	example	mugged
wiggly	congress	exhausted	flagged
neglect	hungry	exempt	begged
angle	regret	exonerate	rigged
single	telegram	executive	tugged
legal	vagrant	exuberant	hugged
snuggle	monogram	exotic	slugged

 ## *Level 3 Practice Sentences for* [g]

1. From this angle it was hard to see the gleam of light from the igloo.
2. You need fertile ground to grow grass.
3. I was exhausted from hunting for exact examples.
4. He shrugged even though his shirt was snagged.
5. The engraving glittered under the glass.
6. I begged her not to put all her eggs in one basket.
7. They asked the guard to show them the executive quarters.
8. The angry captain let the boat go aground.
9. The rig was controlled by a single gear.
10. I asked for the exact name of the gracious angler.
11. I jogged from the Bureau of Engraving to the Department of Agriculture.
12. Are you going to the groundbreaking ceremony?
13. A clove of garlic goes a long way.
14. The greasy telegram was regrettably costly.

Challenge Sentences for [g]

1. Vicky was dragged, kicking and screaming, from the grungy guardroom because of her flagrant neglect.
2. The sluggish English bulldog gave Greg an exuberant kiss with his wiggly tongue.
3. The legal eagle was exhausted from trying to guess the going rate for gumballs.
4. The gregarious gambler gave a good tug on his gloves, glanced at the gas gauge, and gunned his engine.
5. The existence of the angry telegram was guaranteed by the hungry graduate.
6. Englebert egged on the ragged beggar to exaggerate his aggravation.

7. Greg was beguiled by the gorgeous gaggle of Canada geese grazing in his rutabaga garden.
8. "Begone," begged the bedraggled groundskeeper, "I've got graves to gravel."
9. Loggers in the big bogs began digging for soggy logs.
10. Gail was a go-getter, but gosh, after she was gone, what did she get?

[k]
[g]

Challenge Sentences for [k] and [g]

1. The regular caretaker took his gardening with a grain of salt.
2. Be careful to calculate the correct gradations when giving gratis recipes.
3. The groom agreed to create a croquet court that his acquaintances would elect to call classic.
4. The bag lady haggled with the ticket taker over the cost of enclosing her luggage in plastic.
5. Could Captain Queeg have predicted he would end up the subject of an inquest in the excellent book by Herman Wouk, *The Caine Mutiny*?
6. Maggie begged the wicked frog king for a kiss and quickly became a frog queen.
7. Derek described a gargantuan sequoia tree he discovered while trekking through the green glade.
8. Green bagels linger on grocers' counters except around St. Patrick's day, when they become hot commodities.
9. Ricky looked sickly after mistakenly trying to bake an Eskimo Pie in the microwave.
10. Alaska is the biggest state in the country, but its coasts and lakes are becoming increasingly polluted.

Challenge Materials for [k] and [g]

1. The road goes west out of the village, past open pine woods and gallberry flats. An eagle's nest is a ragged cluster of sticks in a tall tree, and one of the eagles is usually black and silver against the sky. The other perches near the nest, hunched and proud, like a griffon. There is no magic here except the eagles. Yet the four miles to the Creek are stirring, like the bleak, portentous beginning of a good tale. The road curves sharply, the vegetation thickens, and around the bend masses into dense hammock. The hammock breaks, is pushed back on either side of the road, and set down in its brooding heart is the orange grove.

Marjorie Kinnan Rawlings, *Cross Creek*

2. *Inclusions in Diamonds*

Many diamonds contain gemlike mineral inclusions that help us understand how diamonds formed. These minute crystals provide valuable information on distribution of chemical elements in Earth's interior, where diamonds crystallized. Some common inclusions are colorless olivine, red-dish-brown chromite, ruby-red chrome magnesian garnet, emerald-green chrome clinopyroxene, yellowish-brown magnesium-iron-calcium garnet, and black graphite.

The Art of Geology

BOB   We have been asked by the National Parks Association to make the following announcement.

RAY   Will tourists and campers please stop throwing things into the Grand Canyon? The Grand Canyon is *your* canyon. It is the deepest canyon we have.

BOB   But it will cease to be the deepest canyon we have if tourists and campers keep throwing things into it. And now a word from Ranger Horace Liversidge of the Parks Service. . .

LIVERSIDGE   Folks, I'm just a grizzled old forest ranger who's grown gray in the National Parks Service. The Grand Canyon is my baby . . . I love it like a son. I've growed up with it. At night I walk the top of the canyon and look down into it. Can't see nothin', but I know what's there. A hole. Mile deep hole. Now, folks, don't throw things in the Grand Canyon no more. This is grizzled old Ranger Horace Liversidge thankin' you from the bottom of his canyon-heart.

BOB   That was grizzled old Ranger Horace Liversidge of the National Parks Service. Thank you, Grizzled.

RAY   If you want to help in this great campaign to preserve our natural wonders, use the litter cans on your city's sidewalks, don't throw things in the Grand Canyon. (*Music: "Grand Canyon Suite"*)

Bob Elliott and Ray Goulding, *Write If You Get Work*

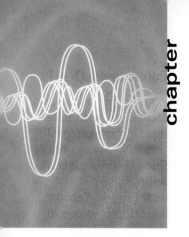

the consonants: fricatives

[f]　　[v]　　[θ]　　[ð]　　[s]　　[z]　　[ʃ]　　[ʒ]

Objectives

After completing the work in this chapter, you should be able to:

- Recognize the consonantal fricatives and the production problems associated with each
- Identify your own misarticulations of the consonantal fricatives (if any), and the nature of each misarticulation
- Distinguish regional and foreign variations of the consonantal fricatives
- Produce the consonantal fricatives correctly, at the instructor's request, in isolation, words, and phrases
- Help others to identify their misarticulations of the consonantal fricatives in a nonjudgmental way

This chapter consists mainly of drill materials for correcting and improving production of the consonantal fricatives. The exercises are organized in ascending order of difficulty; that is, they become increasingly difficult. As you begin a particular phoneme you start with words, phrases, and sentences that are easy to articulate; the material then becomes increasingly difficult as you progress. Finally, when you are very near to mastering the phoneme, you'll find material that is more challenging and, in many cases, more interesting. So that you can be more successful in accomplishing your goals, it's important that you work on the drills in that order. If you haven't already, we suggest that you read Chapter 5, in which the basics of improving diction are outlined.

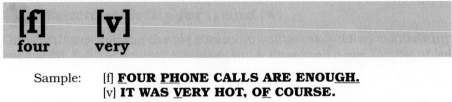

[f]   [v]
four   very

Sample: [f] **FOUR PHONE CALLS ARE ENOUGH.**
           [v] **IT WAS VERY HOT, OF COURSE.**

Spellings: **f** as in **four**   **v** as in **very**
           ff as in **affair**   **f** (only in the word **of**)
           gh as in **enough**   **ph** (only in **Stephen**)
           ph as in **phone**   **vv** as in **savvy**
           lf as in **half**

Description

[f] and [v] are cognate labio-dental sounds. [f] is voiceless, but [v] is voiced. They are fricative sounds that you produce by forcing the breath stream between your upper teeth and lower lip.

Production: [f]

1. Very lightly, rest the cutting edge of your upper front teeth against your lower lip.
2. Let your tongue rest against the floor of your mouth.
3. Start the breath stream moving, and force it between your lower lip and upper teeth. Don't allow any air to escape through your nose. Make sure you use a light touch. If you press too hard, not enough air comes through.

Production: [v]

Follow the same steps you used for [f]. As soon as you feel your teeth and lip touch, add voice.

COGNATE CONFUSION OF [f] AND [v]

Native-born speakers of American English usually don't have many production problems with [f] and [v]. Some non-native speakers, especially native German speakers, may frequently confuse [f] and [v]. The contrast drill below will help you eliminate such confusion.

Contrast Drill for [f] *and* [v]

Say the following words aloud. First read down the list of [f] words, making sure you don't hear or feel voice. Then read down the list of [v] words, this time listening and feeling for voice. For the last step, read across, contrasting pairs of words—the first word voiceless, the second voiced.

[f]	[v]		[f]	[v]
feel	— veal		proof	— prove
fine	— vine		half	— have
fast	— vast		leaf	— leave
fail	— veil		surface	— service
fan	— van		rifle	— rival
fat	— vat		shuffle	— shovel

[f] Level 1

 ### *Level 1 Practice Words for* [f]

Say the words in the following lists slowly and clearly. Listen carefully and correct your production until you're satisfied that the sound is clear. Remember, [f] is voiceless. Start with the *Beginning* words.

Beginning	End	Middle
fee	beef	effect
feed	chief	infect
fit	thief	affect
fin	if	benefit
fate	miff	confident
fake	waif	headphone
fed	deaf	café
fend	chef	infant
fan	tough	magnify
fat	half	jiffy
fact	chaff	muffin
funny	puff	offend
fine	huff	offhand
fight	wife	taffy
fog	off	topography
foe	cough	defend
photo	knife	coffee
phone	enough	confide
foot	goof	confound
food	cuff	affinity

Level 1 Practice Phrases for [f]

fine beef	funny photo	off the cuff
safe by a foot	face the fact	deaf chef
enough affinity	tough muffin	defend the fans

 ### *Level 1 Practice Sentences for* [f]

1. The <u>chef</u> was <u>five</u> <u>feet</u> tall.
2. The <u>funny</u>-tasting <u>coffee</u> was the <u>chief</u> complaint.
3. They charged the <u>photo</u> <u>fee</u> over the <u>phone</u>.
4. The <u>chief</u> was <u>offended</u> by <u>coughing</u> at the <u>benefit</u>.
5. "Where's the <u>beef</u>?" has become a <u>fact</u> of <u>fate</u>.
6. It was <u>fate</u> that <u>confined</u> us to the <u>café</u>.
7. He ate <u>half</u> the <u>muffin</u> but drank all the <u>coffee</u>.
8. The <u>infant's</u> <u>infection</u> <u>confounded</u> the <u>physician</u>.
9. He was <u>confident</u> as he paid the <u>farmer</u> with <u>fake</u> bills.
10. The <u>headphones</u> <u>magnified</u> the <u>effect</u> of the music.

[f] **Level 2**

Words at this level have slightly more difficult combinations of sounds, and some have [v] for contrast. Say them slowly and distinctly, making sure that the [f] doesn't pick up any voicing from adjoining voiced sounds.

 ### *Level 2 Practice Words for* [f]

Beginning	*End*	*Middle*
fear	aloof	before
fever	giraffe	afford
female	playoff	befall
field	bluff	refuse
finish	belief	snowfall
finger	relief	effort
Philip	loaf	breakfast

Beginning	End	Middle
Phyllis	cliff	wishful
face	housewife	satisfy
favor	Joseph	terrify
fair	shelf	glorify
fell	strafe	cupful
ferry	strife	mouthful
fallacy	leaf	steadfast
first	brief	offend
furry	safe	prefect
furnace	proof	rectify
fire	grief	perfect
file	self	kingfisher
five	stiff	rarefy
forest	staff	parfait
four	whiff	default
full	gruff	defer

[f]
[v]

Level 2 Practice Phrases for [f]

fifty-five	famous females	foolish faults
brief whiff	perfect parfait	furnace fire
steadfast effort	breakfast loaf	four fallacies
save face	before the ferry	gruff staff

Level 2 Practice Sentences for [f]

1. The first fall came in fifteen minutes.
2. I was satisfied with a mouthful of breakfast.
3. He could afford to make an effort to be brief.
4. She picked fifty perfect daffodils.
5. The forest was full of rough roads.
6. Joseph saw four terrifying movies.
7. I took a fast ferry to Martha's Vineyard.
8. Phyllis was famous for her vanilla parfait.
9. I was relieved to finish finals before vacation.
10. The field crew removed the snowfall after the playoff.

[f]
[v]

[f] Level 3

Here are practice words for four blends that can cause difficulty. They are [fl], [fr], [fs], and [ft]. Say them carefully, as one sound. Don't let any vowel sound creep in between the consonants in the blends.

 ### Level 3 Practice Words for [f]

[fl]	[fr]	[fs]	[ft]
flake	free	beliefs	raft
floor	frog	skiffs	reefed
flunk	friend	reefs	laughed
flame	frost	graphs	beefed
flush	frenzy	laughs	left
inflexible	infringe	safes	staffed
cauliflower	afraid	chefs	after
sniffle	African	chafes	shafted
raffle	refreshment	calf's	rafted
scuffle	grapefruit	handcuffs	softball
waffle	antifreeze	takeoffs	safety

 ### Level 3 Practice Sentences for [f]

1. His face grew flushed when he won the raffle.
2. I'm afraid I infringed on my friend.
3. He laughs at others' beliefs.
4. We reefed the sail on the raft in complete safety.
5. I left the snowflakes on the frosty shelf.
6. Everyone enjoyed the free refreshments.
7. I found the cauliflower on the floor.
8. He jumped safely from the flaming rafters.
9. Some chefs are inflexible about flush-fitting covers.
10. We beefed up the skiff's frames after it fell.

Challenge Sentences for [f]

1. Florence fried fifty fat cauliflowers for five of her finest friends.
2. Please inform Fred if any funny references are made before breakfast is finished.
3. The chef fixed the food for the afternoon on a flame that was four-fifths safe.
4. The officer fortified his position with an official effort that found favor with the infantry.

5. Finish the furniture with a different polish than you found for us on Friday.
6. Francis frequently affixed a floating fly to his fishing tackle to fortify his fortune with flounders.
7. Frequent fliers often find fault with their favorite flights of fancy.
8. Half a loaf frequently fails to satisfy the food preferences of the affluent folk.
9. A fortunate few are found favorable enough to be specified in the Fortune five hundred.
10. Infant food was fixed fifty-four ways in a formula offered by author Phillip Frost.

[f]
[v]

[v] Level 1

PROBLEM 1: SUBSTITUTION OF [w] FOR [v]

Some nonnative speakers, especially native German speakers who may confuse [f] and [v], frequently substitute [w] for [v]. The following contrast drill will help you eliminate this substitution.

Contrast Drill for [w] *and* [v]

Say the following words aloud. First read down the list of [w] words, making sure that you can feel the pursing movements of the lips; you shouldn't make lip-teeth contact. Then read down the list of [v] words, making sure that you feel the contact between your upper teeth and lower lip. For the last step, read across, contrasting pairs of words.

[w]	[v]	[w]	[v]
west	— vest	went	— vent
wet	— vet	wile	— vile
wine	— vine	wane	— vane
wail	— veil	worse	— verse
waltz	— vaults	wend	— vend

PROBLEM 2: SUBSTITUTION OF [b] FOR [v]

This occurs most often with native Spanish speakers. For example, the word *very* would become *berry.* Try the contrast drill below if you have this substitution.

Contrast Drill for [b] *and* [v]

Say the following words aloud. First read down the list of [b] words, feeling the plosive quality of the sound. Next, read down the list of [v] words, making sure to feel that there is not a buildup of air resulting in a plosive sound. You should feel your teeth touching your lip, not both lips touching each other. For the last step, read across, contrasting pairs of words.

[b]	[v]	[b]	[v]
ban —	van	bend —	vend
berry —	very	saber —	saver
beer —	veer	dub —	dove
bile —	vile	robe —	rove
best —	vest	curb —	curve
bow —	vow	curbing —	curving
boat —	vote	bane —	vane

Level 1 Practice Words for [v]

Say the words in the following lists slowly and clearly. Listen carefully and correct your production until you feel sure that the sound is clear and accurate. Try to start your voicing at the same time that your teeth touch your lip. Start with the *Beginning* words.

Beginning	*End*	*Middle*
veto	weave	even
vee	eve	event
victor	give	given
vintage	native	divide
view	connective	evict
vacate	wave	invent
vague	gave	devote
vain	pave	pivot
vend	concave	heaven
vet	have	devoted
vent	five	paving
van	I've	having
vast	dive	avoid
vow	of	convent
vouch	dove	advance
vitamin	above	nova
vine	wove	avid
voice	cove	advent
void	jove	cave-in
vote	move	moving

Level 1 Practice Phrases for [v]

heaven above	vintage view	voice vote
concave paving	have in advance	moving van
vitamin invention	avoid a cave-in	vowed to veto

 ## *Level 1 Practice Sentences for* [v]

1. The <u>veto</u> was <u>given</u> an <u>advantage.</u>
2. I <u>vowed</u> to take a <u>vitamin</u> in <u>advance.</u>
3. The <u>native</u> <u>dove</u> into the <u>wave</u> in the <u>cove.</u>
4. There was a <u>cave-in</u> in the <u>pavement</u> near the <u>convent.</u>
5. The <u>vent</u> blocked my <u>view</u> so I had to <u>move.</u>
6. The <u>nova</u> exploded in the <u>vast</u> <u>void.</u>
7. <u>Even</u> during the <u>eviction,</u> the apartment was <u>vacant.</u>
8. He <u>divided</u> the <u>van</u> <u>evenly.</u>
9. Number <u>five</u> grape <u>vine</u> has been <u>divided.</u>
10. Out <u>of</u> <u>devotion,</u> she <u>wove</u> the sign <u>of</u> the <u>dove.</u>

[v] **Level 2**

PROBLEM 1: OMISSION OF [v]

Many people tend to omit the [v] when it comes at the end of a word. They also omit it or assimilate it into the next word if that word begins with a consonant. Say the following phrases, making sure to produce a moderately strong [v].

 ## *Drill for Final* [v]

five dollars	five times	five more
five hundred	five million	five months
five thousand	have many	live wire
have one on me	I've done it	give me
give them	save me	leave me
love me	have some	save some

PROBLEM 2: THE PREPOSITION *OF*

The preposition *of* contains the sound [v], but people often omit it or assimilate it into the following word. Say the following phrases, making sure to put the voiced sound [v] in the word *of.* Don't overdo it, though, especially when the consonant that follows is voiceless. In that instance, it's normal to "devoice" the [v] slightly.

 *Drill for of*

loaf of bread	can of worms	nick of time
pair of shoes	one of hers	best of it
two of them	ace of spades	one of the boys
barrels of fun	hill of beans	glass of water
cup of coffee	jug of wine	some of us

Level 2 Practice Words for [v]

The words at this level contain consonants that are more difficult to produce, and may have [f] for contrast. Say the following words slowly and clearly, and listen for a distinct [v].

Beginning	End	Middle	All Positions
veal	leave	fever	divisive
veer	pave	believing	vivid
village	believe	invisible	evolve
vessel	relative	river	vivacious
very	passive	silver	valve
vase	brave	prevent	Vancouver
vapor	enclave	gravy	velvet
valentine	save	shaving	survive
value	arrive	favor	preventive
vulture	glove	cavity	survivor
verse	serve	starving	vivisection
verbal	observe	service	convivial
virtue	stove	device	Vivian
volume	clove	clover	verve
volley	drove	nonverbal	vindictive

Level 2 Practice Phrases for [v]

veal franks	velvet gloves	seven eleven
flu vaccine	very wide	white vanilla
give five	have value	weavers village

 ### Level 2 Practice Sentences for [v]

1. I tried to save five dollars.
2. Give me the vial with the vaccine.
3. I have one of them at the office.

4. I was able to observe the driver arriving five minutes late.
5. Love me, love my dog.
6. Varsity football is regarded positively by most universities.
7. Please leave the gloves for Valerie.
8. The entire village savored the aroma of the clover.
9. The silver river runs through the valley.
10. Many people shiver with a strange fever on Valentine's Day.

[v] Level 3

 ### *Level 3 Practice Words for* [v]

Here are some practice words for three blends that can be troublesome: [vl], [vz], and [vd]. Say them carefully, as one sound. Don't let any vowel sound creep in between the consonants of the blend.

[vl]	[vz]	[vd]
evil	halves	saved
shovel	shelves	loved
marvel	leaves	received
rival	loves	proved
snivel	hooves	lived
grovel	heaves	revolved
gravel	curves	curved
gavel	shoves	shoved
oval	moves	moved
level	carves	carved
hovel	deceives	deceived
weevil	slaves	slaved
survival	grooves	grooved

 ### *Level 3 Practice Sentences for* [v]

1. Vivian was a vivacious vixen, variously proving herself vindictive and benevolent.
2. The oven from Harvey's hovel was moved over to the bottom level of the valley house.
3. Heaven help the evil villain who deceives his virtuous wife with visions of vicarious living!
4. Vincent viewed the bevy of lovelies and vowed he would forever be moved.
5. Did you receive a Valentine from your lover in view of your lively division?

Challenge Sentences for [f] *and* [v]

1. They proved that the levels were uneven.
2. He deceived us in the way he moved on the curves.
3. It's the best work of fiction I've read in five years.
4. Speaking for myself, I've never been happier.
5. I was positive there was a live wire on the pavement.
6. I've told you at least five thousand times never to do it.
7. Half of the shelf was overflowing.
8. I haven't received the load of concrete yet.
9. Make sure to leave some of it for me to give away.
10. I lost the chance for victory in only seven moves.
11. Olivia's fiancé believed that her sylphlike figure was effectively featured in her effervescent offering of flamenco.
12. I often find myself feeling fit in the face of overwhelming evidence of a very different variety.
13. Physical fitness, a fact of life in our environment, is often viewed in a vicarious fashion at physicians' conventions.
14. Vivienne vacations at Puerto Vallarta the first fourteen days of February, or for five days after the first snowfall.
15. Various views of the officiating officials were voiced quite vociferously by the football viewers.

Challenge Materials for [f] *and* [v]

1. The scroll work along the edge of the porch was wet with the fog. The fog dripped from the Monterey cypresses that shadowed off into nothing towards the cliff above the ocean. You could see a scant dozen feet in any direction. I went down the porch steps and drifted off through the trees, following an indistinct path until I could hear the wash of the surf licking at the fog, low down at the bottom of the cliff. There wasn't a gleam of light anywhere. I could see a dozen trees clearly at one time, another dozen dimly, then nothing at all but the fog. I circled to the left and drifted back towards the gravel path that went around to the stables where they parked the cars. When I could make out the outlines of the house I stopped. A little in front of me I had heard a man cough.

My steps hadn't made any sound on the soft moist turf. The man coughed again, then stifled the cough with a handkerchief or a sleeve. While he was still doing that I moved forward closer to him. I made him out, a vague shadow close to the path. Something made me step behind a tree and crouch down. The man turned his head. His face should have been a white blur when he did that. It wasn't. It remained dark. There was a mask over it.

I waited, behind the tree.

Raymond Chandler, *The Big Sleep*

2. Cultural values usually are derived from the larger philosophical issues that are part of a culture's milieu. Hence, they tend to be broad-based, enduring, and relatively stable. Values generally are normative in

that they inform a member of a culture about what is good and bad, right and wrong, true and false, positive and negative, and the like. Cultural values define what is worth dying for, what is worth protecting, what frightens people, what are proper subjects for study and for ridicule, and what types of events lead individuals to group solidarity. Most important, cultural values guide both perception and behavior.

Larry A. Samovar and Richard E. Porter, *Intercultural Communication: A Reader.*

[θ]   [ð]
thin   **the**

Sample: [θ] **I <u>TH</u>OUGHT IT WAS A <u>TH</u>IN SLICE OF BIR<u>TH</u>DAY CAKE.**

[ð] **MY MO<u>TH</u>ER SAID <u>TH</u>EY WERE <u>TH</u>E BEST.**

Spellings: **th** as in **bath**   **th** as in **with**
tth only in **Matthew**   **the** as in **bathe**

Description

[θ] and [ð] are cognate lingua-dental sounds. They are fricatives that you produce by squeezing the breath stream between your tongue and teeth.

Production: [θ]

1. Open your mouth until your teeth are slightly apart.
2. Round the tip of your tongue; don't try to point it too sharply.
3. Place your tongue so that it protrudes very slightly between your upper and lower front teeth.
4. Force the breath stream to come out between your tongue and teeth. Don't press too tightly; you'll end up forcing the sound. Don't let any air escape through the nose.

Production Drill

1. Look in a mirror and say the [θ] sound.
2. Make sure you can see the edge of your tongue protruding between the teeth. Say [θ] again. It may feel unusual and uncomfortable, but don't let that bother you.
3. Say the [θ] sound over and over again. Don't move your tongue between sounds. Try the following:

   [θ] . . . [θ] . . . [θ] . . . [θ] . . . thin
   [θ] . . . [θ] . . . [θ] . . . [θ] . . . thanks
   [θ] . . . [θ] . . . [θ] . . . [θ] . . . thought

Monitor your production visually with the mirror and by listening carefully. If you're unsure, ask your instructor to help.

Production: [ð]

Follow the steps for [θ]. Add voice as soon as you feel your tongue touch your teeth.

Production Drill

1. Review the production notes on [θ] and [ð].
2. Look in a mirror and say the [ð] sound.
3. Make sure you can see the edge of your tongue protruding between the teeth. Say [ð] again. It may feel unusual and uncomfortable, but don't let that bother you.
4. Say the [ð] sound over and over again. Don't move your tongue between sounds. Try the following:

    [ð] . . . [ð] . . . [ð] . . . [ð] . . . the
    [ð] . . . [ð] . . . [ð] . . . [ð] . . . those
    [ð] . . . [ð] . . . [ð] . . . [ð] . . . them

Monitor your production visually with the mirror and by listening carefully. If you're unsure, ask your instructor to help.

Cognate Confusion of [θ] and [ð]

Since both [θ] and [ð] sounds are spelled in exactly the same way, many times people don't know which sound to use. Even if English is your native language and you know instinctively, most of the time, how a word is pronounced, you can still become confused. Maybe these general rules (which have exceptions) can help:

1. Use the voiced sound [ð] when the word ends in *ther.*
   Example: bother [baðɚ]
2. Use the voiced sound [ð] when the word ends in *the.*
   Example: breathe [brið]
3. Use the voiceless sound [θ] when the *th* follows a pronounced consonant. **Example:** month [mʌnθ]

So *rather* uses [ð], *lathe* uses [ð], and *fifth* uses [θ].

[θ] **Level 1**

[θ] and [ð] are sounds that cause trouble for both native and nonnative speakers. They're very weak sounds (hard to hear) and are two of the last sounds children acquire. Since these sounds exist in only a few languages, most nonnative speakers have difficulty with them.

Problem 1: Tongue Placement

Most misarticulations of [θ] result in a sound that is similar to [t]. It happens when you place your tongue too close to the gum ridge behind your upper front teeth or when you press your tongue too firmly on the teeth for fricative production. Instead, you produce a plosive, [t]. If you are misarticulating [θ] in this way, try the following contrast drill.

[θ]
[ð]

🔘 *Contrast Drill for* [t] *and* [θ]

First review the production notes on [θ]. Then read the following words aloud, contrasting the words in the first column, which contain [t], with the [θ] words in the second column.

[t]	[θ]	[t]	[θ]
tin	— thin	tread — thread	
tick	— thick	true — through	
tanks	— thanks	boat — both	
taught	— thought	bat — bath	
tie	— thigh	oat — oath	
tinker	— thinker	bet — Beth	

Problem 2: Substitution of [f] for [θ]

Sometimes people attempt to make the [θ] and [ð] without protruding the tongue. If the lower jaw comes forward and up at the same time, a fricative sound is produced with your lip and teeth instead of with your tongue and teeth. Try the following contrast drill.

🔘 *Contrast Drill for* [θ] *and* [f]

First read down the column of [f] words. Then read down the column of [θ] words. Finally read across, contrasting pairs of words. Feel for contact between your tongue and teeth on the [θ] words. You shouldn't feel any contact between your lip and teeth on those words. Complete the drill and then do it again, this time using a mirror to control your lip movement.

[f]	[θ]	[f]	[θ]
fin	— thin	froze — throws	
fink	— think	free — three	
fought	— thought	miff — myth	
first	— thirst	sheaf — sheath	
Fred	— thread	reef — wreath	

PROBLEM 3: SUBSTITUTION OF [s] FOR [θ]

This substitution is commonly made by nonnative speakers. If you make this substitution, try the following.

💿 *Contrast Drill for* [θ] **and** [s]

Read down the list of [s] words first. Use a mirror, and make sure your tongue stays behind your teeth. Next read down the list of [θ] words. Use the mirror again, and this time, make sure your tongue protrudes slightly between your teeth. For the last step, read across, contrasting pairs of words.

[s]	[θ]	[s]	[θ]
sink	— think	miss	— myth
sought	— thought	pass	— path
sick	— thick	mouse	— mouth
seem	— theme	moss	— moth
sin	— thin	mass	— math
saw	— thaw	worse	— worth
sing	— thing	face	— faith
sigh	— thigh	truce	— truth
sank	— thank		

💿 *Level 1 Practice Words for* [θ]

Say the words in the following lists slowly and clearly. Listen carefully, and correct your production until you are satisfied that it is accurate and clear. You may want to use a mirror so that you can see if your tongue is far enough between your teeth. Remember, [θ] is a voiceless sound. Start with the *Beginning* words.

Beginning	*End*	*Middle*
theme	beneath	ether
thief	heath	anything
thin	myth	nothing
thicken	Judith	ethnic
thing	faith	pathetic
think	Beth	pathway
theta	death	Matthew

Beginning	End	Middle
theft	math	bathmat
thank	bath	methane
thud	path	toothpick
thug	mammoth	Kathy
thumb	Kenneth	pathos
thump	mouth	motheaten
thong	moth	Nathan
thigh	oath	python
thaw	both	anthem
thought	tooth	bathtub
thousand	youth	youthful

[θ]
[ð]

Level 1 Practice Phrases for [θ]

thick thumb	thought nothing	give thanks
think thin	motheaten python	mammoth theft
pathetic thug	beneath the ether	youthful theme
thigh high bath	bathtub bathmat	both thongs
ethnic pathways	a thousand toothpicks	thuds and thumps

Level 1 Practice Sentences for [θ]

1. <u>Math</u> is not my <u>thing</u>.
2. I had <u>faith</u> in a spring <u>thaw</u>.
3. <u>Kathy</u> was headed on a <u>path</u> to <u>tooth</u> decay.
4. He had <u>both</u> a <u>thug</u> and a <u>thief</u> under his <u>thumb</u>.
5. <u>Matthew</u> found <u>methane</u> gas <u>beneath</u> a high <u>heath</u>.
6. According to a popular <u>myth,</u> a <u>toothache</u> you <u>think</u> about won't go away.
7. It was a <u>pathetic</u>, <u>motheaten</u> <u>bathmat</u>.
8. I <u>thought</u> <u>Beth</u> said, "<u>Thank</u> you."
9. A <u>mammoth</u> had an incredibly <u>thick</u> <u>thighbone</u>.
10. <u>Judith</u> didn't <u>think</u> of <u>bathtub</u> accidents.
11. <u>Kenneth</u> broke <u>both</u> <u>thongs</u> <u>thudding</u> and <u>thumping</u> downstairs.
12. She had <u>little</u> <u>faith</u> in <u>anything</u> <u>mathematical</u>.
13. I <u>think</u> I see <u>thousands</u> of <u>toothpicks</u>.
14. I have no <u>thanks</u> for <u>ethnic</u> jokes or <u>thoughts</u>.

[θ] Level 2

 Level 2 Practice Words for [θ]

The words at this level contain certain other consonants that make [θ] more difficult to produce accurately. These include [r], [l], [m], and [p]. Say each word slowly, and distinctly. Make sure you don't add any voice to the [θ]. You may find it helpful to overemphasize the [θ] on the first two or three readings. Start with the *Beginning* column, and don't move on until you are fairly confident that your production is accurate.

Beginning	*End*	*Middle*
theory	wreath	atheist
thistle	fifth	birthday
therapy	wealth	bathtowel
thirst	health	earthy
third	breath	healthy
thermometer	warmth	Southport
Thursday	worth	pathfinder
thorough	earth	something
three	cloth	everything
thrifty	fourth	lethargic
threat	north	stethoscope
thread	south	toothpaste
thirteen	growth	withheld
thrush	truth	truthful
thrive	tablecloth	stealthy
throng	girth	breathy
thrash	zenith	bathrobe
throat	stealth	athlete
threw	fortieth	withhold
thwart	fiftieth	Parthenon

 Level 2 Practice Phrases for [θ]

third Thursday
threw something
thrifty thread
fifth time
sore throat

withheld the truth
three bathrobes
fourth birthday
thirsty throng

Level 2 Practice Sentences for [θ]

1. Truthfully, I'm thrifty about birthday cakes.
2. Southport is a thoughtlessly wealthy town.

   3. A person of girth needs a lot of earth for growth.
   4. Thrushes thrive in the north.
   5. A fourth share was nothing to throw away.
   6. Withholding taxes take a fifth of everything I earn.
   7. He started therapy for his sore throat on Thursday.
   8. We withdrew stealthily under cover of camouflage cloth.
   9. A tablecloth is composed of thousands of threads.
   10. His breathy voice resulted from unhealthy toothpaste.

[θ]
[ð]

[θ] Level 3

 ### *Level 3 Practice Words for* [θ]

When [θ] is surrounded by other consonants in a blend or cluster, the result is a tongue twister. Such clusters are [θs] as in *myths*, [ksθ] as in *sixth*, [pθ] as in *depth*, [nθ] as in *ninth*, [θl] as in *ethyl*, and [dθ] as in *width*. Take these words slowly; they can be very difficult to produce accurately. When [θ] is followed by [s], combine the two into one sound. Don't stop production between the two; keep the breath stream going while you are moving your tongue back. Remember, these words have the voiceless [θ].

[nθ]	[θl]	[dθ]	[θs]	[ksθ]
seventh	ethyl	width	myths	sixth
ninth	faithless	breadth	fifths	six-thirty
tenth	Kathleen	hundredth	tenths	
menthol	lethal	thousandth	sevenths	
synthetic	ruthless		months	
labyrinth	athlete		ninths	
anthology			paths	
Anthony			baths	
month			moths	

Level 3 Practice Sentences for [θ]

   1. I bought a sixth can of synthetic oil.
   2. Two fifths equals four tenths.
   3. Old myths and old athletes can stretch beyond truth.
   4. Kathleen was a ruthless depth-editor.
   5. Length times width equals area.
   6. It was a lethal dose of methyl alcohol.
   7. It sank only three-thousandths of an inch.
   8. His seventh breath was longer than his eleventh.
   9. It was his third faithless love affair.
   10. Surfers set healthy records on ninth waves.

Challenge Sentences for [θ]

1. Theoretical mathematics involves mythical thinking in the third and fourth dimensions.
2. Thirty-three theologians thrust their thirsty tongues through their teeth.
3. Three threadbare travelers threaded their way through isothermal pathways to reach their zenith.
4. The other thermometer has a plethora of mercury at its pith.
5. Thanks for thinking of both of us; it was thoroughly thoughtful of you.
6. The usually thorough mythologist thought Plymouth Rock was a thrilling, though unauthorized, theme song.
7. "Nothing is good, nothing is bad; only thinking makes it so," is theoretically breathtaking if carefully thought through.
8. Bosworth's forthright withdrawal from writing anthologies furthered his thinking both in width and breadth.
9. Thirty thousand synthetic Thanksgiving turkeys gathered in Theo's thatched-roof shanty last Thursday.
10. Without a thesaurus, authoring three growth phrases with the phoneme [θ] is a thankless task.

[ð] Level 1

[ð] causes trouble for native and nonnative speakers alike. It's a weak sound that's hard to hear, and is one of the last sounds children acquire. Because [ð] exists in only a few languages, most nonnative speakers have difficulty with it.

PROBLEM 1: TONGUE PLACEMENT

Most misarticulations of [ð] result in a sound that is similar to [d]. It happens when you place your tongue too close to the gum ridge behind your upper front teeth or when you press your tongue too firmly on the teeth for fricative production. Instead, you produce a plosive, [d]. If you are misarticulating [ð] in this way, try the following contrast drill.

Contrast Drill for [ð] **and** [d]

First review the production notes on [ð]. Then read the following words aloud, contrasting the words in the first column, which contain [d], with the [ð] words in the second column.

[d]	[ð]	[d]	[ð]
day	— they	ladder — lather	
doze	— those	wordy — worthy	
dough	— though	load — loathe	
den	— then	laid — lathe	
dine	— thine	seed — seethe	
dare	— there	breed — breathe	
udder	— other	ride — writhe	
mudder	— mother	fodder — father	

[θ]
[ð]

PROBLEM 2: SUBSTITUTION OF [z] FOR [ð]

This substitution is commonly made by nonnative speakers. If you make this substitution, try the following contrast drill.

Contrast Drill for [z] and [ð]

Read the list of [z] words first. Use the mirror, and keep your tongue behind your teeth. Then read down the list of [ð] words, saying each word carefully. Use the mirror again, and this time make sure your tongue protrudes slightly between your teeth for the [ð] words.

[z]	[ð]	[z]	[ð]
Zen	— then	breezing	— breathing
zee	— thee	close	— clothe
razzer	— rather	seize	— seethe

[z]	[ð]	[z]	[ð]
teasing	— teething	tease	— teethe
closing	— clothing	laze	— lathe

PROBLEM 3. PRONUNCIATION OF THE WORD *THE*

The word *the* is one of the most frequently used in the English language. Yet many people are confused as to how to pronounce it, especially when they see it in print. Here are rules you can use to help you when you read aloud:

1. The word *the* is pronounced [ðə] when it's followed by a consonant.
2. The word *the* is pronounced [ði] when it's followed by a vowel.

So it's [ðə] *beginning* and [ði] *end*.

Level 1 Practice Words for [ð]

Say the words in the following lists slowly and clearly. Listen carefully and adjust your production until you are satisfied with it. You may want

(*continued*)

[θ]
[ð]

to use a mirror so that you can check your tongue to make sure it is far enough out between your teeth. We've saved words that end in [ð] for level 2 since they are fairly difficult to pronounce smoothly. In level 1, we suggest that you start with the *Middle* words first. It's easier to produce [ð] when it's preceded by a vowel. Remember to start your voicing of [ð] early enough.

Middle	*Middle*	*Beginning*	*Beginning*
either	wither	thee	they
within	without	them	then
neither	bathing	their	that
whether	together	though	thou
feather	gather	than	the
father	mother	thy	thine

Level 1 Practice Phrases for [ð]

either one	feather bed	their mother
gather together	father is there	other feather
within and without	that bather	thee and thou

Level 1 Practice Sentences for [ð]

1. The feather bed was very soft.
2. My mother said that it was the end.
3. We can move the furniture together.
4. The critic made a scathing attack after the opening.
5. We were gathering cotton before the hot weather.
6. I like bathing in cool, soothing waters.
7. Neither one cared about the weather.
8. I knew without a doubt that it was the other one.
9. They were within the boundaries.
10. Therein lies the tale of Wuthering Heights.

[ð] Level 2

Level 2 Practice Words for [ð]

The words at this level have consonant combinations in which the [ð] may be hard to produce clearly, and words that end in [ð]. Listen carefully for the [ð]; make sure you voice it when it's preceded or followed by voiceless consonants. Some of the words at this level may also have [θ] for contrast. Start with *Beginning* words and then do the *Middle*. Save the *End* for last.

Beginning	Middle	End
these	although	with
those	rather	bathe
therefore	soothing	soothe
this	smoothly	lathe
thus	teething	tithe
thereafter	breathing	seethe
theirs	clothing	writhe
thence	writhing	breathe
thusly	leather	clothe
therein	rhythms	teethe
themselves	Mother's Day	smooth
that's	southern	scathe

Level 2 Practice Sentences for [ð]

1. Descartes said, "I think, therefore I am."
2. I threw a blanket over the leather couch.
3. Either one is okay with me.
4. Teething rings can soothe a baby's teeth.
5. I have three exams this Thursday, then no more.
6. They attempted to bathe in their clothing.
7. I knew without a doubt the train would run smoothly.
8. The pit was seething with writhing reptiles.
9. Nevertheless, the theater was the oldest.
10. That's the way it is with my father.

[ð] Level 3

Level 3 Practice Words for [ð]

There are three [ð] blends that are difficult: [ðd], [ðz], and [rð]. In practice, you may have to draw the [ð] out slightly and overemphasize it. Try the following words, and listen closely for the [ð].

[ðd]	[ðz]	[rð]
breathed	breathes	farther
bathed	bathes	further
clothed	clothes	northern
seethed	seethes	worthy
smoothed	smoothes	worthiness
soothed	soothes	earthen
writhed	writhes	farthermost
loathed	loathes	swarthy

[θ]
[ð]

🔘 *Level 3 Practice Sentences for* [ð]

The following sentences contain the blends you've just practiced, as well as [ð] words from levels 1 and 2. In addition, you'll find some [θ] words for contrast. Read the sentences a few times. Start off very slowly and carefully, but in subsequent readings, try to imitate normal speech rate and patterns.

1. My mother loathes snakes.
2. The Northern Lights are brighter the farther north you travel.
3. I washed my clothes as I bathed in the river.
4. The seaworthy vessel sailed south by southeast.
5. She was clothed in cotton that breathed.
6. Give him either the Novocain or the ether.
7. Father's brow smoothed, and he breathed easier.
8. Don't bother me with unworthy questions.
9. My brother furthered his career with clear thinking.
10. That is the time that we'll be through.

Challenge Sentences for [ð] **and** [θ]

1. "Lather that leather thong," said the other feather merchant thoughtlessly.
2. "Bother your other brother," the author's father declared wordily.
3. Smooth sailing, thought the sailor, thinking how seaworthy was his sloop from Boothbay.
4. Neither his father nor his mother bothered to clothe him, though they thought he was thoughtless about his appearance.
5. Nothing was further from her mind than the idea of furthering the expedition to the north.
6. As the throng gathered together, they withered at the sight of the thing's clothing.
7. There abide these three: faith, hope and charity. . . .
8. "Breathes there a man with soul so dead, who never to himself hath said, this is my own, my native land." (Sir Walter Scott)
9. Brother against brother—that was the theme of the theatrical *Pathfinder.*
10. "Other times, other thoughts," breathed my brother through the thick ether.
11. Rather than breathe through the other nostril, the father threw the lather away.

12. Math throws many otherwise thoughtful youths, though others go through it without a second thought.
13. "North and South" was a thoroughly breathtaking story, though not as worthwhile as "The Thief Sets Forth."
14. The aftermath of thinking through a thorny problem is worthy of the effort.
15. Length, width, and breadth are the three fundamental measurements lathe operators can't do without.

[θ]
[ð]

Challenge Materials for [ð]

1. I milked the cows, I churned the butter, I stored the cheese, I baked the bread, I brewed the tea, I washed the clothes, I dressed the children; the cat meowed, the dog barked, the horse neighed, the mouse squeaked, the fly buzzed, the goldfish living in a bowl stretched its jaws; the door banged shut, the stairs creaked, the fridge hummed, the curtains billowed up, the pot boiled, the gas hissed through the stove, the tree branches heavy with snow crashed against the roof; my heart beat loudly *thud! thud!*

Jamaica Kincaid, *At the Bottom of the River*

2. *Waiter, There's a Fly. . . .*

"Waiter, there's a fly in my soup."
"That will be thirty cents extra, please."

"Waiter, there's a fly in my soup."
"That's no fly, that's the manager."
"Waiter, there's a fly in my soup."
"Shhh—all the customers will want one."

"Waiter, there's a fly in my soup."
"That's better than half a fly."

"Waiter, there's a fly in my soup."
"Sorry, we ran out of moths."

"Waiter, what's that fly doing in my soup?"
"Looks like the backstroke."

"Waiter, there's a *dead* fly in my soup."
"I know. It's the heat that kills them."

3. *Thank-You Letters and Notes*
"Thank you" is a powerful statement that is heard too seldom. Every thank you is an opportunity to sell your qualifications and to leave a fresh impression in the mind of the reader. Send a thank-

you letter or note to employers and employment contacts whenever they have extended themselves in any way on behalf of your job search. At the minimum, a written thank you should be sent after all interviews.

Thank-you letters and notes should be standard tools in your job search. The thank-you letter should follow a standard business letter format while the note may be a simple hand-written note or card. Which to send depends upon the situation and your personal style.

Minnesota Department of Economic Security
http://www.des.state.mn.us/cjs/cjs_site/letters.htm

[s]   [z]
snake   zoo

Sample: [s] **THE DOG LOST THE SCENT OF THE SNAKE IN THE GRASS.**
[z] **THEY HOSED OUT THE CAGES AT THE ZOO.**

Spellings:
s as in **snake**	**z** as in **zoo**
ss as in **grass**	**x** as in **Xerox**
sc as in **scent**	**se** as in **hose**
c as in **cent**	**zz** as in **blizzard**
ps as in **psychology**	**ss** as in **scissors**
tz as in **waltz**	**s** as in **music**
sch as in **schism**	
x as in **exit**	
(with [**k**])	

Description

[s] and [z] are cognate lingua-alveolar sounds. They are fricatives that you produce by forcing air between your tongue and the upper or lower front teeth.

Production: [s]

1. Place your tongue in the position to say [t], but don't say it.
2. Drop the tip of your tongue down and slightly back, but keep the sides lightly pressed against the middle and back upper teeth. Your tongue should now be pointing at the cutting edges of your front teeth or toward the gum ridge.
3. Make a shallow groove lengthwise along the midline of your tongue. Keep the sides up.
4. Blow the breath stream at the cutting edge of the teeth; create a "hissing" sound. [s] is voiceless.

Production: [z]

Follow the steps for [s]. Start voicing as soon as the air begins to move.

COGNATE CONFUSION OF [s] AND [z]

Because it's often difficult to hear the difference between [s] and [z], and because the letter *s* is frequently pronounced [z], it's no wonder that many people confuse these cognates. Try the following contrast drill if you're not certain of your production of [s] and [z].

 ### *Contrast Drill for* [s] *and* [z]

Read down the list of [s] words first. Notice the absence of voice. Then read down the list of [z] words, feeling for voice. Make sure to start voicing at the start of the sound. The last step is to read across, contrasting pairs of words.

[s]	[z]	[s]	[z]
sue	— zoo	busing	— buzzing
sap	— zap	loose	— lose
sip	— zip	fuss	— fuzz
racer	— razor	spice	— spies
lacer	— laser	device	— devise

Special Problems

[s] and [z] are sounds that can cause you a lot of trouble. They are difficult sounds to produce—they require precision actions by the articulators, especially accurate movements, and fine auditory discrimination to produce just the right amount of "hiss." And, if you don't get it exactly right, people notice.

Although you can correct minor distortions fairly easily, major distortions, such as a frontal or lateral lisp, take more time and usually require trained guidance. If you have a frontal or lateral lisp, ask your instructor for help.

PROBLEM 1: "WHISTLING" [s] OR [z]

If the sound you make is too sharp or too high in pitch, you're probably holding your tongue tip too high and too close to the teeth. Gradually lower the tongue tip a millimeter at a time and, at the same time, draw it back ever so slightly. Listen carefully as you produce an [s] with each adjustment. You'll probably notice that the pitch of the sound drops. Ask your instructor or another student to tell you when you've reached the right pitch. Keep practicing the sound until you're sure you can remember it.

PROBLEM 2: EXCESSIVE SIBILANCE

This is a high-pitched hissiness that seems to pervade a person's entire speech pattern. It usually results from overemphasizing and prolonging the [s]. Many times it's coupled with a whistling [s] and [z]. Try to make the [s] and [z] as short as you can, without actually omitting them when you practice the word lists. Ask your instructor for more help.

PROBLEM 3: "LATERALIZED" [s] AND [z]

**[s]
[z]**

In this problem, the sounds are too low in pitch or too broad. This happens when you let the air go out to one or both sides of the mouth instead of down the central groove or when you fail to make a groove at all. Ask your instructor for additional help.

PROBLEM 4: "WEAK" [s] AND [z]

Some people produce [s] and [z] with the articulators placed correctly, but without enough force in the breath stream to make a strong sound. One way to correct this is by rounding your lips and blowing air out as if you were blowing out birthday candles. Now place your articulators in the position for the [s] and blow out the candles. You should feel a stronger breath stream. For the [z], follow the same procedure, but add voice.

PROBLEM 5: EXCESSIVE TONGUE PRESSURE

[s] and [z] will lose some of their sibilant qualities if your tongue presses upon the upper front teeth during production. Make certain that your tongue does not touch the upper front teeth, and that you form a central channel for the breath stream.

PROBLEM 6: OMISSION OF [s] AND [z]

Frequently non-native speakers of English, especially those whose first language is Chinese, fail to produce the [s] and [z] in final and medial positions. First, ask a native speaker or your instructor to listen as you pronounce Level 1 [s] and [z] words. If you are failing to produce the [s] and [z], review the production of these sounds. Start with the production drills, then read the Level 1 words, exaggerating the target sounds. Ask a listener to check your production.

[s] Level 1

 Level 1 Practice Words for [s]

Say the words in the following lists slowly and clearly. Listen carefully, and adjust your tongue to produce the clearest, strongest [s].

Don't overdo it. Use moderate air pressure. Start with the *Beginning* words.

Beginning	*End*	*Middle*
see	bets	acid
seam	pets	aside
sit	bats	basic
sift	cats	cassette
sin	pats	decent
sing	rats	decide
safe	puts	essay
sane	rates	icing
saint	oats	kerosene
set	pass	Tennessee
send	piece	medicine
sack	pace	baseball
sag	boss	guessing
sand	mass	passing
Sam	kiss	racing
sign	bus	busing
sight	miss	fantasy
soon	mess	foster
suit	hiss	pester
soup	grass	rooster
soak	juice	east
soar	menace	west
soft	purchase	also
sauna	price	mist
soot	goodness	racer
sound	cactus	pricing
sun	caps	bossy
supper	tips	basin
Sunday	tops	presser
someday	pups	messy

[s]
[z]

 ## *Level 1 Practice Phrases for* [s]

sad sack	soft soap	cats and rats
cactus flower	purchase price	new suit
set aside	sing song	pass the soup
kiss me	safe and sound	out of sight

Level 1 Practice Sentences for [s]

1. <u>It's</u> hard to <u>see</u> <u>cats</u> in the <u>grass.</u>
2. The heavy <u>safe</u> made the floor <u>sag.</u>
3. I will <u>send</u> the package <u>soon.</u>
4. He didn't <u>pass</u> the <u>bus.</u>
5. I'm going to <u>sign</u> the <u>lease</u> on the <u>house.</u>
6. He bought the <u>suit</u> at a low <u>price.</u>
7. The <u>sand</u> made a <u>mess</u> on the <u>seat.</u>
8. <u>It's</u> the tip of the <u>iceberg.</u>
9. <u>That's</u> your <u>basic</u> <u>racing</u> car.
10. <u>Set</u> <u>aside</u> a bottle of battery <u>acid.</u>

[s] Level 2

The words at this level are more difficult to produce accurately because of the sounds that precede and follow the [s]. Start with the *Beginning* words, go next to the *End* column, then to the *Middle* column. Make sure the [s] has enough force to be easily heard.

 Level 2 Practice Words for [s]

Beginning	End	Middle
sell	actress	assemble
sail	address	worrisome
salt	blouse	assign
search	endless	icicle
certain	release	saucy
circle	press	sissy
central	furnace	sister
sorry	nauseous	policy
soil	depress	proceed
solve	lettuce	taste
cycle	breathless	jealousy
solar	thoughtless	essential
spite	police	courtesy
sold	worse	classic
Sarah	hearse	bicycle
ceiling	verse	deceive
sulk	curse	blister
solemn	nurse	recent
soccer	face	thermostat

Level 2 Practice Sentences for [s]

1. Sarah lowered the thermostat on the furnace.
2. The soccer game proceeded in spite of the rain.
3. They sent the blouse to the wrong address.
4. The police found the stolen classic car.
5. The actress had to rehearse the role of the nurse.
6. That's the worst lettuce I ever tasted.
7. They searched in an endless circle.
8. Send me a press release.
9. My sister sold her new bicycle at a loss.
10. Problem solving is an endless cycle.

[s]
[z]

[s] **Level 3**

[s] is most difficult to produce when it occurs in *blends* with other consonants. Some blends that can be troublesome are [sw], [sp], [str], [skr], and [sts].

PROBLEM 1: [sw] AND [ʃ] CONFUSION

Sometimes people may substitute [ʃ] as in *shoe* for [s] as in *sue*. Try it. See what happens when the [ʃ] is substituted for the first sound in the word *swim*. This substitution happens when you drop your tongue tip too soon before the [w].

Production Drill

1. Produce a long [s], stop completely, then say the rest of the word.
2. Read across each line. Gradually shorten the [s] and bring the parts together.

sss . . . weet	ss . . weet	s . weet sweet
sss . . . wing	ss . . wing	s . wing swing
sss . . . way	ss . . way	s . way sway
sss . . . well	ss . . well	s . well swell
sss . . . wine	ss . . wine	s . wine swine

Practice Words for [sw] *(Beginning Position Only)*

sweet	sweat	swan	swab
sweep	swept	swallow	swelter
Sweden	swell	swarm	Swiss
swim	swear	swollen	switch
swill	suede	swoosh	swatch
swift	swam	swoon	swindle
sway	swag	swamp	swinger
swing	swine	swum	swale

PROBLEM 2: [sp] AND [ʃ] CONFUSION

The same thing that happens with [sw] can happen with [sp] if you lower your tongue too soon.

Production Drill

1. Produce a long [s], stop completely, then say the rest of the word.
2. Read each line across. Gradually shorten the [s] and bring the parts together.

sss . . . peak	ss . . peak	s . peak	speak
sss . . . pit	ss . . pit	s . pit	spit
sss . . . pare	ss . . pare	s . pare	spare
sss . . . pool	ss . . pool	s . pool	spool
sss . . . pry	ss . . pry	s . pry	spry
sss . . . print	ss . . print	s . print	sprint

 Practice Words for [sp]

Beginning	End	Middle
speak	lisp	respect
speed	hasp	teaspoon
spit	clasp	desperate
spin	grasp	despair
spill	cusp	perspire
Spain	rasp	respond
spare	wisp	Mr. Spock
spat	crisp	respite
span	gasp	inspire
spackle	wasp	desperation

Beginning	*Middle*
spot	respiration
spawn	aspen
spore	rasping
spoke	hospital
spool	conspiracy
spoon	trespass
spunky	conspicuous
sponge	Hispanic
spry	
spurt	
spring	

[s]
[z]

PROBLEM 3: [str] CLUSTER

With [str], the trouble occurs when you prematurely flatten your tongue to make the [t]. This results in [ʃt], so that the word *street* might sound like *shtreet.* This distortion is very common in New York City and other Eastern urban areas.

Production Drill

1. Produce a long [s], stop completely, then say the rest of the word.
2. Read across each line. Gradually bring the two parts together, shortening the [s] at the same time.

sss . . . treet	ss . . treet	s . treet	street
sss . . . trip	ss . . trip	s . trip	strip
sss . . . tray	ss . . tray	s . tray	stray
sss . . . trap	ss . . trap	s . trap	strap
sss . . . truck	ss . . truck	s . truck	struck
sss . . . tripe	ss . . tripe	s . tripe	stripe

3. Read the following pairs of words very slowly, extending the first sound of each word slightly longer than you usually would. Listen carefully; avoid using [ʃ] in the second word.

steam — stream		sting — string
stay — stray		state — strait
stain — strain		stand — strand
stoke — stroke		stole — stroll
stove — strove		stuck — struck
stop — strop		stew — strew

Practice Words for [str]

For this set of words, we'll group *Beginning* and *Middle* separately. There is no *End* group for this set.

Beginning

straddle	street	stream
streak	strip	string
strict	stray	straight
strain	stranger	stretch
stress	strap	strand
strangle	strontium	strop
structure	struck	struggle
strung	straw	strong
stripe	strike	stride

Middle

instrument	construction	frustrate
instruct	restrict	restrain
downstream	Main Street	constrict
destroy	distress	distract
abstract	airstrip	bloodstream
astronaut	mistreat	obstruct

PROBLEM 4: [skr] CLUSTER

Problems with [skr] are usually the result of anticipating the [k]. You raise the back of the tongue too early and, as a result, the tip lowers. You then substitute [ʃkr] for [skr]. If you do this, the word *scrape* might sound like *shcrape*.

Production Drill

1. Produce a long [s], stop completely, then say the rest of the word.
2. Read each line across. Gradually shorten the [s] and bring the parts together.

sss . . . creen	ss . . creen	s . creen	screen
sss . . . cript	ss . . cript	s . cript	script
sss . . . crape	ss . . crape	s . crape	scrape
sss . . . cratch	ss . . cratch	s . cratch	scratch
sss . . . crew	ss . . crew	s . crew	screw
sss . . . crub	ss . . crub	s . crub	scrub

 Practice Words for [skr]

For this set, too, we've grouped *Beginning* and *Middle* separately. There's no *End* list for this sound.

Beginning

screen	scream	screech
script	scribble	scrimmage
scrape	scratch	scrap
scrabble	scramble	scrub
scruffy	scrunch	screw

Middle

describe	discreet	discretion
discrimination	unscrupulous	unscrew
inscribe	postscript	corkscrew
prescription	transcribe	subscribe

[s]
[z]

PROBLEM 5: [sts] CLUSTER

The most common problem with this blend is omitting the [t]. This omission probably occurs because of the precise tongue movements required and because the sounds involved are weak, high-frequency sounds that are hard to hear.

Production Drill

Think of the [sts] cluster as being *two* sounds, not three. It's composed of [s] followed by a [ts] blend. The [ts] is the same sound as the last sound in the word *cats*.

Make a long [s], stop completely, then make a [ts] sound:

sss . . . ts	sss . . . ts	sss . . . ts	sss . . . ts

Read across

beas . . . ts	beas . . ts	beas . ts	beasts
wris . . . ts	wris . . ts	wris . ts	wrists
gues . . . ts	gues . . ts	gues . ts	guests
cas . . . ts	cas . . ts	cas . ts	casts
rus . . . ts	rus . . ts	rus . ts	rusts
coas . . . ts	coas . . ts	coas . ts	coasts

 ### *Practice Words for* [sts] *(End Position Only)*

beasts	feasts	priests	Baptists
fists	wrists	mists	insists
bastes	pastes	pests	nests
bests	rests	guests	tests
casts	masts	blasts	lasts
rusts	busts	dusts	gusts
firsts	bursts	costs	thrusts
rousts	posts	roasts	coasts
boasts	hosts	boosts	roosts
hoists	foists	joists	jests
jousts	frosts	wastes	tastes

PROBLEM 6: REVERSAL OF [k] AND [s]

This inversion is one of the pet peeves of many a speech teacher. It occurs primarily in the word *ask*. If you invert the two consonant sounds, ask [æsk] becomes ax [æks]. Generally, all it takes to correct this problem is a few practice sessions in which you slowly repeat the correct word over and over again. At first it may seem to be a tongue twister, but with a little practice it becomes much easier.

 ### *Contrast Drill for* [ks] *and* [sk]

Say the following pairs of words slowly and carefully. Make the vowel sound in each word longer than usual, and be certain that you hear a [s] before the [k] in the second word of each pair.

axe — ask	backs — bask
max — mask	decks — desk
ducks — dusk	tacks — task

 ### *Practice Words for* [sk]

Say the following words slowly and distinctly. Emphasize the [sk] a little more than you usually would.

cask	husk	tusk	grotesque
disk	picturesque	risk	asterisk
brisk	musk	brusque	mosque
ask	mask	dusk	bask
frisk	desk	arabesque	task

Level 3 Practice Sentences for [s]

1. The screaming guests had been frightened by the snakes.
2. The spilled bleach left a streak in the blouse.
3. The instructor spoke respectfully to the students.
4. She asked him if he could swim to Sweden.
5. The streets were clogged with construction machinery.
6. She soaked her swollen arm discreetly.
7. "It's the last straw," he said with restraint.
8. The Spanish moss swayed in the swampy mists.
9. The mosquito is a pest that makes you scratch.
10. The *Orient Express* stops twice before leaving France.

Challenge Sentences for [s]

1. Amidst the mists and coldest frosts,
   With barest wrists and stoutest boasts,
   He thrusts his fists against the posts,
   And still insists he sees the ghosts.

2. He straddled the stream, rather than destroy the structure of the abstract sculpture.
3. Describe the scrambled inscriptions for your unscrupulous instructor.
4. "Subscribe to the *Main Street Sun*," whispered the sweet young, though strict, Miss.
5. The master's assistant will register your instrument or instruct you in its use.
6. The assistant scoutmaster insisted on destroying the picturesque structure assembled by the scouts.
7. "Please, sir, I want some more," said Oliver Twist to the sinister overseer.
8. The schools known as "The Seven Sisters" may soon be designated as "The Seven Siblings" since suitable males are now admissible.
9. Citizens patronizing fast-food restaurants risk serious consequences from selecting salami or sausages.
10. Narcissus was beset with doubts since his garments didn't enhance either his appearance or prestige.

[s]
[z]

Challenge Materials for [s]

1. Silly Susie went ice-skating.
    The ice was thin, the weather brisk.
    Wasn't Susie slightly stupid,
    Her silly little * ?

2. Each of us, from the very beginning of our lives, has had unique and individual experiences. Scientists tell us that every sensory experience—that is, everything we have ever felt, tasted, heard, seen and so forth—is recorded in the memory banks of our brain. From the very beginning of our lives, we experience things that no other person has experienced in exactly the same way. Each new sensory message received is interpreted in terms of things that we have experienced in the past. The past events color and shade our interpretation of present events.

    Paul R. Timm, *Functional Business Presentations*

3. Consider how we adapt to stress. Stress can be one of the most damaging influences on the biological makeup of the body, to say nothing of its effect on our ability to communicate interpersonally. Stress is a stimulus just like hitting your head on an apple tree. And any stimulus causes one or more reactions. We may have a headache under extreme stress. We may sweat under extreme stress. All of these are biological reactions our bodies are making to signal us that we are overloading our sensory systems.

    How do we adapt to stress? By adapting biologically, we may decide to overeat. Yet overeating may produce just the opposite effect we desire, especially if a stress-prone digestive system can't handle that

[s]
[z]

much food. We may decide to over-drink, but find the consequences of the local pub worse than the cure. We may also lie awake with a case of insomnia while trying to solve a stressful problem and pay for that wakefulness the next day. As we can see, these negative biological adaptations cause more stress, not less.

John R. Bitner, *Each Other: An Introduction*
to Interpersonal Communication

4.   The best material for ties is silk. You can get away with a polyester that looks like silk, or a polyester and silk combination, which can be excellent, but you are safer if you stick with one hundred percent silk. If you have to skimp on your wardrobe, skimp on your suits or shirts before you try to save money on your ties. There is nothing that will destroy a businessman's image as certainly as a cheap tie.

John T. Molloy, *John T. Molloy's New Dress for Success*

[z] Level 1

 Level 1 Practice Words for [z]

Say the following words slowly and distinctly. Listen carefully, and adjust your tongue for the clearest [z] possible. Start with the *Beginning* words and then go on to the *Middle* words.

Beginning	Middle	End
zenith	easy	bees
zip	amazing	ease
zipper	busy	is
zinc	daisy	his
zinnia	fuzzy	gaze
Zen	amusement	days
zany	teasing	as
zephyr	music	because
zombie	noisy	was
zodiac	choosing	buzz
zone	Tuesday	wise
zoom	design	noise
zucchini	using	choose
zygote	hazy	news
zoo	grazing	nose

Level 1 Practice Phrases for [z]

zigzag	zodiac zone	was his
buzzing bees	noisy music	busy Tuesday
using his nose	is it a zoo	hazy days
was it his	as is	amazing design

Level 1 Practice Sentences for [z]

1. She <u>was</u> <u>gazing</u> at a <u>fuzzy</u> wool sweater.
2. <u>Does</u> the <u>amusement</u> park <u>close</u> early on <u>Tuesdays</u>?
3. The goat <u>was</u> <u>grazing</u> through the <u>zinnias</u>.
4. The <u>zany</u> <u>music</u> <u>was</u> <u>noisy</u>.
5. She <u>was</u> <u>always</u> <u>teasing</u>.
6. <u>Is</u> that the right <u>Zip</u> Code <u>zone</u>?
7. I didn't <u>choose</u> that <u>zodiac</u> <u>design</u>.
8. I heard the <u>buzzing</u> of the <u>bees</u> in the <u>daisies</u>.
9. He <u>was</u> <u>using</u> his <u>nose</u> to find <u>news</u>.
10. San Diego <u>has</u> an <u>amazing</u> <u>zoo</u>.

> [s]
> [z]

[z] **Level 2**

 Level 2 Practice Words for [z]

The words at this level are more difficult to produce accurately because of different combinations of consonants, and because they may have [s] for contrast. Start with the *Beginning* words, go next to the *Middle* column, and when you say the *End* words make sure to voice the [z] long enough.

Beginning	Middle	End
zeal	freezing	sees
zero	blizzard	dries
zebra	crazy	prize
zesty	buzzer	refuse
Xerox	disaster	rise
zillion	blazer	trapeze
zilch	rising	bruise
zircon	example	draws
Zurich	causing	lies
zoology	clumsy	falls
xylophone	result	sells
zealous	Brazil	cars

 Level 2 Practice Sentences for [z]

1. She was refusing to wear the violet blazer.
2. The bruise was due to my clumsy move.
3. There are a zillion cars in Brazil.
4. Sometimes it's a disaster when the stock market falls.
5. The river flows zestfully over the sandbars.
6. A trapeze is an example of the height of craziness.
7. The city of Zurich lies next to a river.

(*continued*)

8. He was awarded a prize for braving the freezing blizzard.
9. I was sure a rising tide would cause the warning buzzer to sound.
10. Susan was studying zebras in zoology.

[z] Level 3

Sometimes people have a tendency to unvoice [z] and turn it into an [s] when [s] is blended with other consonants. Say the following words, making sure to voice the [z]. Also, make sure that the two consonants blend into one sound.

[dz]	[nz]	[vz]
reeds	beans	believes
bids	bins	gives
fades	rains	waves
reds	tens	shelves
dads	cans	halves
rods	barns	gloves
cords	lawns	stoves
codes	loans	loves
woods	groans	wolves
foods	spoons	grooves
floods	buns	shoves
rides	lines	hives

UNVOICING OF [z]

This problem is common in the speech of native speakers as well as those with Spanish and German language backgrounds. It happens when you start voicing halfway through the production of [z], and occurs most frequently at the end of words, often when plurals are formed. Although for most English nouns, the addition of *s* forms a plural, the pronunciation can vary. Here are some general rules that may make it easier for you.

Forming English Plurals

1. If the noun ends with a voiceless consonant, the *s* becomes the voiceless sound [s]. **Examples:** books–[bʊks], pants–[pænts]
2. If the noun ends in a voiced consonant, the *s* becomes the voiced sound [z]. **Examples:** legs–[lɛgz], cans–[kænz]
3. If the noun ends with [s], [z], [ʃ], [ʒ], [tʃ], or [ʤ], then the *s* becomes the syllable [ɪz]. **Examples:**

roses	— [rozɪz]	masses	— [mæsɪz]
prizes	— [praɪzɪz]	causes	— [kɔzɪz]
bushes	— [bʊʃɪz]	flashes	— [flæʃɪz]

garages — [gəraʒɪz]	mirages — [mɪraʒɪz]
witches — [wɪtʃɪz]	catches — [kætʃɪz]
judges — [ʤʌʤɪz]	hedges — [hɛʤɪz]

4. The same rules hold true for verbs, too. Here are some examples:

kicks	— [kɪks]	stops	— [staps]
hugs	— [hʌgz]	runs	— [rʌnz]
hisses	— [hɪsɪz]	passes	— [pæsɪz]
fizzes	— [fɪzɪz]	raises	— [rezɪz]
washes	— [waʃɪz]	rushes	— [rʌʃɪz]
hitches	— [hɪtʃɪz]	watches	— [watʃɪz]
urges	— [ɝʤɪz]	wedges	— [wɛʤɪz]

 ### *Level 3 Practice Sentences for* [s] *and* [z]

1. He really shovels in the junk foods.
2. She paints green lawns and red barns.
3. As the saying goes, the race is to the swift.
4. He goes with the flow and rides with the tides.
5. Wood stoves are my answer to the energy crisis.
6. I can't stand long bus lines in the mornings.
7. Deposit cans are worth five cents apiece.
8. She fought her way through the wolves standing outside.
9. My sister groans when she lends me money for school.
10. Sometimes this is an exercise in patience.

Challenge Sentences for [s] *and* [z]

1. Suzie was busy as a bee while Ezra lazed around noisily.
2. Cereals with raisins cause frenzy when dizzy services confuse their orders for those containing pecans.
3. Franz Schubert composed a series of musical interludes.
4. No one believes that cruising packs of wolves bruise herds of cows.
5. Xerox earns zillions of dollars by setting examples for other rising companies.
6. Serious threats face the successful skier, not on the ascent to the summit but on the descent to the base.
7. Cinderella's stepsisters requested assistance in dressing themselves for the Castle Ball.
8. The mysterious mystic asked seven essential questions with respect to the existence of esthetics.
9. Strictly spirited discussions spring swiftly from students' aspirations to sophistication.
10. Despite strong misgivings, the ensign spelled out his instructions to the stalwart sailors.

[s]
[z]

Challenge Materials for [s] *and* [z]

1. To find out if your home business is operating legally, go to your city hall or county office and visit the department responsible for zoning. Zoning regulations may be handled in the planning department, the building-inspection department, or an office of zoning administration. Once you're in the proper department, look for a map that identifies the zoning classification for your area.

Zoning ordinances divide a community into four basic classifications: residential, commercial, industrial, and agricultural. If you live in an agricultural zone, you should be allowed to operate a home business. But chances are you live in an area classified as "Residential"; this classification is the one in which the most problems occur for home-based businesses. Residential zones are further divided into subcategories: Residential Single-Family Units (R1) and Residential Multi-Family Units (R2 through R6).

Paul and Sarah Edwards, "Is Your Business Illegal?"

2. *Right Zipper, Wrong Man*

This man and woman in Asheville had a fight one night . . . a man and wife. Went to bed mad, which they never should have done. Woke up next morning madder still and started off all over again.

Both of them worked, so they were getting ready to go to work. She put on her favorite dress and for some reason she was so mad at him she couldn't reach the zipper. So she backed up to him and just pointed. She didn't talk to him or say anything.

So he grabbed the zipper and zipped it up. And then he zipped it back down. He thought about how funny that was, so he stood there zipping it up and down until he broke the zipper. Then he had to cut her out of her favorite dress, so you can imagine what that did to her disposition. When she got home from work that afternoon she had *revenge* on her mind. She saw two legs sticking out from under his car, so she knew right then what she was going to do. She went over and got his zipper . . . zip, zip, zip, she ran it up and down a few times. "That'll take care of him," she thought.

She went on in the house and there at the kitchen table sat her husband drinking a cup of coffee!

Bob Terrell, *Laughter in Appalachia*

3. *Are the Data Primary or Secondary?*

Secondary information is information that was gathered from other sources and summarized. Secondary sources are useful when you are trying to get some background information or an overview of a field, but these sources are not entirely reliable. Secondary sources synthesize and interpret. So if you rely on secondary sources, you are depending on someone else to draw conclusions for you. Try to rely instead on primary sources.

John A. Courtright and Elizabeth M. Perse,
Communicating Online: A Guide to the Internet

[ʃ] she [ʒ] beige

Sample: [ʃ] **SHE DREAMED THAT HE LIVED IN A MANSION MADE OF SUGAR NEAR CHICAGO'S RUSSIAN EMBASSY.**

[ʒ] **SHE WAS A VISION IN BEIGE AND AZURE AT THE GARAGE.**

Spellings:

sh as in **she**	**s** as in **measure**
c as in **ocean**	**ge** as in **beige**
s as in **tension**	**z** as in **azure**
ss as in **fissure**	**j** as in **bijou**
ch as in **Chicago**	**g** as in **gendarme**
t as in **nation**	
sch as in **schnapps**	
chs as in **fuchsia**	
sc as in **fascist**	

Description

[ʃ] and [ʒ] are cognate sounds. They are lingua-palatal fricatives. You produce them very much like the [s] and [z], except the tongue is farther back.

Production: [ʃ]

1. Open your mouth slightly so that your teeth are apart and your lips are separated.
2. Round your tongue slightly, and raise the sides of your tongue so that they are against the upper molars.
3. Raise the front of the tongue so that it points to the area just behind the gum ridge.
4. Keep the sides of the tongue up and start the breath stream flowing. Force the air against the front teeth, but make sure to keep the front of the tongue elevated. [ʃ] is voiceless.

Production: [ʒ]

Follow the same steps as for [ʃ]. This time add voice at the same instant that the air starts to move.

Special Consideration: Lateral Emission of [ʃ] and [ʒ]

If you don't press your tongue firmly against the upper side teeth, the air can escape from the sides of your mouth. Hold your hands with the forefingers touching the corners of your mouth, as though you were making a megaphone with your hands. Say the sound [ʃ] very forcefully. Do you feel any air on your fingers? If you do, you're emitting the air laterally. Make the sound again, and make sure the sides of your tongue are up and touching the teeth. Hold two fingers about one inch in front of your mouth. Try to direct the stream of air at your fingers. If you have great difficulty directing the air out the front of the mouth, ask your instructor for help.

COGNATE CONFUSION OF [ʃ] AND [ʒ]

💿 *Contrast Drill for* [ʃ] *and* [ʒ]

First read aloud the column of [ʃ] words. You shouldn't feel voice. Then read the column of [ʒ] words. This time feel and listen for voice. The last step is to read across, contrasting pairs of words.

[ʃ]	[ʒ]	[ʃ]	[ʒ]
glacier	— glazier	assure	— azure
Aleutian	— illusion	pressure	— pleasure
shock	— Jacques	fission	— vision
shallow	— jabot		

[ʃ] Level 1

PROBLEM: CONFUSION OF [tʃ] AND [ʃ]

The following contrast drill should help you with this problem, which is common among those whose first language is Spanish.

💿 *Contrast Drill for* [ʃ] *and* [tʃ]

Read the words in the following lists aloud, slowly and clearly. First read down the list of [ʃ] words, then read the list of [tʃ] words. You should not feel any plosive characteristics when you read the [ʃ] words. The last step is to read the words across, contrasting the pairs.

[ʃ]	[tʃ]	[ʃ]	[tʃ]
sheet	— cheat	share	— chair
sheep	— cheap	marsh	— march
ship	— chip	hash	— hatch
shin	— chin	wash	— watch
shoe	— chew	cash	— catch

Level 1 Practice Words for [ʃ]

Say the words in the following lists slowly and clearly. Listen carefully, and correct your production until you are sure you're producing the right sound. If you're not certain, ask your instructor or another member of the class to help. Start with the *Beginning* words.

Beginning	*End*	*Middle*
she	dish	option
sheep	fish	action
ship	finish	addition
Chicago	diminish	condition
shin	Danish	education
shed	wish	temptation
chef	vanquish	notion
champagne	mesh	mention
shabby	mustache	fashion
shack	hash	cushion
shut	ash	punishment
shun	cash	machine
shock	hush	usher
shop	toothbrush	washing
shine	wash	tension
chauffeur	push	tissue
shook	bush	ocean
sugar	posh	pressure
shoe	smash	fissure
shove	mush	insure

 ## *Level 1 Phrases for* [ʃ]

machine shop	push and shove	wash the dish
shook sugar	fashion shoe	shabby chef
shine a shoe	pressure cushion	fish dish

Level 1 Practice Sentences for [ʃ]

1. She shouted a complaint in addition.
2. The usher was shut out of the show.
3. I mentioned that I had shipped the machine.
4. What's your position on voice and diction in education?
5. He mistakenly shook sugar on his corned beef hash.
6. The chef baked Danish pastries in the coffee shop.
7. The sub was shaken by the pressure at the ocean floor.
8. The sheep were shipped to the stockyard in Chicago.
9. The chauffeur stopped at the barber shop for a shave.
10. A shoeshine was always a temptation for me.

[ʃ] Level 2

Words at this level contain some consonant combinations and blends that may be difficult to produce, such as [ʃl] as in *facial* and [ʃr] as in *shrink*. When you say these combinations, try not to make them separate sounds; instead, blend them together, without letting the [ʃ] become hidden or too broad. There are no level 3 drills for [ʃ].

 Level 2 Practice Words for [ʃ]

Beginning	End	Middle
shield	leash	facial
shale	English	partial
shell	fresh	racial
shelf	plush	special
shallow	smash	commercial
chandelier	varnish	martial
shore	Irish	foolishly
short	Welsh	glacier
sheer	harsh	crushed
shower	mustache	crashed
shovel	trash	brushed
schnapps	clash	insurance
sure	foolish	crochet
charades	relish	direction
schwa	establish	discussion
shrink	Polish	wishes
shrank	flush	inflection
shrug	flash	relaxation
shriek	lush	resurrection
shrewd	rush	nationally
shrill	rash	spatial
shrimp	Spanish	vicious
shrub	sash	Russian
shrine	slash	Martian

 Level 2 Practice Phrases for [ʃ]

spatial relations	Polish nation	short shower
crashed on shore	fresh relish	Spanish sash
shrill shriek	foolish charades	brushed varnish

[ʃ]
[ʒ]

Level 2 Practice Sentences for [ʃ]

1. I relished the thought of looking for shells at the shore.
2. He shrank back from the sheer face of the glacier.
3. The flashlight was crushed when the shelter collapsed.
4. She is a commercial insurance underwriter.
5. It's hard to establish a mustache and not seem foolish.
6. Don't brush against the fresh varnish.
7. Are you sure you gave the schwa the right inflection?
8. The boat shook as waves crashed against the shore.
9. She used her shawl as a shield against the showers.
10. The commercials really are what pushed the shovels.

[ʃ]
[ʒ]

Challenge Materials for [ʃ]

1. "First impressions are lasting impressions." You probably heard that saying before, but have you ever given it serious thought? Have you ever contemplated the ramifications of your first impressions on other people? Your first impression is the initial impact you make on another person. In this regard, it covers the areas of dress, voice, grooming, handshake, eye contact, and body posture. The way you choose to manipulate each of these various factors has a profound effect on how other people will perceive you initially. Positive first impressions make initial and subsequent communications with other people much easier and more comfortable. Negative initial impressions can cut off a relationship before it ever gets started. Some people can overcome poor initial first impressions, but it is not easy. Many people give up rather than trying to reverse another person's negative first impression.

Philip L. Hunsaker and Anthony J. Allesandra,
The Art of Managing People

2. In a pile of hundreds of manuscripts, how can you be sure yours will be noticed—and, even better, get a response? After all, publishers call this stack the "slush pile," a demeaning term. But we say "slush" with a mix of frustration, bemusement, and hope—frustration with the volume of material, bemusement at some of the more misguided submissions, and hope that we will find something interesting today (and if not today, then tomorrow). The slush is the future for a publisher, and so many children's publishers still do read the slush, though not always in an organized or speedy way.

Harold Underdown, "Getting Out of the Slush Pile,"
http://www.underdown.org/slush.htm

[ʒ] **Level 1**

PROBLEM: CONFUSION OF [ʒ] AND [dʒ]

Native speakers sometimes "harden up" [ʒ] and produce the affricate [dʒ], due either to confusion over which sound to use or simply a misarticulation caused by excessive tongue pressure against the gum ridge. When you read the level 1 drills, avoid touching the tongue tip to the gum ridge as you produce [ʒ].

 ### *Level 1 Practice Words for* [ʒ]

Say the following words slowly and clearly. Make sure you are voicing the [ʒ]. Correct your production until you're satisfied with the sound. If you're not certain, ask your instructor or a classmate to help. There are no English words that begin with this sound.

End	*Middle*	*Middle*
beige	lesion	decision
garage	leisure	occasion
barrage	casual	conclusion
sabotage	abrasion	vision
massage	illusion	incision
prestige	collision	Asia
rouge	confusion	precision
corsage	evasion	explosion
camouflage	visual	erosion
mirage	pleasure	version
entourage	measure	corsages
collage	treasure	garages

 ### *Level 1 Practice Phrases for* [ʒ]

measure for measure	camouflage rouge
precision explosion	Asian vision
pleasurable leisure	visual mirage
casual decision	beige garage
prestige occasion	

 ### *Level 1 Practice Sentences for* [ʒ]

1. He took <u>pleasure</u> in pointing out the <u>collage</u>.
2. She could always find a <u>treasure</u> in an old <u>garage</u>.
3. The <u>explosion</u> occurred after the <u>collision</u>.
4. He always draws a <u>conclusion</u> with <u>precision</u> thinking.
5. Your <u>version</u> adds to the <u>occasion</u>.
6. It gave the <u>illusion</u> of a <u>casual</u> <u>decision</u>.

7. The art of <u>visual</u> <u>evasion</u> is called <u>camouflage</u>.
8. The <u>beige</u> <u>garage</u> was destroyed in an act of <u>sabotage</u>.
9. The singer's <u>entourage</u> milled about in <u>confusion</u>.
10. He <u>measured</u> the distance of the <u>incision</u> from the <u>abrasion</u>.

[ʒ] Level 2

 Practice Sentences for [ʒ] *and* [ʃ]

Each of the following sentences contains both [ʒ] and [ʃ]. Listen closely, and don't voice the wrong sound.

1. Always shower after a pleasurable massage.
2. They're casual about relaxation in Chicago.
3. I was assured that the ocean would be azure in color.
4. We measured the beach erosion while on our vacation.
5. Teaching is still a prestige occupation.
6. The dog could be vicious on occasion.
7. The sheep were shaken by the explosions.
8. He shouldn't wear that brushed-denim leisure suit.
9. Shoveling sand can be pleasurable.
10. She can't make a decision about shoes.

 Challenge Sentences for [ʃ] *and* [ʒ]

1. Charlotte shoved the brazier aside with pleasure in an unusual display of vicious satisfaction.
2. Fresh fish are an unusually delicious dish when served with Polish sausage and relish.
3. The occasional decision required by the shipping supervisor was foolishly sabotaging the entire entourage.
4. He shaved and showered before brushing his teeth but neglected to massage some polish into his shoes.
5. The mirage showed the result of the camouflaged garage in the process of explosion.
6. George showed rash judgment in measuring the shocks caused by the financial disruptions.
7. Shirley wished for a dish of fresh jumbo shrimp as she shoved the fish aside.
8. The decision to pursue pleasure usually has its resolution in the disillusion caused by delusion.
9. Precision measurement abolishes confusion in the establishment of national averages.
10. Television commercials showed demonstrations of brushless shaving cream as insurance against unusual mustaches.

[ʃ]
[ʒ]

[h]
hot

Sample: **HELEN HEATED THE WHOLE HOUSE UNTIL IT WAS TOO HOT.**

Spellings: **h** as in **hot**
wh as in **whole**

Description

[h] is a voiceless glottal fricative. It is simply a stream of air from the larynx directed through the open mouth.

Production: [h]

1. There's no special position or movement for [h]. Start with your tongue resting on the bottom of your mouth.
2. Open your mouth, constrict your vocal cords as though you were going to whisper.
3. Force the air out of your mouth. Don't produce voice, and don't let any air out of your nose.

Production Drill

The following words begin with [h]. Say the [h] three times, then say the word. Make sure you hear the [h] at the beginning of the word.

[h . . h . . h . .] home
[h . . h . . h . .] him
[h . . h . . h . .] hum
[h . . h . . h . .] ham

Now try the same drill with the level1 practice words for [h].

[h] Level 1

Very rarely does anyone have a problem producing [h]. It's an easy sound to make, and it's one of the first sounds we learn. The only real problem occurs when people *don't* make the sound, as sometimes happens with English speakers from the Caribbean and those whose first language is French. These speakers may omit the [h] when it is in the beginning position of a word.

Practice Words for [h]

There are only a few words that contain the letter [h] in which it isn't pronounced, for example, *hour, heir, honest, honorary* and *herb,* so you're usually safe pronouncing it. Incidentally, there are no English words that end with the [h] sound. Because you can produce this sound so easily, we've only provided level 1 words and sentences.

Beginning	*Beginning*	*Middle*	*Middle*
heat	heed	unheated	behind
hat	happy	ahead	behave
head	hurt	cowhide	anyhow
humid	hungry	Ohio	rehearse
human	who	perhaps	lighthouse
humor	house	somehow	overhaul
huge	health	unharmed	White House
help	here	exhale	coherent

 ### *Practice Sentences for* [h]

1. It isn't the <u>heat</u> that bothers me, it's the <u>humanity</u>.
2. <u>Somehow</u>, I think that <u>lighthouse</u> is beyond <u>help</u>.
3. They were <u>happy</u>, but <u>hungry</u>, after the <u>rehearsal</u>.
4. <u>Perhaps</u> it's not as <u>humid</u> in the western <u>half</u> of <u>Ohio</u>.
5. Too <u>huge</u> a <u>helping</u> can be <u>hazardous</u> to your <u>health</u>.
6. Harry wrote the play *Humor in the White House.*
7. Who ate the other half of the hamburger?
8. He took a huge inhalation at the end of the hallway.
9. The passengers were unharmed in the highjacking.
10. Incoherent sentences are hard to handle.

Challenge Materials for [h]

1. The bat should be held diagonally (neither too vertically nor too horizontally). It should be held completely still, away from the body and as high as is comfortably possible in readiness to lash out instantly at the pitch. There are both advantages and disadvantages to holding the bat either horizontally or vertically. Babe Ruth held his bat in a vertical position, and for that reason was a low-ball hitter. The average batter couldn't possibly hit a high pitch with his bat pointed toward the heavens. Tris Speaker held his bat very flat at shoulder level and looked at the pitcher from over his elbow. As a result he was a good high-ball hitter.

Dell Bethel, *Inside Baseball*

[h]

2. A hero cannot be a hero unless in an heroic world.

Nathaniel Hawthorne

3. People are trapped in history and history is trapped in them.

James Baldwin

4. Happiness does not lie in happiness, but in the achievement of it.

Feodor Dostoevsky

5. I hate the giving of the hand unless the whole man accompanies it.

Ralph Waldo Emerson

6. There is no history of mankind, there are only many histories of all kinds of aspects of human life. And one of these is the history of political power. This is elevated into the history of the world.

Sir Karl Popper

[h]

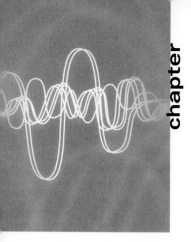

8

the consonants:

nasals [m] [n] [ŋ]

glides [ʍ, w] [r] j

lateral, [l]

affricates [tʃ] [ʤ]

Objectives

After completing the work in this chapter, you should be able to:

- Recognize the consonantal nasals, glides, lateral, and affricates and the production problems associated with each
- Identify your own misarticulations (if any) of the consonantal nasals, glides, lateral, and affricates, and the nature of each misarticulation
- Distinguish regional and foreign variations of the consonantal nasals, glides, lateral, and affricates
- Produce the consonantal nasals, glides, lateral, and affricates correctly, at the instructor's request, in isolation, words, and phrases
- Help others to identify their misarticulations of the consonantal nasals, glides, lateral, and affricates in a nonjudgmental way

This chapter consists mainly of drill materials for correcting and improving production of the consonantal nasals, glides, lateral, and affricates. The exercises are organized in ascending order of difficulty; that is, they become increasingly difficult. As you begin a particular phoneme you start with words, phrases, and sentences that are easy to articulate, then the material becomes increasingly difficult as you progress. Finally, when you are very near to mastering the phoneme, you'll find material that is more challenging and, in many cases, more interesting. So that you can be more successful in accomplishing your goals, it's important that you work on the drills in that order. If you haven't already, we suggest that you read Chapter 5, in which the basics of improving diction are outlined.

[m]
man

Sample:	**THE MAN WAS CALM AFTER HE HIT HIS THUMB WITH THE HAMMER.**
Spelling:	**m** as in **man**
	mm as in **hammer**
	mb as in **thumb**
	lm as in **calm**
	mn as in **column**
	gm as in **diaphragm**

Description

[m] is a voiced bilabial nasal. It is a vowel-like consonant for which you continuously emit the breath stream through your nose.

Production: [m]

1. Close your lips, but keep your teeth very slightly apart.
2. Lower your soft palate, and rest your tongue on the floor of the mouth.
3. Produce voice, allowing the air to come out through your nose.

[m] Level 1

There are very few problems with the production of [m]. This is one of the first and easiest sounds that children learn. When problems do exist, they are usually errors of omission or of assimilating [m] into the next sound.

 ### *Practice Words for* [m]

Say the words in the following lists slowly and clearly. Make sure your lips are closed, and seal off the mouth entirely. Pronounce each [m] distinctly. Don't allow it to become part of the next consonant. Start with the *Beginning* words.

Beginning	*End*	*Middle*
me	thumb	hammer
mitt	team	coming
mate	paradigm	gleaming
metal	fame	demand
mask	time	clamp
moving	name	tomcat
mister	bomb	summer

Beginning	End	Middle
middle	broom	semester
mistake	column	camera
milk	term	woman
minnow	groom	family
mine	psalm	omen
Mike	autumn	remember
mouse	synonym	fireman
month	crumb	somewhere

Practice Phrases for [m]

room full	summer time
I'm going	term paper
some fun	time out
tempt me	time bomb
come true	fame game
remember me	team name

Practice Sentences for [m]

Words with [m] are underlined in the first four sentences.

1. I'm going to school for one summer semester.
2. It was a mistake to wear the metal mask.
3. It's time to make an effort to complete my term paper.
4. He's the only man I know who isn't coming with the team.
5. Don't tempt me with a room full of cameras.
6. The fireman clamped his thumb on the gleaming bomb.
7. You can call me mister, if you can't remember my name.
8. The Romans certainly made mammoth columns.

Challenge Materials for [m]

To be filed under B, for either bizarre, which the following conversation was, or for the Block Drugstore, where the exchange took place.

   Waiting for a prescription to be filled at the drugstore, which is on Third Avenue near 21st Street, Mike Marks became aware of the lovely music on the pharmacist's radio.

MIKE MARKS	That's terrific music? What is it? Wagner?
PHARMACIST	(*busily working on the prescription*) No, Mahler.
MIKE MARKS	Mahler? I don't believe it.
PHARMACIST	What did you ask me?
MIKE MARKS	I asked you who wrote that music.
PHARMACIST	Oh, I thought you asked me what *my* name was.

Ron Alexander, "Metropolitan Diary," *The New York Times*,
October 12, 1988

[m]

[n]
no

Sample: **DUE TO P<u>N</u>EUMONIA HE COULD <u>N</u>OT PICK UP PEN<u>N</u>IES WITH A <u>KN</u>IFE.**

Spellings: **n** as in **no**
nn as in **penny**
kn as in **knife**
gn as in **gnat**
pn as in **pneumonia**
mn as in **mnemonic**

[n]

Description

[n] is a voice lingua-alveolar nasal. It's a vowel-like consonant you produce by blocking the airstream at the gum ridge with your tongue and emitting it nasally, in a continuous release.

Production: [n]

1. Open your mouth slightly. Place the tip of your tongue on the upper gum ridge. At the same time, place the sides of your tongue along the upper inside surface of the molars.
2. Lower the soft palate so that air can leave via your nostrils.
3. Produce voice.

Problems

There are very few problems with [n]. We learn this sound very early in life, so misarticulations are seldom serious. The most common problems are omission of [n] and assimilating it into the sounds surrounding it. [n] is most often assimilated when it is followed by another consonant. It then takes on the characteristics of that consonant. For example, in the phrase *in cold water* [ɪn kold wɔtɚ], the [n] changes to [ŋ] and the word becomes *ink*. Here are some phrases and words in which this happens. Try them slowly, making sure to produce the [n].

income tax	in cold water	concrete
in capitals	in front	unpopular
infrequent	unbiased	in back
in fact	tin whistle	incomplete

[n] **Level 1**

 ### *Practice Words for* [n]

Say the following words slowly and clearly. Listen to your production and feel it as well. Make sure you use only the tip of your tongue for the [n]. Don't omit it and don't assimilate it.

Beginning	*End*	*Middle*
knee	keen	penny
knit	tin	peanut
name	mane	cannot
nap	pan	many
north	mine	honey
nose	began	finish
next	token	cleaner
nation	satin	lightning
nail	alone	flint
needle	spoon	opener
knowledge	mitten	bench
gnarled	brown	tunnel
pneumatic	burn	blend
number	drawn	blond
know	scorn	concert
nearing	mention	incomplete
nil	barn	inquire

[n]

 ### *Practice Sentences for* [n]

Words with [n] are underlined in the first five sentences.

1. She <u>began</u> <u>knitting</u> the cap <u>in</u> <u>November</u>.
2. The <u>flint</u> <u>knife</u> was <u>found</u> <u>in</u> the <u>abandoned</u> <u>tin</u> <u>mine</u>.
3. I <u>inquired</u> about the <u>tenpenny</u> <u>nails</u>.
4. He used <u>satin-finish</u> <u>varnish</u> <u>on</u> the table.
5. The price of <u>peanuts</u> is <u>nearing</u> a <u>penny</u> a <u>pound</u>.
6. The old brown barn burned last night.
7. Nancy didn't have any subway tokens.
8. With all our knowledge, thunder and lightning still frighten many of us.
9. Some students get incomplete grades because they procrastinate.
10. He put his sore hand in cold water for an hour.

Challenge Materials for [n]

The Earth is spinning on its axis like a top, once a day. We define the points where this axis intersects the Earth's surface as the North and South Poles. If you stood at the North Pole (brrrr!) over the course of one day you would spin around once. Now, since we are stuck on the surface of the Earth, we don't really perceive this spin. We do see the sky, however, and our spin makes it look like the sky is revolving around us once a day.

Imagine someone standing on the equator. If he looks straight up, he will see stars fly past him all night long as the Earth spins, sweeping him around the circumference of the Earth. The stars would appear to rise in the East and set in the West. However, if he were at the North Pole, it would look like the stars are spinning around a point straight up in the sky. This point is called the North Celestial Pole (NCP), and is basically the same as the North Pole on the Earth projected up into the sky. All the stars seem to spin around this point, just as the Earth spins around its own North Pole.

Phil Plait's Bad Astronomy,
http://www.badastronomy.com/bad/misc/badpole.html

[ŋ]

[ŋ]
sing

Sample:	**I THINK THAT SINGING IS GOOD EXERCISE FOR YOUR TONGUE.**
Spellings:	**ng** as in **sing**
	n as in **think**
	nc as in **anchor**
	n as in **anxious**
	ngue as in **tongue**

Description

[ŋ] is a voiced lingua-velar nasal. It is a vowel-like consonant you produce by blocking off the breath stream with the tongue and soft palate and letting the air out through the nostrils, in a continuous stream.

Production: [ŋ]

1. Open your mouth fairly wide.

2. Place the back of your tongue against your soft palate, as though you were going to say the first sound of the word *go.*

3. Lower your soft palate, produce voice, and let the air and sound leave through your nose.

Production Drill

Let's borrow a word from baseball—*inning.* This word contains the sound [n] in the middle, and the sound [ŋ] at the end. Say the word slowly, and feel the way the tongue moves. Maintain the same pause in the middle as you read across the page.

in . . . ning   in . . . ning   in . . . ning   in . . . ning   in . . . ning

Repeat this line another five or six times. Make sure you feel the back of your tongue touching the soft palate in the second syllable.

Now say the following, slowly and distinctly, reading across. Again, be sure to make contact between your tongue and soft palate.

sing . . . sing . . . sing . . . sing . . . sing . . . sing . . . sing . . . sing
sing . . . ing   sing . . . ing   sing . . . ing   sing . . . ing
singing . . . singing . . . singing . . . singing . . . singing . . . singing
kink . . . kink . . . kink . . . kink . . . kink . . . kink . . . kink . . . kink
kink . . . ing   kink . . . ing   kink . . . ing   kink . . . ing
kinking . . . kinking . . . kinking . . . kinking . . . kinking . . . kinking

Now try the following words. Say them slowly.

sing	king	ring
sting	wing	bring
long	strong	wrong
hang	gang	rang

If you're satisfied with your production of [ŋ], you can go on to the contrast drill below.

[ŋ] Level 1

Problem 1: Deciding Whether to Use [ŋ] or [n]

This is a sound we learn very easily as children, and it's easy to produce. Almost no one has problems with accurate production. But a good many people have difficulty deciding *when* to use [ŋ], and many inadvertently substitute [n] for [ŋ].

This substitution is commonly called "dropping the *g*." From a phonetic point of view there is no "g" to be dropped, but people are inclined to describe pronunciations such as *goin'*, *thinkin'*, *askin'*, and *workin'* with such a phrase. Actually, these pronunciations result from the substitution of [n] for [ŋ]. It is very common and very ancient in English speech, but it may be viewed as too informal in many situations. Your instructor can tell you about the social standing of [n] for [ŋ] in your area.

Try the following drill.

[ŋ]

Contrast Drill for [n] and [ŋ]

Read across the page, contrasting the pairs of words. Notice the difference between [n] in the first word and [ŋ] in the second. You should be able to feel and hear the difference. Read slowly and distinctly. If you're not sure of your production, ask your instructor or a member of the class to help.

[n]	[ŋ]		[n]	[ŋ]
thin	— thing		lawn	— long
sin	— sing		ton	— tongue
win	— wing		stun	— stung
ban	— bang		run	— rung
fan	— fang		gone	— gong
pan	— pang		sun	— sung

[ŋ]

PROBLEM 2: [ŋ] SPELLING CONFUSION

A great many people, especially nonnative speakers, become confused by English spelling and don't know when to use [ŋ] alone and when to follow it with [g]. For example, *finger* is pronounced [fɪŋgɚ], with [g] following the [ŋ]. But the word *singer* has no [g]. It's pronounced [sɪŋɚ]. Here are some simple rules that should clear up some of the confusion.

1. Use [ŋ] when the word ends in *ng.* **Example:** *sing* [sɪŋ]
2. Use [ŋ] when *ng* or another suffix is added to a root word ending in *ng.* **Example:** *singing* [sɪŋɪŋ]
3. Use [ŋ] + [g] when the *ng* is in the middle of the original word. **Example:** *finger* [fɪŋgɚ]
4. **Exceptions:** Use [ŋ] + [g] in the superlative and comparative forms of certain words such as *long, longer, longest; strong, stronger, strongest; young, younger, youngest.*

Here are more examples:

	[ŋ] + [g]	
longer	stronger	linger
finger	hunger	language

	[ŋ] alone	
singing	ringing	banging
hanging	prolonging	bringing
hangar	belonging	flinging
singer	swinger	ringer

Note: nge is *not* pronounced [ŋ], but [ndʒ] as in *lunge.* For example, *stranger, arrange, hinge, orange, sponge,* and *change* do not contain the sound [ŋ]

PROBLEM 3: INTRUSION OF [k] AND [g]

Even if you do know the rules, you may be adding these sounds and not be aware of it. For example, adding [k] to *thing* turns it into *think*. If this is a problem for you, try this:

 Contrast Drill for [ŋk] *and* [ŋ]

Say the following pairs of words. The first word in each pair ends in [ŋk]; the second ends in [ŋ].

[ŋk]	[ŋ]		[ŋk]	[ŋ]
think	— thing		hank	— hang
sink	— sing		bank	— bang
rink	— ring		rank	— rang
wink	— wing		tank	— tang
stink	— sting		sunk	— sung
clank	— clang		bunk	— bung

[ŋ]

Production Drill

Now say the words below very slowly. Don't remove your tongue from your soft palate until you have completed the [ŋ]. Listen for any telltale "clicking" sound.

sing . . . . sing . . . . sing . . . . sing . . . . sing

sing . . . ing   sing . . . ing   sing . . . ing   sing . . . ing

 Level 1 Practice Words for [ŋ]

At this level, you won't have to worry about the rules of usage. All the words in the level 1 drills have [ŋ] alone, not followed by [g].

Say the words in the following lists slowly and clearly. Make sure you feel contact between the back of your tongue and your soft palate. Monitor your production carefully. If you have doubts, ask your instructor or a member of the class to help. There are no words in English that begin with the [ŋ] sound.

End	*End*	*Middle*	*Middle*
amazing	herring	hangman	bangs
among	icing	wings	ringer
jogging	king	tongs	singer
racing	tongue	youngster	length
nursing	gang	stingers	strength
dancing	strong	things	gangster
staying	asking	gongs	thronged
doing	wrong	hanger	ringed

Level 1 Practice Phrases for [ŋ]

staying among	amazing throng	doing wrong
racing and jogging	strong hanger	amazing wings
gongs and things	asking the singer	buying rings

 ### *Level 1 Practice Sentences for* [ŋ]

1. I'm always <u>asking</u> the <u>wrong</u> questions.
2. Those are <u>amazing</u> <u>racing</u> shoes.
3. <u>Nursing</u> is one of the <u>helping</u> professions.
4. The <u>king</u> was <u>staying</u> in the middle of <u>things</u>.
5. We stopped <u>jogging</u> and started <u>dancing</u>.
6. <u>Running</u> and <u>jumping</u> conflict with <u>eating</u> and <u>relaxing</u>.
7. <u>Insulting</u> words can be <u>damaging</u> to <u>youngsters</u>.
8. The <u>gangster</u> wore a <u>sterling</u> silver <u>ring</u> on his <u>pinkie</u>.
9. "<u>Hangman</u>" is a good game for <u>playing</u> on <u>long</u> trips.
10. <u>Singing</u> in the rain can be <u>dampening</u> to your spirits.

[ŋ]

[ŋ] **Level 2**

 ### *Level 2 Practice Words for* [ŋ]

The words at this level have been divided into two lists: words containing [ŋk] and words with [ŋg]. Read them slowly and carefully. Be sure you have them right before you go on to the sentences.

[ŋk]	[ŋk]	[ŋg]	[ŋg]
bank	junk	England	finger
anchor	donkey	angle	longer
drinker	larynx	penguin	stronger
thinker	thanks	younger	hunger
jinx	planks	tangle	hungry
ink	bankrupt	mingle	angry

 ### *Level 2 Practice Sentences for* [ŋ]

These sentences contain the [ŋk] and [ŋg] blends as well as words from level 1.

1. Thanks for taking my change to the bank.
2. I'm still hungry after I eat junk food.

3. The tongue is located above the larynx.
4. I don't have the strength for jogging.
5. English vowels are longer than Spanish vowels.
6. Two triangles make one rectangle, I think.
7. The song they were singing so strongly was annoying.
8. She's staying later for the dancing.
9. Donkeys have an amazing amount of strength.
10. Thanks to you I didn't get a single one wrong.

Challenge Sentences for [ŋ]

1. The singer fulfilled his secret longing by learning a song while clinging to a cliff.
2. Nothing is as fine as finding a single perfect wedding ring.
3. The winning goal was banked into the netting by the smiling right wing of the English hockey team.
4. "Your Anchor Banker understands" was the advertising slogan of a leading savings bank.
5. The angry child was wringing wet when he hung his wrinkled swimming trunks from the swinging shingle.
6. The long anchor was hanging alongside the dinghy swinging at the mooring.
7. It is wrong to think that hungry donkeys in England don't mingle when grazing.
8. The bankrupt banker sang inspiring songs while musing over money-making pranks.
9. Frank was angry at having to hang around the savings bank for long, rambling meetings.
10. The quaking singer with the quivering voice sang haltingly at the beginning of the "Star-Spangled Banner."

[ŋ]

Challenge Materials for [ŋ]

1. If you stopped to think about how much time you spend communicating, you would probably be surprised. Responding to sounds from alarms, turning on radios, reading morning papers, answering phones, stopping at traffic lights, buying gas from local dealers, getting messages and giving instructions to assistants, writing memos, ordering coffee, and so on—within a few hours you have sent and received thousands of communication messages.

Lyman K. Steil, Larry L. Barker, Kittie W. Watson,
Effective Listening: Key to Your Success

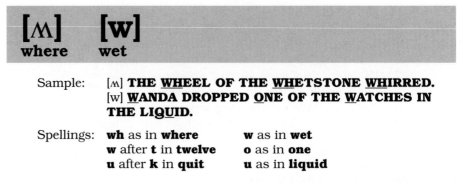

Sample: [ʍ] **THE <u>WHEEL</u> OF THE <u>WHETSTONE</u> <u>WHIRRED</u>.**
[w] **<u>WANDA</u> DROPPED <u>ONE</u> OF THE <u>WATCHES</u> IN THE <u>LIQUID</u>.**

Spellings: **wh** as in **where**   **w** as in **wet**
w after **t** in **twelve**   **o** as in **one**
u after **k** in **quit**   **u** as in **liquid**

Description

[ʍ] and [w] are bilabial glides you make by moving your lips while you're producing the sound. The air is emitted between the lips. They are cognate sounds; the [ʍ] is voiceless, while the [w] is voiced.

Production: [ʍ]

1. Round your lips and purse them. Raise the back of your tongue toward the soft palate, but don't let it touch. Keep your mouth slightly open.
2. Blow air out of your mouth with enough force to make an audible rush of air.
3. As you create the sound, open your mouth slightly. Keep this sound very short and don't add voice.

Production: [w]

Follow the same steps used for [ʍ]. This time add voice as soon as you purse your lips. Continue to voice it as your lips open slightly.

Production Drill

This drill is designed to help you learn to produce the [w] sound. First say the sound [u] (as in cool), then say the word that follows. Read across, and gradually shorten the spacing between [u] and the word.

[u] . . . air	[u] . . air	[u] . air	wear
[u] . . . itch	[u] . . itch	[u] . itch	witch
[u] . . . end	[u] . . end	[u] . end	wend
[u] . . . ache	[u] . . ache	[u] . ache	wake
[u] . . . aid	[u] . . aid	[u] . aid	wade

THE DISAPPEARANCE OF [ʍ]

Chances are you don't know very many people who use the [ʍ] sound consistently. As a matter of fact, the [ʍ] sound seems to be going out of our language fairly rapidly. Listen to your pronunciation of these words: *what, why, when, where, anywhere.* Do you use [ʍ] or [w]? How about other people around you? What do they say? Do they contrast *witch* and *which*?

So the question is, what's the standard way to pronounce those words? Should you use [ʍ] or [w]? Well, community standards where you live may dictate whether you make the distinction between [ʍ] and [w] or not. Your instructor can offer you the guidance you'll need to decide on your own pronunciation.

COGNATE CONFUSION OF [ʍ] AND [w]

⊙ *Contrast Drill for* [ʍ] *and* [w]

Say the words in the following lists aloud, reading across. Contrast the word pairs. The left column should contain the sound [ʍ] and the right column, the sound [w].

[ʍ]	[w]	[ʍ]	[w]
where	— wear	whirred	— word
which	— witch	whetstone	— wet stone
whether	— weather	while	— wile
whale	— wail	whey	— way
whine	— wine	when	— wen

This is the only contrast drill we've included for [ʍ]. Since the decision to use [ʍ] is a matter of choice, and to avoid confusion, we'll try to avoid using that sound in the word drills that follow for [w]. You will find [ʍ] in some of the practice sentences.

[w] **Level 1**

PROBLEM: SUBSTITUTION OF [v] FOR [w]

This problem is most prevalent among nonnative speakers, especially native German speakers, and usually is caused by confusion over how to pronounce the letter *w*. An example of this substitution would be to pronounce the word *west* as if it were *vest*. If you haven't already done so, try the production drill for [w]; when you're sure you can pronounce the [w] correctly, try the contrast drill for [v] and [w].

[ʍ]
[w]

Contrast Drill for [v] *and* [w]

Once you can produce the [w] correctly, you're ready to try contrasting [w] and [v]. Say the following words aloud. First read down the list of [w] words. Use a mirror and check to see that there is no lip-teeth contact. Then read the list of [v] words. Finally, read the pairs across. Try to feel and hear the difference between the [w] andthe [v].

[v]	[w]	[v]	[w]
vine	— wine	vee	— we
vet	— wet	vane	— wane
veil	— wail	vaults	— waltz
vest	— west	visor	— wiser
vend	— wend	viper	— wiper
verse	— worse	vow	— wow
vent	— went	veal	— weal

 ### *Practice Words for* [w]

Say the words in the following lists slowly and clearly. Note that there are no words in English that end with the [w] sound.

Beginning	*Beginning*	*Middle*	*Middle*
we	woman	awake	quack
wake	woods	byway	reward
witty	weird	cobwebs	unwise
wave	waffle	midweek	backward
weak	wash	thruway	dwarf
wife	welcome	highway	dwindle
wide	weld	everyone	seaweed
window	walk	quick	quiz
with	wedding	quiet	required

Practice Sentences for [w]

Words with [w] are underlined in the first five sentences.

1. The <u>thruway</u> <u>was</u> closed for <u>one</u> hour due to high <u>winds</u>.
2. I <u>was</u> late for the <u>quiz</u> because I <u>woke</u> up at <u>twelve</u>.
3. The supply of <u>wood</u> had <u>dwindled</u> by <u>Wednesday</u>.
4. Grapes are really <u>wine</u> on the vine.
5. Young men in the <u>west</u> frequently <u>wear</u> vests.
6. It was the last waltz at the wedding.
7. It takes me until midweek to brush away the cobwebs.
8. I rewarded the dog with a sandwich.
9. The weather has been wetter than usual.
10. We walked through the seaweed in the backwash.

[ʍ]
w]

Challenge Sentences for [ʍ] *and* [w]

1. We awoke while the wives of the highway workers wondered whether the weather would worsen.
2. The quiet woman squeezed water out of the seaweed without a backward glance seaward.
3. "A quick quiz," quoted the professor, quieting the qualms of the quivering students.
4. "Which witch is the one working weirdly in Ipswich on Wednesdays?" queried the quack.
5. It is unwise to reward widows of White House workers who wickedly wield weapons to bushwhack their spouses.
6. The weird tightrope walker was worried about when and where he was to work.
7. Which words are worthwhile when working with wide-awake car washers?
8. We welcomed the dwindling and waning of the wet winter as well as we were able.
9. Where, oh where, dwell women and men as wise as one would wish?
10. Why wasn't the "Wide World of Walking" contest held where we could watch waves from the boardwalk while it was swept?

Challenge Materials for [ʍ]

1. I keep six honest serving men
   (They taught me all I knew);
   Their names are What and Why and When
   And How and Where and Who.

   Rudyard Kipling, "The Elephant's Child"

2. Why are grocery carts made with one wheel that has a mind of its own and runs cockeyed to the other three?

   Why do so many people close their eyes when they brush their teeth?

   Why do people believe that pushing an elevator button several times will make the car come quicker?

   Why can't we just spell it "orderves" and get it over with?

   Why do people drop a letter in the mailbox and then open the lid again to see if it really went down?

   Why are there zebras?

   Why do people put milk cartons back into the fridge with just a tiny bit of milk left in the bottom?

   Why aren't there any traditional Halloween carols?

   Why does every tree seem to have one old stubborn leaf that just won't let go?

   Robert Fulghum, *All I Really Need to Know I Learned in Kindergarten*

[ʍ]
[ð]

3. Waterwheels: How They Work

There are three main kinds of waterwheels. One kind is the horizontal waterwheel, in which water flows from an aqueduct and the forward action of the water turns the wheel. Another kind of waterwheel is the overshot vertical waterwheel, in which water flows from an aqueduct and the gravity of the water turns the wheel. The last kind is the undershot vertical waterwheel; a large vertical waterwheel placed in a stream is turned by the river's motion.

Water Power, Inc., http://hydroelectricity.hypermart.net/waterwheels.html

[r]
red

Sample: **THE <u>R</u>ED FE<u>RR</u>Y WENT IN THE <u>WR</u>ONG DI<u>R</u>ECTION.**

Spellings: **r** as in **red**
             rr as in **ferry**
             rh as in **rhythm**
             wr as in **wrong**

Description

[r] is a voiced lingua-alveolar sound that can be produced in two ways. The first way, usually at the beginning of words, you produce it rather like a fricative by curling the tip of the tongue up and back. In the second way, usually after a vowel or at the end of a word, you produce it as a glide that sounds like a vowel. Both ways produce a glide because the articulators are in motion.

Production Method 1: [r]

1. Open your mouth slightly. Protrude your lips just a bit.
2. Raise the tip of your tongue to a point slightly behind the gum ridge, but don't make contact. At the same time, spread the sides of your tongue so that they touch the upper side teeth. You don't want air to escape from the sides of your mouth.
3. Produce voice.

Production Method 2: [r]

This time keep the tongue tip down and slightly in back of the lower front teeth while you raise the center portion. This position is not used as much as method 1.

[r]

[r] **Level 1**

[r] is one of the most troublesome sounds in our language and for a variety of reasons. Normally, it's one of the last sounds children master, and many times certain nonstandard productions, such as substituting [w] for [r], as in *wed* for *red,* can be continued into adult speech patterns. Many nonnative speakers have difficulty producing [r] due to the fact that it may not exist in their language at all or is very similar to another sound. The use of [r] varies from region to region in American speech, so it's confusing even to native speakers. We'll cover the problems in production first and then go over regional usage.

PROBLEM 1: TRILLED [r]

The sound of a trilled [r] is almost that of a [t] or [d]. It's produced by tapping the tongue very lightly and quickly against the gum ridge. Try this: say the word *car.* If you've trilled the [r], you'll feel the tongue tip touch.

Production Drill

Say the word *are* very slowly, almost separating it into vowel-consonant. Say it a few times. Monitor your production carefully. Try to keep the tip of your tongue from touching anything. Now try the following drill: say the word *are,* stop completely, but don't move your tongue at all. Then add the [r] word that follows. As you read across, make your pause shorter and, finally, drop the *are.*

are . . . red	are . . red	are . red	are red	red
are . . . ripe	are . . ripe	are . ripe	are ripe	ripe
are . . . rode	are . . rode	are . rode	are rode	rode

Here's another way. Say the vowel [ɝ] as in the word *turn.* Hold it for a moderately long time, then add the [r] word that follows. Read across.

er . . . red	er . . red	er . red	er red	red
er . . . rose	er . . rose	er . rose	er rose	rose
er . . . rye	er . . rye	er . rye	er rye	rye
er . . . rain	er . . rain	er . rain	er rain	rain
er . . . raw	er . . raw	er . raw	er raw	raw

PROBLEM 2: OVERLABIALIZATION AND [w] FOR [r]

One of most common problems is an [r] that sounds rather like a [w]. This happens if you purse your lips too much or if your tongue is inactive while the [r] is produced. Try the following:

[r]

🔘 *Contrast Drill for* [w] *and* [r]

Say the following words aloud. Use a mirror and note the position of your lips. Try to minimize lip movement for the [r] words. First read the list of [w] words, then the list of [r] words. Then read across, contrasting the pairs of words. Repeat the words and watch your lips in the mirror.

[w]	[r]	[w]	[r]
weep — reap		wage — rage
weed — reed		wise — rise
wed — red		twice — trice
wing — ring		twain — train
wipe — ripe		twist — tryst
west — rest		twill — trill
wait — rate		tweeze — trees
won — run		tweet — treat
woe — row		away — array

PROBLEM 3: SUBSTITUTION OF [l] FOR [r]

If English is your second language, your [r] may sound like an [l], so that *red* becomes *led.* This is especially true of people whose first language was an Asian one. Native speakers of Asian languages tend to produce the [r] with the tongue tip touching the gum ridge, which is an unacceptable practice in English.

🔘 *Contrast Drill for* [r] *and* [l]

Say the words in the following list aloud. First read the list of [l] words. Notice the contact between your tongue and the gum ridge. Then read the list of [r] words. Try to keep your tongue tip from touching anything as you produce the [r]. Purse your lips slightly. Finally read across, contrasting the pairs of words.

[l]	[r]	[l]	[r]
leaf — reef		blew — brew
leap — reap		blight — bright
lid — rid		bland — brand
lip — rip		bled — bread
late — rate		class — crass
lend — rend		clew — crew
lag — rag		cloud — crowd
law — raw		glass — grass
lot — rot		flesh — fresh
lug — rug		flank — frank

[r]

[l]	[r]		[l]		[r]
light — right			flay	—	fray
play — pray			fly	—	fry

PROBLEM 4: INTRUSIVE [r]

When a word that ends with a vowel is followed by a word that begins with a vowel, some people will bridge the gap between the words with an [r]. We call this type of [r] *intrusive.* This is widespread in New England and New York City.

Practice Phrases

Say the following phrases carefully making sure you don't add an intrusive [r].

law and order
saw a man
vanilla ice cream
drama and speech

Alaska and Alabama
go to Africa on vacation
Havana is the capital of Cuba.
The idea is okay.

PROBLEM 5: SUBSTITUTION OF [v] FOR [r]

[r] is very difficult to articulate accurately. So, some speakers replace it with [v] in initial position and between vowels by using a light lip-teeth contact instead of the more precise adjustments required by the [r] glide. The result is that *berry* may sound like *bevy.* If you have this problem, try the following practice drills.

Contrast Drill for [v] and [r]

Say the following words aloud. Use a mirror to note the position of your lips when you say [v]. Avoid any contact between your lower lip and upper front teeth while you say the [r] words. During the actual moment when you are saying the [r], you should not feel contact between your articulators.

[v]	[r]		[v]	[r]
vain — rain			avail — a rail	
veal — reel			avid — arid	
vice — rice			heaven — heron	
vote — wrote			divide — deride	
vat — rat			moving — mooring	
van — ran			cleaver — clearer	
vest — rest			bevy — berry	

[r]

🔘 *Practice Phrases*

The [v] for [r] substitution occurs also in the [br] and [pr] blends. This is due to giving the [b] and [p] a fricative quality by not pressing the lips together tightly enough. Try the following phrases, making sure to articulate distinctly and precisely.

Brooklyn Bridge	his brother's bride	Great Britain
broken promises	bring back	brain drain
broad protection	bright eyes	Bryn Mawr

Special Problems

It's possible that you still are having difficulty in producing an acceptable [r] sound even after trying all the drills. If so, talk to your instructor about this, or check with a local speech and hearing center to see if you can get (or need) additional help.

How [r] is pronounced varies with the regions of the country. Pronunciations of [r] preceding a consonant in middle position (as in *tired*) and in final position (as in *care*) are seldom heard in the South and in New England, and can be considered to be optional in many other areas. Ask your instructor and listen to the way educated people in your area talk before you decide on the correct pronunciation.

🔘 *Level 1 Practice Words for* [r]

Say the words in the following lists slowly and clearly. Listen carefully and adjust your production until you are satisfied you have produced the desired sound. Start with the *Beginning* words. Even though the final [r] may be optional, say the [r] in the *End* words so that you can get an auditory and tactile feeling for it. Don't overdo it by curling your tongue too far back. The final [r] is just a small amount of [r] shading in the form of the vowel [ɚ] added to another vowel or diphthong. For example, the word *tire* is formed by adding [ɚ] to [aɪ] as in *tie*, resulting in [taɪɚ]. See page 270 for more examples of the use of [ɚ].

Remember that in many areas of the South pronunciation of *Middle* words, such as *Mary, Carolina,* and *very,* may or may not include [r]. Your instructor is the best guide to the acceptable pronunciation in your locality.

Beginning	*End*	*Middle*
reap	peer	marry
reed	dear	carry
rim	mere	Harry

Beginning	End	Middle
rig	near	arrow
ring	wear	narrow
raid	there	merit
rake	care	berry
rate	tear	hurry
rain	bear	Karen
red	affair	carrot
wreck	hair	around
ran	pair	orange
rap	air	terrific
rub	chair	wearing
run	war	caring
write	chore	direct
ride	door	very
rock	cure	tomorrow
rob	tire	furrow
round	tour	tearing
roam	tar	worry
wrote	car	borrow
room	far	turkey
rug	or	pouring

[r]

 ## Level 1 Practice Phrases for [r]

red hair	worry tomorrow	very direct
hurry around	wreck the car	terrified bear
narrow room	orange carrot	near here
marriage rite	pouring rain	write to Harry

Level 1 Practice Sentences for [r]

1. I roamed around the room to find the rake.
2. I put the rock near the rim of the tire.
3. He hurried to borrow the carfare.
4. The pirate told a terrific tale of raiding the port.
5. The wedding ring was neither here nor there.
6. Harry wanted to tour Arizona by car.
7. The rain poured down at a rate of one inch per hour.
8. She rang the bells without very much care.
9. He worried that the tar would ruin the rug.
10. I wrote to Karen asking her to fly here tomorrow.

[r] **Level 2**

The [r] words at this level are more difficult to produce because of the presence of other sounds such as [l]. In addition, the *Middle* words contain [r] preceding a consonant, so you may have doubts as to local pronunciation. We suggest that you pronounce the [r] (even if others in your area don't) simply to get experience. Take your time with these words. Say them slowly and clearly. If you have doubts as to the accuracy of your production, ask your instructor or another member of the class.

 Level 2 Practice Words for [r]

Beginning	*End*	*Middle*	*Combination*
reel	leer	barrel	rather
rile	peer	florist	burger
race	velour	warm	farther
rail	clear	alarm	armory
roll	implore	spiral	roar
royal	lair	Lawrence	rare
rasp	pear	fork	rural
Ralph	father	storm	barrier
rules	mother	burn	carrier
ruffle	sister	birthday	purser
raffle	elsewhere	girl	farmer
rubble	welfare	Cheryl	dormitory
rectangle	sphere	choral	runner
reassure	square	glory	racer
riddle	stare	parallel	writer
rusty	flair	pearl	career
roost	lure	flowered	reader

 Level 2 Practice Sentences for [r]

1. It's rare to find a real pearl.
2. The carrier was on a rural route.
3. Ralph has the list of rules for the raffle.
4. I burned the burgers on the barbecue fork.
5. My mother said I'd be a millionaire.
6. The weather was clear after the storm.
7. The florist climbed the spiral staircase.
8. I implore you not to bother my sister.
9. The purser threw the roll over the rail.
10. The bear chased my father with a roar.

[r] **Level 3**

This level has some difficult blends you might want to practice.

 Level 3 Practice Words for [pr]

If you purse your lips too much, the [pr] blend may sound like [pw]. Use a mirror and try these words:

preach	priest	pretty	preserve
prince	price	prank	prepare
prime	prize	pray	pronounce
appraise	approve	apricot	appropriate
appreciate	improve	April	impress
waterproof	depress	interpret	enterprise
oppress	express	shipwreck	surprise

 Level 3 Practice Words for [br]

This blend can be misarticulated the same way as [pr].

breed	bred	broad	briefcase
bring	brown	bread	Brooklyn
breeze	broom	bride	Libra
brought	abrasive	abrupt	upbringing
abridge	abroad	Hebrew	celebrate

 Level 3 Practice Words for [gr] **and** [kr]

Make sure to produce these as true blends. Don't let a vowel creep in between the two consonants.

[gr]	[gr]	[kr]	[kr]
gracious	diagram	crouch	secret
granddad	congress	crude	concrete
grillwork	telegraph	crumb	cockroach
groggy	kilogram	cry	aircraft
grinder	pedigree	crash	democrat

 Level 3 Practice Words for [fr]

Don't let a consonant separation occur here, either.

friend	fried	French	fraction
freedom	fragile	freeze	deepfry
front	frown	frame	girl friend
affront	African	afraid	bullfrog
defraud	belfry	defrost	waterfront

Level 3 Practice Words for [tr]

If you press your tongue too firmly against the gum ridge when you make the [t] and then slide your tongue back, the sound produced is somewhat like [tʃr]. To avoid this, press the tongue lightly against the palate and make a clean break on the way back to making the [r].

trim	tree	troop	triple
true	trash	train	neutral
tribe	trend	track	mattress
trunk	trigger	try	metric
entreat	oak tree	attractive	patriotic
entrance	trestle	atrium	electricity

 Level 3 Practice Words for [dr]

Produce these the same way as [tr]. Just add voice early enough.

dream	drink	drew	gumdrop
drip	drape	drive	withdrawn
drum	dragon	drain	hundred
address	Andrew	undress	raindrop
children	Mildred	quadrant	foundry

Level 3 Practice Sentences for [r]

1. The prime rate rose three points this year.
2. April gives us freedom from the trials of winter.
3. I put the French vanilla ice cream in the freezer.
4. I'll have a burger, rare, and an order of fries.
5. When you're angry, a frown spreads across your face.
6. He broke the bottle of apricot brandy.
7. She prided herself on her freeze-frame photography.
8. That's where the schooner ran aground.
9. I purchased an unabridged dictionary.
10. It was a plot to defraud the African prince.
11. He was a firm believer in law and order.
12. The bumpy drive aggravated my injuries.
13. The fragile crystal broke in the crate.
14. I brought red roses home for our anniversary.
15. She won the blue ribbon for her brown bread.

[r]

Challenge Sentences for [r]

1. The crooked criminal cried gratingly around the grimy court.
2. Friday afternoon traffic across the Brooklyn Bridge increases abruptly at approximately three-thirty.
3. Fred affronted his friend who was reading an African tome regarding the approved way to cross the Nile River.
4. Borrowing a brush before entering a store in order to purchase one is purely breeding trouble.
5. Prince Andrew prayed with his priest to produce a present for his pretty princess.
6. Transit authority trains travel on thoroughly straight rails.
7. The dreary day was characterized by a drenching drizzle of no paltry proportions.
8. The gray grizzly grunted and grimaced as he grasped the great round beehive in the tree.
9. The brown rock was rubbed with vigor by the gray-bearded old prospector.
10. Fame and fortune follow forth from earning a richly deserved reward.
11. Ferdinand the bull, terror of the ranch, grazed really greedily around the range while ignoring the surrounding herd.
12. Are we ready to reserve our customary places for the regular three o'clock presentation?
13. Orson Welles frightened America seriously with his broadcast of the War of the Worlds.
14. Roberta proposed a rally supporting a broad spectrum of worthy charities.
15. Presenters of oral readings should peruse the ready references wherever they occur.

[r]

Challenge Materials for [r]

1. Talking on the radio does not require a permit—anyone can do that. But the operator of broadcasting equipment must have one, just as the operator of a motor vehicle must have a license. If you control technical functions of a station, by turning on the transmitter or regulating the volume of sound that will be broadcast, the Federal Communications Commission says that you must hold the proper license or permit. Recently the FCC had modified its requirements for broadcast operators. Under the new regulations, all that is required is a *Restricted Radiotelephone Operator Permit,* which can be obtained by any United States citizen simply by filing an application.

John Hasling, *Fundamentals of Radio Broadcasting*

2. Row, row, row your boat
Gently down the stream.
Merrily, merrily, merrily, merrily,
Life is but a dream.

3. Refrigerators. On a very local scale, a refrigerator is the center of the universe. On the inside is food essential to life, and on the outside of the door is a summary of the life events of the household. Grocery lists, report cards, gems of wisdom, cartoons, family schedules, urgent bills, reminders, instructions, complaints, photographs, postcards, lost and found items, and commands. When the word *GARBAGE* appears there, somebody had better move it and soon.

The door of the refrigerator is a chronicle of current events not found on TV or in the daily newspapers.

Robert Fulghum, *Uh-Oh*

[j]
yes

Sample:	**YES. IN MY OPINION THAT VIEW IS FAMILIAR.**

Spellings: **y** as in **yes**   **e** as in **few**
io as in **opinion**   **ia** as in **familiar**
ie as in **view**   **j** as in **hallelujah**
u as in **use**

Description

[j] is a voiced lingua-palatal glide. You produce it by raising the tongue toward the palate and gliding it toward the position of the next sound. [j] is voiced.

Production: [j]

1. Open your mouth slightly.
2. Place the tip of your tongue behind your lower front teeth.
3. Raise the front of your tongue toward the hard palate. Keep the tip in place behind your lower front teeth and pull your lips slightly back.
4. Produce voice and let your tongue and lips glide to the position of the next sound. Don't let any air out your nose.

Problems

Because of its vowel-like qualities, most people don't have much trouble producing [j] accurately. Most of the problems involve regional usage or result from learning English as a second language but are not misarticulations.

PROBLEM 1: SUBSTITUTION OF [ʤ] FOR [j]

If your native language doesn't have this sound, you will probably substitute the sound associated with the letter *j*. In other words, *yet* would become *jet*. The opposite can occur, too. That is, if the letter *j* is pronounced as a *y* in another language, speakers new to English might pronounce *jam* as if it were *yam*. Use the contrast drill below to reinforce the difference between the two sounds.

🔘 *Contrast Drill for* [j] *and* [ʤ]

Say the words in the following lists aloud. Read the list of [ʤ] words first. Feel the way the tongue tip touches the gum ridge. Then read the list of [j] words. As you say the first sound of each word, be sure to keep your tongue tip down behind the front teeth. Finally, read across, contrasting the pairs of words.

[ʤ]	[j]		[ʤ]	[j]
jet	— yet		Jack	— yak
jam	— yam		jeer	— year
juice	— use		jail	— Yale
Jell-O	— yellow		jowl	— yowl
Jess	— yes		jarred	— yard
joke	— yoke		jot	— yacht

PROBLEM 2: OMISSION OF [j]

Even native English speakers become confused as to whether to pronounce [j] when it's represented by a letter other than *y*. The general rule is that you use [j] after consonants such as [k, b, f, v, h, p] with such spelling as:

> *cu* as in *cupid*
> *eau* as in *beauty*
> *ew* as in *few*
> *ue* as in *hue*
> *ie* as in *view*
> *pu* as in *putrid*

Pronounce the [j] when it is followed by [n] as in *union*. It almost doesn't make sense to state rules such as these when they have a great many exceptions. Perhaps the best solution is simply to observe usage.

[j]

[j] **Level 1**

Since there are few production problems with [j], the drills are all at level 1. Note that there are no words ending with [j]. The pronunciation of [j] is optional in those words that are starred, and occurs much more in the South than in the West and Northeast.

 Practice Words for [j]

[j] is optional in starred words.

Beginning	Middle	Beginning	Middle
year	figure	universe	onion
yes	employer	U.S.	senior
use	regular	eurythmics	communicate
you	student*	Utah	beyond
Yankee	million	uranium	usual
yawn	popular	Jung	cue
yard	distributor	yield	Tuesday*
youth	triangular	Uganda	reduce*
unit	royalty	university	institute*
Europe	J. R. Ewing	Johannes	cute
yellow	New York	yogurt	duke*

 Practice Sentences for [j]

1. Yes, you can have the yacht tonight.
2. The Institute sent Jeff to Europe last year.
3. They sold millions of lemon yellow units.
4. Bakers use egg yolks by the yard.
5. I tried to communicate with that cute senior.
6. The problem of uranium disposal has become universal.
7. The Eurythmics used to be a popular group on U.S. campuses.
8. Johannes was a transfer student from the University of Uganda.
9. High-yield onion seeds are grown in Utah.
10. Many New Yorkers think J. R. Ewing comes from a royal oil family.

Challenge Sentences for [j]

1. Yorick loved yellow yams and yogurt during his university years.

[j]

2. Young Frankenstein yearned for used electrodes from Uganda to restore his youthful looks.

3. More than a few army units situated in Europe reduced unusual yields of uranium.

4. Some musicians use popular folk tunes to produce music which goes beyond the usual.

5. Onions grown in the yard usually produce yearnings for yeasty bouillons.

Challenge Material for [j]

1. The term "Yankee," as slang for Americans or Northerners, or specifically, New Englanders, mysteriously cropped up in America around 1700. Speculation on its origin has offered such far-flung guesses as Indian (a Native American mispronunciation of "English"), Spanish (*Yankey* was a buccaneer nickname), Cherokee (*eankke*, meaning slave), and Dutch (*Jan Kees*, which translates as John Cheese—the tasty equivalent of our John Doe). The word's nuances have ranged from flattery (remember Yankee ingenuity?) to slur (who'd ever forget the imperialist *Yanqui* of the '60s?). Yankees have been damned and doodled.

Susan Orlean, *Red Sox and Bluefish*

2. You can be a Yo Yo hero. Teach your beginner friend how to get the Yo Yo to the end of the string and back successfully—on the first try. You be the coach.

Start with the string on your finger, Yo Yo ready to go. Show your friend the following technique (relax and visualize this technique before you try it):

1. Hold the Yo Yo in your cupped hand, palm facing down, and with your string finger curled comfortably in the Yo Yo groove.
2. Elbow at your side, hold the Yo Yo hand forward at waist height.
3. Ease your grip on the Yo Yo; as it falls from your hand move your hand and arm upward in a smooth easy motion.
4. When the Yo Yo reaches the end of the string, move your hand and arm down toward the Yo Yo in a smooth easy motion to . . .
5. Catch the Yo Yo in your cupped hand at waist height, the same position where you released it! And its perfectly OK for any beginner to use the left hand to help catch the Yo Yo to help things along for awhile.

Moving the hand upward (Step 3) while the Yo Yo is on the way down imparts spin energy to the Yo Yo, giving the Yo Yo a better chance to get back to your hand when it starts back up the string. Moving your hand downward (Step 4) makes it easier for the Yo Yo to rewind the string all the way back to your hand.

American YO-YO Association, http://ayya.pd.net/dwrl.html

[j]

[l]
left

Sample: **LAURA LEFT THE YELLOW PILLOW IN THE HALL.**

Spellings: **l** as in **left**
             ll as in **pillow**
             ln as in **kiln**

Description

[l] is a voiced lingua-alveolar lateral. You produce it by dropping the sides of the tongue and allowing air to escape around the sides.

Production: [l]

1. Place the tip of your tongue against your upper gum ridge.
2. Open your mouth wide enough to slip the tip of your finger between your teeth.
3. Keep the sides of the tongue down.
4. Produce voice. Don't let any air through your nose.

Special Problems

PROBLEM 1: SUBSTITUTION OF [w] FOR [l]

You are making this substitution if you pronounce the word *late* so that it sounds like *wait*. Talk to your instructor before you start on the level 1 drills in this chapter.

PROBLEM 2: UVULAR PRODUCTION OF [l]

The uvula is a small fleshy structure that hangs in the rear of the mouth from the center of the soft palate (velum). English speakers don't ordinarily use this structure in speech, but some speakers may make it into an articulation point by excessive "darkening" of the [l] by raising the back of the tongue rather than the tip. Talk to your instructor about this problem.

[l] Level 1

PROBLEM 1: DISTINGUISHING BETWEEN "DARK" [l] AND "CLEAR" [l]

The [l] we described above is called the "clear" [l]. It's the [l] that occurs at the beginning of a word or immediately after a beginning consonant.

Try the word *let*. You should feel as though you're making the sound entirely with the front of your tongue. The tongue tip remains touching the gum ridge throughout the [l] and the back stays down.

The "dark" [l] is called dark because it is produced, to a great extent, by the back of the tongue and is slightly muffled. Say the word *ball*. You should feel your tongue tip still touching the gum ridge, but the back of your tongue lifts slightly. Now say the word *lull* slowly a few times; the difference between the two [l] sounds should become more apparent. Some people, however, may even drop the tongue tip from the gum ridge and produce the [l] entirely with the back portion near the palate. If you produce the [l] this way, you probably won't feel the tip of the tongue.

Many foreign languages do not make use of the dark [l] at all. It does, however, exist in all dialects of English, usually at the end of words and sometimes in the middle. Some people, especially in the West and Midwest, use the dark [l] in beginning position. Try the contrast drill below to see how you produce the [l].

Contrast Drill for Clear [l] *and Dark* [l]

Read the following pairs of words aloud. Make sure your tongue tip is touching the gum ridge each time you produce the sound [l]. Use the "clear" [l] in the first word of each pair and the "dark" [l] in the second.

clear [l]	dark [l]		clear [l]	dark [l]
let	— tell		lap	— pal
lip	— pill		lean	— kneel
lead	— deal		lick	— kill
late	— tail		led	— dell
load	— dole		Luke	— cool
lost	— stall		light	— tile

If you are having difficulty producing the clear [l], we suggest that you speak to your instructor.

PROBLEM 2: SUBSTITUTING [r] FOR [l]

If your first language was one of the Asian languages, you may have difficulty with the [l]. Chances are you produce this sound with your tongue tip *behind* the gum ridge. The result is a sound similar to the [r]. Try the following contrast drill.

[l]

🔘 *Contrast Drill for* [r] *and* [l]

Read the words in the following list aloud. Read them across, in pairs. The first word of each pair will start with [r], the second with [l]. Notice how the tongue is back farther in the mouth for [r] and is more in the front for [l]. Make sure the part of the gum ridge you're touching for [l] is just behind the upper teeth.

[r]	[l]		[r]	[l]
red	— led		brew	— blue
reed	— lead		pray	— play
right	— light		frame	— flame
rode	— load		fry	— fly
rate	— late		grow	— glow
rush	— lush		graze	— glaze
rise	— lies		prod	— plod

Practice these words a few times, concentrating on the differences between [l] and [r]. Ask your instructor or a classmate to listen to you. When you're satisfied, try the level 1 practice words.

PROBLEM 3: OMISSION OF [l]

This happens usually when [l] either precedes or follows another consonant such as in the word *already.* When you're trying the practice words, make sure you pronounce the [l] in each word.

🔘 *Level 1 Practice Words for* [l]

Say the words in the following lists slowly and clearly. Make sure the tip of your tongue touches the gum ridge behind your upper front teeth: not on the teeth, and not behind the gum ridge, but squarely on the gum. Listen carefully and monitor your production until you're sure that you are producing the clear and dark [l] accurately and that you're using the dark [l] only where it's appropriate. Start with the *Beginning* words.

Beginning	*End*	*Middle*
lean	kneel	allow
lid	deal	alike
late	bail	daylight
let	fell	pillow
led	mill	yellow
laugh	bell	eleven
lot	tall	always
lawn	bill	follow
long	call	dollar

[l]

Beginning	End	Middle
like	style	telling
look	pile	along
lunch	motel	believe
loud	pool	balloon
leave	cruel	fill-up
law	hotel	belong
love	feel	only
low	will	valley
lip	fool	fellow

 Level 1 Practice Phrases [l]

late lunch	look alike	laugh a lot
always believing	follow a balloon	daylight yellow
motel pool	tall pile	fell in the pool

 Level 1 Practice Sentences for [l]

1. I <u>let</u> <u>lunch</u> go on too <u>long</u>.
2. <u>Eleven</u> <u>always</u> <u>follows</u> ten.
3. That <u>motel</u> <u>pool</u> has <u>style</u>.
4. I don't <u>believe</u> how <u>loud</u> that <u>laugh</u> was.
5. I was <u>kneeling</u> on the <u>railing</u> over the <u>mill</u>.
6. She was <u>telling</u> me about the "<u>look alike</u>" contest.
7. Take the <u>yellow</u> <u>pillow</u> <u>along</u>.
8. They're <u>always</u> too <u>late</u> to make a <u>deal</u>.
9. <u>While</u> I waited for you, I <u>located</u> a <u>dollar</u> <u>bill</u>.
10. <u>Let's</u> <u>call</u> from <u>Long Island</u>.

[l] Level 2

The words on this level are generally more difficult to produce because the sounds in them may require a wider range of movement by the articulators and because of the [pl], [bl], and [lp] blends. If you say each word carefully and make sure that your tongue tip touches your gum ridge, you should be ready to try these blends.

One additional difficulty results with the production of the syllabic [l]. You produce the syllabic [l] when it is in an unstressed syllable following [t], [d], or [n], as in the words *petal*, *pedal*, and *channel*. To produce the syllabic [l], you leave your tongue touching the gum ridge; you don't remove it after producing the sound before the [l]. The [l] is made by simply dropping the sides of the tongue.

[l]

Production Drill

Read down each column. Don't remove your tongue from the gum ridge before making the [l].

[tl]	[dl]	[nl]
petal	pedal	channel
bottle	paddle	panel
little	muddle	funnel
settle	middle	kennel
rattle	candle	arsenal

Listen carefully and try the words again. If you are producing the syllabic [l] correctly, you won't hear a vowel between the [l] and the sounds that go before.

 ## *Level 2 Practice Words for* [l]

Read the words in the following lists slowly and carefully. Take special time with the words that contain [pl], [bl], [lp], [fl], and syllabic [l]. Don't let a vowel creep in between the two consonants of the blend.

Beginning	*End*	*Middle*
lure	apple	plank
leaves	bobble	blue
lapse	quarrel	filling
leases	schedule	weld
lustrous	quail	railing
lair	pearl	help
link	curl	twelve
liar	dimple	garlic
leer	triple	belt
laws	shrill	ugly

 ## *Level 2 Practice Sentences for* [l]

1. I love the smell of garlic.
2. I heard the shrill call of the owl.
3. A liar is a person with a lot of memory lapses.
4. You don't find cultured pearls in clams.
5. He had a triple black belt.
6. Lorraine tried to weld the broken railing together.
7. I like long gold necklaces.
8. The plank started to curl in the moist climate.
9. The falling leaves were red and yellow.
10. The apple rolled along the trail.

[l]

[l] **Level 3**

The following drills are more difficult than the ones you've done so far. The words combine the blends you practiced in level 2, and we've added others, such as [lz], along with words containing more than one [l]. Remember, if a word starts and ends with [l], the first [l] will be clear and the second will sometimes be dark.

 Level 3 Practice Words for [l]

lonely	fields	cleverly	wrinkle
bells	lulls	lilt	boggle
lately	jails	literally	legal
rolls	lollipop	collegial	eclectic
helpless	scheduled	swelter	exclaim
eagle	likely	glue	lethal
liability	faultless	exclaim	clavicle

 Level 3 Practice Sentences for [l]

1. She's not likely to be lonely.
2. The sweltering heat leaves me feeling helpless.
3. I'm planning for limited liability.
4. I was wallowing in the glow of collegial smiles.
5. The lock was literally welded closed.
6. The colors blended together beautifully.
7. He scheduled the hearing for his helpless client.
8. She liked to be awakened by little bells, not alarms.
9. There will likely be hail or sleet late tonight.
10. Fields of clover and alfalfa dotted the landscape.

Challenge Sentences for [l]

1. Lilly slowly ladled little Letty's lentil soup into the lemon-yellow bowl.
2. Lawrence flew to the Italian Alps to listen to the local yokels yodel.
3. "Will you lift the ladder later?" lisped Lester as he looked longingly at a cold cola.
4. "No man who has once heartily and wholly laughed can be altogether irreclaimably bad." (Thomas Carlyle)
5. Laura laughed as she sang, "Merrily we roll along, roll along, roll along, o'er the bright blue sea."
6. Blair mumbled a lengthy litany as he loaded the barrel of his flintlock rifle.

(continued)

[l]

7. Will Alfred listen along with Lucy and Leslie to Lester's tales of gloom?
8. Little lollipops belong in the clasp of children who long for empty calories.
9. Puzzle lovers get ruffled feathers when raffles baffle their tallies.
10. Lately, people complain bitterly about untangling world problems.

Challenge Materials for [l]

1. Lollipops
Ingredients: 1 cup light corn syrup, 1 cup water, 2 cup sugar, flavoring, coloring, Lollipop sticks.

1. Place corn syrup, water and sugar in small saucepan, stir over low heat until sugar is dissolved.
2. Brush sides of pan with a wet pastry brush to dissolve sugar crystals.
3. Increase heat, cook until syrup reaches 325 degrees F when tested with a sweets thermometer or until syrup reaches hard crack stage.
4. Remove from heat, add a little flavoring and coloring to syrup, stir through.
5. Pour spoonfuls of mixture in desired shapes onto foil-covered trays. Press a lollipop stick into each shape; allow lollipops to cool at room temperature.

Lollipops are best made on the day you wish to serve them.

Gail's Food Swap, http://food4.epicurious.com/HyperNews/
get/archive_swap27101-27200/27148/2.html

2. Literary works become important as they develop themes of universal interest, but to understand a culture's uniqueness study must also be directed to local nonuniversal cultural patterns.

Even in situations where the legitimate objective of a course is the study of fine literature, a knowledge of culture is not an irrelevant digression. One writer whose sympathies were definitely literary in nature came to the conclusion through teaching a course in English as a second language that in the study of literature the whole area of a cultural comprehension is more likely than language to cause difficulty.

H. Ned Seelye, *Teaching Culture*

3. A meeting of meeting planners is really two meetings rolled into one. First, it's a regular meeting. Second, it's an *example* of a regular meeting, a sort of metameeting. At the regular meeting the attendees eat terrible food, listen to boring speeches, and take part in boring seminars. It's just like any other meeting. But at the metameeting the attendees view every meal, speech, and seminar as a failed or successful representation of an abstract ideal of meetingness.

David Owen, *The Man Who Invented Saturday Morning*

[l]

[tʃ] [ʤ]
chair **judge**

Sample: [tʃ] **THE KITCHEN CHAIR HAD A NATURAL WOOD COLOR.**
[ʤ] **THE JUDGE SAT ON THE EDGE OF HIS SEAT AS HE HEARD THE SOLDIER ACCUSE THE GYPSY.**

Spellings: **ch** as in **chair**   **j** as in **judge**
tch as in **kitchen**   **g** as in **gypsy**
tu as in **natural**   **dg** as in **edge**
ti as in **question**   **dj** as in **adjective**
c as in **cello**   **d** as in **soldier**
te as in **righteous**   **gg** as in **exaggerate**
                    di as in **cordial**
                    du as in **gradual**
                    ge as in **George**

Description

[tʃ] and [ʤ] are cognate sounds. [tʃ] is voiceless and [ʤ] is voiced. They are affricate sounds, which you produce by blocking off the breath stream between the tongue and gum ridge, for a plosive *and* a fricative. The [tʃ] is a blend combined of [t] and [ʃ]. The [ʤ] is a blend of [d] and [ʒ].

Production: [tʃ]

1. Open your mouth slightly.
2. Place the tip of your tongue against the gum ridge, and lift the sides to touch the teeth, as though you were going to make the sound [t].
3. Build up air pressure.
4. Release the air pressure very suddenly, but only allow a very small portion of your tongue tip to leave the gum ridge. Although you started with [t], you'll finish with [ʃ].

Production: [ʤ]

Follow the same steps used for [tʃ]. The only difference is voice. Produce voice as soon as you feel your tongue touch the gum ridge.

Special Considerations

If you have difficulty producing any of the sounds that make up [tʃ] and [ʤ], read the sections of this chapter that apply to those sounds. Once you or your instructor are satisfied with your production of the component sounds, you can go ahead and work on [ʤ] and [tʃ].

[tʃ]
[ʤ]

Cognate Confusion of [tʃ] and [dʒ]

If you don't produce enough voice, you make the sound [tʃ] instead of [dʒ]. This turns the word *joke* into *choke*. To avoid this, you must start voicing at the very beginning of the [dʒ] and hold it all the way through the [dʒ]. Try the following contrast drill.

Contrast Drill for [tʃ] *and* [dʒ]

Read the words in the following lists aloud, slowly and carefully. First read down the column of [tʃ] words. Notice how your voicing begins in the middle of the words after the [ʃ] is complete. Then read down the list of [dʒ] words. You should feel voicing right at the start. Then read across the page, contrasting pairs of words, listening and feeling for the differences between the voiceless and voiced sounds. Read the lists a few times until you're sure you can distinguish the two sounds.

[tʃ]	[dʒ]	[tʃ]	[dʒ]
choke	— joke	lunch	— lunge
cheer	— jeer	etch	— edge
chest	— jest	britches	— bridges
cheap	— Jeep	searches	— surges
chew	— Jew	riches	— ridges
chin	— gin	batches	— badges
chip	— gyp	cinches	— singes
chump	— jump	perches	— purges

[tʃ] Level 1

Problem: Substitution of [ʃ] for [tʃ]

Nonnative speakers often make this substitution. Here is a contrast drill that may help.

Contrast Drill for [tʃ] *and* [ʃ]

Say the following words aloud. First read down the list of [ʃ] words. Then read the list of [tʃ] words, making sure you say the [t] portion of the blend. Finally read across, contrasting pairs of words. Feel for the hard contact between the tongue and alveolar ridge for [tʃ]. Notice how there isn't any hard contact for [ʃ].

[ʃ]	[tʃ]	[ʃ]	[tʃ]
sheet	— cheat	wash	— watch
ship	— chip	dish	— ditch
share	— chair	marsh	— march
shanty	— chanty	lashing	— latching

[tʃ]
[dʒ]

[ʃ]	[tʃ]		[ʃ]	[tʃ]
shop	— chop		washed	— watched
shore	— chore		mashing	— matching
shoe	— chew		wishing	— witching
cash	— catch		busher	— butcher

Level 1 Practice Words for [tʃ]

Say the words in the following lists slowly and clearly. Listen carefully and correct your production until you are sure it is accurate. Make sure to produce the full blend, and not just a [ʃ]. Start with the *Beginning* words.

Beginning	*End*	*Middle*
chief	beach	kitchen
chin	each	butcher
chain	peach	hatchet
champion	winch	hitchhike
chat	inch	patching
chime	catch	coaching
chowder	match	bunching
choose	patch	munching
chew	watch	watching
China	coach	teaching
chop	ouch	enchant
chow	hitch	matching
chug	itch	hatching
chunky	much	penchant

Level 1 Practice Phrases for [tʃ]

cheap chalk	chitchat	chief coach
kitchen match	catch much	teach a child
watching China	inch of ketchup	Chowder Beach

Level 1 Practice Sentences for [tʃ]

1. The clam <u>chowder</u> was <u>much</u> too <u>chewy</u>.
2. He <u>chose</u> to <u>question</u> the <u>teacher</u>.
3. He was the <u>champion catcher</u> and <u>pitcher</u>.
4. <u>Peach</u> fuzz will make you <u>itch</u> if you <u>touch</u> it.
5. The <u>coach</u> ate <u>lunch</u> in the <u>kitchen</u>.
6. Plant <u>bunches</u> of <u>beech</u> trees in <u>chalky</u> soil.
7. The <u>matching China</u> plates <u>chipped</u> easily.
8. <u>Hitchhikers</u> are always <u>watching</u> for <u>cheap</u> rides.
9. The <u>butcher</u> used a <u>hatchet</u> to open the <u>ketchup</u>.
10. A <u>winch</u> pulls <u>inch</u> by <u>inch</u> by <u>inch</u>.

[tʃ]
[dʒ]

[tʃ] Level 2

 Level 2 Practice Words for [tʃ]

Say the words in the following lists slowly and distinctly. Make sure you produce the full [tʃ] blend, even where it appears with other sounds that may be difficult to make.

Beginning	*End*	*All Positions*
chair	bleach	achieved
cheer	reach	fracture
chill	rich	church
charm	scorch	ritual
chest	mulch	ratchet
chicken	porch	chinchilla
chili	leach	researching
chocolate	clutch	cha-cha
choice	breech	bachelor
chuckle	crouch	preaches
chance	grouch	choo-choo
chirp	French	watched
cello	wrench	actual
children	ranch	sculpture
Charley	branch	satchel

 Level 2 Practice Phrases for [tʃ]

chocolate chips	French chili	actual choice
choice chinchilla	grouchy bachelor	cheery children
chirping cello	church sculpture	charming ranch

Level 2 Practice Sentences for [tʃ]

1. I gave a bowl of chili to each child.
2. Charley actually led the marching.
3. The mulch pile reached almost to the porch.
4. We bleached the stain out of the birch chair.
5. I drew a sketch of the preacher at the church.
6. Do you want to purchase that Chinese chest?
7. Do French restaurants serve chocolate chip cookies?
8. The branch fractured under the weight of the chicken.
9. I chuckle every time I watch them dance the cha-cha.
10. Bachelor-watching is a ritual at dude ranches.

[ʤ] **Level 1**

PROBLEM: SUBSTITUTION OF [j] FOR [ʤ]

This substitution usually results from confusion between the letter *j* and the sound [j]. This is due to the fact that the letter *j* is pronounced as [j], as in *yes*, in some other languages, and this problem is usually experienced only by nonnative speakers. To correct this problem, you must replace one association pattern with another. Here's a contrast drill that will help.

 Contrast Drill for [j] ***and*** [ʤ]

Read the following words aloud. Read across the page, contrasting the pairs of words. The first word contains the sound [j], and so shouldn't have the tongue tip touching at all. Feel for tongue-gum ridge contact in the second word. Read the lists a few times until you're satisfied that you're pronouncing the words correctly. Then go on to level 1 words.

[j]	[ʤ]	[j]	[ʤ]
yoke	— joke	year	— jeer
use	— juice	yell	— gel
yule	— jewel	yard	— jarred
yellow	— Jell-O	yaw	— jaw
yam	— jam	paying	— paging
yet	— jet	Yale	— jail

 Level 1 Practice Words for [ʤ]

Say the following words slowly and carefully. Listen closely. Make sure to voice the entire consonant blend. Start with *Beginning* words.

Beginning	End	Middle
jeep	age	imagine
gee	bandage	enjoy
gyp	cabbage	budget
gin	damage	agent
Jane	vintage	gadget
gem	teenage	digit
gent	fudge	object
gender	wedge	pigeon
Jack	hedge	magic
John	cage	edgy
job	package	major
junk	wage	manager
jump	badge	budging
jaw	budge	paging
joy	baggage	damaging
join	page	aging
joke	nudge	fidget

[tʃ]
[ʤ]

Level 1 Practice Phrases for [ʤ]

jump for joy	magic pigeon	paging Jack
join the pageant	baggage agent	vintage cabbage
aging major	jab at the jaw	gypped John

 Level 1 Practice Sentences for [ʤ]

1. John ripped the gem from the guard's cage.
2. In the package was a gadget.
3. Jane enjoyed the wedge of fudge.
4. The major lost his badge in the jeep.
5. The managing agent would not pay a high wage.
6. Don't damage the hedge.
7. The magician used an imaginary pigeon.
8. There was a joke written on the edge of every page.
9. Jack's new job is balancing the budget.
10. Jack's old job was jumping on baggage.

[ʤ] Level 2

 Level 2 Practice Words for [ʤ]

These words combine sounds with more difficult articulatory movements. Say the words slowly and distinctly. Make sure to voice the [ʤ]. Start with the *Beginning* words.

Beginning	*End*	*All Positions*
genius	garbage	ginger
jeans	courage	judge
jester	large	dodged
Jill	message	exaggerate
geranium	strange	agile
gelatin	village	bulges
jelly	pledge	fragile
jealous	college	registrar
genial	foliage	suggest
journalism	wreckage	grudge
gentle	gorge	Georgia
jarred	barge	lounging
gerbil	bridge	region

 Level 2 Practice Phrases for [ʤ]

ginger jar	strange village	gentle judge
college registrar	dodged wreckage	large barge
regional foliage	fragile genius	agile gerbil

[tʃ]
[ʤ]

Level 2 Practice Sentences for [ʤ]

1. Attending college is a privilege.
2. The judge was gentle as well as genial.
3. Sausage and ginger don't mix.
4. I was jarred by the wreckage of the garage.
5. George was jealous of my beautiful geraniums.
6. The registrar let me take psychology at another college.
7. The garbage can was wedged rigidly against the wall.

Challenge Sentences for [ʤ] *and* [tʃ]

1. He majored in lunch at college.
2. That was a strange choice to make.
3. I almost choked when I saw the damage to my jeans.
4. I suggested that the children chew more quietly.
5. Charley was known to exaggerate about his courage.
6. He actually worked his way through college selling gadgets.
7. Jeff caught a big striped bass in the channel near the beach.
8. He was teaching seamanship as we watched.
9. Jane lost her gold chains and engagement ring.
10. She wrote about range wars and prairie justice.
11. Justin was just in time for jury duty when the village engaged a new judge.
12. While chasing the ketch along the beach, Charlie fractured his leg jumping over a ditch.
13. The agitated French chef clutched the jar of natural jelly and gestured rashly for a wrench.
14. Imagine the joy of chewing chocolate chip cookies while watching juniors perform jumping jacks.
15. Jane dispatched her journals on high-temperature fashions while on a research venture to Fiji.

[tʃ]
[ʤ]

Challenge Materials for [tʃ] *and* [ʤ]

   1. The desk clerk at London's finest intercontinental hotel discovers the hazards of body language when checking in a line of foreign guests. When an Italian in line asks her a question, she tugs at her itching ear, a gesture with no special meaning in England. The Italian is insulted, and say so. In Italy, tugging the earlobe implies effeminity. The Spaniard thinks she is calling him a sponger. The Maltese reads her action to mean, "You're a sneaky spy." The Greek considers it a threat. Only the Portuguese is pleased; in Portugal the gesture signifies something good.
   Later a Sardinian woman asks the clerk to call a taxi, and the clerk responds with a thumbs up. The woman slaps the unfortunate clerk's face for making such a devastatingly obscene gesture. In the lobby, a

(continued)

Japanese businessman asks an American what the hotel is like. The American replies with the well-known "A-OK" ring gesture. To the Japanese this means "money," and he concludes that the hotel is expensive. The Tunisian onlooker thinks the American is telling the Japanese that he is a worthless rogue and is going to kill him. But the Frenchman, overhearing the questions, thinks the hotel is cheap because the ring gesture in France means "zero."

Donald W. Klopf, *The Fundamentals of Intercultural Communication*

2. Peaches

A mouthful of language to swallow:
stretches of beach, sweet clinches,
breaches in walls, pleached branches;
britches hauled over haunches;
hunched leeches, wrenched teachers.
What English can do: ransack
the warmth that chuckles beneath
fuzzed surfaces, smooth velvet
richness, plashy juices.
I beseech you, peach,
clench me into the sweetness
of your reaches.

Peter Davison,

The Poems of Peter Davison 1957–1995

[tʃ]
[dʒ]

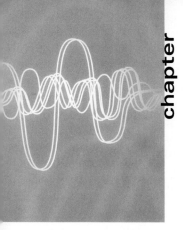

vowels and diphthongs

Front Vowels [i] [ɪ] [e] [ɛ] [æ]

Back Vowels [u] [ʊ] [o] [ɔ] [ɑ]

Mid Vowels [ʌ] [ə] [ɝ] [ɚ]

Diphthongs [ɑɪ] [ɑʊ] [ɔɪ] [eɪ] [oʊ]

[ɚ] Diphthongs [ɪɚ] [ɛɚ] [ɑɚ] [ʊɚ] [ɔɚ]

Objectives

After completing the work in this chapter, you should be able to:

- Recognize the vowels and diphthongs and the production problems associated with each
- Identify your own misarticulations (if any) of the vowels and diphthongs, and the nature of each misarticulation
- Distinguish regional and foreign variations of the vowels and diphthongs
- Produce the vowels and diphthongs correctly, at the instructor's request, in isolation, words, and phrases
- Help others to identify their misarticulations of the vowels and diphthongs in a nonjudgmental way

On the following pages you'll find drills for working on vowels and diphthongs. Because of regional dialects, some of the words we use as examples for particular vowels may be pronounced differently in your area of the country. For example, in upstate New York the word *Florida* generally is pronounced with the vowel [ɑ] as in *top,* while in Orlando it is generally pronounced with the vowel [ɔ] as in *tall.* When you come across such words, either skip the examples that don't match the pronunciation in your region or say them in the way that is standard for your area.

Don't, however, assume that a different pronunciation is always regional; it could be nonstandard for your area. Check with your instructor or someone else who is knowledgeable about pronunciation in your region. We don't advocate any particular regional dialect as being preferable over another. We do, however, advocate "standard for your area" as being preferable to nonstandard.

We have organized the exercises in ascending order of difficulty; that is, they become increasingly difficult. As you begin a particular phoneme you start with words, phrases, and sentences that are easy to articulate; then the material becomes increasingly difficult as you progress. Finally, when you are very near to mastering the phoneme, you'll find material that is more challenging and, in many cases, more interesting. So that you can be more successful in accomplishing your goals, it's important that you work on the drills in that order. If you haven't already, we suggest that you read Chapter 5, in which the basics of improving diction are outlined.

We've arranged the vowels and diphthongs in the following order:

<table>
<tr><td colspan="2">*Front Vowels*</td><td colspan="2">*Back Vowels*</td></tr>
<tr><td>[i] as in *see*</td><td>p. 214</td><td>[ʊ] as in *book*</td><td>p. 239</td></tr>
<tr><td>[ɪ] as in *sit*</td><td>p. 218</td><td>[u] as in *too*</td><td>p. 237</td></tr>
<tr><td>[e] as in *ate*</td><td>p. 223</td><td>[o] as in *rope*</td><td>p. 241</td></tr>
<tr><td>[ɛ] as in *bet*</td><td>p. 227</td><td>[ɔ] as in *awful*</td><td>p. 244</td></tr>
<tr><td>[æ] as in *bat*</td><td>p. 231</td><td>[ɑ] as in *calm*</td><td>p. 252</td></tr>
</table>

<table>
<tr><td colspan="2">*Mid-Vowels*</td><td colspan="2">*Diphthongs*</td></tr>
<tr><td>[ʌ] as in *up*</td><td>p. 263</td><td>[ɑɪ] as in *ice*</td><td>p. 255</td></tr>
<tr><td>[ə] as in *banana*</td><td>p. 266</td><td>[ɑʊ] as in *how*</td><td>p. 260</td></tr>
<tr><td>[ɝ-ɜ] as in *early*</td><td>p. 269</td><td>[ɔɪ] as in *coin*</td><td>p. 249</td></tr>
<tr><td>[ɚ] as in *father*</td><td>p. 272</td><td>[eɪ] as in *raid*</td><td>p. 223</td></tr>
<tr><td></td><td></td><td>[oʊ] as in *robe*</td><td>p. 241</td></tr>
</table>

<table>
<tr><td colspan="2">[ɚ] *Diphthongs*</td></tr>
<tr><td>[ɪɚ] as in *gear*</td><td>p. 219</td></tr>
<tr><td>[ɛɚ] as in *pair*</td><td>p. 228</td></tr>
<tr><td>[ɑɚ] as in *car*</td><td>p. 252</td></tr>
<tr><td>[ʊɚ] as in *poor*</td><td>p. 239</td></tr>
<tr><td>[ɔɚ] as in *pore*</td><td>p. 239</td></tr>
</table>

[i]

[i]
see

Sample: **SHE̲ COULD SE̲E̲ THE RE̲APING MACHI̲NES IN THE FI̲E̲LD.**

Spellings:
e as in **he**	**ee** as in **see**	**ay** as in **quay**
ea as in **eat**	**ie** as in **field**	**oe** as in **Phoenix**
eo as in **people**	**ei** as in **receipt**	**y** as in **easy**
ey as in **key**	**is** as in **debris**	
i as in **marine**	**ae** as in **Caesar**	

Description

[i] is a high, front, tense vowel.

Production: [i]

1. Open your mouth very slightly. Spread your lips just a little and pull the corners back slightly, as though you were going to smile. Your teeth should be almost touching.
2. Touch the back molars with the sides of the back of the tongue.
3. Put the tip of the tongue behind the lower teeth and arch the tongue up and forward. Continue to touch the rear upper teeth. Keep the soft palate tensed so that there's no nasal emission of air.
4. Produce voice.

[i] **Level 1**

 Level 1 Practice Words for [i]

Say the words in the following lists slowly and clearly. Alter your production until you are sure you are saying the sound acceptably. If you're not sure of the standard sound, ask your instructor to identify a word that you do say correctly. Use that word as your comparison word when you're in doubt.

Beginning	*End*	*Middle*
eat	be	mean
evening	he	need
each	knee	Pete
eager	pea	team
Eden	we	teach
even	fee	keep
Egypt	tea	heat
eke	me	week
eating	gee	weep
Eve	vee	deep
equip	handy	feet
ego	gooey	beat

Level 1 Practice Phrases for [i]

each week	tea for me	even heat
Pete and Eve	need to eat	keep the team
deep vee	equip to teach	be mean

 Level 1 Practice Sentences for [i]

1. <u>He</u> paid the <u>fee</u> for the new <u>key</u>.
2. <u>Teach</u> <u>me</u> how to <u>heat</u> the <u>tea</u>.
3. <u>We</u> were <u>eager</u> to bring <u>the</u> <u>equipment</u> for the <u>team</u>.
4. <u>Keep</u> heading toward <u>me</u>.
5. <u>Each</u> <u>week</u> <u>we</u> had a new <u>teacher</u>.
6. <u>Eve</u> <u>eked</u> out a living selling <u>beehives</u>.
7. <u>We</u> were <u>eating</u> marshmallows that were <u>gooey</u>.
8. <u>Pete</u> was a <u>handyman</u> who was quick on his <u>feet</u>.
9. <u>We</u> <u>even</u> had to <u>feed</u> ourselves on the trip to <u>Egypt</u>.
10. <u>He</u> hurt his <u>knee</u> when <u>he</u> fell into the <u>deep</u> hole.

[i] Level 2

PROBLEM: ADDITION OF [ə] AFTER [i]

[i] is not a difficult sound to produce. Probably the most frequently occurring problem is the addition of the schwa ([ə]) after [i] when it is followed by [l], as in *feel.* This is very common, but not standard, in the southern United States. Try the following drill.

Production Drill

If you add [ə] to [i], you should feel your jaw drop slightly as you say it. If there is no extra sound, your jaw will remain steady. Say the words in the following list slowly and carefully, reading across the page. First you'll break a word into two parts. Then you'll join the parts together. As you say the words, place the back of your hand so that it is touching the underside of your jaw to feel if your jaw drops. You can also use a mirror for this.

fee . . . l	fee . . l	fee . l	feel
mee . . . l	mee . . l	mee . l	meal
dee . . . l	dee . . l	dee . l	deal
whee . . . l	whee . . l	whee . l	wheel

ree . . . l	ree . . l	ree . l	reel
hee . . . l	hee . . l	hee . l	heel
stee . . . l	stee . . l	stee . l	steel

The following drills contain [i] in more difficult contexts, including words in which [l] follows [i].

Level 2 Practice Words for [i]

Say the following words slowly. Start with *Beginning* words.

Beginning	*End*	*Middle*
ear	see	steel
eel	she	heel
eagle	agree	receive
easy	glee	speed
east	plea	increase
either	flee	cheese
eerie	three	please
equal	free	deal
evil	ski	believe
easel	tree	sleet

Level 2 Practice Phrases for [i]

agree to flee	cheesy meal	either easel
steel heel	speech speed	easy to believe
receive three	eerie eagle	see no evil

Level 2 Practice Sentences for [i]

1. That's easy for me to equal.
2. We agreed that my dog really has fleas.
3. The guilty plea was part of the deal.
4. See no evil, hear no evil, speak no evil.
5. The three greeting cards were free.
6. She didn't hear you speak last evening.
7. The early eagle catches the eel.
8. Sleet came from the eastern sky like drops of steel.
9. These readings are in a book called *Speaking Clearly*.
10. The cheese spread made a greasy meal.

[i]

Challenge Materials for [i]

Killer Bees Make Honey to Die For

Reed Booth has a love-hate relationship with killer bees.

The Bisbee, Ariz., resident claims to be the only beekeeper in the country who sells honey produced by the Africanized honeybee. He used to make his living with honey from the tamer European honeybee, until the killers moved in about seven years ago.

The European bees would let him walk up to their hives, harvest the honey and walk away. Dressed only in a hood that covered his face, he could gently brush the bees aside as he went about his task.

Now when he approaches the 16 hives he maintains at Reed's Aviary he's covered head-to-toe in protective clothing. "Beekeeping used to be a lot of fun, but not anymore. When I get within 20 feet of the hives it feels like hail hitting my suit. I can smell the venom dripping from their stingers," he said.

A graceful exit is no longer possible.

Booth runs to his van, throws the honey into the back and speeds off. But he doesn't go straight home from his honey farm in the desert. "I drive around with the windows down until all the bees are gone. They'll chase me for a mile," he said.

Jerry Fink, *Las Vegas Sun*, May 15, 2000

[ɪ]
sit

[ɪ]

Sample: **THE R<u>I</u>CH S<u>Y</u>RUP SP<u>I</u>LLED ON THE <u>E</u>NGL<u>I</u>SH BOOK.**

Spellings:

i as in **it**	**y** as in **syrup**	**o** as in **women**
e as in **English**	**u** as in **busy**	**ei** as in **forfeit**
ui as in **build**	**ee** as in **been**	**ie** as in **sieve**

Note: [ɪ] does not normally occur at the ends of words, except when the letter *y* occurs in unstressed position, as in the word pretty. Speakers in the South and New England will frequently use [ɪ] instead of [i] at the ends of such words.

Description

[ɪ] is a high, front, lax vowel. It is very much like [i], being made in almost the same place and the same way. The difference is that [ɪ] is lax, and [i] is tense, so [ɪ] is a shorter, slightly lower pitched sound.

Production: [ɪ]

1. Open your mouth very slightly. Your upper and lower teeth should be close together, but not quite as close as for [i]. Spread your lips slightly, but don't smile for this vowel.
2. Touch the back sides of your tongue to the upper molars. Place the tip behind the lower front teeth. The back of the tongue will be slightly lower than it was for [i].
3. Produce voice.

Diphthong [ɪɚ]

The vowel [ɪ] is frequently combined with [ɚ] to produce the diphthong, [ɪɚ], as in the word *here.* We'll cover this diphthong in the level 2 drills.

[ɪ] Level 1

PROBLEM 1: DISTINGUISHING BETWEEN [i] AND [ɪ]

[ɪ] is actually not a difficult vowel for native English speakers to produce. Some people who have learned English as a second language, however, may have difficulty if the sound [ɪ] does not appear in their native language. The Romance languages—Spanish, French, Italian, and other languages developed from Latin—are examples. If you have difficulty distinguishing between [ɪ] and [i], try the following contrast drill.

Contrast Drill for [i] *and* [ɪ]

Read the words in the following lists aloud slowly and carefully. First read down the columns, then read across. When you read across, contrast the pairs of words, listening for the differences between the [i] in the first word and the [ɪ] in the second.

[i]	[ɪ]		[i]	[ɪ]
eat	— it		jeep	— gyp
seat	— sit		bean	— been
heat	— hit		peak	— pick
meat	— mitt		cheek	— chick
cheap	— chip		bead	— bid
Jean	— gin		deep	— dip
reach	— rich		beat	— bit
peel	— pill		steal	— still

PROBLEM 2: ELONGATION OF [I]

If you hold on to [I] too long, as many speakers do in the South, you may add an extra sound, the schwa ([ə]), to it. For example, the word *pill* becomes [pɪəl] instead of [pɪl]. [I] is a shorter sound than [i]. Read the words presented in the contrast drill above to feel the difference in length. When you read the words in the drills that follow, make sure to cut off the [I] without adding [ə].

 ### *Level 1 Practice Words for* [I]

Read the words in the following lists slowly and carefully. Monitor your production until you're sure it's correct. Ask your instructor to identify a word that you say correctly. Use that word for comparisons. Start with the *Beginning* words.

Beginning	End (y)	Middle
it	any	bit
in	funny	big
if	baby	wind
imply	heavy	dinner
infer	candy	fit
ignite	handy	committee
into	tiny	hit
impact	honey	wit
inborn	money	knit
invent	dandy	king

 ### *Level 1 Practice Phrases for* [I]

funny baby	into money	whipped honey
big committee	heavy dinner	invented candy

Level 1 Practice Sentences for [I]

1. The <u>dinner</u> was <u>fit</u> for a <u>king</u>.
2. <u>Many</u> people confuse the words <u>infer</u> and <u>imply</u>.
3. <u>Did</u> you <u>invent</u> that <u>funny</u>-flavored <u>candy</u>?
4. We felt the <u>impact</u> of the <u>big</u> <u>wind</u>.
5. The <u>committee</u> spent all the <u>money</u>.
6. <u>Many</u> a <u>tiny</u> <u>baby</u> likes a <u>bit</u> of <u>honey</u>.
7. <u>It</u> felt like a <u>bit</u> of rain.
8. One car <u>hit</u> hard <u>into</u> the other.
9. <u>Did</u> you enjoy the <u>funny</u> <u>movie</u>?
10. Rags can <u>ignite</u> <u>if</u> left under the <u>sink</u>.

[ɪ]

[ɪ] **Level 2**

💿 *Level 2 Practice Words for* [ɪ] *and* [ɪɚ]

The vowel [ɪ] is frequently combined with [ɚ] to produce the diphthong [ɪɚ]. It's not a difficult diphthong to produce, but whether or not you produce it with "r-shading," that is, use the [ɚ] or the [ə], can cause heated criticism and arguments between speakers of the same regional dialect. Here's an example: Many people in New York and in much of New England (as well as other parts of the country) pronounce the word *Korea* in such a way that others might confuse it with *career.* Our advice is to determine which pronunciation is standard for your region and then try to be consistent.

Try the following practice words. They all contain [ɪɚ] in different sound contexts. Listen to hear if you pronounce the words with [ɚ] or [ə].

ear	steers	bier	fears
eerie	weird	clear	cheers
fear	shears	career	gears
appear	jeers	hear	smears
we're	tear	near	beard

In the lists below, we've included some words that have the letter *i* in an unstressed position, as it is in the word *Africa.* The alternate standard pronunciation of these words is with a schwa [ə] instead of [ɪ]: [æfrəkə].

Make sure that you are cutting off the [ɪ] and not adding a schwa to it.

Beginning	*End (y)*	*All Positions*
ill	busy	pretty
irritate	foamy	silly
igloo	tally	chilly
isn't	rally	script
Illinois	Sally	wilt
Indiana	slimy	flinch
itch	rainy	English
its	briny	printing
is	shiny	city
ingenious	seedy	written

💿 *Level 2 Phrases for* [ɪ]

chilly igloo	it's written	English script
irritating itch	pretty shiny	busy city

[ɪ]

Level 2 Sentences for [ɪ]

1. Chicago is a big city in Illinois.
2. Read it as it's written in the script.
3. My English teacher irritates me immensely.
4. The Indy 500 rally is run even if it's rainy.
5. I'm itching from sitting in poison ivy.
6. Is he too ill to pitch this spring?
7. Isn't that printer's ink a pretty color?
8. The fire extinguisher made a slimy, foamy mess.
9. The wilted flowers were on the window sill.
10. It wasn't a silly idea, it was ingenious.

Challenge Sentences for [ɪ]

1. Sitting in the rear seat, he cleaned the windows in minutes.
2. Rip Van Winkle reaped the winter wheat in ripped denim jeans.
3. The slim slipper seemed simple when seen in brilliant sunlight.
4. "The difference between the reason of man and the instinct of the beast is this, that the beast does not know, but the man knows that he knows." (John Donne)
5. "If a man sits down to think, he is immediately asked if he has a headache." (Ralph Waldo Emerson)
6. The bee flitted over the little silver weed seed and alit in the willows.
7. James McNeill Whistler lived in the impressionist period, and his painting, now called simply *Mother,* was immediately a big hit.
8. Rumpelstiltskin used to sit and spin bit by bit, until one day she tired of it.
9. Richard saw Miss Fitch sitting and sipping cinnamon tea and eating vanilla ice cream.
10. "A million miles, a million smiles," said the eager, if still impatient, in-flight assistant.

Challenge Materials for [ɪ]

1. How the Singing Fish Works

Lately it seems that every time you turn around, there's a fish singing a song to you! Boogie Bass, Big Mouth Billy Bass, Rocky

[ɪ]

Rainbow Trout and other variations have become enormously popular as novelties and gag gifts. You've probably seen one at a store in the mall, at the flea market or on television. Looking deceptively like a normal stuffed fish mounted on a plaque, it is actually a robot that begins to sing and move when someone walks up to it. As the fish swings his head out from the plaque, he lip-syncs to a prerecorded 30-second clip of a popular song or spits out a savvy one-liner. For the unsuspecting viewer, a singing mounted fish can be quite a humorous surprise, which seems to be the key to its charm.

Jeff Tyson, *How the Singing Fish Works*,
http://www.howstuffworks.com/singing-fish.htm

2. Around every activity there develops a unique language, a special jargon or list of terms, the use of which saves time and trouble and prevents confusion. Import-export is no exception. There is a set of standard *shipping terms* to specify who makes the arrangements for each step in international shipping and who pays the charges. Most important, these terms indicate where the transfer of title takes place. Who has title determines who bears the risk for loss or damage to the cargo at each point in its voyage.

Kenneth D. Weiss, *Building an Import Export Business*

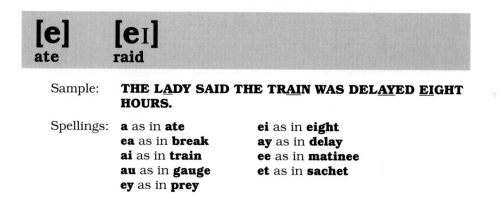

[e] [eɪ]
ate   raid

Sample: **THE LADY SAID THE TRAIN WAS DELAYED EIGHT HOURS.**

Spellings: **a** as in **ate**   **ei** as in **eight**
            ea as in **break**   **ay** as in **delay**
            ai as in **train**   **ee** as in **matinee**
            au as in **gauge**   **et** as in **sachet**
            ey as in **prey**

[e]
[eɪ]

Description

[e] is a mid, front, tense vowel. In stressed syllables, especially those in final position, and when the vowel is followed by a voiced consonant, we tend to use a diphthong, [eɪ], which is longer than [e] and drops in pitch. Using the diphthong instead of the vowel (or vice versa) doesn't change the meaning of a word.

Production: [e]

1. Lower your tongue to a point just a bit lower than the position for [ɪ]. Open your mouth slightly. Only the rear of your tongue should touch the upper back teeth, and the tip should be behind the lower front teeth.
2. Produce voice. As you do, pull the corners of your lips back very slightly.

PROBLEM: CLIPPED [eɪ]

American English speakers in some regions tend to "clip" the diphthong [eɪ] and use the vowel [e] most of the time. Many other languages don't use the diphthong [eɪ] at all, and when speakers of those languages learn American English, they frequently use the vowel [e] exclusively.

Do you use only the vowel [e]? If so, does your speech sound "clipped"? You can find out by trying the following contrast drill.

Contrast Drill for [e] *and* [eɪ]

Read slowly across the columns. The first word in each pair should have a shorter [e] than the second. The second word should use the noticeably longer diphthong [eɪ]. If the vowel sounds seem to be the same length, try dropping your pitch as you extend the vowel.

[e]	[eɪ]	[e]	[eɪ]	[e]	[eɪ]
rate	— raid	face	— faze	lace	— laze
mate	— maid	race	— raze	mace	— maze
state	— stayed	grace	— graze	safe	— save
plate	— played	wait	— wade	fate	— fade
grate	— grade	eight	— aid	trait	— trade

[e] and [eɪ] Level 1

PROBLEM 1: ADDITION OF [ə]

When [e] is followed by [l], we sometimes add the schwa ([ə]) between the [e] and the [l]. If you do this, try the following:

Production Drill

Say the following words, reading across the page. The words will be broken at first, but you'll join the parts together as you go across. Make sure to stop producing voice entirely during the breaks, which will become shorter and shorter.

[e]
[eɪ]

may . . . l	may . . l	may . l	mail
say . . . l	say . . l	say . l	sail
pay . . . l	pay . . l	pay . l	pail
ray . . . l	ray . . l	ray . l	rail
fay . . . l	fay . . l	fay . l	fail
tray . . . l	tray . . l	tray . l	trail

PROBLEM 2: LOWERED [e]

In the metropolitan New York area, speakers tend to lower [e] when it comes before [l]. The result is to replace [e] with [ɛ] so that *fail* [fel] sounds like *fell* [fɛl]. Try the drills in the section on [ɛ] (p. 227) and the following contrast drill.

 ## *Contrast Drill for* [ɛ] *and* [e]

Read the words in the following lists aloud slowly and carefully. First read down the columns, then read across. When you read across, contrast the pairs of words, listening for the difference between the [ɛ] in the first word and the [e] in the second.

[ɛ]	[e]		[ɛ]	[e]
fell	— fail		jell	— jail
shell	— shale		hell	— hail
weld	— wailed		sell	— sale
meld	— mailed		tell	— tale
bell	— bail		dell	— dale

 ## *Practice Words for* [e] *and* [eɪ]

Say the words in the following lists slowly. Listen carefully as you say them, and try to make the vowel [e] the correct length. Avoid adding the schwa or lowering [e] before [l]. Since [e] is a sound of relatively few problems, all the drills are at level 1.

Beginning	End	Middle
able	delay	break
eight	matinee	train
age	away	label
ace	gray	great
ache	repay	place
April	pray	flake
angel	replay	scrape
aim	relay	slate
ape	weigh	relation
acorn	stay	belated
acre	sleigh	chaotic
aid	stray	aggravate

[e]
[eɪ]

Phrases for [e] *and* [eɪ]

great place	break the label	matinee day
able to repay	relay race	weigh acorns

Sentences for [e] *and* [eɪ]

1. It would be <u>great</u> to <u>take</u> the <u>day</u> off.
2. I'll <u>pay</u> you back on <u>Thursday</u>.
3. We'll be <u>able</u> to meet you at the <u>train</u> by <u>eight</u>.
4. Show the instant <u>replay</u> of the <u>relay</u> <u>race</u>.
5. <u>Wednesday</u> and <u>Saturday</u> are <u>matinee</u> <u>days</u>.
6. <u>Scrape</u> the <u>snowflakes</u> off the <u>slate</u>.
7. This backache won't go away today.
8. They won't take it if you break the label.
9. They attacked the ape on the Empire State Building.
10. Did you enjoy your April vacation in Asia?
11. They don't serve ale in jail.
12. It was great to awaken to that view of the bay.
13. The sleigh can't stay on the frozen lake.
14. The acorns caused chaos when they rolled in the way.
15. Aim the bug spray away from your face.

Challenge Materials for [e] *and* [eɪ]

1. Cake Baking Lesson

A moist, beautifully frosted cake is the crown jewel of baking accomplishments. The art of baking perfect cakes is still the highest achievement of baking technique.

Premix cakes are very good, but are also expensive and require much of the same baking knowledge as baking from scratch. You must always carefully follow each step of the formula's directions.

Your baking environment is different from anyone else's. Your oven will bake differently, your mixer will mix differently, the temperature of the pre mix ingredients or your fresh ingredients will be different. Even the humidity of your kitchen will be different. You are unique and because of your being unique, the problems you face will be different from anyone else's.

Cake baking isn't difficult, it just demands close attention to each detail of the project. Cake baking technique is not forgiving, when you make a mistake . . . the project is ruined.

Baking Masters, http://bakingmasters.com/bakery/cake.htm#Baking Lesson

2. Are Raindrops Shaped Like Teardrops?

The artistic representation of a raindrop as presented by popular culture is that of a teardrop. Actually, real raindrops bear scant resemblance

[e]
[eɪ]

to this popular fantasy (except after they have ceased to be raindrops by splattering on a window, say). Virtually everyone from advertisers to illustrators of children's books represent raindrops as being tear-shaped.

Small raindrops (radius < 1 millimeter [mm]) are spherical; larger ones assume a shape more like that of a hamburger bun. When they get larger than a radius of about 4.5 mm they rapidly become distorted into a shape rather like a parachute with a tube of water around the base—and then they break up into smaller drops.

This remarkable evolution results from a tug-of-war between two forces: the surface tension of the water and the pressure of the air pushing up against the bottom of the drop as it falls. When the drop is small, surface tension wins and pulls the drop into a spherical shape. With increasing size, the fall velocity increases and the pressure on the bottom increases, causing the raindrop to flatten and even develop a depression. Finally, when the radius exceeds about 4 mm or so, the depression grows almost explosively to form a bag with an annular ring of water, and then it breaks up into smaller drops.

United States Geological Survey, http://ga.water.usgs.gov/edu/raindrop-
shape.html

[ɛ]

bet

Sample: **I DIDN'T USE MY H<u>EA</u>D WHEN I MADE A B<u>E</u>T WITH MY FR<u>IE</u>ND.**

Spellings: **e** as in **bet**   **ea** as in **head**   **ai** as in **again**
           a as in **any**   **ie** as in **friend**   **ei** as in **heifer**
           eo as in **leopard**   **ae** as in **aesthetic**
           u as in **burial**

Description

[ɛ] is a mid, front, lax vowel. It is shorter than [e] and lower-pitched.

Production: [ɛ]

1. Open your mouth slightly wider than for [e].
2. The very back of the tongue is touching the upper molars, and the tip is behind the lower front teeth.
3. Produce voice.

This is one of the most often used sounds in the English language. There are few real difficulties in producing the sound, but there are some substitutions and one common, but still nonstandard, regional variation to consider.

Diphthong [εɚ]

The vowel [ε] is frequently combined with [ɚ] to produce the diphthong, [εɚ]. It's a simple diphthong to produce, but whether or not you produce it with "r-shading" will be noticed quickly by speakers of your regional dialect. Our advice is to determine which pronunciation is standard for your region and then try to be consistent.

Try the following practice words. They all contain [εɚ] in different sound contexts. Listen to hear if you pronounce the words with [ɚ] or [ə].

bear	scares	cares
scare	wears	dares
aware	snares	fairs
share	fared	stared

PROBLEM 1: SUBSTITUTION OF [e] FOR [ε]

Some speakers, especially nonnatives, substitute [e] for [ε]. As a result, the word *sent* sounds like the word *saint.* This may be due to an inability to hear the differences between the two sounds or to producing [ε] as a tense vowel with the mouth not open enough. Try the following contrast drill.

Contrast Drill for [e] *and* [ε]

Read the following words in contrasting pairs, down each column. Try to feel your mouth open slightly and tongue tension reduce as you move from [e] to [ε].

[e]	[ε]	[e]	[ε]	[e]	[ε]
late	— let	mail	— Mel	freight	— fret
bait	— bet	rake	— wreck	wait	— wet
fade	— fed	rain	— wren	trade	— tread
pain	— pen	braid	— bread	flayed	— fled
paste	— pest	saint	— scent	stayed	— instead

PROBLEM 2: SUBSTITUTION OF [ɪ] FOR [ε]

A common substitution, especially in the southern United States, is [ɪ] as in *pin* for [ε] as in *pen.* In many southern speakers this is not an allophonic variation; it is a true substitution of one phoneme for another that can change the meaning of a word. As a result, listeners from other areas may have to depend on context to determine a speaker's meaning. Although the substitution occurs frequently, it is still not considered standard. Try the following contrast drill to determine if you make this substitution.

Contrast Drill for [ɪ] *and* [ɛ]

Say the words in the following lists slowly, reading across the page. The first word of each pair contains the sound [ɪ] and the second contains the sound [ɛ]. Ask your instructor or a fellow student to listen to you and to correct your pronunciation.

[ɪ]	[ɛ]	[ɪ]	[ɛ]	[ɪ]	[ɛ]
pin	— pen	sit	— set	bit	— bet
tin	— ten	wrist	— rest	lid	— led
him	— hem	lint	— lent	been	— Ben
mint	— meant	hid	— head	rid	— red
since	— cents	sinned	— send	will	— well

[ɛ] Level 1

[ɛ] is a relatively easy sound to produce accurately, so we've provided only level 1 drills. Just make sure you're producing [ɛ] and not another vowel in these drills.

 Practice Words for [ɛ]

Say the words in the following lists slowly. Monitor your production to make sure you are producing the desired sound. Ask your instructor or a class-mate to listen to you if you're not sure of your pronunciation. Start with the *Beginning* words. Note: [ɛ] does not occur in end position in English.

Beginning	*Beginning*	*Middle*	*Middle*
end	any	pen	rent
edge	echo	pledge	center
eggs	elderly	again	ledge
extra	exit	gentle	forget
every	elbow	tent	energy
enter	engine	sent	said
ever	educate	heaven	mess

 Practice Words for [ɛɚ]

End	*End*	*Middle*	*Middle*
air	dare	stared	bares
chair	care	cared	careful
wear	stare	pared	wary
bare	hair	hairs	barefoot
spare	pair	wears	spared
flare	fare	flared	fared

[ɛ]

Practice Phrases for [ε] *and* [εɚ]

heaven sent	extra echo
forget the rent	any exit
every edge	a mess again
gentlemen's pledge	center entrance
bent elbow	spare pair
airfare war	tear one's hair
spare the stairs	a flair for chairs

 Practice Sentences for [ε] *and* [εɚ]

1. Eggs again?
2. I sent the rent on Wednesday.
3. I pledged my help to the Center for the Elderly.
4. The squeak of Fred's pen set my teeth on edge.
5. I need every bit of extra energy I can get.
6. I missed the exit because of the mess.
7. The sunset tinted the tent a pale yellow.
8. The engineers couldn't get rid of the extra echoes.
9. Don't forget to give me the fifty cents.
10. He got his education sitting in front of the TV set.
11. Today's airfare wars are enough to make one tear one's hair.
12. The square room was carefully fitted with flared chair rails.
13. Mary always carried a spare pair of keys for her rare treasure warehouse.
14. Be careful where the bare carpet on the stairs has begun to tear.
15. Mares walking barefoot stare at carefree bears walking bearfoot.

[ε]

Challenge Materials for [ε] *and* [εɚ]

1. There are several good reasons for making your own bread. Anyone who has ever taken a golden loaf fresh from the oven knows that special joy of eating the first warm slice, and breathing its heady fragrance.

Beyond the earthy pleasures of savoring the flavor, aroma and texture of homemade bread, the best reason for doing your own baking is knowing that the produce is thoroughly edible, comprising purely nutritious ingredients with names a child could understand. Children can smell a fresh loaf down the block. If you want company, leave the kitchen door open and a pot of jam on the table.

The American Heart Association Cookbook

2. Hear the sledges with the bells—
     Silver bells!
What a world of merriment their melody foretells!
     How they tinkle, tinkle, tinkle,
     In the icy air of night!
     While the stars that oversprinkle
     All the heavens, seem to twinkle
     With a crystalline delight;
     Keeping time, time, time,
     In a sort of Runic rhyme,

To the tintinnabulation that so musically wells
     From the bells, bells, bells, bells,
     Bells, bells, bells—
From the jingling and the tinkling of the bells.

Edgar Allan Poe

3. "Good morning."
"Today we will take up the broken chair. The thing to do with a bro-ken chair is this. First, carefully carry the chair to the driveway and put it in the back of the car. Next, get in the car and take the broken chair to someone who knows how to fix it. Ask how long it will take. On the day it's supposed to be finished, return with a great deal of money. The chair will not be finished that day. Keep returning until finally the chair is fixed. This is how to repair a broken chair. Broken chairs may also be taken to the dump."

Andy Rooney, *Word for Word*

[æ]
pat

[æ]

Sample: **A FL<u>A</u>T TIRE IS NO L<u>AU</u>GHING M<u>A</u>TTER.**

Spellings: **a** as in **pat**   **au** as in **laugh**
             ai as in **plaid**

Description

[æ] is a low, front, slightly tense vowel. It is a longer sound than [ɛ] and lower pitched.

Production: [æ]

1. Drop your lower jaw noticeably from the position for [ɛ].
2. Place your tongue tip behind the lower front teeth. Flatten the entire tongue slightly, and raise the middle and back slightly.
3. Produce voice. Make sure to keep the soft palate energized to prevent nasal emission of air.

> ***Note:*** There is another vowel that frequently takes the place of [æ] and is used mostly in New England. This is a low, front vowel, [a], as in the words *ask, half, chance,* that is commonly called the "Boston a." It is produced in a position somewhere between [æ] as in *hat* and [ɑ] as in *father.* This is simply a regional pronunciation and there is nothing "nonstandard" about it.

[æ] **Level 1**

PROBLEM 1: DISTINGUISHING BETWEEN [ɛ] AND [æ]

If you raise the back and sides of the tongue just a little too much, you change an [æ] word to an [ɛ] word. For example, *bat* becomes *bet.* There are some regional differences, too. Say the words, *merry, marry, Mary.* If you live in the Northeast, you probably say each word with a different vowel. Elsewhere you may be saying them the same, with the vowel [ɛ]. For words in which there's an [r], then, we would consider the use of [ɛ] to be regional. Substituting [ɛ] for [æ], as in *bet* and *bat,* is common in the Great Lakes region. Try the following contrast drill:

Contrast Drill for [ɛ] *and* [æ]

Say the words in the following list slowly, reading across the page, contrasting the pairs of words. The first word of each pair will contain the vowel [ɛ], the second word will contain [æ]. Listen carefully to hear the difference between the two. Ask your instructor to check your pronunciation.

[ɛ]	[æ]		[ɛ]	[æ]
bet	— bat		fed	— fad
ten	— tan		led	— lad
end	— and		head	— had
Ed	— add		set	— sat
Ken	— can		lend	— land
send	— sand		bed	— bad
said	— sad		pest	— past
left	— laughed		leg	— lag

[æ]

PROBLEM 2: DIPHTHONGIZATION

You may be in the habit of producing [æ] with your jaw too high, near the position for [ε]. This will result in a diphthong, [εæ], instead of the pure vowel [æ]. This most often happens before voiced consonants, especially the nasals. To prevent this, you must move the articulators quickly. The following transfer exercise will help. (The exercise is adapted from Hilda B. Fisher, *Improving Voice and Articulation*, 2d ed., Houghton Mifflin, Boston, 1975.)

 ### *Transfer Exercise*

The beginning word of each line below is one in which [æ] is not as likely to change to a diphthong as in some of the words following on that line. Avoiding diphthongization is likely to be more difficult in later words on the same line. Listen carefully to your production of [æ] in the first word of a line. Then, in producing every other word in the line, try to copy the same pure [æ] vowel you produced in the first word. Circle the words you find most difficult and practice them repeatedly, transferring the vowel sound from a "safe" word in that line to your troublesome word.

1. at add ant act actor actual
2. bat bad bath bash batch balance back bag bang bank
3. fat fad fan fast fact fang fashion
4. sat sad sand sash sack sang sank
5. hat had half hand hash hatch hack hang hank
6. pat pad pan path pass patch pack pang
7. cat cad can cash catch can't
8. mat mad matter mass man mash match mangle
9. lad laugh lass lash latch lap lab lamb lamp lank
10. dad Dan dash dab dam damp dank
11. tat tan tap tab tam tack tag tang tank
12. rat radish rather raft wrap rash ran ram rang
13. gap, gaff gander gallon gash gag gang
14. gnat nab nap nasty gnash knack nag
15. chat chatter chap chastise champion chant
16. plaid plastic plan plant plaque
17. blab bland blast black blank
18. glad glass gland glance
19. grad grab grand grass gramp
20. trap tramp trash track
21. stab stamp stand staff stash stack stank
22. slap slab slash slant slam slack slang
23. snap snack snatch snag
24. flat flap flab flash flask flack flag flank
25. exact example examine examination

[æ]

Level 1 Practice Words for [æ]

Say the words in the following lists slowly. Listen carefully as you say them. If you're not sure of your production, ask your instructor or a classmate to listen to you and identify a word you say correctly to use for comparison. Start with the *Beginning* words. Do not go on to the phrases or sentences until you have had enough practice on single words. There are no English words ending with the [æ] sound.

Beginning	*Beginning*	*Middle*	*Middle*
at	add	bat	pat
actor	annex	fat	canned
after	attic	habit	fact
act	atom	Jack	have
ant	adding	ham	handy
Anthony	apt	had	band
anchor	Andy	banner	happy
and	am	hat	cat

 ### *Level 1 Practice Phrases for* [æ]

after the fact	at bat	handy map
bad habit	added an act	canned ham
happy band	fat cat	have a hat

 ### *Level 1 Practice Sentences for* [æ]

1. <u>Anthony</u> <u>packed</u> his <u>bag</u>.
2. <u>Can</u> I <u>have</u> a <u>hand</u> with this <u>anchor</u>?
3. The <u>fact</u> is, he was <u>acting</u>.
4. <u>Jack</u> bought a <u>canned</u> <u>ham</u>.
5. The <u>handyman</u> cleaned the <u>attic</u>.
6. He <u>had</u> three turns <u>at</u> <u>bat</u>.
7. <u>Happiness</u> <u>can</u> get to be a <u>habit</u>.
8. The <u>banner</u> was <u>at</u> the head of the <u>band</u>.
9. The <u>fat</u> <u>cat</u> ate a whole <u>can</u> of sardines.
10. <u>Andy</u> <u>and</u> <u>Pat</u> <u>can't</u> ride in the <u>back</u>.

[æ]

[æ] Level 2

 ### *Level 2 Practice Words for* [æ]

Say the words in the following lists slowly and carefully. Make sure you don't nasalize the vowel when there's a nasal consonant in the word. Also, many of the words at this level are easily diphthongized. Listen carefully. If you're not sure of your production, ask your instructor or a classmate to listen to you.

Beginning	Middle	Middle	Middle
angle	fast	class	plant
amplify	bland	grant	grand
ankle	sandwich	brand	placid
angry	fans	grass	pants
asking	lands	strand	pangs
Alice	sank	flapping	standing
ample	jam	slant	bath
antler	clash	slang	plank
as	bashful	clang	shrank
ask	ranch	than	mask

 ## Level 2 Phrases for [æ]

bland sandwich	plank shrank	ample antlers
ask the class	fast flapping	angry answer

 ## Level 2 Sentences for [æ]

1. I can't stand an unwaxed car.
2. I'll have a stab at it after exams.
3. The fans were standing while the band played the National Anthem.
4. He gets angry when we ask too many questions in class.
5. They were stranded on the grass strip after the crash.
6. The ham sandwiches in the snack bar are pretty bland.
7. Sandy is never ready with a pat answer.
8. Alice felt hassled on the last trip to Lake Placid.
9. No matter how fast I flap my wings, I can't fly.
10. There's an ample planting season in southern California.

[æ]

 ## Challenge Sentences for [æ]

1. Hand me the black hat on the back of that hat stand, Stanley.
2. The standard stereo amplifier has collapsing handles to grasp when being carried.
3. Matthew clasped his hands where the asp's fangs had clamped on his badly damaged ankle.
4. Spanish apples have lasting flavor and have tangy sap as well.
5. The blast of a saxophone can be hazardous unless random cancellation can be applied to damp its racket.

Challenge Materials for [æ]

1. A canner exceedingly canny
One morning asked of his granny
A canner can can anything that he can,
But a canner can't cancan, can he?

2. Clamps Every Woodworker Needs

The first rule of woodworking is that you can never have too many clamps. A corollary of this rule states that you'll find your stock of clamps to be lacking whenever you're holding a newly glued project in place with your left hand while rooting through your toolbox with your right. For general woodworking projects, keep these clamps close at hand:

C-clamps: Anyone who took wood shop in the seventh grade knows about C-clamps. They're simple, relatively cheap, and come in handy for every sort of job. Whether you want to hold a tabletop to a frame for gluing or set up a quick-and-dirty stop on your radial arm saw, C-clamps can do the job.

F-clamps: F-clamps pick up where C-clamps leave off. F-clamps are similar to bar clamps, with one fixed jaw and a second jaw that slides. There's a screw for fine pressure adjustments, too. F-clamps in 8-, 12-, and 18-inch sizes are useful to have around the shop.

One-handed quick clamps: A real boon to woodworkers, quick clamps allow you to position their jaws on a workpiece and apply pressure, all using only one hand. You hold a pistol grip and squeeze a trigger (resembling that of a caulking gun) to bring the jaws together. There's a switch to release the pressure when it's time to remove the clamp. Quick clamps do much the same work as F-clamps, but cost more because of the one-handed feature.

David Wall, *Woodworking Clamps,* http://www.amazon.com

[æ]

3. Dance is one of the most fundamental of human activities. It is an idea both reasonable and acceptable that, when primitive man had satisfied his basic needs for food and shelter, he should express his emotions through movement, through rudimentary dance, through the most natural and immediate channel of expression— his body. Dance, even in this lowly form, became the earliest of the arts, the germ from which other arts evolved. To guide his movement man must have marked out rhythms, and with the first chants and music he then embroidered that rhythmic base. With costume and mask, he then decorated the dance, and the first seeds of the arts had been sown. Were it not for the fact that a few animals may be said to 'dance,' in that they perform repeated

rhythmic actions for display or to mark out territory, or, as in the case of bees, to indicate sources of food, man might well be identified as 'an animal who dances.' For in the creations of shapes and patterns of movement, both spatial and temporal, man can be seen to define himself, as well as his dancing.

Mary Clarke and Clement Crisp, The History of Dance

[u]
too

Sample: **HE WAS TOO LATE TO GO ON THE CRUISE AS A CREW MEMBER.**

Spellings: **o** as in **to**   **oe** as in **shoe**   **u** as in **tuba**
             ew as in **crew**   **oo** as in **too**   **ue** as in **true**
             ou as in **you**   **ui** as in **cruise**   **eau** as in **beauty**

Description

[u] is a high, back, tense vowel. It's the highest back vowel, and we make it with our lips considerably rounded.

Production: [u]

1. Put your jaw in the same place as for [i]. Round your lips so as to leave only a small opening, as for [w].
2. Raise the back of your tongue so that it almost touches your soft palate. The tip should be just touching the gum behind the lower front teeth.
3. Produce voice. Make sure there's no nasal emission.

[u] Level 1

PROBLEM: CONFUSION OF [ʊ] AND [u]

[u] is not often misarticulated. It's fairly easy to produce, so only level 1 drills are given. Sometimes, though, nonnative speakers may be confused as to which sound to use—[u] or [ʊ]. And there are some regional variations in the pronunciation of words such as *roof* and *root*. Here's a contrast drill to help reinforce the differences between [u] and [ʊ].

[u]

Contrast Drill for [u] *and* [ʊ]

Say the words in the following lists slowly, reading across the page. Contrast the pairs of words. The first word of each pair uses a [ʊ] and the second a [u]

[ʊ]	[u]	[ʊ]	[u]	[ʊ]	[u]
soot	— suit	pull	— pool	stood	— stewed
look	— Luke	full	— fool	cookie	— kooky
would	— wooed	could	— cooed	should	— shooed

 ### Practice Words for [u]

Say the words in the following lists slowly. Make sure you're not saying [ʊ] for [u]. Ask your instructor or a classmate to listen to you if you're not sure. There are only a few words beginning with [u].

Beginning	End	End	Middle	Middle
oodles	crew	two	pool	stool
ooze	true	through	fool	coupon
oolong	stew	blue	dues	moon
	shoe	grew	dunes	whose
	flew	glue	tube	soup
	knew	who	food	stoop

Practice Sentences for [u]

1. He jumped in the <u>pool</u> like a <u>fool</u>.
2. <u>Food</u> <u>tubes</u> are the <u>stews</u> of tomorrow.
3. We found a <u>coupon</u> for a <u>soup</u> <u>spoon</u>.
4. Is it <u>true</u> he <u>flew</u> the <u>coop</u>?
5. I carried my <u>shoes</u> while we walked <u>through</u> the <u>dunes</u>.
6. <u>Newton</u> <u>booed</u> while the <u>crooner</u> sang the <u>blues</u>.
7. <u>Louis</u> Armstrong <u>blew</u> a <u>cool</u> trumpet with <u>true</u> enthusiasm.
8. <u>Whose</u> newspaper is due to arrive sooner than Tuesday?
9. Cape Cod has two temperatures: too hot and too cold.
10. U Nu was the premier of Burma many moons ago.
11. They put on a new crew to fly to the moon.
12. Should you pay the dues so soon?
13. I could eat oodles of noodles.
14. Would you please stand on that stool?
15. The huge shadow grew in the moonlight.

[u]

Challenge Materials for [u]

Piano Tuning

A concert artist has his piano tuned before each performance. The frequency of tuning depends on the use the piano receives and the conditions peculiar to its location. A piano will stay in tune better if the atmospheric conditions are uniform. Changes from moist to dry air cause wood to swell and shrink, thus changing the tension on the strings. Keep the humidity as constant as possible and your piano will need less frequent tunings.

Pianoworld, July 31, 2000, http://www.pianoworld.com/care.htm

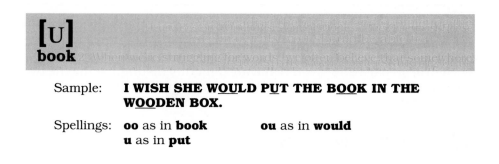

[ʊ]
book

Sample:	**I WISH SHE WOULD PUT THE BOOK IN THE WOODEN BOX.**
Spellings:	**oo** as in **book** **ou** as in **would**
	u as in **put**

Description

[ʊ] is a high, back, lax vowel. Your lips are slightly rounded.

Production: [ʊ]

1. Open your mouth to a position slightly higher than for [ɪ]. Round and slightly protrude your lips.
2. Touch your lower front teeth with the tip of your tongue.
3. Produce voice. Make sure there's no nasal emission.

 ## Diphthong [ʊɚ]

The vowel [ʊ] is frequently combined with [ɚ] to produce a diphthong, [ʊɚ], as in the word *lure*. Some regions don't distinguish between the diphthongs [ɔɚ] and [ʊɚ] as in *pore* and *poor*. Sometimes, this can cause confusion and, perhaps, misunderstandings. Another factor to consider is that oftentimes, r-shading on the diphthong varies regionally, too. It doesn't matter if you use the [ɔɚ] or [ʊɚ], just be consistent.

[ʊ]

Say the following words slowly and carefully. Make sure you distinguish between [ɔɚ] and [ʊɚ]. Also, listen for the "r-shading" at the end of the diphthong, regardless of which diphthong you use.

[ɔɚ]	[ʊɚ]		[ɔɚ]	[ʊɚ]
pore	— poor		tore	— tour
shore	— sure		lore	— lure
more	— moor		yore	— you're
chore	— chewer		store	— stewer

[ʊ] and [ʊɚ] Level 1

[ʊ] is a fairly easy vowel to produce. Most of the problems occur when a nonnative speaker isn't sure of how to pronounce a word and substitutes [u] for [ʊ]. For example, *should* becomes *shooed*. Try the contrast drill on page 238 if you're having difficulty distinguishing the two sounds. The drills for [ʊ] are all level 1. Just be sure you're using [ʊ] and not [u].

🔘 *Practice Words for* [ʊ]

Say the words in the following lists slowly and carefully. Listen closely, and be sure you are not saying [u] instead of [ʊ]. [ʊ] does not occur in end or beginning positions.

wood	book	could	put	hoof
stood	should	sugar	pull	push
look	cook	bushel	bully	shook
hook	hood	wooden	couldn't	nook
brook	butcher	wool	bush	rook
wouldn't	cookie	took	good	crook

Practice Sentences for [ʊ] *and* [ʊɚ]

1. I couldn't push the wood through the bush.
2. I was sure I would do it by hook or by crook.
3. He took the meat off the butcher block.
4. The bully stood still against the pull.
5. The sugar cookies were too good to crumble.
6. The tour book stood where all could look at it.
7. Wouldn't you like a woolen hood?
8. The horse splashed his hoof in the brook.
9. The poor cook pushed the saltshaker back in its nook.
10. They lifted the bushel with a wooden pulley.

[ʊ]

Challenge Sentences for [u] *and* [ʊ]

1. Hughie Boone used a new broom to sweep up his room.
2. The mud oozed through the flue in the sluice.
3. *Who Is Suing Whom* is the title of the soon-to-be-released movie starring Susan Pool and Steward Goodwood.
4. The foolish cook stood looking at the book while the pudding shook.
5. Do you know how Newton knew his new shoes were in the new schoolroom?
6. Nanook pushed his canoe through the brook looking like a man from Brooklyn.
7. Lucy Bloom rudely pushed her bushel basket through the wooden hood.
8. Hugh hooked the huge pulley to two blue spruces in June.
9. The crooked bully stood without moving because he couldn't pull his foot off the stool.
10. Too few fumes from the burning wood could be consumed in the chimney flue.

Challenge Materials for [u] *and* [ʊ]

The best material from which a suit can be made is wool. Wool takes dyes better than any other fabric. It does not snag; it fits well; it does not lose its shape; it is resilient; it lies better on the body; in winter, it's warmer; it outlasts any other fabric. It can also be woven into many different textures and looks.

The second-best suit fabric is a polyester and wool blend. The general rule is the more wool the richer looking the material and the better the suit. Avoid any suit made with less than forty-five percent wool, as well as those made of a blend that has the shiny look of polyester.

John T. Molloy, *John T. Molloy's New Dress for Success*

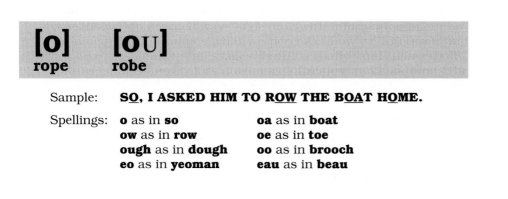

[o] [oʊ]
rope   robe

| Sample: | **SO, I ASKED HIM TO ROW THE BOAT HOME.** |

Spellings:
- **o** as in **so**
- **ow** as in **row**
- **ough** as in **dough**
- **eo** as in **yeoman**
- **oa** as in **boat**
- **oe** as in **toe**
- **oo** as in **brooch**
- **eau** as in **beau**

Description

[o] is a mid, back, tense vowel. The jaw is up slightly higher than for [ʊ], and the lips are rounded. In stressed syllables, especially those in final position, and when the vowel [o] is followed by a voiced consonant, we tend to use a diphthong, [oʊ], which is longer than [o] and drops in pitch. Using the diphthong instead of the vowel (or vice versa) doesn't change the meaning of a word.

Production: [o]

1. Open your mouth about halfway. Round your lips and slightly purse them. Touch the tip of your tongue to the back of your lower teeth, but do it lightly.
2. Raise the back of your tongue as you purse the lips. Produce voice. Make sure there's no nasal emission.

[o] **and** [oʊ] **Level 1**

[o] is fairly easy to produce accurately. Actually, most native speakers produce the diphthong [oʊ] more than the pure vowel [o], especially in stressed syllables and before voiced consonants. People living in the upper midwest tend to use the pure vowel [o] consistently, as do nonnative speakers who have only the pure vowel [o] in their languages. It doesn't really matter which one you use for meaning.

See if you can hear a difference in length in the following pairs of sounds. The second word should use the noticeably longer diphthong [oʊ].

Contrast Drill for [o] *and* [oʊ]

[o]	[oʊ]	[o]	[oʊ]	[o]	[oʊ]
rope	— robe	coat	— code	post	— posed
lope	— lobe	boat	— bowed	host	— hosed
dose	— doze	rote	— rowed	gross	— grows

Practice Words for [o]

Say the words in the following lists slowly. Listen for length: do you use the vowel [o] or the diphthong [oʊ]?

Beginning	*End*	*Middle*
open	flow	road
over	toe	boat
oh	dough	bowl

Beginning	End	Middle
oak	throw	sewing
oats	show	pole
ocean	mow	coal
own	grow	grown
omit	follow	stone
odor	glow	whole

 ### Practice Sentences for [o] and [ou]

1. He <u>owned</u> an <u>oceangoing</u> <u>boat</u>.
2. Put the <u>oatmeal</u> in the <u>bowl</u> next to the <u>stove</u>.
3. We <u>opened</u> the <u>coal</u> <u>stove</u> and began to <u>choke</u> on the <u>smoke</u>.
4. She was <u>sewing</u> <u>closed</u> a <u>hole</u> in the <u>toe</u>.
5. It's hard to <u>follow</u> such a <u>glowing</u> <u>show</u>.
6. I'm told that eating oats lowers cholesterol.
7. Only the lonely enjoy flying solo polar flights.
8. I know you would like stone-ground whole wheat toast.
9. Flo owed the owner of the grocery store for the rolled oats she stole.
10. The roly-poly roll baker was rolling in dough from years of rolling dough.

Challenge Materials for [o] and [ou]

When the snow clouds retreated, the gray slopes and jagged cliffs were gone, as were the livestock trails and raw stumps of felled oak. Several inches of fresh snow softened all contours. Hunched against December's cold, I scanned the slope, looking for the snow leopard which was somewhere a thousand feet above near a goat it had killed the previous day. But only cold prowled the slopes. Slowly I climbed upward, kicking steps into the snow and angling toward a spur of rock from which to survey the valley. Soon scree gave way to a chaos of boulders and rocky outcrops, the slopes motionless and silent as if devoid of life.

Then I saw the snow leopard, a hundred and fifty feet away, peering at me from the spur, her body so well molded into the contours of the boulders that she seemed a part of them. Her smoky-gray coat sprinkled with black rosettes perfectly complemented the rocks and snowy wastes, and her pale eyes conveyed an image of immense solitude. As we watched each other the clouds descended once more, entombing us and bringing more snow. Perhaps sensing that I meant her no harm, she sat up. Though snow soon capped her head and shoulders, she remained, silent and still, seemingly impervious to the elements. Wisps of clouds swirled around, transforming her into a ghost creature, part myth and part reality. Balanced precariously on a ledge and bitterly cold, I too stayed, unwilling to disrupt the moment.

George B. Schaller, *Stones of Silence: Journey in the Himalaya*

[o]
[ou]

awful

Sample: **I THOUGHT THE LAUNDRY DID AN AWFUL JOB IN A SHORT TIME.**

Spellings: **aw** as in **awful**   **au** as in **laundry**   **oo** as in **door**
o as in **wrong**   **ough** as in **thought**   **augh** as in **taught**

Description

[ɔ] is a mid, back, lax vowel. The lips are usually rounded.

Production: [ɔ]

1. Close the mouth very slightly from the position of [æ], and slightly round your lips. Elevate the back of your tongue a bit, but don't touch your upper teeth.
2. Produce voice. Make sure there's no nasal emission.

Diphthong [ɔɚ]

The vowel [ɔ] is frequently combined with [ɚ] to produce a diphthong, [ɔɚ], as in the word *four.* We'll cover this diphthong in the level 2 drills.

[ɔ] Level 1

Use of [ɔ] varies almost from word to word, region to region. Words that are pronounced with [ɔ] in one region may be pronounced with [ɑ] or [ɒ] in others. For example, the word *water* may be pronounced with [ɑ] in upstate New York and with [ɔ] in downstate New York. Floridians usually say *Florida* with [ɔ], but northerners say it with [ɑ]. How do *you* say such words as *fog, wash, caught, coffee,* and *auto*?

In the drills that follow, we've used words that are pronounced with [ɔ] in at least one regional dialect. You'll have to determine the usage in your area by consulting your instructor and others knowledgeable on the subject.

PROBLEM: NONSTANDARD [ɔ]

Although use of [ɔ] varies greatly around the country, there is a nonstandard production. It occurs when you round your lips too much and close your mouth slightly. It frequently is associated with the dental and gum ridge consonants because they require a slight closing of the mouth. Look at your mouth in a mirror as you say *awful.* Do your lips suddenly round before you make the sound? Is your mouth almost closed? If so, you are probably producing the nonstandard sound. Here's another test: put the back of your hand lightly against the underside of your chin and say *all.* Did your jaw drop? It should, but only very slightly.

If your jaw drops a great deal, you're probably producing a nonstandard diphthong that sounds close to [ɔə]. This sound is produced for two reasons: you're saying the [ɔ] with too much lip-rounding, and the [ə] results because you're dropping your jaw *before* you stop producing the [ɔ]. This nonstandard production is very common in the New York metropolitan area. Ask your instructor to listen to you, and if you produce the nonstandard diphthong, try the following drill.

Production Drill

Say the following pairs of words. The first word of each pair contains the sound [ɑ]. The second has the sound [ɔ]. Hold your chin and look in a mirror while you say the words. Don't let your jaw rise or your lips round—go from the position for [ɑ] to the position for [ɔ] without moving anything except your tongue. Ask your instructor to listen.

[ɑ]	[ɔ]	[ɑ]	[ɔ]	[ɑ]	[ɔ]
cot	— caught	hock	— hawk	la	— law
on	— awning	wok	— walk	tot	— taught
lot	— lawn	knot	— gnawed	don	— dawn

 ### *Level 1 Practice Words for* [ɔ]

Say the following words slowly and carefully. If a particular word is not pronounced with [ɔ] in your area, eliminate it. (Check with your instructor first.) Find a word you consistently pronounce correctly, and use that word for comparison.

Beginning	*End*	*Middle*
awful	draw	tall
often	law	stall
August	straw	thought
auction	jaw	wrong
autumn	saw	chalk
also	flaw	hawk
author	craw	fought
audio	claw	caught
awesome	maw	yawn
awkward	gnaw	song
awning	paw	long
offer	raw	dawn
auburn	slaw	ball
always	thaw	fawn

[ɔ]

Level 1 Practice Phrases for [ɔ]

raw coleslaw	also an author	August auction
gnaw its paw	awesome audio	long song
wrong awning	tall ballplayer	chalk talk
falling straw	flawed thought	all offers

Level 1 Practice Sentences for [ɔ]

1. I <u>always</u> <u>thought</u> he would break the <u>law</u>.
2. <u>August</u> can be <u>awfully</u> <u>long</u>.
3. We <u>saw</u> her last <u>autumn</u> at the <u>auction</u>.
4. That <u>dog</u> <u>always</u> <u>offers</u> its <u>paw</u>.
5. I <u>bought</u> the <u>wrong</u> kind of <u>coleslaw</u>.
6. We <u>all</u> like to <u>draw</u> with <u>chalk</u>.
7. The <u>straw</u> baskets hung from the <u>awning</u> in the <u>stall</u>.
8. He <u>fought</u> to <u>cross</u> the ice during the <u>thaw</u>.
9. <u>Authors</u> don't <u>always</u> admit their <u>flaws</u>.
10. <u>Dawn</u> <u>often</u> colors her hair <u>auburn</u>.

[ɔ] and [ɔɚ] Level 2

PROBLEM: DISTORTION OF THE DIPHTHONG [ɔɚ]

Many words couple the [ɔ] and [ɚ] sounds in the minor diphthong [ɔɚ]. Make an extra effort to stop your jaw from rising and your lips from rounding too much. If you don't, the first part of the diphthong, mostly the sound [ɔ], will become distorted and the diphthong will seem to separate into two distinct sounds as your jaw drops again. Check your production, using a mirror, and make a special effort to open your mouth open wide as you begin to produce the [ɔɚ].

[ɔ]

Level 2 Practice Words for [ɔ] *and* [ɔɚ]

Say each of the following words slowly, reading down the columns. Compare each word with a word you're sure you say correctly. If you're uncertain about your production, ask your instructor or a classmate to listen.

Beginning	*Middle*	*Middle*	*Middle*
oar	born	morning	sports
orchid	store	torn	thorn
organ	four	cork	gauze
ornate	corn	horn	born
orchestra	north	fourth	storm
Orient	core	cord	ward
orphan	score	more	door
ornament	bore	war	tore
Orlando	floor	lore	forty
ordeal	fortune	shore	spore
order	snore	fourteen	dormant
orator	dorm	warm	swarm
oral	dorsal	dory	story
oracle	glory	forceps	force
orbit	horse	course	forbid

 Level 2 Practice Phrases for [ɔ]

ornate store	fourteen stories	warm floor
morning course	north forty	more corn
dormant spore	force ashore	born in a storm

Level 2 Practice Sentences for [ɔ]

1. I bought a totally awesome audio system.
2. The storm washed an oar up on the shore.
3. He steered a broad course by the North Star.
4. I had an awful cough all morning.
5. I ordered it all at the store.
6. Have you ever stored corn in straw?
7. The orator spoke of law and order.
8. It was an ordeal listening to the snoring in the dorm.
9. The score was fourteen to four.
10. The horse forced its way through the door.

[ɔ]

Challenge Sentences for [ɔ]

1. Norton ordered audio equipment from a store in the north ward of Boston.
2. The mortician often saw long cordons of autos swarming along the boardwalk.
3. Orlando, Florida, has long been called a city of the fourth glory.
4. The law office was warm despite the strong autumn storm of the morning.
5. The haughty horseman was ordered off the course because of his unsportsmanlike oratory.
6. Some authors ought to be brought up on charges of disorderly construct.
7. The war horse bore his master with a strong show of loyal support.
8. Foster lost a quarter of the course materials for the four courses he taught.
9. Fourteen actors sought to audition for the naughty Broadway show.
10. The sawyer's foreman walked the boards across the courtyard to the sawmill.

Challenge Materials for [ɔ]

1. Basic Monthly Telephone Service
Use Flat Rate if:
   You use the phone often for local calls.
Use Message Rate if:
   You make few outgoing calls in the local areas.
   You usually talk longer than 4 minutes.
Use Select-a-Call Residence Rate if:
   You make fewer than 3 local calls a day.
   You make most calls within your toll-free calling area.
   You usually talk less than 4 minutes.
Use Select-a-Call Business Rate if:
   You make fewer than 5 local calls each business day.
   You make most calls within your toll-free calling area.
   You usually talk less than 3 minutes.

Adapted from *Fairfield Community Directory,*
Southern New England Telephone

2. Malls
   Although they are designed to always seem familiar, not all malls are alike. The big ones have at least two major department stores, one at each end (known in the mall trade as "anchors"), so that shoppers who want to visit both are forced to walk past all the stores in between.

[ɔ]

The West Edmonton Mall in Canada—the world's largest—has 11 department stores, 821 other shops, an amusement park with twenty-two water slides, and more spaces than any other parking lot on earth. (Mall parking lots are striped and restriped according to how good business is. A mall in a slump offers fewer parking spaces, making the lot appear full, and thus attracting customers who crave to be where everybody else is—the exemplary mall shopper's mentality; a mall doing booming business cuts down spaces to a minuscule 8 × 17½ feet to squeeze in more customers.) Minimalls, also known as pod-malls, are anchored only by a 7-Eleven or Stop-N-Go convenience store and are at best a stopgap measure for any shopper who craves the neurological bombardment of a full-featured mega-mall.

Jane and Michael Stern, *The Encyclopedia of Bad Taste*

3. Autumn is the season between summer and winter.

The Northern Hemisphere, the northern half of the earth, has autumn weather during late September, October, and November. Autumn weather does not last so long in the polar region, where extremely cold winter weather begins earlier. In tropical regions, seasonal changes are not great.

The Southern Hemisphere has autumn from March until early June.

Many people call this season fall because it is the period of falling leaves. Autumn is also harvest time for many crops. In North America, early autumn days are generally warm and nights are cool. As winter approaches, the air becomes chillier and frost often occurs at night. In much of North America, the end of autumn is marked by the freezing of lakes and streams, southern migration of birds, and prewinter snowstorms.

Autumn—especially September—is the season when most hurricanes occur. Hurricanes cause great damage along the coasts of the Gulf of Mexico and the western North Atlantic Ocean.

World Book, Inc.,
http://www.worldbook.com/fun/seasons/html/autumn.htm

[ɔɪ]
coin

Sample: **ROY TOOK GREAT JOY IN COIN COLLECTING.**

Spellings: **oy** as in **joy**   **oi** as in **coin**

Description

[ɔɪ] is a diphthong beginning with a low, back vowel and gliding to a high, front vowel. Your lips should be slightly rounded.

Production: [ɔɪ]

1. Open your mouth almost to the position for [ɔ]. Raise the back of your tongue slightly and round your lips just a tiny bit.
2. Produce voice. As you do, your jaw should drop slightly. Then let your tongue lift toward the position for [ɪ], relax your lip-rounding, and draw the corners of your mouth back. Make sure there's no nasal emission of air.

[ɔɪ] **Level 1**

PROBLEM 1: NONSTANDARD [ɔ]

The problems with [ɔɪ] are generally caused by too much lip-rounding and by not opening the mouth wide enough. If you distort the vowel [ɔ] this way, you will almost certainly distort the diphthong [ɔɪ]. Try the drills for [ɔ] on page 245.

PROBLEM 2: SUBSTITUTION OF [ɝ] FOR [ɔɪ]

If you make this substitution, you would say, for example, *curl* for *coil.* This substitution happens occasionally in the New York area and in some areas of the south. Although it does happen rather infrequently, it's very noticeable to those who don't make the substitution. If you make this substitution, try the following contrast drill.

  Contrast Drill for [ɔɪ] ***and*** [ɝ]

Say the following word pairs slowly and carefully. Read across the page, contrasting [ɔɪ] in the first word with [ɝ] in the second.

[ɔɪ]	[ɝ]		[ɔɪ]	[ɝ]
coil	— curl		loin	— learn
poise	— purrs		foist	— first
poison	— person		oil	— Earl
boys	— burrs		voice	— verse

[ɔɪ]

Practice Words for [ɔɪ]

The drills for [ɔɪ] are all at level 1. Say the following words slowly and carefully. Listen to your production and make sure you're not substituting [ɝ] or closing your mouth too much.

Beginning	*End*	*Middle*
oil	Roy	boil
oyster	employ	join
ointment	destroy	appointment
oily	boy	soy sauce
	enjoy	toys
	annoy	boycott
	coy	coin
	alloy	point
	toy	anoint

 ### *Practice Sentences for* [ɔɪ]

1. They served <u>oysters</u> cooked in <u>soy</u> sauce.
2. Please <u>oil</u> that <u>noisy</u> hinge.
3. I have an <u>appointment</u> for an <u>employment</u> physical.
4. The little boys really enjoyed the toys.
5. I need some ointment for that annoying boil.
6. The coins were made of a copper alloy.
7. The boycott destroyed his profits.

Challenge Sentences for [ɔɪ]

1. The noisily toiling boys coiled the lines boisterously.
2. Burt employed the third toy maker to avoid an employees' boycott.
3. Helen of Troy played it coy with the boys.
4. Always try to avoid poison ivy's annoying, burning oils.
5. The unsoiled ointment was kept in five poison-proof foil containers.

[ɔɪ]

Challenge Materials for [ɔɪ]

Identifying Poison Ivy

1. Although the appearance of poison ivy, oak, and sumac may vary depending on where the plant grows—the leaves may be smooth-edged or scalloped, for example—here are some characteristics to watch for:

- Poison ivy's leaves are usually glossy green in the spring and summer and reddish in the fall.
- Poison ivy and poison oak most commonly grow in three-leaf groupings. Poison sumac, on the other hand, generally has seven to eleven leaves along its stems—one at the tip and others in pairs across the stem.
- Poison-oak leaves often resemble those of the oak tree.
- Poison ivy grows throughout the United States, except in the extreme southwest. Poison oak is found along the West Coast and from New Jersey to eastern Texas. Poison sumac thrives in moist soil east of the Mississippi River.

"Vital Signs," *McCall's*, July 1988

2. Buying and Storing Olive Oil

Buying oil in small sizes, or splitting larger bottles with friends, is a practical way to buy expensive oils. Oil purchased in bulk should always be poured into smaller containers, preferably in a can or a dark-colored bottle.

Air, heat, and light will cause olive oil to turn rancid, so it should be stored in a cool place in an airtight container. Store at a temperature of 14 degrees C. or 57 degrees F. If you have a wine cellar, store your olive oils there and keep a small amount in your kitchen. Always replace the cap on the bottle. Do not put olive oil in a container without a tight cap.

When chilled, or in cold weather, the oil may turn cloudy and even solidify. Such oil will clear again as it warms, so cloudiness should not be taken as an indication that the oil is past its prime. Be sure bottles are tightly sealed. Never store olive oil in the refrigerator.

Linda Stradley, *What's Cooking America*

[ɑ]   ([ɒ])   ([a])
calm

[ɑ]
[ɒ]
[a]

Sample: **IT DIDN'T BOTHER HIM AS HE CALMLY LOCKED THE CAR.**

Spellings: **a** as in **calm**   **o** as in **lock**
ea as in **heart**   **ow** as in **knowledge**
e as in **sergeant**   **aa** as in **bazaar**
al as in **palm**

Description

[ɑ] is a low, back, lax vowel. The mouth position is the widest open of all the vowels. The tongue has only the very back part slightly raised, the rest of it is relaxed. There are two alternate forms that are very close in placement, and are regional variations in some American dialects. One variation, [ɒ], is slightly higher and more tense. This variation occurs notably in New England and parts of the South. The other is [a], a low, front vowel, and often occurs in the Northeast. Note that [ɒ] and [a] are not nonstandard productions; they are simply regional variations. If you're unsure of the usage in your area, or of your own production, consult with your instructor or someone else knowledgeable about local usage.

Diphthongs [ɑɪ], [ɑɪ] and [ɑʊ]

The vowel [ɑ] combines with [ɪ] to produce the diphthong, [ɑɪ] as in *time*, and with [ʊ] to produce the diphthong [ɑʊ] as in *house*. Because these diphthongs occur so frequently in American English, we have provided separate sections beginning on page 254 for [ɑɪ] and on page 259 for [ɑʊ]. Another diphthong forms when the vowel [ɑ] combines with [ɚ] to produce the diphthong [ɑɚ], as in *car*. Its use varies from region to region, so we won't provide separate drills for [ɑɚ].

Production: [ɑ]

Open wide, and say ahhh.

[ɑ] **Level 1**

Very few problems exist with [ɑ]. There are a couple of substitutions, but they tend to be regional. For example, New Englanders tend to say *park* with the vowel [a] and, along with certain New Yorkers and West Indians, might say the word *hot* with the vowel [ɒ]. It probably doesn't matter which you say as long as you are consistent.

Before [r] many New Yorkers raise and round [ɑ], resulting in a nonstandard vowel resembling [ɔ]. *Card* then may sound like *cord*, *star* sounds like *store*, and *far* sounds like *four*. Listen for this when you do the practice words, and check for lip-rounding with a mirror. Opening the mouth a little bit wider and relaxing the lips will change *tore* back to *tar*.

[ɑ]
[ɒ]
[a]

Practice Words for [ɑ] *and* [ɑɚ]

Listen carefully as you say each word. Some of the words contain the diphthong [ɑɚ]. It doesn't matter if you pronounce it with r-shading, that is with [ə] as opposed to [ɚ]. Just be consistent with your regional pronunciation.

Say the words in the following lists slowly. All the drills for [ɑ] are at level 1. There are no English words that end in [ɑ].

Beginning	*Beginning*	*Middle*	*Middle*
ah	on	calm	top
are	arms	frog	father
honest	alarm	bomb	stars
obvious	occupy	locker	guard
art	onset	spot	response
argue	arson	palms	stopping
arch	army	smart	follow
article	operation	hot	modern
olive	almonds	knowledge	heart

 ### *Practice Phrases for* [ɑ]

obvious response	calm frog	card shark
argue about art	smart bomb	farmyard barn
on top of	spot the guard	Charlie's cart

Practice Sentences for [ɑ]

1. They had an <u>honest</u> <u>argument</u> with their <u>father</u>.
2. <u>Stopping</u> is the <u>obvious</u> <u>response</u> when the <u>guard</u> is <u>armed</u>.
3. The <u>fog</u> crept into the <u>harbor</u> on little <u>frog's</u> feet.
4. Sighing "<u>ahh</u>" can be <u>calming</u>.
5. Watch them <u>stop</u> the <u>cars</u> at the <u>top</u> of the <u>yard</u>.
6. Star-gazing is a pleasurable occupation on some nights.
7. The pool shark spotted the ball on the mark.
8. The palm trees arched into the sky over the dark oasis.
9. Sorry, this locker room is occupied.
10. The arson squad turned the bomb over to the army.

Challenge Materials for [ɑ] and [ɑɚ]

Build a Frog Pond

Having a frog pond full of frogs in your backyard is a joy few of us think of when planning our gardens. Having a frog pond is fun, allows you to do your bit for the conservation of wildlife, and is a great conversation point when strolling around your garden with friends. Children can be

[ɑ]
[ɒ]
[a]

fascinated for hours, giving you a much-needed rest. Frogs can be easily attracted to your garden whether you live in the country or the city.

You can design ponds for different types of frogs. There are two types of frogs, ground dwelling and tree frogs. A raised pond will only allow tree frogs in while a sunken pond will suit those frogs that like to keep their feet on the ground. A pond with a lot of vegetation such as reeds will attract swamp-loving frogs.

Frogs will then naturally gravitate towards your pond. However, if there is a delay in colonisation, it may be due to the local population's severe depletion. If this is the case, you can introduce some locally caught tadpoles from the area. Only catch local tadpoles because the introduction of a new species to the area may have catastrophic effects on the existing populations.

Most states have some protection on frogs and tadpoles, so please check with your local wildlife authorities because you may need a permit.

Peninsula Community Access News, July 1999

[ɑɪ]
ice

Sample: **I WOULD LIKE TO BUY SOME ICE SKATES SOMETIME.**

Spellings: **i** as in **ice**   **y** as in **cry**   **ye** as in **dye**
             ie as in **lie**   **uy** as in **buy**   **ui** as in **guile**
             igh as in **light**   **ei** as in **height**   **ey** as in **eye**
             ais as in **aisle**   **ia** as in **diamond**

Description

[ɑɪ] is a diphthong beginning with a low back vowel and gliding toward a high front vowel. A regional variation [aɪ], beginning with a low front vowel, occurs in many parts of New England and in large portions of the Southeast and the South.

Production: [ɑɪ]

1. Open your mouth to the position for [ɑ]. Your tongue should be flat in the bottom of your mouth, relaxed. Your lips should not be rounded.
2. Produce voice. As you do, lift the back of your tongue toward the position of [ɪ]. Don't close your mouth very much; there should be more tongue movement than jaw movement. Allow your jaw to move only very slightly, and straight up, not inward.

[ɑɪ]

[ɑɪ] **Level 1**

PROBLEM 1: SUBSTITUTION OF [a] FOR [ɑɪ]

In many areas the [ɑɪ] is "broadened"; in other words, the first part of the diphthong has its normal value, but the second part, though still present, is greatly diminished. This happens particularly in the South and Southeast. There is a nonstandard pronunciation, however, where the vowel [a] replaces the vowel [ɑ], and the second part of the diphthong is entirely missing. An example of this nonstandard production is when the word *time* [tɑɪm] becomes *tahm* [tam]. Check with your instructor to see if you make this substitution. If you do, try the following production drill.

Production Drill

Read across the page, saying the "broken" words slowly. Bring the parts together as you read across. Say the first part with the vowel [ɑ] as in *calm,* and say the second part with the vowel [ɪ] as in *sit.*

ta . . . it	ta . . it	ta . it	ta it	tight
la . . . it	la . . it	la . it	la it	light
na . . . it	na . . it	na . it	na it	night
ba . . . it	ba . . it	ba . it	ba it	bite
ka . . . it	ka . . it	ka . it	ka it	kite
ra . . . it	ra . . it	ra . it	ra it	right
sa . . . it	sa . . it	sa . it	sa it	sight

PROBLEM 2: SUBSTITUTION OF [ɔɪ] FOR [ɑɪ]

If you raise your jaw a little too much, you'll produce a diphthong, [ɔɪ], instead of [ɑɪ], the same sound you'd get if you substituted *loin* for *line.* The problem seems to occur most often in words in which [ɑɪ] is followed by a voiced consonant. Do you hear a difference between *right* and *ride*? Between *sight* and *side*? If you make this substitution, try the problem 1 drill presented above. Then try the following contrast drill:

💿 *Contrast Drill for* [ɑɪ] *and Nonstandard* [ɔɪ]

Read the words in the following lists slowly. First read down the *vs* (voiceless) column, next down the *v* (voiced) column, and then across the page. When you contrast the pairs of words, try to hold your jaw position constant: don't let it move up.

[ɑɪ]

ʊs	ʊ	ʊs	ʊ
right	— ride	ice	— eyes
sight	— side	slights	— slides
height	— hide	strife	— strive
lice	— lies	ricing	— rising
rice	— rise	slighting	— sliding
light	— lied	sighting	— siding
a bite	— abide	righting	— riding
tight	— tide	device	— devise

If you seem to have difficulty, try using a mirror to look for lip-rounding, which would be associated with lifting your jaw.

Level 1 Practice Words for [ɑɪ]

Say the words in the following lists slowly and carefully. You may want to use a mirror and feel your lower jaw to see if you're closing too much. Start with the *Beginning* words. [ɑɪ] doesn't occur in unstressed syllables.

Beginning	*Middle*	*End*
ice	sight	tie
item	kite	sigh
eye	rice	shy
ice cream	bite	hi
isotope	fright	thigh
isometric	nice	pie
isolate	dice	pry
icon	price	sky
icing	night	fry

Level 1 Practice Phrases for [ɑɪ]

an eye for an eye	sky high	out of sight
bite the ice	thigh high	shy sigh

Level 1 Practice Sentences for [ɑɪ]

1. I read an <u>item</u> about <u>isotopes</u>.
2. The <u>kite</u> was so <u>high</u> it was out of <u>sight</u>.
3. I was too <u>shy</u> to say <u>hi</u>.
4. He spilled <u>rice</u> pudding all over his <u>tie</u>.
5. He wants an <u>ice</u> pack for his mosquito <u>bites</u>.
6. I won it on "The <u>Price</u> is <u>Right</u>."
7. He had a <u>night</u> job as a <u>fry</u>-cook and <u>pie</u>-maker.
8. We became <u>frightened</u> when we were <u>isolated</u>.
9. The <u>right</u> <u>icon</u> would bring a <u>high</u> <u>price</u>.

[ɑɪ]

[aɪ] **Level 2**

 Level 2 Practice Words for [aɪ]

These words contain [aɪ] in more difficult sound contexts. Say the words slowly and listen carefully. If you're not sure of your production, ask your instructor or a classmate to listen to you.

Beginning	*End*	*Middle*	*All Positions*
idea	lie	rise	itemize
iron	cry	dime	Irish eyes
island	buy	alive	finite
I've	dry	dried	Mai-tai
I'm	try	tried	typewriter
idle	rely	crime	finalize
I'll	deny	climb	idolize
aisle	why	pliers	ninety-nine
ideal	guy	hide	jai alai

 Level 2 Practice Sentences for [aɪ]

1. He said he didn't find the pliers at the scene of the crime.
2. I tried to buy some dry clothes.
3. I'm sure I dropped the dime in the aisle.
4. He climbed the cliffs on the north side of the island.
5. I try not to rely on ideal solutions.
6. We could see the steam rising from the iron.
7. I tried to time the engine and adjust the idle.
8. Diane started to cry when she realized he was alive.

Challenge Sentences for [aɪ]

1. It was five after nine by the time the white-gowned bride sidled down the aisle.
2. The tired pirate tried to hide his eyes with a wide blindfold.
3. Simon sighed with pride as he eyed his island paradise.
4. The ideal crime implies buying iron pliers and shying away from prying eyes.
5. The idle guide fried the spiced rice with dry white wine.
6. Lionel denied he tried to hide the archives behind the pile of white binders.
7. I like five bright lights in my room while I write at night.
8. The idea behind priceless icons is that they light religious fires in our minds.
9. Bridey told Ike to kindly rise and go fly a kite.
10. Jeff ties dry flies with pliers on nights when the moon is high in the sky.

[aɪ]

Challenge Materials for [ɑɪ]

1. Time ripens all things. No man's born wise.

Cervantes, *Don Quixote*

2. Time is a file. It wears but makes no noise.

English Proverb

3. Time flies over us, but leaves no shadow behind.

Nathaniel Hawthorne

4. Half our life is spent trying to find something to do with the time we have rushed through life trying to save.

Will Rogers

5. A stone thrown at the right time is better than gold given at the wrong time.

Persian Proverb

6. But at my back I always hear
   Time's winged chariot hurrying near.

Andrew Marvell, "To His Coy Mistress"

7. Time is life. It is irreversible and irreplaceable. To waste your time is to waste your life, but to master your time is to master your life and make the most of it.

Alan Lekein, *How to Get Control of Your Time and Your Life*

8. Why Are Dalmatians the Traditional Mascots of Firehouses?

In the days before firehouses even existed, Dalmatians were bred and trained for the specific purpose of preventing highway robbery. Dalmatians, or "coach dogs," ran alongside of horse-drawn stagecoaches, and acted as buffers and as bodyguards to ward off robbers, also known as highwaymen, who attempted to ambush the carriages and, quite literally, to lighten their loads.

When horse-drawn fire engines arrived on the scene, firemen naturally chose Dalmatians to assist them, since the breed was accustomed to running long distances and to being around horses. Their bright white coats, covered with large black spots, made them a highly visible warning sign to bystanders and onlookers, as the dogs ran ahead of, and cleared the path for, fire engines racing towards a fire.

With technological advancement, horse-drawn fire engines became obsolete, and the need for Dalmatians to clear the way for fire engines no longer existed. People knew better than to get in the way of motorized fire engines speeding towards them with blaring sirens!

Fortunately, firemen did not fire the gentle Dalmatian from his position in the department. Instead, they honored him, by adopting the breed as the official firehouse mascot. The tradition continues to this day, and Dalmatians can even be spotted at some fire stations!

Useless Knowledge,
http://www.uselessknowledge.com/explain/dalmatians.shtml

[ɑɪ]

[ɑʊ]
how

Sample: **THE CROWD SHOUTED AND HOWLED WHEN THE BALL WENT FOUL.**

Spellings: **ou** as in **shout**   **ow** as in **crowd**   **ough** as in **bough**

Description

[ɑʊ] is a diphthong beginning with a low, front vowel and gliding to a high, back vowel.

Production: [ɑʊ]

1. Open your mouth for the position of [ɑ]. Your tongue should be relaxed and flat in the mouth. Your lips should not be rounded.
2. Produce voice. As you do, close your mouth slightly and round your lips. Your tongue should elevate. Move toward the position for [ʊ].

[ɑʊ] Level 1

PROBLEM 1: SUBSTITUTION OF [o] FOR [ɑʊ]

This regional substitution occurs frequently in the southeast, in the upper midwest near the Canadian border, and often in areas where people use the pure vowel [o] consistently instead of the diphthong [oʊ]. It results from not lowering the jaw enough at the start of the diphthong. The result is that a word such as *about* sounds something close to "a <u>boat</u>" and can sometimes confuse a listener from another area. Try the following contrast drill.

Contrast Drill for [o] *and* [ɑʊ]

Read down each column first, then across. When reading across, try to make each pair of words distinctly different.

[o]	[ɑʊ]	[o]	[ɑʊ]
know	— now	a boat	— about
groaned	— ground	phoned	— found

[o]	[aʊ]	[o]	[aʊ]
hoe	— how	oat	— out
coach	— couch	moaned	— mound
bow	— bough	clone	— clown
tone	— town	crowed	— crowd
honed	— hound	toll	— towel

PROBLEM 2: SUBSTITUTION OF [ɛaʊ] FOR [aʊ]

This substitution happens if you don't open your mouth enough and if you draw back the corners of your mouth. If you smile when you say this diphthong, it will be distorted. This substitution is a frequent nonstandard production. Check with your instructor to see if you produce [aʊ] in this way. If you do, try the following production drill.

Production Drill

Say the following "broken" words, reading across the page. The first part of each word has the sound [ɑ] as in *calm*. The second has the sound [ʊ] as in *push*. Gradually join the parts together as you read across. It may be very helpful to use a mirror to see your lips.

ba . . . u	ba . . u	ba . u	ba u	bow
ka . . . u	ka . . u	ka . u	ka u	cow
na . . . u	na . . u	na . u	na u	now
ha . . . u	ha . . u	ha . u	ha u	how
va . . . u	va . . u	va . u	va u	vow
ta . . . un	ta . . un	ta . un	ta un	town
da . . . un	da . . un	da . un	da un	down

 ### *Practice Words for* [aʊ]

All the practice exercises for [aʊ] are on level 1. Say the following words slowly and carefully. You may want to use a mirror to see lip-rounding and to help prevent the smile. Having someone else watch and listen to who can also help.

Beginning	*End*	*Middle*
out	cow	town
ouch	allow	couch
hour	plow	cloud
ours	how	towel
ounce	now	powder
outside	eyebrow	allowance
oust	endow	growl
outlaw	chow	about

Practice Phrases for [ɑʊ]

our couch	allow an hour	allowance now
how to plow	brown towel	how about

 ### *Practice Sentences for* [ɑʊ]

1. It took an <u>hour</u> to get <u>downtown</u>.
2. They didn't raise an <u>eyebrow</u> about the <u>cow</u>.
3. Where's the <u>brown</u> <u>towel</u> you took <u>outside?</u>
4. An <u>ounce</u> of prevention is worth a <u>pound</u> of cure.
5. The <u>outlaws</u> <u>growled</u> at the <u>crowd</u>.
6. Some flowers don't open on cloudy days.
7. I said more than ouch when I dropped the couch.
8. Coffee grounds were floating around in my cup.
9. The county raised our mileage allowance.
10. My stomach gave a loud growl in the crowded elevator.

Challenge Materials for [ɑʊ]

1. What makes sounds different from each other? There are three characteristics that can be used to differentiate one sound from another. One of these characteristics is pitch. Pitch is how low or high a sound is. A high pitch is produced by high-frequency sound waves and a low pitch is produced by low frequency sound waves. Another characteristic used to differentiate between sounds is loudness and softness. The louder the sound is the more energy it has. Therefore, the greater the amplitude is the louder the sound will be. The other characteristic is quality or whether or not the sound is pleasant or just noise. A pleasant sound has a regular wave pattern that is repeated over and over. A noise is made by irregular sound waves that are not in a repeating pattern.

Michelle Byington, DeSoto Senior High School,
http://www.desoto.k12.mo.us/html/dhs/

2. It is important to develop an eye for the "geography" of power in the office.

[ɑʊ]

. . . an "outside" office, however desirable it may be because of its window, is in fact a less powerful place to be than an inside office within the area of power, and it may well be better to stay inside the power area, forgoing a window, until such time as one can acquire a corner office. People who move to "outside" offices in the middle of the row, in the power deadspace, tend to stay there forever.

Michael Korda, *Power! How to Get It, How to Use It*

[ʌ]
up

Sample:	**HE WAS LUCKY TO DOUBLE HIS MONEY IN UNDER A MONTH.**

Spellings: **u** as in **up**   **o** as in **month**
              ou as in **double**   **oo** as in **blood**
              oe as in **does**

Description

[ʌ] is a low, central, stressed vowel that occurs in stressed syllables and words.

Production: [ʌ]

1. Open your mouth about as wide as for [ɔ] and slightly higher than for [ɑ]. Don't round your lips.
2. Raise the center of your tongue very slightly. Produce voice. Make sure there's no nasal emission.

[ʌ] Level 1

PROBLEM: SUBSTITUTION OF [ɑ] FOR [ʌ]

[ʌ] is one of the least complicated vowels to produce. But because it doesn't exist in many other languages, nonnative speakers will frequently substitute another sound for [ʌ]. Most often, [ɑ] is substituted, so here's a contrast drill to help you distinguish between [ɑ] and [ʌ].

[ʌ]

Contrast Drill for [ɑ] and [ʌ]

Read the words in the following lists aloud. First read down the list of [ɑ] words. Then read down the list of [ʌ] words. Finally read across the page, contrasting the pairs of words. The first word of each pair will contain [ɑ], and the second [ʌ].

[ɑ]	[ʌ]	[ɑ]	[ʌ]	[ɑ]	[ʌ]
hot	— hut	rob	— rub	cob	— cub
cop	— cup	lock	— luck	bomb	— bum
not	— nut	rot	— rut	got	— gut
calm	— come	mock	— muck	Don	— done
cot	— cut	dock	— duck	Ron	— run
gone	— gun	sob	— sub	shot	— shut

Note: [ʌ] occurs *only* in stressed words and syllables. It does not occur at the ends of words.

Practice Words for [ʌ]

Say the words in the following lists slowly. Monitor your production to make sure you are producing the sound correctly and not substituting [ɑ] for [ʌ]. If you aren't sure of your production, ask your instructor or a classmate to listen to you. Start with the *Beginning* words.

Beginning	*Beginning*	*Middle*	*Middle*
up	under	double	month
uncle	other	nothing	mother
oven	us	brother	discuss
onion	ugly	instructor	tough
usher	ultimate	enough	bubble

Practice Phrases for [ʌ]

nothing under	tough and ugly	the other onion
enough ushers	double up	under discussion

Practice Sentences for [ʌ]

1. There's <u>nothing</u> cooking in the <u>oven</u>.
2. We have <u>enough</u> ushers this <u>month</u>.
3. My <u>uncle</u> and my <u>brother</u> have the matter <u>under</u> <u>discussion</u>.
4. My mother doesn't cry when she peels onions.
5. The other instructor is a tougher grader.
6. I blew the ultimate bubble with that ugly-looking gum.
7. What's coming up for us next?

[ʌ]

Challenge Materials for [ʌ]

1. A lesson that our country learned early and well, and which some countries unfortunately never learned or learned too late, is that each citizen had better take an active interest in running his country or he may suddenly find the country running him.

Art Linkletter, A Child's Garden of Misinformation

2. A prominent banker gave his teen-age daughter, a student at the Actor's Studio, a pedigreed pup for her birthday, warning her that the little dog had not yet been house broken. Sure enough, an hour later, when he wandered into his daughter's study, he found her contemplating a small puddle in the center of the room. "My pup, " she murmured sadly, "runneth over."

Bennett Cerf's Treasure of Atrocious Puns

3. If you want to tour Europe at the least expense, and you can arrange your timetable with a certain degree of flexibility, here's what to do: buy a one-way (or roundtrip) ticket to London. When you arrive in London purchase onward tickets from a "bucket-shop."

London is where you'll find the most bucket-shops. The term "bucket-shop" doesn't refer to the product they sell, rather to the fact that unsold tours and airline tickets are sold by this kind of business; sort of like putting the leftovers in a bucket so to speak.

Bucket shops are nothing new, in fact airline tickets and tours have been sold through this kind of outlet for years in London. Only since airline deregulation have bucket-shops come into being in the United States. Typical U.S. "bucket-shops" usually operate as "Discount Travel" clubs. Some require membership (and a yearly fee), others can be used at no cost.

Capt. Richard A. Bodner, Money Saving Secrets of Smart Airline Travelers

4. Donald Duck

Donald debuted in the cartoon "The Wise Little Hen" June 9, 1934. His first appearance in comics was in the comics adaptation of that same year in the *Silly Symphonies* comic series.

Donald lives in Duckburg with his three nephews Huey, Dewey, and Louie. Other than that his most important relatives are his uncle Scrooge McDuck, his cousin Gladstone Gander, and Grandma Duck.

Probably the only time he refers to his mother is in a story by Barks where he has disguised himself and says, "My own mother wouldn't know me now!" He has a girlfriend, Daisy Duck. In some Italian stories Donald has a super-hero alias, Superduck.

Adapted from Disney Comics Mailing List.
http://stp.ling.uu.se/~starback/dcml/chars/donald.html

[ʌ]

[ə]
banana

Sample: **THE PRICE OF BANANAS WENT DOWN AGAIN.**

Spellings: **a, e, i, o, u,** plus virtually any vowel combination, in unstressed syllables.

Description

[ə] is a low, mid-central, unstressed vowel. It does not occur in any stressed syllables or in stressed single-syllable words.

Production: [ə]

1. [ə] is produced in the same way as [ʌ]. The only difference is in stress (loudness). Open your mouth to a position about the same as for [ɔ]. Rest your tongue in the bottom of your mouth.
2. Produce voice, but not as loud as for [ʌ] or as long.

[ə] is the vowel we use more than any other in our language. That's because the *other vowels tend to change from their original form to* [ə] *when they are unstressed.* This vowel actually can't be pronounced alone, since it only occurs in unstressed positions, so you may be confused as to what its sound is. For now, let's say that *it sounds just like* [ʌ], *but weaker.* As a matter of fact, the name of this vowel, schwa, is from the German word for "weak."

Here are some words that may explain this. Say the word *above.* It has the stress on the second syllable, so the vowels are [ə] and [ʌ]: [əbʌv]. Say the word a few times to get the feeling of the first sound. Make sure to say the word normally, with the first sound so weak that it's almost not there. Now say *above* with equal stress on both syllables, as you would in a word such as *Ping-Pong.* Sounds strange, doesn't it. When you said *above* that way, you used the vowel [ʌ] twice. Here's another example: the word *the* can be said in two ways. Try these phrases: *the beginning, the end.* Say them a couple of times. You should hear a difference: in phrases in which *the* comes before a consonant sound, we say [ə]; in phrases in which *the* comes before a vowel sound, we say [i]. You have to listen to the stress to decide which vowel was used.

[ə]

In summary, [ə] is produced in the same way and sounds just like [ʌ], only it is weaker. You use [ə] when other vowels change because they are in unstressed syllables.

[ə] **Level 1**

PROBLEMS

The difficulties with [ə] are really not production difficulties. They are basically difficulties caused by confusing [ʌ] and [ə], omission of [ə], and addition of [ə] in the word *athlete.* Here's a contrast drill to help you distinguish between [ə] and [ʌ].

Contrast Drill for [ə] *and* [ʌ]

Say the following words and phrases slowly. Each word or phrase contains both the [ə] (marked _) and the [ʌ] (marked ‾).

abōve	come ūp	sūn up	abrūpt
cūt up	cut ūp	stuck ūp	būttercup
seven ūp	amōng	hūndred	undōne

 ## *Level 1 Practice Words for* [ə]

The words in the following lists all contain the vowel [ə]. Because you can spell [ə] so many ways, and the same letter can be pronounced differently in the same word, we've underlined the letters that are to be pronounced [ə]. Say the words slowly and carefully, but make sure to use the conventional stress pattern. Check with your instructor or a classmate if you're not sure.

Beginning	*End*	*Middle*
about	soda	lion
around	Canada	banana
another	sofa	connect
again	tuba	official
agree	vanilla	option
away	Carolina	elephant

[ə]

[ə] **Level 2**

Level 2 Practice Words for [ə]

Here are more words containing [ə]. This time, though, there's no underlining. Check with your instructor if you're not sure of pronunciation.

Beginning	*End*	*Middle*	*All Positions*
afraid	Roberta	dictionary	apology
amend	area	university	astronomical
aloud	camera	parade	biological
asleep	arena	possible	electrical
across	visa	zoology	culpability
appreciate	panda	professor	agenda

Level 2 Practice Sentences for [ə]

Since you can spell [ə] with any vowel, you may have to double-check the pronunciation of some of the new words in these sentences.

1. Look it up in the dictionary.
2. Did you bring your camera to the parade?
3. Roberta was afraid she would fall asleep in class.
4. I was in that professor's class last semester.
5. I understand that rain is possible later in the day.
6. He walked across the restricted area.
7. I learned about the giant panda in zoology.
8. The elephant charged around the arena.
9. He was an undercover agent.
10. They couldn't agree on an official solution.

Challenge Materials for [ə]

Banana and Peanut Butter Sandwich
   Preparation: Spread creamed butter on half the slices of bread and peanut butter on the others. On each of the latter slices place a leaf of crisp lettuce, or shredded lettuce, and cover with sliced bananas. Spread with mayonnaise, add a dash of salt, and put sandwiches together.
   Yield: single serving per banana

United Fruit Company, *The New Banana*

[ə]

[ɝ]
early

Sample: **THE EARLY TURTLE IS THE FIRST ONE IN THE HERD.**

Spellings: **er** as in **herd**   **ur** as in **turtle**
            ear as in **early**   **ir** as in **first**
            our as in **journey**   **or** as in **world**
            yr as in **myrtle**   **olo** as in **colonel**
            yrrh as in **myrrh**

Description

[ɝ] is a mid, central, stressed vowel that occurs only in stressed words and syllables. It has an [r] sound to it, but it is different from the consonant in that it is longer and can form a syllable on its own.

The amount of [r] varies in different areas of the country. Less [r] is used in large areas of the South, East, and Northeast. That pronunciation can be transcribed with another symbol, [ɜ]. We won't use that symbol because we don't think it's important to distinguish between the [ɝ] and [ɜ] symbols, except in the New England dialect.

Production: [ɝ]

1. Open your mouth to the position to say [ɔ], about halfway. Don't round your lips.
2. Raise the middle section of the tongue slightly, and *curl the tip back* until it's pointing to the palate just behind the upper gum ridge. Produce voice. Make sure there's no nasality.

[ɝ] Level 1

PROBLEM: SUBSTITUTION OF [ɔɪ] FOR [ɝ]

There is a nonstandard pronunciation that occurs mostly in the east when [ɔɪ] is substituted for [ɝ]. In this substitution, the word *bird* would become something like *boid* because of the addition of the [ɪ] after the [ɝ]. This pronunciation is considered nonstandard in New York City and the Northeast, but is standard in New Orleans and other areas along the Gulf of Mexico.

[ɝ]

Here's a contrast drill to help you distinguish [ɔɪ] and [ɝ]. Read each pair of words slowly and carefully, listening for a distinct difference in each word. You can use either [ɝ] or [ɜ] in the second word.

[ɔɪ]	[ɝ]	[ɔɪ]	[ɝ]
boil — burl		foist — first	
foil — furl		oil — earl	
loin — learn		boy — burr	

This substitution is used by only a small number of speakers, so we suggest you check with your instructor or see page 250 for more help.

Practice Words for [ɝ]

Say the words in the following lists slowly and carefully, but don't overdo it. Determine the amount of [r] used in your area by checking with your instructor or some other person knowledgeable about your regional dialect.

Beginning	*Beginning*	*Middle*	*Middle*
early	earnest	first	turtle
earn	urn	nervous	word
irk	urban	attorney	burn
earth	urgent	learn	girl
urge	herb	curve	whirl

Level 1 Practice Sentences for [ɝ]

1. They <u>turned</u> when they <u>heard</u> the <u>first</u> <u>words</u>.
2. She <u>learned</u> why the map of the <u>world</u> was <u>curved</u>.
3. The <u>attorney</u> <u>nervously</u> awaited the <u>urgent</u> message.
4. <u>Certain</u> <u>words</u> can <u>hurt</u>.
5. <u>Herbs</u> are grown in many <u>urban</u> gardens.
6. He was so earnest, he began to irk me.
7. I worked hard to read the words on the Grecian urn.
8. Where on earth did you get that turtle?
9. He burned his early travel journals.
10. Let's give it a whirl.

Challenge Sentences for [ɝ]

1. Her version of the third verse was truly absurd.
2. The bird chirped nervously, reversing an early worm.
3. Herbert observed the curved urn and preferred to earn it.
4. The surly gardener was irked as he turned over the moist earth.
5. Ferdinand was an attorney who heard the good word about Robert Burns.
6. Bernard learned about the curvature of the earth by observing early birds searching for late worms.

[ɝ]

7. Burglar alarms disturb people in both urban areas and the suburbs.
8. Irma's purse was filled with lists of words she learned for her merchandising midterm.
9. Richard Burton rehearsed in earnest, although he was always nervous at first.
10. Whereas the attorney urged the jury to be merciful, it's not certain they heard.

Challenge Materials for [ɝ] *and* [ɚ]

1. Touch the earth, love the earth, honor the earth, her plains, her valleys, her hills, and her seas; rest your spirit in her solitary places.

Henry Beston, "Orion Rises on the Dunes," *The Outermost House*

2. When we're struggling for words, we often believe that somewhere there exists "the perfect word." Actually, there's no such thing as the perfect word. Rather than worrying about striving for perfection, the practical question for us to ask is, "Which word communicates the best?"

All of us have our favorite words based on our personal taste. And taste in words is about as predictable as taste in ice cream. We also select our words on the basis of experience. Our choice is influenced by the words we heard and used at the dinner table while growing up, the words our community uses, the words that are popular in our region of the country, and the words that are well respected in our business environment.

Sherry Sweetnam, *The Executive Memo*

3. The Parts of a Search Engine

Search engines have three major elements. First is the spider, also called the crawler. The spider visits a web page, reads it, and then follows links to other pages within the site. This is what it means when someone refers to a site being "spidered" or "crawled." The spider returns to the site on a regular basis, such as every month or two, to look for changes.

Everything the spider finds goes into the second part of a search engine, the index. The index, sometimes called the catalog, is like a giant book containing a copy of every web page that the spider finds. If a web page changes, then this book is updated new information.

Sometimes it can take a while for new pages or changes that the spider finds to be added to the index. Thus, a web page may have been "spidered" but not yet "indexed." Until it is indexed—added to the index—it is not available to those searching with the search engine.

Search engine software is the third part of a search engine. This is the program that sifts through the millions of pages recorded in the index to find matches to a search and rank them in order of what it believes is most relevant. You can learn more about how search engine software ranks web pages on the aptly-named How Search Engines Rank Web Pages page.

[ɝ]

Danny Sullivan, *Search Engine Watch*, http://searchenginewatch.com/

[ɚ]
father

Sample: **HER FATHER'S LETTER GAVE THE GOVERNOR
             PLEASURE.**

Spellings: **Any vowel and r combination.**

Description

[ɚ] is a mid-central, unstressed vowel with an [r] quality. In large areas
of the south, east, and northeast, the pronunciation is optional, with the
[ə] being used instead. [ɚ] *is used only in unstressed syllables and words.*
It is a shorter, unstressed version of [ɝ] and may be contrasted with it
in the word *murmur* [mɝmɚ].

Production: [ɚ]

1. [ɚ] is produced in the same way as [ɝ]. The only difference
   is in stress (loudness). Open your mouth to the position to
   say [ɔ], about halfway. Don't round your lips.
2. Curl the tongue tip back until it points just behind the
   upper gum ridge and raise the center. Produce voice, but
   not as loud or as long as for [ɝ].

Diphthongs

[ɚ] is an element in five diphthongs: [ɪɚ] as in *near* (page 221), [ɛɚ] as in
air (page 228), [ɑɚ] as in *car* (page 235), [ʊɚ] as in *tour* (page 253), and
[ɔɚ] as in *floor* (page 247). The use of these diphthongs varies regionally,
as does the vowel [ɚ]. We've included explanations and drills for each minor diphthong in the appropriate section for each vowel.

[ɚ] Level 1

[ɚ] is a relatively simple sound to produce. One problem may be that of
the "optional" pronunciation. That could occur should you relocate to an
area of the country where [ɚ] isn't optional from an area where it is. In
that case, you may want to consider pronouncing the [ɚ].

    Only level 1 drills are given for [ɚ].

[ɚ]

Practice Words for [ɚ]

Say the words in the following lists slowly. Although all the drills for [ɚ] are on level 1, you may have some difficulty deciding when to use [ɚ] and [ɝ]. When both sounds occur in a word or a sentence, we've marked [ɚ] with __. Ask your instructor about the optional pronunciation of [ə] in your area. Remember, [ɚ] is unstressed.

End	*End*	*Middle*	*Middle*
father	dollar	eastern	western
wonder	after	perhaps	cover
bother	caller	answered	sisterly
actor	sailor	modern	government
matter	tire	sisterhood	b<u>er</u>serk
buyer	tar	anchorman	counterfeit
burg<u>er</u>	tur<u>ner</u>	summertime	interstate
earn<u>er</u>	runner	lumberyard	letterhead

 ## Practice Sentences for [ɚ]

1. A <u>burger</u> and fries cost a <u>dollar</u>.
2. I'd <u>rather</u> <u>surrender</u> first.
3. <u>Are</u> those <u>American</u> <u>sailors</u>?
4. That <u>actor</u> looks like a TV <u>anchorman</u>.
5. The <u>tire</u> goes on the <u>eastern</u> end of the street.
6. Answer the other caller first.
7. My sister ordered a western omelet.
8. Something's bothering my father.
9. Perhaps you'd like more modern furniture?
10. They caught the counterfeiters on Interstate 95.

Challenge Materials for [ɚ]

1. Culture affects our communication in various ways. It provides us with patterned ways of dealing with information in our environment. It determines what we perceive, how we interpret, and how we respond to messages both verbally and nonverbally. Culture shapes and colors our image of reality and conditions the way we think.

[ɚ]

Our communication patterns are often subtle, elusive, and unconscious. It is difficult for even well-informed members of a culture to explain why, in their own culture, the custom is thus-and-so rather than so-and-thus. For example, it would probably be hard for one to explain the "rule" governing the precise time in a relationship when the other person becomes a friend. One simply "feels right." Fortunately, members of the same culture share a great number of such taken-for-granted assumptions about interpersonal relationships and the corresponding "appropriate" behavior.

William B. Gudykunst and Young Yun Kim, *Communicating with Strangers:*
An Approach to Intercultural Communication

2. People often say that hard times build character. I think sometimes they're just hard times, and when they're over we move on in the best way we can. There'll still be dreams for us, albeit with less expectations of grandeur. And there's a peace in knowing that if those dreams don't come true there will always be new ones to take their place.

Jayne Gilbert, "The Family Car: A Metaphor for Life?"
Newsweek, July 31, 2000

part three

voice

Voice *and* diction. You can't separate the two. Think about it; you can't get along with just one. Imagine trying to make yourself understood speaking without consonants and vowels. And what about voice? You could whisper, but most people wouldn't be able to hear you.

Your voice carries a great deal of meaning not only about what you say, but about *you.* Yet most of us don't' know very much about voice. As a matter of fact, a great many people have no idea that the voice they hear in their heads isn't the voice that other people hear; they have no idea what their own voices sound like.

Part III is devoted to improving vocal skills, so you'll learn a great deal about your own voice and how you use it. In Chapter 10 you'll learn about voice production: how you control loudness, pitch, and quality. In Chapter 11 you'll learn the factors of vocal expressiveness and you'll get a chance to put them into practice.

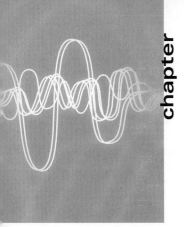

chapter

10

voice production

Objectives

After reading this chapter, and practicing the drills and exercises presented, you should be able to:

- Show understanding of the principles and procedures by which we produce and modulate voice
- Identify your own vocal tendencies, and distinguish between those that enhance your communication and those that may interfere with it
- Demonstrate the techniques that are helpful in overcoming phonatory problems
- Produce, in class, voice that is free from attributes which interfere with communication and which, in the judgment of the instructor, may result in physical abuse to the vocal mechanism
- Speak, in class, with sufficient vocal flexibility and variety to meet the needs of most speaking situations

Guide to Voice Production Exercises

Who taught you how to produce and use your voice? Not just one person, surely, and you probably did not learn in any kind of formal setting. Most of us learn how to use our voices simply by using them. We don't think about voice, we *do* it. Sometimes, though, we don't do it in efficient ways. This can result in voices that may cause physical discomfort, such as a sore throat after loud talking, or voices that others find unusual, unpleasant, or hard to hear.

It's our purpose in this chapter to present the basics of voice production: breathing for speech, loudness, pitch, and quality. By the end of the chapter you should know considerably more about your own voice: how you produce it and how you use it. And, if your voice is one that is not loud enough to hear or one that calls undue attention to itself, you'll have plenty of exercises to work on. These exercises are listed in Table 10-1, which you can use as a reference after you have completed the work in the chapter.

If you haven't read Chapter 3, we suggest that you do so before you go on with this chapter. In fact, even if you have read it, a review wouldn't hurt. Chapter 3 explains the structures we use for voice production and how we physically make the sound of voice. You should be familiar with that material before you read this chapter.

Table 10-1
Voice Improvement Exercises

Exercise	Page	Breath control	Loudness	Pitch	Tense quality	Strident quality	Metallic quality	Hoarse quality	Nasal quality	Hard glottal quality
1. Abdominal breathing	280	■	■		■			■		■
2. Breath control—duration	281	■	■	■						■
3. Breath control—breathiness	282	■	■							■
4. Loudness—force	284	■	■							
5. Loudness—projection	285		■						■	
6. Loudness—control	286		■						■	
7. Loudness—practice	287		■						■	
8. Habitual pitch	289			■	■	■	■	■		■
9. Relaxation—progressive	291	■			■	■	■	■		■
10. Relaxation—fantasy	291	■			■	■	■	■		■
11. Relaxation—head rolling	292	■			■	■	■	■		■
12. Relaxation—sighing	292	■	■		■	■	■	■		■
13. Relaxation—yawning	293				■	■	■	■		■
14. Nasality—ear training	295								■	
15. Nasality—pulling	297								■	
16. Nasality—pushing	297								■	
17. Denasality	298								■	
18. Vocal fry	299			■	■					
19. Hard glottal attack	301				■	■		■		■

Breathing

As we explained in Chapter 3, the breath stream is the powerhouse of voice production. It's difficult to produce effective voice if you don't breathe efficiently; you'll put a strain on the entire vocal mechanism. If you're like most people, you probably don't have any real problems with breathing for speech, but don't stop reading here. If you want to be a more effective oral communicator, you can benefit from an understanding of the hows and whys of breathing for speech.

Breathing for Speech

You breathe differently when you're breathing for speech than you do when you're breathing for purely biological purposes. The difference is not in how much air you take in; you don't have to breathe more deeply for speech. The difference is in how you control your exhalations. In rest breathing, the time taken for inhalation and exhalation is usually about the same. In speech breathing, you take a quick breath in, then gradually let the air out, pacing the exhalation so that it lasts long enough for what you want to say. If you don't control the exhalation efficiently, you may run out of breath, sound strained or breathy, or not be loud enough. So the major difference between speech breathing and biological breathing is breath control.

Breath Control

You control your rate of exhalation in a couple of fairly simple ways. One form of control is by far the most important—the way you use your abdominal muscles. You could almost consider your abdominal muscles to be the pump that pushes air out of your respiratory system. And, just like a bicycle pump, the harder you push, the faster the air moves. In breathing for speech, the major part of breath control consists of contracting the abdominal muscles, but just the right amount for the level of loudness you want for the sounds you are making. The other form of control is in the use of the vocal folds; here's where they can function as a valve during phonation to help control the rate of air flow.

Not everyone uses the muscles of respiration in exactly the same way, and not everyone uses the abdominal muscles to the same degree in breath control. Most voice and speech experts, however, advocate "abdominal breathing" as the most desirable breathing pattern. What if you're not an abdominal breather—should you change your breathing pattern? Before you answer, ask the following questions about your breathing pattern: *Can you breathe comfortably? Can you breathe unobtrusively? Does your breathing pattern allow you to speak effectively? If you (or a qualified evaluator) answered no to any of these questions, you should attempt to learn the abdominal (also called central and diaphragmatic) style of breathing. We think it's the most efficient style—the most air for the least work—and the most effective for producing and sustaining loud, clear tones.*

WHAT'S YOUR BREATHING TYPE?

How do *you* breathe? Are you an abdominal breather, or are you using clavicular or thoracic breathing? This activity will help you find out.

1. Find a partner with whom you can do this activity. Stand and face your partner at a comfortable distance. If either of you is wearing loose-fitting clothing, try to hold it closer to your body—you need to be able to see the shoulder, chest, mid-central, and diaphragmatic areas.
2. Begin by having a conversation with your partner about some pleasant, unemotional topic. Try to relax. When you start, you'll probably be very conscious of your breathing. Thinking about it may cause you to breathe in a way that's not your normal pattern.
3. Observe your partner's breathing pattern by looking to see which area of the body moves during inhalation for speech. Continue your observation for two to three minutes to make sure the pattern is consistent.
4. Identify the noticeable areas of movement. If the shoulders are showing the most movement (lifting), what you are seeing indicates *clavicular* breathing. If the greatest movement is in the chest area, you are seeing *thoracic* breathing. When the expansion is near the sternum (breast bone), it indicates *mid-central* breathing. If the expansion is mostly at the abdomen, you are seeing *abdominal* breathing.
5. Now switch partners.
6. If you have difficulty identifying your breathing type, ask your instructor for help.

EXERCISE 1.   *Abdominal Breathing*

The following exercise provides a relaxing way to practice abdominal breathing. Try it, even if you are already an abdominal breather; everyone can benefit from a "refresher course."

1. Lie on your back on a comfortable but firm surface.
2. Make sure your knees are supported in a slightly flexed position; your arms should be by your side, with your elbows slightly bent.
3. Place a moderately heavy weight (a book two or three times heavier than this one, for example) on your abdomen near the navel.

4. Begin breathing in and out, through your mouth, so that you push the book up when you breathe in; the book should sink down as you breathe out.

5. Keep one hand on your chest, about three inches below your neck, to make sure you are keeping chest movement to a minimum.

6. Once you are able to move your abdomen in coordination with your breathing in and out, remove the book and put your hand in its place. Continue to move your abdomen up when you inhale and down when you exhale.

7. When you feel you have abdominal breathing under control while lying down, move to a comfortable sitting position. Continue the exercise, keeping one hand on your chest and the other on your abdomen.

8. Take a deep breath with the new breathing pattern. Exhale slowly, sighing the vowel *ahh* with each exhalation. Sustain the vowel for five seconds.

9. Take a deep breath. Exhale slowly, counting from 1 to 5, holding each number for one full second.

10. Take a deep breath, abdominally. Exhale slowly, naming the days of the week at a rate of one per second.

11. Repeat steps 8 through 10 while standing.

Learning to use abdominal breathing comes somewhat slowly. It's important to practice at least once a day for about a week until the process becomes automatic.

EXERCISE 2.   *Breath Control—Duration*

This exercise is designed to help you develop improved breath control while speaking. It will also help to increase the depth of your breathing.

1. Take three normal rest breaths. Make a mental note as to how much air is going in and out.

2. Take a normal breath in and, as you let the air out, count to 3, holding each number for one second. Do it almost like singing. Make sure to hold each number for one full second and not pause between numbers.

3. Repeat step 2, but this time continue counting until you begin to run out of breath. Do it again, stopping at the same point.

4. Now take a deep breath and count again until you begin to run out of breath; you've counted as high as you can. Repeat this twice, then stop the exercise for a while.

5. Allow at least 15 minutes after step 4 and start the whole procedure again.

6. Take a deep breath, then say the names of the days of the week, one word per breath. Then do the same saying, first, two words per breath, then three words per breath.

7. Say each of the following phrases on one abdominal breath:
   a. Going home
   b. New moon
   c. Low down
   d. Hard heart
   e. Look sharp

8. Using abdominal breathing, say each of the following phrases using only one breath:
   a. Look at me
   b. Time for lunch
   c. Make my day
   d. Practice makes perfect
   e. Haste makes waste

9. The following exercise will also help you improve your breath control. Using abdominal breathing, say each of the following sentences in one breath. Even though each time you add an item to the sentence it will become longer and longer, continue to say each sentence in one breath. We've started you off with five items to buy at the "store," and you can add more on your own until you reach the maximum number you can do comfortably in one breath. Take a deep breath and say.
   - I went to the store.
   - I went to the store and bought some eggs.
   - I went to the store and bought some eggs and milk.
   - I went to the store and bought some eggs, milk, and cheese.
   - I went to the store and bought some eggs, milk, cheese, and juice.
   - I went to the store and bought some eggs, milk, cheese, juice, and popcorn.
   - I went to the store and bought some eggs, milk, cheese, juice, popcorn, and . . .

The object of these exercises is to gradually increase the length of the phrases you can say until you reach your maximum. Don't push until you feel uncomfortable, and don't do too much deep breathing all at once; you might get dizzy. Try this drill every day, and you'll soon have more efficient breath control.

EXERCISE 3.   *Breath Control—Breathiness*

Sometimes, people tend to waste so much air that their voices take on a noticeably breathy quality. This breathiness can be deliberate (trying to sound sexy, perhaps) or simply the result of poor breath control owing to failure to bring the vocal folds together. In any case, a breathy voice is usually hard to hear, may call considerable attention to itself, and may distract the listener from the speaker's message. You'll need a small hand mirror for this exercise. Make sure it's clean and cold enough so that your breath will condense on the surface.

1. Hold the mirror about an inch away from your mouth. Say *ahh.* Quickly take the mirror away from your mouth and look at it. Check for fogging. Repeat this procedure, and try to see the pattern of fogging on the glass.
2. Hold the mirror in front of your mouth again. Say *ahh* more loudly. Check what's happened to the fogging on the glass. Repeat, and try to reduce the fogging when you say *ahh.*
3. Try the same drill with the other vowels. First, see how much condensation occurs when you say the vowel the way you usually do. Then try to reduce the area of glass that gets covered.
4. Compare the breathy and nonbreathy production. Visually, the breathy production will have a large area of condensation. The nonbreathy production will result in a small area. You should also begin to *hear* the difference.
5. Now go back and do steps 6, 7, and 8 in exercise 2 again. Make sure to use the nonbreathy voice. (You can monitor your breath flow by placing your fingers about an inch in front of your mouth as you speak.) You will notice a change in the number of words you can comfortably speak on one inhalation.

Loudness

The loudness of your voice says a lot about you. We tend to think of people with weak or soft voices as being shy and timid, perhaps afraid to speak up because they're so unsure of themselves. On the other hand, people with loud, booming voices may be thought of as overbearing, over-confident, and boorish. When a person speaks too loudly, we often pull back—both physically and mentally.

To many people, the person who doesn't talk loudly enough to be easily heard is the more annoying. It's frustrating to continually ask a person to speak up or, even worse, to miss much of what that person says.

Loudness problems are usually caused by a person's *inability to produce and sustain* the proper loudness or *failure to monitor* his or her own voice. The result is loudness that is inappropriate for the listeners and the environment as well as for the content of the communication. Chapter 11 discusses monitoring your loudness level to produce a voice that fits the content, listeners, and environment. But before you can do those exercises, you must be able to produce a tone of adequate loudness. Let's work on that now.

Controlling Loudness

Have you ever gone to an exciting sporting event such as a hockey match or football game or soccer game? Remember how much you enjoyed yourself? Until the next day, that is, when your throat was so sore you could hardly talk. That sore throat may have lasted for a couple of days or longer. Your sore throat and loss of voice were probably the result of the way you were trying to produce a loud voice.

A loud voice does *not* require a lot of muscular action by the vocal folds and larynx (though that is what hurts). The force behind a loud voice should be supplied primarily by the abdominal muscles.

The vocal folds are set into vibration by the air you force out of the lungs. So, to increase the strength of their vibrations, you must increase the force behind the breath stream. You do that by contracting the abdominal muscles.

Try this: Place one hand flat against your abdomen just below your breastbone. Say *ahh* and hold it. While you're saying *ahh,* hit the back of your hand with your other fist (not too hard, though). You should have heard a sudden increase in loudness. Now try this: Place both hands on your abdomen. At the rate of one number per second, count to 4. Start quietly but make each number louder. You should feel your abdominal muscles contract suddenly for each number.

The following exercises should help you develop the proper support for a loud voice. In some exercises, you'll see certain words or syllables printed in type that increases or decreases in size. Those changes provide a visual guide to help you change loudness levels, much in the same way as sheet music shows you a tune. Here's how the system works.

THIS IS NORMAL LOUDNESS.

THIS IS VERY LOUD.

This is soft.

Your voice should grow louder as the words increase in size, and softer as the words become smaller. Use your loudest voice for the largest words.

EXERCISE 4.   *Loudness—Force*

This exercise is designed to help you increase the force with which your breath stream pushes the vocal folds apart during phonation. Practice abdominal breathing for about five minutes before you do this exercise for the first time.

1. Hold a piece of paper, about the size of this page, lengthwise just under your lower lip. Hold it by the corners closest to you, with the edge of the paper touching your skin.
2. Blow across the surface of the paper and try to make the paper rise to a horizontal position. Do this five times, feeling for contraction of your abdominal muscles as you blow.
3. Now use a slightly larger piece of paper. Make the paper rise five times.
4. Repeat step 3 a few times every hour for two or three days. You'll find that it will probably take less effort each day to make the paper rise.
5. Now try saying each of the following phrases and sentences using a very loud voice. Don't strain; use breath energy.

   a. ***HELLO, THERE.***
   b. ***SIT STILL.***
   c. ***CLIMB DOWN.***
   d. ***SPEAK LOUDER.***
   e. ***HAVE HOPE.***
   f. ***GO AWAY.***
   g. ***I WANT MY ICE CREAM.***
   h. ***TAKE THAT THING AWAY.***
   i. ***DON'T START ANYTHING WITH ME.***
   j. ***THAT BOOK IS TERRIBLE.***
   k. ***HAVE A NICE DAY.***

EXERCISE 5.   *Loudness—Projection*

This exercise should generate some of the same physical feelings as the previous exercise for force, but this time you'll actually be speaking.

1. Have another person stand facing you, about 5 feet away. His or her right hand should be at shoulder height, slightly cupped, and facing you.
2. From your position, count to 5. *Try to speak into the other person's hand.* Yes, you may feel a little silly, but do it anyway. Project your voice, throw it or whatever else you may call it, but speak into the other person's hand.
3. Have the other person take one step backward, and repeat step 2. Continue the procedure until the other person is about 40 feet away from you.

4. Now have the other person walk back, one step at a time, reversing the procedure.

5. Now read the following phrases and sentences aloud, again placing them in the other person's hand as he or she moves closer and farther away.

   a. Hello, there. HELLO, THERE. ***HELLO, THERE.***

   b. Ship ahoy. SHIP AHOY. ***SHIP AHOY.***

   c. The other way. THE OTHER WAY. ***THE OTHER WAY.***

   d. Watch out. WATCH OUT. ***WATCH OUT.***

   e. On a roll. ON A ROLL. ***ON A ROLL.***

   f. I like my new car. I LIKE MY NEW CAR. ***I LIKE MY NEW CAR.***

   g. Color my hair purple. COLOR MY HAIR PURPLE. ***COLOR MY HAIR PURPLE.***

   h. I don't have a favorite book. I DON'T HAVE A FAVORITE BOOK. ***I DON'T HAVE A FAVORITE BOOK.***

   i. Where are the snows of yesteryear? WHERE ARE THE SNOWS OF YESTERYEAR? ***WHERE ARE THE SNOWS OF YESTERYEAR?***

   j. Hold the low tone as long as you can. HOLD THE LOW TONE AS LONG AS YOU CAN. ***HOLD THE LOW TONE AS LONG AS YOU CAN.***

EXERCISE 6.   *Loudness—Control*

You don't need anyone to help you with this one. We do suggest, though, that you find a place where you won't bother other people. Again, feel for abdominal muscle contractions.

1. Pick a series of items: numbers, months, letters, and so forth. (Here we'll use numbers to describe the exercise.)

2. Count to 5; start with low intensity, and increase intensity with each number. Take a breath between each number and the next. Repeat this twice.

3. Count backward, starting from 5. *Start with high intensity and gradually decease intensity.* Again, take a breath between productions. Repeat twice.

4. On one breath, count to 5. This time you should be loudest at *3*. In other words, gradually increase loudness until you reach *3*, then decrease. Do the entire exercise once a day.

5. Read the following sentences aloud. Start each in a very soft voice, gradually becoming louder until you reach the end.

   a. I'm GOING **HOME.**

   b. Look AT THE **TIME.**

   c. He's A GOOD **MAN.**

   d. What ARE YOU **DOING?**

   e. Where IS MY **HAT?**

6. Read the following sentences aloud. Begin each sentence softly, and gradually increase the loudness level until you reach the middle of the sentence. Then, decrease the loudness until you reach the end. This may be a bit difficult at first, but stick with it. It will become easier as you go along.

   a. You can COME WITH ME **OR STAY HOME** alone.

   b. I tried MY HARDEST, **AND I** FINISHED the puzzle.

   c. My soup IS TOO **HOT;** I'LL DRINK IT FROM the saucer.

   d. When you GET TO **THE TOP,** LOOK AROUND and ski down.

   e. My professor IS **LAZY,** HE MAKES US WORK on our own.

EXERCISE 7.   *Loudness—Practice*

Read aloud using whatever materials you would like, but we especially recommend the Letters to the Editor in your local or school newspaper. The late comedian Steve Allen included this as a regular feature of his late-night TV show. He would read angry letters to the editor in a loud, angry voice. As he made the writers' points for them, the audience would cheer or otherwise show approval. Try this yourself. Ask a friend to sit across the room while you read angry letters to him or her. Make sure your voice is adequately loud and that you *project* your voice to your friend.

Pitch

The pitch of your voice—its highness or lowness—is another variable of speech that says a lot about you. As a rule, we apply certain stereotypes to our expectations of what a person's voice should sound like. For example, we have learned to expect that women will generally have higher voices than men. We also expect that there will be an inverse ratio between a person's size and the pitch of his or her voice. In other words, the larger the person, the more low-pitched you expect that person's voice to be. These are just a few examples of common vocal stereotypes and, yes, many times our expectations are incorrect. Were you ever surprised to discover that someone you had only heard speaking over the phone, but had never seen in person, looked quite different from what you had expected?

We all probably know someone who attempts to influence the impression he or she makes on others by speaking in a voice that's too low- or high-pitched to use comfortably for a long time. By doing so, though, the person puts a strain on the vocal mechanism and also restricts the voice to a narrow pitch range. The vocal mechanism is strained because the person is using his or her vocal folds to produce a pitch they weren't designed to produce for long periods of time.

In Chapter 3 we discussed the factors that determine the frequency of vibration of your vocal folds and the pitch of your voice. You may recall that the main factors in determining the pitch of your voice are the length of your vocal folds and the size of your resonating cavities. The pitch that your vocal folds and resonating cavities are naturally suited to produce is called your *optimum pitch,* and you produce it with less effort than other pitches. The pitch you use all the time is called your *habitual pitch.* It is best, for the vocal mechanism, if your habitual pitch is the same as your optimum, because using a habitual pitch that's far from your optimum can result in voice problems. Put it this way: you don't ask a trumpet to do a tuba's job.

Try the following procedure. You can use it to determine your optimum pitch.

Determining Optimum Pitch

For this procedure, you need another person and a piano, electronic keyboard, or other musical instrument capable of playing a musical scale. Don't worry: neither one of you needs to be a musician. The other person is there to help you confirm your judgments.

1. Pick a voice pitch near the middle of your range. Determine the corresponding note on the musical instrument. You do this simply

by playing different notes until you decide you've matched the pitch of your voice.

2. Chant *ah* down the scale to the lowest possible pitch your voice can reach. Locate that pitch on the musical instrument. For chanting, which is really a combination of talking and singing, you can use *do, re, me,* and so on or *me, me, me* or any vowel you like.

3. Now chant up the scale to the highest pitch your voice can reach. Locate that pitch on the piano.

4. Count the number of notes in the range, from the lowest to the highest pitch. Include both the highest and lowest pitches and count both black and white keys.

5. Divide the number of notes by 4. Count this number of keys up from the lowest pitch. This should be at (or no more than one key above or below) your optimum pitch.

6. Try phonating at all three of those pitches (one above, optimum, and one below) to determine which is the most comfortable for you. The spread between the lowest and highest notes you can reach is your *pitch range.*

Determining Habitual Pitch

Now that you know your optimum pitch, you should see if your habitual and optimum pitches are the same. You'll need the piano and a listener.

Read the following passage aloud, at a normal conversational loudness level. Read it three or four times, each time making it more monotonous and more like machine talk. Ask your listener to find the note on the piano that's closest to the average pitch of your reading. Here's the passage. It's from a booklet published by the Environmental Protection Agency.

The decibel is the most commonly used unit to measure sound intensity at its source. The decibel level starts at 0, the hearing threshold, and goes to 180, the level heard when a rocket is launched. Brief exposure to levels over 140 decibels, however, causes pain and can rupture eardrums, resulting in permanent hearing loss. But one can suffer hearing loss or impairment at much lower levels. According to some scientific opinion, continuous exposure for 8 hours to noise levels of approximately 85 decibels can also cause permanent hearing loss.

Compare your habitual pitch with your optimum pitch. Are they just about the same? If they're more than two tones away from each other, you should work on changing your habitual pitch.

Changing Habitual Pitch

Changing your habitual pitch to coincide with your optimum pitch is not very complicated. It requires nothing more than ample practice speaking at your optimum pitch, using some form of reference point when you start and listening periodically to make sure you haven't strayed off target. For example, when you have determined your optimum pitch you might tape record yourself saying a few phrases at that pitch. Or you might record the sound of a musical instrument playing a note at that pitch. Listen to that tape recording and immediately practice saying some phrases or sentences at the pitch that you hear. *Caution:* If you use a tape recorder for this purpose, be sure to use one that plugs into an AC wall socket; a battery-operated recorder may play back at a different speed from that at which it recorded. This could make the pitch vary from your optimum pitch.

For practice, we suggest that you start with the following drill materials. Then you may go on to use any of the selections in Chapter 11 or other readings from literature, magazines, and so forth. You may want to check your pitch regularly against the standard you are using for your optimum pitch, be it a tape recording, musical instrument, or other sound source. Read your selections aloud at conversational loudness. For best results, and to avoid vocal fatigue, practice twice a day, in the morning and evening. Limit yourself to two readings at each session. Continue your practice session every day until you are satisfied that your optimum and habitual pitch levels are the same.

EXERCISE 8.   *Changing Habitual Pitch*

Say the following sentences three times each at your optimum pitch. Try not to vary the pitch as you go through each one.

1. Give me a light.
2. Sing us a song.
3. Pick up your litter.
4. Lend him a pencil.
5. Let's take a break.
6. I like to pick flowers in the field.
7. Hand her gloves to her before you go out.
8. Learning the decimal system can be very exciting.
9. The sum of two numbers added together will always be the same regardless of the order in which they are added.
10. Persistence is essential to successful achievement.

Extending Pitch Range

Often we use only a small number of the notes available from the total pitch range. We tend to stay more or less in one general location on the scale; and when we do move away from that place, we tend to go up rather than down.

RELAXATION

Relaxation is one good way to extend your pitch range. Ever notice that your voice seems lower in the morning after a good night's sleep? That's because you, and your vocal folds, had a chance to relax. Before you deliberately try speaking at a lower pitch, you should be relaxed. Try the relaxation exercises below. They'll make a difference.

EXERCISE 9.   *Progressive Relaxation*

The purpose of this exercise is to reduce tension. You can do this alone, but it's better if someone reads the directions to you, slowly and in a gentle, soothing voice.

1. Sit with your back touching the back support of your chair. Cross your legs at the ankles. Hold your hands out in front of you at chest level. Shake them energetically for about 5 seconds, then let them fall loosely into your lap. Keep them there.
2. Do the following exercise *in your mind only,* without moving any parts of your body. Concentrate on the toes of your left foot. Let the muscles go loose. Then the sole of your foot, then the ankle. Now loosen the muscles of your right foot. When your feet have no tension left in them, move on. First to your lower legs, knees, thighs, then buttocks, back, spine, moving very slowly. Then go on to your stomach, chest, shoulders, arms, hands, and fingers, then back up to your neck, jaws, face, and scalp. As you go along, slowly and methodically untie the knots in your muscles until there is no tension left in your body. When you've finished, stand up, stretch, and yawn or take as deep a breath as you can, with your mouth wide open, and then release it.

EXERCISE 10.   *Fantasy*

This is a very pleasant exercise designed to reduce tension. It can also help you fall asleep at night when you're tense and jumpy. The exercise is really quite simple. Find a comfortable position, one that you can hold for a few minutes. Close your eyes and mentally transport yourself to a place that's calm and relaxing. Don't pick a place where you'll get involved in any kind of activity. We recommend that you imagine you're sitting on a deserted beach—just clean, white sand and the ocean waves rolling in with eternal regularity, one after the other. Imagine that you're sitting there listening to the waves breaking against the shore. You'll feel more relaxed after a couple of minutes of this. Just make sure that you concentrate on the waves; block out everything else.

EXERCISE 11.   *Head Rolling*

This exercise focuses specifically on the neck.

1. Take a comfortable sitting position in a chair with a medium or low back. Holding your body erect, let your head drop forward so that your chin is resting on your chest. Keeping your face pointing forward, roll your head to the right so that your right ear is close to your right shoulder. Make sure not to raise your shoulder. Now roll your head back and look up at the ceiling. At the same time, let your lower jaw drop. Next roll your head to the left so that your left ear is near your left shoulder. Don't raise your shoulder. Now roll your head forward again.
2. Repeat this exercise three times, slowly.
3. If you feel some tightness at the back of your neck during the exercise, try to relax the muscles of your neck and shoulders. The tightness should disappear. If the tightness doesn't ease or if you feel pain, discontinue the exercise. *Caution:* do not let your head roll all the way back; that sometimes can be painful.
4. Now roll your head around as before, but this time roll it all the way around in one continuous circle. Repeat the exercise, rolling your head in the opposite direction.

EXERCISE 12.   *Sighing*

This exercise helps relax the vocal folds and the neck during voice production.

1. Take as deep a breath as possible. Hold it for a count of 3. When you release the air, all at once, sigh. That is, say the vowel *ahh* in a very breathy voice. Repeat four or five times, speaking more softly with each sigh.
2. Sigh while you count to 3; then try *a, b, c.* In each case, take a deep breath, hold it for a count of 3, then sigh. Repeat four or five times.
3. Make sure you monitor the quality of your voice by listening carefully. As you sigh more softly, the amount of air expelled

should decrease and your voice should become less breathy. Even though the breathy quality leaves, it's important to keep production relaxed.

EXERCISE 13.   *Yawning*

Take a comfortable sitting position in a chair. Open your mouth wide. (Make sure your mouth is wide open. You can't yawn properly with your mouth half shut.) Take as deep a breath as you can. Stretch both arms out to the sides. Now let the air out in as easy a manner as possible. Repeat this several times and notice how you begin to feel more and more relaxed. If you have some difficulty in achieving a real yawn the first several times you try this, don't worry; you'll get it. Yawning is very contagious; you can even catch it from yourself. If you are still having difficulty, ask someone else to yawn; you'll probably find yourself yawning in imitation.

SINGING

This is probably one of the best ways to extend your pitch range, especially downward. The only problem is many people think they "can't" sing or are just plain embarrassed to sing in public. That's why we suggest that you do your singing in the shower; it's a great place for it. Here's why: first, a shower's in a room that's usually square or rectangular with walls that are hard and smooth. That makes it a good resonator, so your voice sounds richer and fuller than it does outside. Second, the sound of the running water makes it hard for other people to hear you and affords you some privacy. Finally, the shower relaxes you, and you can reach those low notes more easily.

So try singing in the shower. After a few days you should notice that your range is increasing. Then it's time to *speak* in the shower. Try such things as Hamlet's soliloquy that beings "To be or not to be. . . ." or whatever else you can have fun with.

Quality

It has been said of the human voice that it is the best and most accurate indicator of a person's physical and emotional state. Think for a moment of the way people you know sound when they are tired, tense, upset, angry, happy, or sad. It's likely that just by listening to the person's voice you can tell which of those emotions he or she may be feeling. The variations you hear, as well as others, are the reflections of changes in what we call *voice quality.*

Resonance

Let's review the physiological processes affecting voice quality. You may recall that the voice is produced by a series of puffs of air that are emitted between the vocal folds in your larynx. The complex sound created by these puffs is then bounced around (resonated) in several hollow spaces in your neck and head. This process amplifies and modifies some tones of the voice, depending on the sizes and shapes of the cavities in use.

Each person's voice quality is unique. Because no two people have resonating cavities that are exactly the same in size and shape, no two people produce voices with exactly the same acoustic characteristics. That's why it's possible for you to identify people you know when they call you on the phone. In addition, people vary the manner in which they use these resonating cavities according to their physical and emotional states. When you're tense and anxious, you generally hold your vocal folds tense, and the sound you produce has qualities that we have come to recognize as indicating tension. When you are relaxed, your voice reflects that feeling, too.

It's possible for you to assess, by the variations in voice quality, a good deal of meaning over and above what meaning is contained in the context of an utterance. Suppose you detect a note of impatience in your professor's or supervisor's voice. Even though that person's words may be telling you it's okay to be turning your work in late, you know that your next assignment had better be on time or else. Another example might be a person expressing some positive feeling toward you verbally, but there's something in the voice that tells you all is not well in the relationship. It would be difficult, wouldn't it, for a salesperson to sell a group of people on the desirability of an idea, product, or some action if he or she sounded tense or uncertain?

We've all met, at one time or another, people who told us a lot about their personalities just by the kind of voice quality they characteristically used. The person for whom all of life is one terrible catastrophe after another, for whom everything is difficult and unpleasant, will frequently have a voice quality that is petulant and complaining. Who of us has not had our nerves stretched almost to the breaking point while listening to a parent, boss, or teacher whose voice was what we call *strident?* (Stridency is a combination of a very tense quality and high pitch.) Chances are you distinctly remember people with some of these voice qualities, and the memories may not always be pleasant.

To repeat what we said earlier: your voice quality is determined, for the most part, by the size and shape of your resonating cavities. Since you can adjust those cavities and change their sizes and shapes, you can change the quality of your voice. The following sections contain a number of exercises designed to help you work on various voice qualities. We designed these exercises for students in voice and diction classes; they may not suit the purposes of voice coaches and acting teachers whose approach to resonance is planned for a different purpose.

Nasality and Resonance

The way you alter and select the resonating cavities is very important in determining voice quality and in helping to support a loud tone. The following exercises should help you increase and decrease the resonance of different cavities as necessary. We're assuming that the problems in nasality and resonance we describe are not due to any physical problems. If you have physical problems, we advise you to discuss the condition with your instructor.

TYPES OF NASALITY

Nasality problems fall into two types—too much and too little. Let's call "too much" *excessive* and "too little" *denasal*. Sometimes excessive nasality can be characteristic of a person's entire speech pattern, with all sounds having a nasal quality; or excessive nasality could occur only when there are nasal sounds in a word. In either case, the cause usually is failure to make firm contact between the soft palate and the pharynx (throat) to prevent nasal emission. Denasality is just the opposite: very close and firm contact is made, not allowing enough nasal emission.

EXERCISE 14. *Nasality—Ear Training*

1. Pinch your nostrils closed using your thumb and index finger. Read the following sentence aloud:

   Robert took a good look at the spotted puppy.

   Now release your nostrils and read the same sentence. Did you hear any difference in voice quality between your first and second readings? If you're not sure, try reading each word two times, alternately pinching and releasing your nostrils.

   If there is a difference, chances are your voice tends to be excessively nasal. If your voice has this quality, the likelihood of reducing the nasality depends, in part, on your being able to recognize when you are being excessively nasal and when you are not.

2. Place a clean, cool mirror directly under your nostrils in a horizontal plane and read the following sentence aloud:

Many people enjoy summer more than winter.

Immediately remove the mirror and look at it. You should notice two cloudy spots on the mirror. Now wipe the mirror clean again, place it under your nose, and read the following sentence aloud:

The weather report calls for cloudy skies today.

Again, remove the mirror immediately and examine it. Are there any traces of cloudiness this time? If there are, you're probably using excessive nasal resonance. Repeat these two steps until you are sure you can hear when you are using excessive nasal resonance and when you're not.

3. This part of the exercise consists of contrast drills. Say the following pairs of words, reading down each column from the left. The first word in each pair contains a nasal sound, the second does not.

ban — bat	may — say	annoy — alloy
bin — bill	might — light	sinning — sitting
fin — fill	moose — loose	hunt — hurt
flame — flake	now — how	glimmer — glitter
roam — road	nor — for	taint — taste
seem — seep	more — tore	under — udder
rung — rug	nose — rose	lent — lest
no — dough	nap — lap	sing — sit

Did you hear the difference between the nasal and nonnasal sounds in each pair?

4. Read the following sentences aloud. There should be no nasal emission during any of the sentences.
   a. Paul was the first of several quarterbacks to try out.
   b. Susie liked school a lot.
   c. Where will you go for your holiday?
   d. I'd like a glass of water, please.
   e. It's all right for you to stay.
   f. I hope you like the picture.
   g. Look for the lifeguards at the beach.
   h. Take the key to your father.
   i. Write the essay at your desk.
   j. Save your cash for the right purchase.

5. The following sentences contain some nasal sounds. As you say each sentence, listen for the nasal sounds. Are you producing any nasal sounds where you should not?

   a. Nobody likes to be left in the lurch.

   b. Bird in Hand is the name of a town in Pennsylvania.

   c. A stitch in time saves an executive headache.

   d. Sticks and stones may break my bones.

   e. Abraham Lincoln was in error. You *can* fool all the people all the time.

   f. Lewis Carroll's other book, *Through the Looking Glass,* is not as popular as *Alice in Wonderland.*

   g. "Neither a borrower nor a lender be."

   h. Muscle men of the cinema seek fame and fortune by knocking other people's heads.

Exercise 15. *Nasality—Pulling*

This exercise is designed to help you energize the area of the soft palate and pharynx.

1. Curl the fingers of both hands toward the palms. Lift your elbows to chest height. Rotate your left hand so that the curled fingers and palm are facing outward, away from you; one thumb should be up, the other down. Hook the fingers of your left hand to the fingers of your right.

2. Begin to count aloud, slowly, from 1 to 10, and listen carefully to voice quality as you count.

3. At the number 5, pull your arms away from each other. Use a strong pull, but make sure to keep your fingers hooked.

4. Did you notice a reduction in the amount of nasality? Did you notice a change in loudness? Most often this exercise produces an energizing effect on the entire body, including the soft palate, and increases the intensity of the voice.

5. Repeat this exercise three times, varying the number at which you begin pulling.

6. Say the names of the days of the week, starting with Sunday; but this time pull when each day is named. Do you hear a decrease in the amount of nasal emission and/or resonance? Repeat the exercise, saying the months of the year.

7. Now go back and do steps 4 and 5 of exercise 14.

EXERCISE 16.　*Nasality—Pushing*

Do this sitting down.

1. Place both hands, palms down, on the front corners of your chair. Count aloud from 1 to 10. Listen carefully as you count. At the number five, try to push yourself off the seat by pushing down on the chair. Continue to count up to 10. Did you notice any change? What kind of change? Repeat the exercise three times.
2. Repeat the pushing exercise. First name the days, then the months, pushing downward throughout the entire exercise. You should be able to hear a marked reduction in nasality as you go through the exercise. You can use the same exercise for practice with other words.
3. Now go back and do steps 4 and 5 of exercise 14.

DENASALITY

Does your voice lack sufficient nasal resonance (the reinforcement of the high frequency vocal overtones that give voice its brilliance and clarity)? Do others believe that you are constantly suffering from a "stuffy nose"? The muffled, dull-sounding voice of a person whose nose is stuffed up is characteristic of the denasal voice quality. Try the following exercise.

EXERCISE 17.　*Denasality*

1. Vocalize the consonant [m]. Sustain it for 10 seconds, repeating it five times.
2. Chant the following group of nonsense syllables five times. Prolong the nasal consonants in the two middle syllables.

   ohh—nee—hung—ahh

   Repeat this five times.
3. Read aloud the following words, emphasizing and prolonging the nasal sound or sounds in each. Be careful to confine the nasality to just the nasal consonant. Don't let it move into the vowel.

no	on	sing	single
knee	in	ring	finger
my	time	song	monkey
neck	him	hand	spangle
now	hum	along	England
may	name	wing	mangle
kneel	calm	bang	mingle
more	loom	wrong	uncle
mill	moon	sting	dunking
mood	fine	fling	ringer

4. Try the drills for the nasal consonants starting on page 295. Again, emphasize the nasals, but don't let the nasality spread to the vowels or other consonants.

Tense, Strident, Metallic, and Hoarse Qualities

With the exception of the hoarse voice, these qualities are usually fairly high-pitched and seen to be "hard-hitting." The quality we call *hoarseness* is a combination of breathiness and harshness resulting in a voice that sounds very rough. Hoarseness can be associated with physical problems of the larynx, so we suggest you see your physician if your voice has been hoarse for a long time.

EXCESS TENSION

The common denominator of these qualities seems to be tension—excess tension in the area of the larynx. Sometimes the tension may be caused by inadequate breath support of loudness. If your instructor feels this is the case, we recommend that you review and practice exercise 1, "Abdominal Breathing" (page 280). If the excess tension is caused by something other than breath support, relaxation exercises (exercises 9–13 above) can physically relax the laryngeal area. It takes time for the effects of these exercises to be felt, though, so don't expect overnight miracles. Think, instead, in terms of days or a few weeks before you notice significant changes in your voice quality.

VOCAL OR GLOTTAL FRY

This strangely named quality supposedly sounds like bacon frying. That may be stretching the imagination, but the voice does get a rough, bubbly quality, especially at the ends of sentences or thought groups. At these times, the pitch lowers considerably and the voice weakens. Many times this quality is indicative of a more serious ailment, so we suggest a visit to your physician. Vocal fry can sometimes be eliminated with the following exercises:

EXERCISE 18.   *Vocal Fry*

Work on holding your pitch level at the end of the sentence or phrase. A piano can be especially helpful with this. Read phrases and sentences aloud. Find the note on the piano that is close to your pitch at the beginning of the phrase. Play the note again at the end of the phrase, and notice if your pitch has lowered. Try to keep matching your pitch to the note played all the way through your utterance. Repeat often, using various reading materials. We suggest that you use the materials for "High Key" on page 323 in your practice.

EXERCISE 19.   *Vocal Fry—Questions*

In American English, questions frequently end in rising pitch. Read the following "frequently asked questions" adapted from the website of Monmouth University Office of Residential Life. Try to keep your pitch level until the end of each question, when your pitch should rise slightly. Make certain your pitch doesn't fall at the end of a question.

1. When will I get my room assignment?
2. What is my room like?
3. May I see my room before I move in?
4. Are the beds bunked? Can they be?
5. When do I move in?
6. Can I request a roommate?
7. Do I have to purchase a meal plan?
8. What banks are local?
9. Are there computers on campus?
10. Do we have cable TV?
11. Is housing guaranteed?
12. Can I request a building?

EXERCISE 20.   *Vocal Fry—Questions and Answers*

Read the following questions so that they end with rising pitch, and say the last words (in bold) with a slight increase in loudness. Read the corresponding answers with level pitch throughout, and say the final words (in bold) slightly louder than the rest.

1. Did you have a good **day?** . . . I had a good **day.**
2. Did you work **hard?** . . . I worked **hard.**
3. Will you be home **late?** . . . I won't be home **late.**
4. Can you get this computer to **work?** . . . I can't get this computer to **work.**
5. Can we do research on the **Internet?** . . . We can do research on the **Internet.**
6. Can we send out for **pizza?** . . . We can send out for **pizza.**
7. Do you like the **winter?** . . . I like the **winter.**
8. Did you say make them **louder?** . . . I said make them **louder.**
9. Have you known them a long **time?** . . . I've known them a long **time.**
10. Will the weather be **snowy?** . . . The weather will be **snowy.**

EXERCISE 21.   *Additional Vocal Fry Reading*

1. Read the following nursery rhyme using moderate loudness and level to rising pitch.

> As I was going to St. Ives,
> I met a man with seven wives.
> Each wife had seven sacks,
> Each sack had seven cats,
> Each cat had seven kits.
> Kits, cats, sacks, and wives,
> How many were going to St. Ives?

2. Use the sighing technique explained in exercise 22 on page 301.
3. Use the abdominal breathing explained in exercise 1 on page 280.

THROATY QUALITY

The throaty quality is characterized by the voice that doesn't seem to project at all, staying in the throat with a muffled sound to it. Frequently, the voice is also denasal. Exercises 17 to 21, which help eliminate denasality and vocal fry, will help with this problem as well.

HARD GLOTTAL ATTACK

If you have this quality, you seem to hit your vowels hard, especially when the vowel is the first sound in a word. After a long period of using this type of attack, your voice may begin to crack and may become harsh or hoarse. Do the following exercise to try to change your method of attack.

EXERCISE 22.   *Hard Glottal Attack*

1. Sigh the vowel *ahh*, beginning it with a slight *h* sound so that it sounds like *hahhh.* Repeat three times.
2. In order, sigh the following: *ohh, aww, eee, aye* five times each, starting with an *h: hohh, haww, hee, haye.*
3. Repeat the previous steps, this time without the beginning *h* sound, but be careful to bring the vocal folds together gently; begin the sound without a hard attack by easing into it. Think the *h*, but don't say it.
4. Repeat, this time gently phonating each sound, rather than sighing. Be sure to initiate each sound gently and without a hard attack.

5. Say each of the following words two times. The first time, think the *h* before the vowel but don't say it. The second time, initiate the vowel sound gently and without a hard attack.

I	own	another
owe	order	arson
ear	army	evening
owl	awning	over
oar	aisle	open
arm	inn	aiming
up	under	above

6. Say the following phrases and sentences out loud, being careful to initiate each word with a soft attack.
   a. All alone.
   b. In advance.
   c. Eleven o'clock.
   d. Eight hours.
   e. Open ocean.
   f. Enough apples.
   g. I am awake and aware.
   h. All of us are going.
   i. Order your anchors early.
   j. Every army is orderly.
   k. The owl didn't give a hoot about anything.

7. Read the following sentences aloud, again being careful to initiate each word beginning with a vowel using a soft attack.
   a. If we are all looking for answers, what are the questions?
   b. *Annie Hall* is an excellent film.
   c. Is your aunt expecting to get her pen off the table?
   d. "Alexander's Ragtime Band" isn't among my favorite songs.
   e. We were able to observe the evening star through the awning.

vocal expressiveness

Objectives

After reading the chapter and completing the appropriate drill and practice materials, you should be able to:

- Demonstrate your understanding of the vocal variables of rate, stress, and pitch
- Develop the skills necessary to maintain control of those variables during oral reading and, to a lesser degree, instill meaning and interest into spontaneous speech
- Display mastery of those skills during the presentation of a prepared oral reading

In every school there's at least one teacher who has the nickname "Mr. Excitement." If you were in one of his classes, you'd understand why. He gives his lectures in a dull, dry, and deadly tone, never changing his rate, never varying his pitch, never saying words any louder or softer, speaking in a monotone that puts his students to sleep almost instantly. Faculty members also tend to go to sleep when talking with him in a meeting or conference because his speech pattern is very much like his personality: dull, dry, and deadly.

Perhaps you know or have heard of someone like Mr. Excitement. Maybe you've dozed off in church, in class, or in a meeting. Would you want to get to know someone who speaks in such an expressionless manner? And there are worse things than just falling asleep during a monotonic delivery. We all can probably recall misinterpreting someone's remarks because the right words weren't emphasized.

Vocal expressiveness is what this chapter is all about. We're going to work on how to bring appropriate variety to the way we speak and read aloud. We think that working on vocal expression is important for the following reasons:

1. Vocal expressiveness is one of the major factors necessary for gaining and keeping your listener's attention and interest. By the way, that's *your* job. You're the one with the communication purpose to be achieved.

2. Vocal expressiveness can make meanings clear when the actual words leave some doubt.

3. Vocal expressiveness tells your listeners what you think of them, what you think about the words you're saying, and how you feel about yourself. Listeners tend to respect and believe a person who uses vocal expression effectively.

Reading Aloud

Unfortunately, there's a little of Mr. Excitement in most of us. It usually doesn't appear when we're speaking spontaneously, though it can. It generally is noticeable when we read aloud; that's when we "put on" our reading voices. You know what we mean by reading voice; it's an artificial, unemotional, impersonal way of speaking aloud. It's usually very different from the way we speak spontaneously, and it's usually much less effective.

Even though you may be saying to yourself, "I really don't do much reading aloud," chances are that you will. Most of us do a considerable amount of reading aloud during the normal course of living and working. We read newspaper articles to other people; directions on how to make, build, or cook things; letters and business reports during meetings and conferences; stories and fairy tales to our children, brothers and sisters, nieces and nephews. We could add to the list, but we've made our point: you *do* read aloud. You do it for the same reasons that you speak spontaneously, but you may not be reading effectively.

We'll tell you first what we're *not* going to do: we're not going to teach you to be a professional radio or TV announcer, or a Broadway or film actor, or any such thing. That's beyond the scope of this text. We *do* want to help you become more effective in your everyday speaking and reading. So, we'll teach you how to use the components of vocal expression; *rate, phrasing, intonation,* and *stress*. We'll provide you with some theory and plenty of practice.

Components of Vocal Expression

Rate

Can you imagine yourself at Gettysburg listening to Abraham Lincoln deliver the famous address at the same rate of speech as a stand-up comic in a Las Vegas nightclub act? In all likelihood, the very idea of such a rapid rate of delivery for that somber, serious message would appeal to your sense of the ridiculous rather than the sublime.

Rate has a definite effect on our perceptions of people and the relative importance of their messages. Perhaps in your work or school environment you have come across a person who speaks at a very rapid rate. Chances are that you tend to place less value on what that person has to say than you would if he or she spoke at a slower rate.

As a rule, we deliver spoken messages at a rate that is appropriate for the content. A rapid rate usually carries the unspoken message, "What I'm saying now is light, frivolous, unimportant, humorous, not meant to be taken too seriously." A slow, deliberate rate, on the other hand, implies, "This message is meant to be considered important and weighty and is to be taken seriously."

The rate of speech also reflects the speaker's physical and emotional states. When you're feeling calm or sad or tired, you'll probably speak relatively slowly. When you are in a state of physical or mental excitement, though, you'll most likely speed things up considerably.

The rate at which you speak affects understanding. The process whereby you take in and interpret messages is a highly complex one. To understand a spoken message, your brain must "hear" all the acoustic elements of the message, then translate them into the concepts or ideas they symbolize, then associate those concepts with the meanings you've attributed to them as a result of all the experiences you've had in your life. You can understand, therefore, that although you can *hear* words just as rapidly as they are spoken, it takes you longer to understand and integrate the message in some meaningful and usable form. When you are presented with a message delivered at a high rate of speed, you have more difficulty dealing with it in a meaningful way. This is especially true if the message is complex or abstract. Then you work particularly hard to understand everything the speaker is saying or you give up trying. In either case, there's a good chance that the speaker's purpose has not been achieved.

If a speaker delivers a relatively unimportant message slowly and deliberately, you may become impatient or bored waiting for the message to be completed because you understood the speaker's intent long before the delivery ended. For communication to be effective, it is important for the rate of delivery to match the meaning the speaker wishes to convey.

DETERMINING YOUR OWN RATE

Most people don't accurately know their rate of speaking or reading. So before you practice the exercises for rate, you should learn what your average rate actually is. To do this, try the following exercise. You can time yourself or have someone time you. You'll need either a stopwatch or a watch with a second hand.

1. Time yourself as you *silently* read through the *entire* selection. The piece you'll be reading is from the U.S. Department of Commerce publication *A Basic Guide to Exporting.* We selected this passage because of its average word length and because of the unemotional nature of its content. When you've finished reading silently, write the time in seconds in the "silent" reading box in Figure 11–1.

2. Now time yourself while you read the selection *aloud.* Try to make the contents of the passage understandable to a listener, real or imagined. If you're doing this outside of class, pretend that you are addressing the entire class. Write the time in seconds in the "oral reading" box in Figure 11–1.

3. Now use a tape recorder and time yourself while you give a brief extemporaneous or impromptu talk to a real or imagined listener. Talk about your job or your hobbies. Describe a movie you've seen or a book you have read, or tell about a significant personal experience. The subject itself isn't important as long as you can talk about it for at least two minutes. Write the speaking time, in seconds, in the "conversational speaking rate" box in Figure 11–1. Then replay the tape and count the number of words you said. Write this number in the "words spoken" box in Figure 11–1.

4. Follow the instructions in Figure 11–1 to determine the rate for each situation.

APPROPRIATE RATE

Most people find that the silent reading rate is the highest and the conversational speaking rate the lowest. If your oral reading rate falls between 150 and 180 wpm, it's within the normal range for this type of material. The middle of the range, 160 to 170 wpm, would be considered by most listeners to be the most effective and easiest to understand. Your speaking rate should be slower, probably below 150 wpm. In both speaking and reading, of course, the rate will reflect the content of the material, the listener's state of mind, and so forth.

If you've determined that your rate is too fast or too slow, try the following exercises for adjusting rate.

Figure 11–1
Rate of Speech for Silent Reading, Oral Readng, and Conversational Speech.

SILENT READING RATE

full selection: (281 words) 281 ÷ _____ (secs.) × 60 = ___ (rate in words per minute)

partial selection: ___ words read ÷ ___ (secs.) × 60 = ___ (rate in words per minute)

ORAL READING RATE

full selection: (281 words) 281 ÷ _____ (secs.) × 60 = ___ (rate in words per minute)

partial selection: ___ words read ÷ ___ (secs.) × 60 = ___ (rate in words per minute)

CONVERSATIONAL SPEAKING RATE

words spoken ÷ _____ (secs.) × 60 = ___ (rate in words per minute)

Number of Words	
12	The international freight forwarder acts as an agent for the exporter in
24	moving cargo to the overseas destination. These agents are familiar with the
35	import rules and regulations of foreign countries, methods of shipping, U.S.
43	Government export regulations, and with the documents connected with
45	foreign trade.
57	Freight forwarders can assist with an order from the start by advising
70	the exporter of the freight costs, port chargers, consular fees, cost of special
82	documentation, and insurance costs, as well as their handling fees—all of
95	which help in the preparation of a price quotation. They may also recommend
108	the type of packing that should be considered to help protect the merchandise
123	in transit and can arrange to have the merchandise packed at the port or to
136	have it containerized. The cost for their services is a legitimate export cost
147	that should be figured into the price charged to the customer.
160	When the order is ready to ship, freight forwarders should be able to
172	review the letter of credit, commercial invoices, packing list, etc., to ensure
185	that everything is in order. If desired, they can also reserve the necessary
191	space on board an ocean vessel.
205	If the cargo arrives at the port of export and the exporter has not
215	already done so, freight forwarders may make the necessary arrangements
227	with custom brokers to ensure that the goods comply with customs export
238	documentation regulations. In addition, they may have the goods delivered to
251	the carrier in time for loading aboard the selected vessel. They may also
264	prepare the bill of lading and any special documentation that may be required.
277	After shipment, they forward all documents directly to the customer or to the
281	paying bank if desired.

Timed Readings for Rate

Use the following selections for correcting either slow or fast rate. Each selection contains 160 to 170 words and should take exactly one minute for you to read aloud. Continue to read each selection (without looking at your watch) until it takes you one minute.

1. You've just been given a big assignment! You're in charge of co-ordinating a large off-site meeting, and you'll manage the details that will help make that event a success. Can this be a nerve-wracking assignment? You bet! But by putting your organizing and planning skills to work and using your ability to produce everything from the invitations sent out in advance to the handouts that the attendees will take home with them, you'll find that this is a great opportunity to show-case your skills.

Your first step will be to meet with the person in charge of the meeting so that you are clear on specifics—the old journalism formula of who, what, when, where and why. During this meeting, you should also learn what materials you're expected to produce. Once you know the particulars—and have the big picture—you can begin working out the details. Creating a plan and breaking it down by activities will make your task less overwhelming and a lot more manageable.

"Mastering the Meeting" in *Great Results,* Avery Dennison Corp., La Brea, CA:
Vol. 1, No. 3, 2000

2. Earthquakes have an uncanny knack of picking on the weakest part of a house's structure and focusing their energy there. That could be a disaster if the weak link is the cripple walls, since they carry the weight of a wood frame house. One of the smartest precautions you can take is to brace them with plywood.

First, replace any rotten wood and bolt the mudsill to the foundation if it isn't bolted already. The difficulty of the project depends largely on how cramped the space is under the house.

Brace the walls at least four feet out from every corner. For maximum strength, brace their whole length. If you can't, brace all corners and at least half of each wall—more if the house is two stories. Ask a structural engineer or your local building department for specifications for the bolts, plywood and nails to use. Even if you do the work yourself, it is wise to hire a professional to inspect under the house and advise you.

Sierra Home, *Home Repair Essentials*

3. Here are some typing and editing tips:

- Don't use the space bar to indent the beginning of a paragraph or to center text—the text in your document may not align properly when you print it. To indent the first line of a paragraph, press **Tab.** To center a line, choose **Line** from the **Format** menu, then choose **Center.**

- Don't use the space bar to go to the next line. If you use the space bar to go to the next line, those extra spaces will remain when you edit your document. As a result, you may have gaps in your paragraphs. Instead, press **Enter** to go to the next line.

- Don't use the Enter key to move to the next page. If you press Enter several times to move to the next page, you may end up with unwanted blank lines in the middle of a page after you edit your document. Instead, press **Control + Enter** to start a new page.

WordPerfect User's Guide, 1994

4. Our listeners and viewers have come to expect us to provide them with news, whether impromptu news occurs or not. If we've scheduled five minutes of news every hour on the hour on radio, we're obliged to provide five minutes of news each hour. If we've scheduled an early evening hour and a late evening half hour for news on television, we must appear at the scheduled hour prepared to deliver news.

Reporters cannot wait for news to come to them. They must look for it. They cannot wait for the National Weather Service to announce a tornado, the police dispatcher to radio a detective to investigate a possible murder, the fire dispatcher to call a third alarm on a fire, the highway patrol to announce a traffic tie-up on an interstate highway, the FBI agent in charge to reveal a bank robbery, the prison warden to reveal a riot—they must *dig* for news.

Roy Gibson, Radio and Television Reporting

It's important for you to read these passages a number of times at the rate of 160 to 170 wpm to get the feeling in your mouth, tongue, and jaw of what that rate is like. You must also get accustomed to that rate in your mind. We'd bet that the first couple of times you read them at the desired rate, it felt awfully strange. After a while the feeling of strangeness will go.

Practice speaking spontaneously at 160 to 170 wpm. Use a tape recorder and count your words afterward, or ask a friend to listen and to tell you if you speed up or slow down.

Now we'd like you to try reading a few passages at an average rate of 120 to 150 wpm. This rate is appropriate for serious, somber material, or for material which is difficult for others to grasp (for the authors, such material might be on economic theory). In addition, learning to select various rates will give you a good deal of flexibility in your vocal expressiveness.

The following passages should take from 50 seconds to 1 minute to read.

1. This crisis model of young people caught in a turbulent passage between their late teens and early twenties has come to be equated with the normal process of growing up. We all recognize hallmarks of this sensitive condition: kids who are at once rebellious, listless, and jumpy. Kids who are seized by sudden and riotous swings of mood. When cramped by anxiety, they cannot sleep or work. They may suffer from mysterious maladies and hold to inflexibly high ideals. Often they seem to be gripped by a negative view of themselves and by hostility to the family. They are likely to drop out of school, the job, the romance, or to stay in and be actively resentful.

In short, it's like having flu of the personality.

Gail Sheehy, *Passages;* 126 words

2. People of all ages come to Maine hoping to spot a moose. Maine has more moose per square mile than any state or province in North America including Alaska. Most experts say the ideal time to see a moose is between mid-May and late July; either early in the morning or late in the afternoon—and be patient. At other times during the year, while hiking or driving in any of Maine's rural locales, sighting moose is always a possibility.

Here are a few words of caution: While the moose you spot may appear to be docile, don't underestimate its ability to do severe damage to your vehicle or person. The moose is a wild animal and you need to treat it with respect.

Maine Publicity Bureau, *Maine Invites You;* 124 words

Duration

Rate is partly determined by how you produce your vowels. If you sound them very quickly, they become clipped and the words become shorter. Even if you reduce the number of words you say each minute, your speech would still sound rapid. On the other extreme is prolongation. If you hold on to the vowels too long, your speech may be too slow. Use the following drill to vary duration.

Duration Practice

We've found it convenient to use the following system to indicate duration: ˘ for short duration; ‾ for long duration; no marking for average duration.

Exercise 1.   *Contrast Drill for Duration*

Say the following pairs of words aloud. Listen for a difference in how long the vowel sounds in each word are held. Try to exaggerate the difference by making the vowel in the first word of each pair very short, and the vowel in the second word very long.

căp	— cāme	spĕnt	— spānned
slĭp	— slēēve	rĭch	— rīde
grĭp	— grīēve	dŏt	— dūde
poŭt	— pound	hŏp	— hōme
tŏte	— tōēs	flăp	— flāw
rŏtten	— rōses	spăt	— Spāin
făce	— fāze	shŏt	— shāme
frŏnt	— frōnd	brăt	— brāīn
păce	— pāge	thĭn	— thīgh
măt	— māde	shĭp	— shȳ

Exercise 2. *Contrast Drill for Duration*

Read the following words aloud, giving the vowels the duration as marked. Remember, ˘ means short duration, ‾ means long duration, no mark means average duration.

hăppȳ	wōnder	sĭck
lōngĭng	shāmefŭl	blŭff
sŭrprīse	ĭnhăbĭtĕd	lĭkely
sādly	fūtŭre	ăfrāīd
pĕppy	smīle	sŭppōse

Exercise 3. *Contrast Drill for Duration*

Read the following words aloud at an average loudness. First read the entire list, giving the vowel sounds average duration. Then read the list again, making the vowel sounds as short as possible. Then give the vowel sounds average duration again. Finally, make the vowel sounds as long as possible.

afraid	inch	clothing	narcotic
backache	snore	rotten	republic
ashamed	pout	total	submerging
prank	browse	creeping	polluted
grieve	doze	speaker	improvement
sleep	grunt	garden	newcomer
glib	swoop	paper	bakery
divide	girl	quarrel	saleable
voodoo	sided	nickname	commitment
fragile	shallow	dynamic	eloping

Now go back over the above list of words and mark the vowels with the symbols for whatever duration you believe to be appropriate. Pronounce the words in accordance with your duration markings.

Here are more selections for duration. Read them silently first, planning the duration of certain words, perhaps marking them in the text as you did above. Then read them aloud.

1. Outside the open door
    Of the whitewashed house,
    Framed in its doorway, a chair,
    Vacant, waits in the sunshine.

    A jug of fresh water stands
    Inside the door. In the sunshine
    The chair waits, less and less vacant.
    The host's plan is to offer water, then stand aside.

    Galway Kinnell, "The Supper after the Last"

2. When English children begin to crawl, they find carpets on the floor, carelessly turned up at the corners. They find walls soft with wallpaper, thick curtains they can haul themselves up on, deep sofas smothered in cushions, big quilts on top of the bed, fluff and dustballs beneath. The English domestic world is a soft, soft place. Perhaps there is a hearthrug. Perhaps there is a cat or a dog on the rug. The child moves from one softness to another.

    When Italian children begin to crawl, they find tiles or at best polished wood. Carpets are too hot for hot summers and unhygienic. Every day a wet cloth spreads disinfectant on shiny ceramics. There is no soft paper on the walls but rough whitewash, or solid waxed stucco, which is the fashion now. The stairs to the outer world are polished stone. The windows are shuttered. It's a harder, cleaner, smoother, more controlled environment, bright by day, jet dark at night. With the shutters tight, no shadows flit softly about the curtain hem. Bang your head on the window ledge, and you find marble. Take a tumble, or *capitombolo,* as they say here, on ceramics, and the bruises go deep.

    Tim Parks, *An Italian Education*

Try this same exercise with poetry and literature selections of your own choosing. Continue to be aware of overall rate while you're working on duration.

Pausing

We can't consider rate without discussing pausing. But the relationship is secondary; we use pausing for much more than simply controlling rate. Often, in fact, rate is subordinate to pausing.

We use pauses for a number of purposes: emphasis, clarity, meaning, attention, reflection, variety, change of ideas, change of mood, and last but not least, for breathing. Without pausing, you tend to lose your listener because pauses act as verbal punctuation marks. Furthermore, we use pausing to regulate the back and forth nature of conversation. If you're a listener, you wait for the speaker to pause before you begin to speak; speaking before you hear the pause is considered an interruption.

Major, or long, pauses are controlled by *thought groups.* A thought group is analogous to the written sentence; it is complete and can stand by itself. Your pause is the verbal punctuation mark. Minor, or short, pauses are used for all the purposes we listed above. Notice that of all the purposes, we listed breathing last. That's right. You should pause for meaning, not just to get air. Pausing should be frequent enough that you don't run out of breath. If you do, it means you're not pausing enough or you're not controlling your breath flow efficiently. Remember, you can only take a quick inhalation during most pauses, so breath control is very important.

Pausing Exercises

1. Read the following telephone conversation from *Come Blow Your Horn* by Neil Simon. First read it through silently, then aloud, pretending that you're actually talking on the phone. The pauses were indicated by the author (—), but he didn't indicate their length; that's up to you. Remember, this is a conversation between Alan and Chickie, so the pauses indicate when it's Chickie's turn to talk. When you pause, imagine what Chickie might be saying, and give her enough time to say it.

   Alan: Hello?—Chickie? Don't you know you could be arrested for having such a sexy voice?—Alan—How could I? I just got in from Europe an hour ago—Switzerland—A specialist there told me if I don't see you within a half an hour, I'll die—Yes, tonight—A friend of mine is having a little party—Wonderful guy—hundred laughs — Hey, Chickie, is your roommate free? The French girl? — Wonderful. Yes. Bring her— No, I can't. I've got to get the pretzels. Can you meet me there? The Hotel Croyden, Room 326, Marty Meltzer—A half hour—Marvelous. I just love you — What? — Yes, Alan *Baker.*

2. Meaningful pauses don't have to be long. Many times we use pauses just for that little extra bit of emphasis; we can set things apart by pausing slightly before or after a word. Mark the following selections for meaningful pauses. Use / to indicate a slight pause and // to indicate a longer pause, as in the following example:

   To be / or not to be. // That / is the question.

   Notice how we can change the feeling by changing the pauses:

   To be or / not to be. // That is // the question.

Here's one for you to try. First read it as we've marked it. Then change the pausing and mark the second listing to represent the way you'd like to read it.

Tomorrow // and tomorrow // and tomorrow // creeps in this / petty pace / from day / to day. . . .

Tomorrow and tomorrow and tomorrow creeps in this petty pace from day to day. . . .

3.   Here are more practice selections for pausing. Make light marks in pencil so you can change the pauses if they don't seem right when you read the passages aloud. Try each selection a few times, and change the pausing each time.

a.   A hundred feet in the sky he lowered his webbed feet, lifted his beak, and strained to hold a painful hard twisting curve through his wings. The curve meant that he would fly slowly, and now he slowed until the wind was a whisper in his face, until the ocean stood still beneath him. He narrowed his eyes in fierce concentration, held his breath, forced one . . . single . . . more . . . inch . . . of . . . curve . . . Then his feathers ruffled, he stalled and fell.

Richard Bach, Jonathan Livingston Seagull

b.   For the fashion of Minas Tirith was such that it was built on seven levels, each delved into the hill, and about each was set a wall, and in each wall was a gate. But the gates were not set in a line: the Great Gate in the City Wall was at the east point of the circuit, but the next pointed half south, and the third half north, and so to and fro upwards; so that the paved way that climbed toward the Citadel turned first this way and then that across the face of the hill. And each time that it passed the Great Gate it went through an arched tunnel, piercing a vast pier of rock whose huge out-thrust bulk divided in two all the circles of the City save the first. For partly in the primeval shaping of the hill, partly by the mighty craft and labor of old, there stood up from the rear of the wide court behind the Gate a towering bastion of stone, its edge sharp as a ship-keel facing east. Up it rose, even to the level of the topmost circle, and there was crowned by a battlement; so that those in the Citadel might, like mariners in a mountainous ship, look from its peak sheer down upon the Gate seven hundred feet below.

J. R. R. Tolkien, The Lord of the Rings

c.   **Rounding Off to Whole Dollars.** You may find it easier to do your return if you round off cents to the nearest whole dollar. To do so, drop amounts under 50 cents and increase amounts from 50 to 99 cents to the next whole dollar. For example, $129.39 becomes $129 and $235.50 becomes $236. If you do round off, do so for all amounts. But if you have to add two or more amounts to figure the amount to enter on a line, include cents when adding and only round off the total.

Internal Revenue Service, 1999 1040EZ

d. Pace has always had a student-centered focus and is committed to providing access to those who range widely in age, ethnicity, socio-economic background and academic preparation. The use of increasing amounts of institutional financial aid to help students meet the growing costs of a private education; locations in New York City and Westchester County; evening, weekend and summer scheduling; and special counseling and academic tutoring services are ways in which the University has sought to enhance the accessibility and opportunities of a Pace education. A significant tradition of Pace University is its strong relationship with business, civic and community organizations.

Pace University, The Pace Story

e. In moving-slow he has no Peer
You ask him something in his Ear
He thinks about it for a Year;
And, then, before he says a Word
He will assume that you have Heard—

A most Ex-as-per-at-ing Lug.
But should you call his manner Smug
He'll sigh and give his Branch a Hug;

Then off again to Sleep he goes,
Still swaying gently by his Toes,
And you just know he knows he knows.

Theodore Roethke, "The Sloth"

Stress

If someone were to say to you, in a soft, weak voice, "Pay attention; this is very important," chances are you wouldn't immediately drop what you were doing to listen. If, however, you heard the same command given in a loud, strong voice, you would probably respond immediately. As a rule, in our society, we tend to place more importance on things said loudly than we do on things said softly. This also holds true for the way we customarily *stress* (accent by loudness) the various parts of speech. Nouns, for example, are the primary conveyors of meaning, and as such, we ordinarily give them the most stress. Next come verbs, then adjectives, then adverbs. Those parts of speech getting the least amount of stress, or sometimes no stress at all, include pronouns, articles, prepositions, and conjunctions. In other words, we indicate the relative importance of parts of speech, or the importance of particular things we say, by making them louder (we call this stress).

There are, however, certain situations for which you want to give a special twist of meaning to what you are saying. Let's take the sentence, "The boy took his dog to the park" as an example. Spoken as a simple statement, you would stress the nouns <u>boy</u>, <u>dog</u>, and <u>park</u> and the verb <u>took.</u> Using double underlining to indicate primary stress and single underlining to indicate secondary stress, we would indicate the stress pattern of that sentence as:

The <u>boy</u> <u>took</u> his <u>dog</u> to the <u>park</u>.

Suppose you wished to use the very same sentence to answer a series of questions. We can predict the ways in which your stress pattern would vary. Let's ask the questions and listen to the answers:

Question: Did just any boy take his dog to the park?
Answer: No, <u>the</u> <u>boy</u> <u>took</u> his <u>dog</u> to the <u>park</u>.
Question: Did a girl take a dog to the park?
Answer: No, the <u>boy</u> <u>took</u> his <u>dog</u> to the <u>park</u>.
Question: Did the boy take someone else's dog to the park?
Answer: No, the <u>boy</u> <u>took</u> <u>his</u> <u>dog</u> to the <u>park</u>.

A whole series of similar questions could be asked, and for each, the word receiving primary stress would change with the change of information asked for in the various questions.

Word Stress

The example above illustrates the way we use word stress; that is, how we make different words louder to transmit special meaning. In the example, each time we said the sentence, using different stress but not different words, we changed the meaning of the sentence. Try the following:

Word Stress Drill

Following are some simple sentences. Read each one aloud. Begin by stressing the first word of each sentence, then move the stress to the second word, and so on, just as we did with "The <u>boy</u> <u>took</u> his <u>dog</u> to the <u>park</u>."

1. This is my favorite.
2. I'm buying a new car.
3. Where are you going?
4. I don't like him.
5. This is a great book.
6. Do you like my new hat?

7. How much did that cost?
8. Things are sure different around here.
9. Make my day.
10. Don't come home late.

In the following sentences, underline the words to show where you would place primary and secondary stress. Then read the sentences aloud making sure you stress the words the way you planned.

1. Please don't do that again.
2. If I've told you once, I've told you a thousand times.
3. Where are those keys of mine?
4. Which book are you going to buy?
5. I really need a rest.
6. Excuse me, but I believe that seat is mine.
7. I know where I'm going.
8. Tim was certainly not feeling well.
9. Please don't eat the daisies.
10. Just how safe do you think that is?

SYLLABLE STRESS

In words of more than one syllable (polysyllabic words), one syllable will receive more stress than the others. The stress pattern is agreed to by the speakers of the language; look up a word in the dictionary and you'll see a diacritical mark indicating stress. Sometimes we stress a different syllable for special emphasis; most of the time, though, a word is considered mispronounced if the wrong syllable stress is used.

When we join two nouns to form a compound word, we usually stress the first noun more than the second. Try the following list.

Compound Word Stress Drill

Read the following words aloud. Place primary stress on the first syllable of each word:

<u>air</u>plane	<u>hot</u>house	<u>Sun</u>day
flatfoot	beefsteak	downtown
bluefish	notebook	paperback
motorboat	butterfly	forestfire
rubberband	sometime	overcharge
driveway	underpass	football
windchime	textbook	noonday
surfboard	software	grandstand

Polysyllabic words, other than compound words, usually follow a pattern in which the stress moves farther along in the word as the word becomes longer. Try the following:

Polysyllabic Stress Drill

Read the following words aloud, reading *across* the page. Place the primary stress on the appropriate syllable:

major	majority	
sacrifice	sacrificial	
reference	referee	
incident	incidental	
continent	continental	
simplify	simplification	
occupy	occupation	
product	productive	
beautify	beautification	
converse	conversational	
nominate	nomination	nominee
photograph	photography	photographic
object	objective	objectification
subject	subjective	subjectification
person	personify	personification

Practice Readings for Stress

Read the following selections aloud. It may be helpful for you to underline words for primary and secondary stress. Remember, there's no right way: interpretation of the authors' words is up to you. Just be aware of how your stress patterns may change the meaning.

1. The idea of <u>you</u> lynching anybody is amusing. The idea of you thinking you had pluck enough to lynch a <u>man</u>! Because you're brave enough to tar and feather poor friendless castout women that come along here, did that make you think you had grit enough to lay your hands on a <u>man</u>? Why, a <u>man's</u> safe in the hands of ten thousand of your kind—as long as it's daytime and you're not behind him.

Mark Twain, *Huckleberry Finn*

2. Climb to a thousand feet. Full power straight ahead first, then push over, flapping, to a vertical dive. Then, every time, his left wing stalled on an upstroke, he'd roll violently left, stall his right wing recovering, and flick like fire into a wild tumbling spin to the right.

Richard Bach, *Jonathan Livingston Seagull*

3. **Harmony** refers to the way chords are constructed and how they follow each other. A **chord** is a combination of three or more tones

sounded at once. Essentially, a chord is a group of simultaneous tones, and a melody is a series of individual tones heard one after another. As a melody unfolds, it gives clues for harmonizing, but it does not always dictate a specific series—or **progression** of chords; a melody may be harmonized in several musically convincing ways. Chord progressions enrich a melody in adding emphasis, surprise, suspense, or finality. New chords and progressions continually enter the language of music, but the basic chordal vocabulary has remained fairly constant.

Roger Kamien, Music: An Appreciation

4. . . . the boat is caught by the wave and, gathering speed, begins to rush forward. The speedometer needle starts its climb—9, 10, 11 knots. Once in a while, a big one, a real graybeard comes along and we hit 12 and 13 knots. The helmsman, the wheel vibrating in his hands as the rudder is locked in a fore and aft position by the force of the water rushing by its sides, lets out a howl of triumph. It is almost an animal cry, a natural outlet, welling up in a geyser of exhilaration. He has the feeling of having harnessed the angry forces of nature to beat it at its own game. He has pulled Poseidon's beard.

William Snaith, On the Wind's Way

5. Tyger, tyger, burning bright
In the forests of the night,
What immortal hand or eye
Could frame thy fearful symmetry?

In what distant deeps or skies
Burnt the fire of thine eyes?
On what wings dare he aspire?
What the hand dare seize the fire?

And what shoulder and what art?
Could twist the sinews of thy heart?
And, when thy heart began to beat,
What dread hand and what dread feet?

What the hammer? What the chain?
In what furnace was thy brain?
What the anvil? What dread grasp
Dare its deadly terrors clasp?

When the stars threw down their spears,
And water'd heaven with their tears,
Did He smile His work to see?
Did He who made the lamb make thee?

Tyger, tyger, burning bright
In the forests of the night,
What immortal hand or eye
Dare frame thy fearful symmetry?

William Blake, "The Tyger"

6. The year's at the spring,
   And day's at the morn;
   Morning's at seven;
   The hill-side's dew-pearl'd

   The lark's on the wing;
   The snail's on the thorn;
   God's in His heaven—
   All's right with the world!

   Robert Browning, "Pippa Passes," Part 1

7. It seemed to me that I should have to have a desk, even though I had no real need for a desk. I was afraid that if I had no desk in my room my life would seem too haphazard.

The desk looked incomplete when I got it set up, so I found a wire basket and put that on it, and threw a few things in it. This basket, however, gave me a lot of trouble for the first couple of weeks. I had always had TWO baskets in New York. One said IN, the other OUT. At intervals a distribution boy would sneak into the room, deposit something in IN, remove the contents of OUT. Here, with only one basket, my problem was to decide whether it was IN or OUT, a decision a person of some character could have made promptly and reasonably but which I fooled round with for days—tentative, hesitant, trying first one idea then another, first a day when it would be IN, then a day when it would be OUT, then, somewhat desperately, trying to combine the best features of both and using it as a catch-all for migratory papers no matter which way they were headed. This last was disastrous. I found a supposedly out-going letter buried for a week under some broadsides from the local movie house. The basket is now IN. I discovered by test that fully ninety per cent of whatever was on my desk at any given moment were IN things. Only ten per cent were OUT things—almost too few to warrant a special container.

E. B. White, "Incoming Basket," in *One Man's Meat*

Intonation

We spoke about pitch in Chapter 10. We also discussed it in Chapter 3. What we've talked about so far is mainly the overall pitch of your voice—pitch range and optimum and habitual pitches. Now we'll look at pitch in a different way: how you use pitch to bring additional meaning to or clarify or reinforce what you say.

Listen to someone whom you consider to be a good speaker. Close your eyes and concentrate mainly on that person's voice, not the actual words. Begin to focus on pitch—not the overall pitch but the changes in pitch that are occurring. After a while, you should begin to notice a pattern of pitch changes, up and down, that emerges. If you're successful in blocking out the actual words, it will almost seem as though the person is singing rather than speaking.

We *are* singing, to a certain extent, when we speak. Our language, just like every language, has its own unique melody that all native speakers learn from the beginning. We know that the melody adds a lot to the message.

We call the melody of language *intonation.* Intonation refers to the total pattern of pitch changes within an utterance. The intonation patterns we use are familiar and required by our language. For example, say the following sentence five times: *I am going to the store.* Listen closely to the pitch of your voice. You should hear that your voice started off at one pitch, rose slightly during the first couple of words, and then descended gradually during the rest of the utterance. This is a characteristic intonation pattern for a declarative statement. Now try asking some questions aloud. For example, ask "Am I going to the store?" Did you notice a different intonation pattern? You probably noted that rather than a descending pitch pattern at the end, there was a rising pitch. That pattern is characteristic of questioning utterances but not interrogatives. Notice the difference between "Are you going?" and "Why are you going?" The second question actually has a falling pitch.

It's important for you to use the appropriate intonation patterns when you speak. Otherwise, you may be sending messages using intonations that contradict what you want your words to say. Intonation patterns that disagree with the content of the utterance may indicate doubt, sarcasm, or confusion. And speech with a monotone intonation pattern may not be listened to at all. We're going to discuss the types of pitch changes that you make and give you exercises that you can use for practice. The drills and exercises should be helpful to you whether you're a native speaker or have learned English as a second language.

KEY

You're most likely aware that there's a relationship between the content and purpose of your utterance and the general pitch level you use. It wouldn't be appropriate for you to, let's say, resign "regretfully" from a job and use the higher notes of your pitch range to tell your boss. Nor would it be appropriate to announce that you just won a million dollar lottery prize using the lower part of your range. Try it: say, "I'm so happy! I just won a million dollars," using a low-pitched voice. You certainly don't sound happy, do you?

What we're talking about is called *key*—the average pitch level of an utterance. Generally, we refer to three keys—*low, middle,* and *high.* The middle key should be comfortable for you because it should correspond to your optimum pitch. Here are some selections for you to read aloud using the different keys. Try reading each sentence five times: first at middle key, then at high key, then back to middle key, then low key, and finally at middle key again:

1. Please take a seat and the dentist will be with you in a few minutes.
2. If I had it to do all over again, I'd do it all over again.
3. An old German proverb says, "It is a bad bridge that is shorter than the stream."
4. "Peace in space will help us nought once peace on Earth is gone." (John F. Kennedy)
5. "A fool and his money are soon parted." (*The New York Times,* October 20, 1987.)
6. The camel has been called "the ship of the desert," I guess because of seasickness.

The following exercises provide connected passages to read at the three levels.

Middle Key Readings

1. Learning is finding out what you already know. Doing is demonstrating that you know it. Teaching is reminding others that they know just as well as you. You are all learners, doers, teachers.

Richard Bach, Illusions

2. When you move to a new city it always seems mysterious. Filled with unknown people and businesses, strange addresses, and streets that interconnect at weird angles. After a few days of carefully following maps, or weeks of aimless wandering, the city begins to form into a logical concept in your mind. You are subconsciously aware of landmarks. If the clock tower is off to your right, you must be heading toward the coffee shop. You learn how the bus, subway, and back alleys carry you from point to point. After a while, even the biggest city starts to shrink as your mental image grows to encompass it.

Steve Lambert and Walter Howe, Internet Basics

3. One of my purposes was to listen, to hear speech, accent, speech rhythms, overtones and emphasis. For speech is so much more than words and sentences. I did listen everywhere. It seemed to me that regional speech is in the process of disappearing, not gone but going. Forty years of radio and twenty years of television must

have had this impact. Communications must destroy localness, by a slow, inevitable process. I can remember a time when I could almost pinpoint a man's place of origin by his speech. That is growing more difficult now, and will in some foreseeable future become impossible. It is a rare house or building that is not rigged with spiky combers of the air. Radio and television speech becomes standardized, perhaps better English than we have ever used. Just as our bread, mixed and baked, packaged and sold without benefit of accident or human frailty, is uniformly good and uniformly tasteless, so will our speech become one speech.

I who love words and the endless possibility of words am saddened by this inevitability. For with local accent will disappear local tempo. The idioms, the figures of speech that make language rich and full of the poetry of time and place must go. And in their place will be a national speech, wrapped and packaged, standard and tasteless. Localness is not gone but it is going.

John Steinbeck, Travels With Charley

4. Use a comma only when you have a definite reason for doing so in accordance with the guidelines below. A safe rule to follow, "When in doubt, leave it out."

The Random House Dictionary

5. There is an electricity about friendship relationships; they are like no other. Though we might not be able to choose our neighbors, relatives or the people with whom we work, friendships are an act of pure intention. Very few associations allow for such a free exchange of loyalty, trust, affection and, sometimes, doubt, hurt and anger. Friendship not only begins on a voluntary basis, but it continues by choice. The depth and rhythm of the relationship, the desire and willingness to respond to each other are open to negotiation. The process of choice may not be quick nor may it develop spectacularly—the yearning for a good friend is frequently frustrated—but make no mistake about it, most of us are involved in the search: Friendship matters.

Joel D. Block, Friendship: How to Give It, How to Get It

Low Key Readings

1. I leaned on the gate for a moment, breathing in the sweet air. There had been a change during the last week; the harsh winds had dropped, everything had softened and greened and the warming land gave off its scents. On the lower slopes of the fell, in the shade of the pine woods, a pale mist of bluebells drifted among the dead bronze of the bracken and their fragrance came up to me on the breeze.

James Herriot, All Things Bright and Beautiful

2. "I'm afraid he's dead, Mr. Barnett."

The big man did not change expression. He reached slowly across and rubbed his forefinger against the dark fur in that familiar gesture. Then he put his elbows on the desk and covered his face with his hands.

I did not know what to say; I watched helplessly as his shoulders began to shake and tears welled between the thick fingers. He stayed like that for some time, then he spoke:

"He was my friend," he said.

James Herriot, *The Lord God Made Them All*

3. The tree began softly to sing a hymn of twilight. The sun sank until slanted bronze rays struck the forest. There was a lull in the noises of insects as if they had bowed their beaks and were making a devotional pause. There was silence save for the chanted chorus of the trees.

Stephen Crane, *The Red Badge of Courage*

4. For a full day and two nights I have been alone. I lay on the beach under the stars at night alone. I made my breakfast alone. Alone I watched the gulls at the end of the pier, dip and wheel and dive for the scraps I threw them. A morning's work at my desk, and then, a late picnic lunch alone on the beach.

Anne Morrow Lindbergh, *Gift from the Sea*

5. May the sun bring you new energy by day,
   May the moon softly restore you by night.
   May the rain wash away your worries
   And the breeze blow new strength into your being.
   And all of the days of your life may you walk
   Gently through the world and know its beauty.

Apache Blessing

High Key Readings

1. Things to remember about saying hello—and goodbye:

The first one to offer his or her hand to the other is the hero. When you see someone you recognize (other than a celebrity) on the street or in an office, restaurant, movie or wherever, put a smile on your face and say cheerily, "Hello." The other person is immediately put at ease and thinks you're great for having gotten things moving.

Perfect a strong handshake. Have someone in your family or inner circle test your handshake. Do you give people a limp-fish grip? Do you crush the bones of the other person? Do you offer your fingertips instead of your hand (the worst thing you could possibly do)? Practice your handshake until it is warm, friendly and properly brief. If you are afflicted with sweaty palms, brush your right hand quickly over the back of your trousers or skirt so that the other person won't notice what you're doing, and then quickly bring your hand forward for the handshake.

Letitia Baldridge, *USA Today*

2. If you shut your eyes and are a lucky one, you may see at times a shapeless pool of lovely pale colors suspended in the darkness; then if you squeeze your eyes tighter, the pool begins to take shape, and the colors become so livid that with another squeeze they must go on fire. But just before they go on fire you see the lagoon. This is the nearest you ever get to it on the mainland, just one heavenly moment; if there could be two moments you might see the surf and hear the mermaids singing.

James Barrie, Peter Pan

3. I spun the periscope. Nothing. Putting it down, I grabbed for the extra earphones and heard it. No doubt about it, O'Brien was right. It sounded very much the same as one of our own torpedoes— the same high-pitched whine I had heard hundreds of times. It crossed our stern, came back up the starboard side, veered to the left as if to cross our bow. That was enough. My hair tingled as I thought of the secret magnetic exploder in the warheads of our torpedoes.

Edward L. Beach, Run Silent, Run Deep

4. So let freedom ring—from the prodigious hilltops of New Hampshire, let freedom ring; from the mighty mountains of New York, let freedom ring—from the heightening Alleghenies of Pennsylvania!
Let Freedom ring from the snowcapped Rockies of Colorado. Let freedom ring from the curvaceous slopes of California! But not only that; let freedom ring from Stone Mountain of Georgia.
Let Freedom ring from every hill and mole hill of Mississippi. From every mountainside, let freedom ring.

Martin Luther King, Jr., "I Have a Dream"

Inflection

Inflectional changes are those changes in pitch that occur within words while you're producing voice. You can think of them as being pitch glides or slides; they are done very smoothly. For example, say the word *yes* to mean, "Who is it?" You probably said that with a rising inflection. Now say the word *no* to mean "Absolutely not!" That word probably fell in pitch.

In English, we generally use rising inflection to indicate:

Questions
Incomplete series (Monday, Tuesday, Wednesday. . . .)
Doubt or uncertainty
A stressed word or syllable

We generally use falling inflection to indicate:

Ending or finality—positive statements
End of a phrase
Interrogatives (Where are you?)
A greater amount of stress

Drills for Inflection

Here are some drills for inflection. Doing these with a tape recorder or a fellow student can be helpful. Some of the following sentences have been diagrammed to indicate inflection: ⌣ means rising inflection; ⌢ means falling inflection; — means no change (level pitch). Read the sentences aloud using the inflection indicated by the marks.

Drill for Rising Inflection

Read each of the following words aloud three times, each time asking more of a question. In other words, you're going to read them with rising pitch, and each time you read a word you're going to exaggerate, making the pitch rise more than the time before. Try to start each word at the same pitch levels as the word before; don't "step" each word higher.

1. Where?   Where??   Where???
2. When?   When??   When???
3. Who?   Who??   Who???
4. Why?   Why??   Why???
5. What?   What??   What???

Now read each of the following sentences three times, and each time exaggerate the rise in pitch at the end. Continue to start each sentence at the same pitch level as the previous one; don't start progressively higher.

1. Is it my book?   Is it my book??   Is it my book???
2. Is the TV on?   Is the TV on??   Is the TV on???
3. Are you sure?   Are you sure??   Are you sure???
4. Can we go?   Can we go??   Can we go???
5. Want some coffee?   Want some coffee??
   Want some coffee???

Drill for Falling Inflection

Read each of the following words aloud, three times. Each time make it more of a definite, positive statement. Each time you read the statement, exaggerate the falling inflection. Try to start each word at the same pitch level as the previous word; don't "step" each word lower.

1. No!   No!!   No!!!
2. Now!   Now!!   Now!!!
3. Sure! Sure!! Sure!!!
4. Yes!   Yes!!   Yes!!!
5. Go!   Go!!   Go!!!

Now do the same with the following sentences. Read each one aloud three times, each time exaggerating the falling pitch more than the time before. Start each sentence at the same pitch level as the previous one; don't start progressively lower.

1. Yes, I'm sure!   Yes, I'm sure!!   Yes, I'm sure!!!
2. The TV's on!   The TV's on!!   The TV's on!!!
3. Have some coffee! Have some coffee!! Have some coffee!!!
4. Gosh, I'm tired!   Gosh, I'm tired!!   Gosh, I'm tired!!!
5. Let's go now!   Let's go now!!   Let's go now!!!

There's another pattern of inflection that we call *circumflex.* It's a combination of rising and falling inflections. Here's an example. Say the word *yes* in a way that indicates a confident, positive answer. You probably said it with a definite falling inflection. Now say the word *yes* to indicate you're not sure. Notice the change? You probably said it this time with circumflex inflection: both rising and falling inflections in the same utterance.

Drill for Circumflex Inflection

Say each of the following words aloud four times. The first time you say the word, use falling inflection to indicate a positive, final statement. The second, third, and fourth times follow the markings and use circumflex inflection, exaggerating the pitch rise and fall more than the time before. As in the previous drills, start each word at the same pitch level.

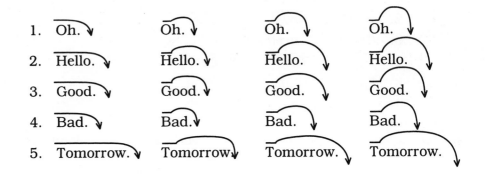

1. Oh.
2. Hello.
3. Good.
4. Bad.
5. Tomorrow.

Practice Sentences

The following sentences contain both rising and falling inflections. Read each sentence using the pattern of inflection indicated by the arrows.

1. Here's your tea.
2. Did you go?
3. I want it now.
4. I bought some books,   pens,   and ink.
5. Up,   up,   and away.
6. Are you alone?
7. Can you say *please?*
8. Do you want a peach,   a plum,   or a pear?
9. I see.
10. Do you?

We have not marked the following sentences, nor have we provided punctuation. Mark them yourself, being as creative as you like, and then read them according to your directions.

11. Go down that road and make a left

12. Yesterday was hot humid and horrible

13. A word of advice after injury is like a dose of medicine after death

14. Never try to teach a pig to sing—it only wastes your time and makes the pig angry

15. The Greek philosopher Heraclitus said "It is not possible to step into the same river twice"

Steps

We also change pitch *between* utterances. It's an abrupt change, almost a jump, that we call a step. You make this type of change between syllables and words.

Drill for Steps

Read the following phrases and sentences aloud. The steps have been diagrammed as follows:

I can jump/up\or down.

The word *up* steps up to a higher pitch, the word *down* steps down to a lower pitch.

Now, diagram the following sentences and say them aloud according to the way you have marked them.

1. He\did.

2. What/time?

3. Next\week.

4. On/top\of the/desk.

5. On top of/the\desk.

6. The/next\time.

7. This\is a/shift.

8. Come/here\right/now!

9. A/piece\of paper.

10. Do\you/want\it?

11.   Come   back   tomorrow.

12.   Write   to   me.

13.   Ask   me   a   question.

14.   Are   you   hungry?

15.   Read   this   sentence   aloud.

16.   A   man   and   a   woman.

17.   Let's   take   a   walk.

18.   Do   you   have   today's   paper?

19.   What   time   is   it?

20.   I've   got   a   case   of   new   car   fever.

Readings for Intonation

Read the following selections silently first, and decide on the appropriate pitch patterns to use. Plan your readings by marking the selections in advance for overall key, inflectional changes, and steps. Each selection can be read in a number of ways, so make your markings erasable.

1. Sunlight powers the world. It strikes the earth as radiant energy, and as it strikes it is changed into a bewildering variety of other forms. It lifts the waters of the oceans high above the earth, providing a store of potential energy in the clouds. It appears in awesome forms in hurricanes and lightning bolts. It is also a form of chemical energy, stored silently by the green plants of the oceans—chemical energy to be transformed in many ways to serve the energy needs of man. Each of these many pathways—whether in living or in non-living systems—conforms to the law of conservation of energy.

The flashing of a firefly on a hot summer night, the flow of electricity from the generators of Hoover Dam, the surging power of a swordfish, all conform to this same universal law.

Ritchie Ward, *Into the Ocean World*

2. I go down.
Rung after rung and still
the oxygen immerses me

the blue light
the clear atoms
of our human air.
I go down.
My flippers cripple me,
I crawl like an insect down the ladder
and there is no one
to tell me when the ocean
will begin.

First the air is blue and then
it is bluer and then green and then
black I am blacking out and yet
my mask is powerful
it pumps my blood with power
the sea is another story
the sea is not a question of power
I have to learn alone
to turn my body without force
in the deep element.

Adrienne Rich, "Diving into the Wreck"

3. I wanted to be a Boy Scout, but I had all the wrong traits. They were looking for kids who were trustworthy, loyal, helpful, friendly, courteous, kind, obedient, cheerful, thrifty, brave, clean, and reverent. Whereas I tended to be devious, fickle, obstructive, hostile, impolite, mean, defiant, glum, extravagant, cowardly, dirty, and sacrilegious.

George Carlin, *Brain Droppings*

4. To every thing there is a season, and a time to every purpose under the heaven;
   A time to be born, and a time to die; a time to plant, and a time to pluck up that which is planted;
   A time to kill, and a time to heal; a time to break down, and a time to build up;
   A time to weep, and a time to laugh; a time to mourn, and a time to dance;
   A time to cast away stones, and a time to gather stones together; a time to embrace, and a time to refrain from embracing;
   A time to get, and a time to lose; a time to keep, and a time to cast away;
   A time to rend, and a time to sew; a time to keep silence, and a time to speak;
   A time to love, and a time to hate; a time of war, and a time of peace.

Ecclesiastes 3:1–8

Integration

Now you can practice putting all the pieces of vocal expression together by integrating them for effective readings. We've provided a number of fiction and nonfiction selections for you to work with. We suggest that you read a piece silently first. Consider the mood, the author's purpose. Determine how you're going to emphasize stress, rate, duration, inflection, pausing, and so on. You may notice we've spaced the lines of these readings slightly farther apart than usual. That's to make it easier for you to mark your directions with the arrows, slash marks, underlines, and other marks we've shown you in this chapter. Tape-record your readings. Ask for feedback from your instructor or someone in your class.

The selections are organized in two separate levels. Level 1 is general and contains a variety of selections covering a range of materials as well as different subjects. They are all average in level of difficulty. Level 2 contains selections that are more challenging to read aloud—not only because they have unusual requirements for vocal variety but also because they may contain difficult-to-produce sounds or sounds in intricate combinations. The selections are numbered according to group.

Level 1

1-1. "Dead on the Road," in Mama Makes Up Her Mind, Bailey White *(237 words)*

My mother eats things she finds dead on the road. Her standards are high. She claims she won't eat anything that's not a fresh kill. But I don't trust her. I required documentation. I won't eat it unless she can tell me the model and tag number of the car that struck it.

Mama is an adventurous and excellent cook, and we have feasted not only on doves, turkeys, and quail, but robins, squirrels, and, only once, a possum. I draw the line at snakes. "But it was still wiggling when I got there," she argues. "Let's try it just this once. I have a white sauce with dill and mustard."

"No snakes," I say.

And she won't even slow down for armadillos, although they are the most common dead animal on the road these days. "They look too stupid to eat," she says.

We have a prissy aunt Eleanor who comes to dinner every third Friday. We always get out the linen and polish the silver when she comes. She expects it. Last month we sat her down to an elegant meal, complete with the Spode china and camellias in a crystal bowl.

"The quail are delicious," my aunt sighed. And I haven't found a single piece of shot. How do you manage it?"

"Intersection of 93 and Baggs Road," recites Mama. "Green late model pickup, Florida tag. Have another one. And some rice, El."

1-2. *"A Lifetime of Chances"* in Harvest Moon: A Wisconsin Outdoor Anthology, Timothy L. Personius *(224 words)*

I remember certain fall days. The first fall days, really, when an uncertain cold front would drop out of Canada, temporarily pushing the muggy air of summer out of the upper Midwest. If you've ever lived there, you know how refreshing those suddenly clear, brisk days can be—days when you want to live just to breathe that clear, cool air from the tundra.

Those fronts also brought thousands of geese to my home in Wisconsin, on the edge of Horicon Marsh. Canada geese—big, black, white and gray. I'd hear the murmuring rumor of them for some days; a late night whisper of honking, far away in the dark. I'd look for them every morning, sometimes calling my father at the federal wildlife refuge headquarters to ask if anyone had yet seen them.

Finally they'd arrive—chevron after chevron traced thinly against the sky, looming larger in their descent—some nearly overshooting the refuge and resorting to a spectacular side-slip stall, plummeting like skydivers until they unfurled their wings with a rifle-sharp crack of suddenly compressed air. For a moment, even now, the air is filled with the snapping reports of barking geese, and I am standing outside our house, watching them settle softly over the marsh. In my commonest memory, they arrive all at once, changing summer into fall, instantly, by their presence.

1-3. *Dracula,* Bram Stoker *(380 words)*

I looked out over the beautiful expanse, bathed in soft yellow moonlight till it was almost as light as day. In the soft light the distant hills became melted, and the shadows in the valleys and gorges of velvety blackness. The mere beauty seemed to cheer me; there was peace and comfort in every breath I drew. As I learned from the window my eye was caught by something moving a storey below me, and somewhat to my left, where I imagined, from the lie of the rooms, that the windows of the Count's own room would look out. The window at which I stood was tall and deep, stone-mullioned, and though weather-worn, was still complete; but it drew back behind the stonework, and looked carefully out.

What I saw was the Count's head coming out from the window. I did not see the face, but I knew the man by the neck and the movement of his back and arms. In any case I could not mistake the hands which I had had so many opportunities of studying. I was at first interested and somewhat amused, for it is wonderful how small a matter will interest and amuse a man when he is a prisoner. But my very feelings changed to repulsion and terror when I saw the whole man slowly emerge from the window and begin to crawl down the castle wall over that dreadful abyss, *face down*, with his cloak spreading out around him like great wings. At first I could not believe my eyes, I thought it was some trick of the moonlight, some weird effect of shadow; but I kept looking and it could be no delusion. I saw the fingers and toes grasp the corners of the stones, worn clear of the mortar by the stress of years, and by thus using every projection and inequality move downwards with considerable speed, just as a lizard moves along a wall.

What manner of man is this, or what manner of creature is it in the semblance of man? I feel the dread of this horrible place overpowering me; I am in fear—in awful fear—and there is no escape for me.

1-4. "How the Popsicle Got on the Stick," in How the Cadillac Got Its Fins, Jack Mingo *(174 words)*

How many things have been invented by eleven-year-old boys? Lots, no doubt. But how many of them would you want to stick in your mouth?

Eleven-year-old Frank Epperson, the story goes, accidentally left a glass of soda pop mix and water on his back porch. The stirring stick was still in it. That night the temperature got well below freezing. Absent-minded Frank went out and found the stick emerging from a frozen block of soft drink. His friends and family were amazed. On that night in 1905, the Popsicle was invented.

You could question the details of the story. On a cold winter day, after all, how many people take a cold drink out to the back porch? How often do eleven-year-olds mix up a soft drink and then forget to drink it? Isn't it more likely that Epperson had figured out what would happen and left the glass outside on purpose? Or even more likely that he simply made the story up years later when his patent application came under question? Hmmm.

1-5. The Hound of the Baskervilles, Sir Arthur Conan Doyle *(138 words)*

With tingling nerves but a fixed purpose, I sat in the dark recess of the hut and waited with sombre patience for the coming of its tenant.

And then at last heard him. Far away came the sharp clink of a boot striking upon a stone. Then another and yet another, coming nearer and nearer. I shrank back into the darkest corner and cocked the pistol in my pocket, determined not to discover myself until I had an opportunity of seeing something of the stranger. There was a long pause which showed that he had stopped. Then once more the footsteps approached and a shadow fell across the opening of the hut.

"It is a lovely evening, my dear Watson," said a well known voice. "I really think that you will be more comfortable outside than in."

1-6. "The Tide Rises, The Tide Falls," Henry Wadsworth Longfellow *(101 words)*

> The tide rises, the tide falls,
> The twilight darkens, the curlew calls;
> Along the sea-sands damp and brown
> The traveller hastens toward the town,
>   And the tide rises, the tide falls.
>
> Darkness settles on roofs and walls,
> But the sea, the sea in the darkness calls;

The little waves, with their soft, white hands,
Efface the footprints in the sands,
  And the tide rises, the tide falls.

The morning breaks; the steeds in their stalls
Stamp and neigh, as the hostler calls;
The day returns, but nevermore
Returns the traveler to the shore,
  And the tide rises, the tide falls.

1-7. *Love and Will,* Rollow May *(179 words)*

During the long summers in New Hampshire I would often get up early in the morning and go out on my patio where the valley, stretching off to the mountain ranges in the north and east, was silver with predawn mist. The birds eloquent voices in an otherwise silent world, had already begun their hallelujah chorus to welcome in the new day. The song sparrow sings with an enthusiasm which rocks him almost off his perch atop the apple tree, and the goldfinch chimes in with his obligato. The thrush in the woods is so full of song he can't contain himself. The woodpecker beats on the hollow beech tree. The loons over the lake erupt with their plaintive and tormented daemonic, to save the whole thing from being too sweet. Then the sun comes up over the mountain range revealing an incredibly green New Hampshire overflowing through the whole long valley with a richness that is almost too abundant. The trees seem to have grown several inches overnight, and the meadow is bursting with a million brown-eyed Susans.

1-8. *Mister Roberts,* Thomas Heggen *(265 words)*

He walked back to the wing, leaned against the windshield, and looked out at the sea and the night; and for the first time he noticed what an incredible night it was. The moon—what an enormous moon! It had risen yellow and round and fat, and now that it was higher it had shrunk a little, but still it was round and full, and no longer yellow, but molten, incandescent silver. The light it spread was daylight with the harshness filtered out, unbelievably pure and even and dimensionless. On the bridge you could have read a newspaper: it was that bright. The moon now was on the port quarter and all the way to the horizon it parted the water in a wide, white glistening path that hurt the eyes; and back where the horizon should be there was really none at all, there was only this pale blue, shimmering haze where sky and water merged without a discernible break. And the sea was even more remarkable: Roberts had never seen the sea quite like this. There wasn't a ripple anywhere; there was only the faintest hint of a ground swell, an occasional bulge of water. The surface, glazed as it was with moonlight, looked heavy, coated, enameled: it was that perfect. The ship slid through the water with an oily hiss, and the bow cut the fabric like a casual knife. At the stern, the wake was a wide, frothing rent, but further back it was healing and not so wide, and far, far back the fabric was whole and perfect again.

1-9. "Your Guide Deserves Better," in Saltwater Fly Fishing, Captain John Kumiski *(119 words)*

It's happened to me more than once. I get up at 4:30 a.m. and drive blearyeyed to the boat landing while drinking strong black coffee. I need the caffeine because I want my brain in gear for that 5:30 appointment. I launch my boat and make sure things are in working order. Five-thirty comes and goes. I fight off mosquitoes. I finish my coffee. I watch the sky get light. Six o'clock comes and goes. I fight off mosquitoes. I apply sunsreen. I watch the sunrise. Six-thirty comes. I decide whether to pull the boat out and go home, or go fishing alone, since the charter isn't showing up. I spend time wishing I had gotten a deposit.

1-10. Fire and Ice, Paul Garrison *(247 words)*

He dozed and woke shivering. Dozed some more, starting awake with anxious looks at his watch. The hours crept by—two, three, four. He thought of the chances he must take and grew crazy with doubt. He slept from four to five-thirty and woke feeling little refreshed, his stomach alive with hunger, his mouth dry, craving coffee.

He was gazing across the enclosure, studying the wooden posts that studded the distant ground, before he realized that dawn had already broken, casting enough light through the overcast for him to see the far walls. The posts—for that was what they definitely were, wooden posts sunk in the ground—stood like the sentinels he had imagined in the dark. Warily, he stirred, studying the walls to the left and right. The light revealed a scruffy field of uncut grass and very little cover. If anyone at the home plate end were to study the far walls carefully, they'd spot him. The light grew stronger.

He cursed himself for waiting too long. He should have awakened earlier. On the other hand, what fog there was lay thinly on the ground. Was it the same beyond the walls, or did the walls block the fog on its route from the river? Sarah would make her move half an hour after the fog was thick. Only by climbing the wall could he see, and if he tried they would surely spot him. Yet better to try now before more people came.

1-11. Inaugural Address, New York City Mayor David N. Dinkins *(166 words)*

Human rights is the most powerful idea in human history. And now we know—and yes, we don't just hope, we know—that some day soon the bells of freedom will also ring in Tianaymen Square and Soweto.

We are all foot soldiers on the march to freedom, here and everywhere. We all belong to the America that Lincoln called "the last, best hope of earth."

In advancing that hope, our most powerful weapon is example. And this year, this city has given powerful proof of the proposition that all of us are created equal.

I stand here before you today as the elected leader of the greatest city of a great nation, to which my ancestors were brought, chained and whipped in the hold of a slave ship.

We have not finished the journey toward liberty and justice. But surely we have come a long way.

This day is not a tribute to me; it is a tribute to you, the people of New York.

1-12. *"This New England Sea Smoke,"* in Yankee Magazine, Susan Hand Shetterly, *(200 words)*

Often during the night in winter, air from the vast snow barrens far to the north of Prospect Harbor, Maine, slips down and rests against the water. Then, in the morning, you can't see the sun coming up beyond Lighthouse Point to the east of the harbor and the lighthouse, but you can see the pale colors of sunrise as they shimmer through curtains of sea smoke.

A mast or a radar antenna from one of the moored fishing boats pokes into the sky. A brightly painted bow or a gunwale or a stern with a name on—the *Miss Rita,* perhaps—appears and vanishes as the gauzy curtains close. Usually, there is hardly a wind. Everything is quiet, except for a few eider ducks conversing in low-pitched voices somewhere beyond the boats. Invisible.

The men who fish and haul traps out of Prospect Harbor know weather. They maneuver their boats through it with the same skill it takes to lower drag doors and a net onto soft bottom or to set a trawling line for cod. Weather out on the water is something so familiar it is almost beyond words. It is a look. A feel. A smell.

1-13. *The Airborne Buffet Takes Off,* Heath Eden *(148 words)*

Although no one ever fondly remembers a meal served during an airline flight, passengers complained loudly in late 1993 when major carriers started forgoing meals for lower airfares. Now food is back, with a vengeance.

Hungry travelers on flights that offer full meals now have more choices that just chicken or beef. For example, if you order ahead, United Airlines offers such special menu and dietary choices as vegetarian, Asian vegetarian, vegetarian nondairy, child, toddler, baby, seafood, kosher, Obento, low-cal, low-sodium, diabetic, Hindu, gluten-free, high-fiber, low protein, bland, lactose-free, halal, skinless boneless chicken, chef's salad, and that longtime favorite, the fruit plate. Other major airlines have also expanded their menus to avoid offending any person.

With all the emphasis on health meal choices, however, snacks remain a favorite: In a Harris survey commissioned by United Airlines of its passengers, fliers preferred peanuts to pretzels by a 2-to-1 margin.

1-14. *"Sign and Pun-ishment,"* Fred L. Schroder *(162 words)*

The sign over a Brooklyn, New York, café reads "Warm Beer—Lousy Food." Hardly inviting at first gland, but after an involuntary double take, one somehow gets a strong feeling that the beer must really be super-cold and the food terrific. It's artful psychology: Aren't chances better you'll remember that place than if its sign read simply, "Cold Beer—Good Food"?

And who couldn't admire the play on words of the Recovery Room, a Salt Lake City upholstery shop, or the San Francisco eatery specializing in hot dogs called Franks for the Memory. Then there's an auto-rental agency in Mahopac, New York, whose sign hints at a famous movie title: Chariots for Hire.

Unlike their counterparts in most foreign countries, American merchants love to inject humor and sparkle when naming their places of business. All over the United States dealers in products and services have coined odd-ball names for their companies in an effort to make them stand out.

1-15. Aunt Erma's Cope Book, Erma Bombeck (54 words)

My son, Jaws II, had a habit that drove me crazy. He'd walk to the refrigerator-freezer and fling both doors open and stand there until the hairs on his nose iced up. After surveying two hundred dollars' worth of food in varying shapes and forms he would declare loudly "There's nothing to eat."

1-16. Sein Language, Jerry Seinfeld (140 words)

Men seem to flip around the television more than women. Men get that remote control in their hands, they don't even know what the hell they're not watching. You know we just keep going, "Rerun, that's stupid, he's stupid, she's stupid, go, go, go."

"What are you watching?"

"I don't care, I gotta keep going."

"Who was that?"

"I don't know what it was, doesn't matter, it's not your fault, I gotta keep going."

"I think that's a documentary on your father."

"Don't care, what else is on?"

Women don't do this. Women will stop and go, "Well let me see what the show is, before I change the channel. Maybe we can nurture it, work with it, help it grow into something." Men don't do that. Because women nest and men hunt. That's why we watch TV differently.

1-17. If Life Is a Bowl of Cherries, What Am I Doing in the Pits? Erma Bombeck *(97 words)*

Did you ever notice how in reporting sports no one ever "wins" a game?

They crush, stomp, triumph, trounce, bomb, outscore, outclass, overthrow, run over, edge out, hammer and victimize, but they never use the word "win."

The other night after a sportscast where there were three assaults, four upsets, one humiliation, a squeaker, and a rout, I said to my husband, "These guys must be fed intravenously by a thesaurus each night to come up with all those words that mean 'win.'"

"They have to," he said. "You'd get bored hearing who 'won' all the time."

Level 2

2-1. Third Inaugural Address, President Franklin D. Roosevelt (247 words)

Democracy is not dying.

We know it because we have seen it revive—and grow.

We know it cannot die—because it is built on the unhampered initiative of individual men and women joined together in a common enterprise—an enterprise undertaken and carried through by the free expression of a free majority.

We know it because democracy alone, of all forms of government, enlists the full force of men's enlightened will.

We know it because democracy alone has constructed an unlimited civilization capable of infinite progress in the improvement of human life.

We know it because, if we look below the surface, we sense it still spreading on every continent—for it is the most humane, the most advanced, and in the end the most unconquerable of all forms of human society.

A nation, like a person, has a body—a body that must be fed and clothed and housed, invigorated and rested, in a manner that measures up to the objectives of our time.

A nation, like a person, has a mind—a mind that must be kept informed and alert, that must know itself, that understands the hopes and the needs of its neighbors—all the other nations that live within the narrowing circle of the world.

And a nation, like a person, has something deeper, something more permanent, something larger than the sum of all its parts. It is that something which matters most to its future—which calls forth the most sacred guarding of its present.

2-2. Inaugural Address, President Harry S. Truman *(367 words)*

The American people desire, and are determined to work for, a world in which all nations and all peoples are free to govern themselves as they see fit, and to achieve a decent and satisfying life. Above all else, our people desire, and are determined to work for, peace on earth—a just and lasting peace—based on genuine agreement freely arrived at by equals.

In the pursuit of these aims, the United States and other like-minded nations find themselves directly opposed by a regime with contrary aims and a totally different concept of life.

That regime adheres to a false philosophy which purports to offer freedom, security, and greater opportunity to mankind. Misled by this philosophy, many peoples have sacrificed their liberties only to learn to their sorrow that deceit and mockery, poverty and tyranny, are their reward.

That false philosophy is communism.

Communism is based on the belief that man is so weak and inadequate that he is unable to govern himself, and therefore requires the rule of strong masters.

Democracy is based on the conviction that man has the moral and intellectual capacity, as well as the inalienable right, to govern himself with reason and justice.

Communism subjects the individual to arrest without lawful cause, punishment without trial, and forced labor as the chattel of the state. It decrees what information he shall receive, what art he shall produce, what leaders he shall follow, and what thoughts he shall think.

Democracy maintains that government is established for the benefit of the individual, and is charged with the responsibility of protecting the rights of the individual and his freedom in the exercise of his abilities.

Communism maintains that social wrongs can be corrected only by violence. Democracy has proved that social justice can be achieved through peaceful change.

Communism holds that the world is so deeply divided into opposing classes that war is inevitable.

Democracy holds that free nations can settle differences justly and maintain lasting peace.

These differences between communism and democracy do not concern the United States alone. People everywhere are coming to realize that what is involved is material well-being, human dignity, and the right to believe in and worship God.

2-3. *First Inaugural Address,* President Dwight D. Eisenhower *(326 words)*

We must be ready to dare all for our country. For history does not long entrust the care of freedom to the weak or the timid. We must acquire proficiency in defense and display stamina in purpose.

We must be willing, individually and as a nation, to accept whatever sacrifices may be required of us. A people that values its privileges above its principles soon loses both.

These basic precepts are not lofty abstractions, far removed from matters of daily living. They are laws of spiritual strength that generate and define our material strength. Patriotism means equipped forces and a prepared citizenry. Moral stamina means more energy and more productivity, on the farm and in the factory. Love of liberty means the guarding of every resource that makes freedom possible—from the sanctity of our families and the wealth of our soil to the genius of our scientists.

And so each citizen plays an indispensable role. The productivity of our heads, our hands, and our hearts is the source of all the strength we can command, for both the enrichment of our lives and the winning of the peace.

No person, no home, no community can be beyond the reach of this call. We are summoned to act in wisdom and in conscience, to work with industry, to teach with persuasion, to preach with conviction, to weigh our every deed with care and with compassion. For this truth must be clear before us: whatever America hopes to bring to pass in the world must first come to pass in the heart of America.

The peace we seek, then, is nothing less than the practice and fulfillment of our whole faith among ourselves and in our dealings with others. This signifies more than the stilling of guns, easing the sorrow of war. More than escape from death, it is a way of life. More than a haven for the weary, it is a hope for the brave.

2-4. *Inaugural Address,* President John F. Kennedy *(261 words)*

My Fellow Citizens: We observe today not a victory of party but a celebration of freedom—symbolizing an end as well as a beginning—signifying renewal as well as change. For I have sworn before you and almighty God the same solemn oath our forebears prescribed nearly a century and three-quarters ago.

The world is very different now. For man holds in his mortal hands the power to abolish all forms of human poverty and all forms of human life. And yet the same revolutionary beliefs for which our forebears fought are still at issue around the globe—the belief that the rights of man come not from the generosity of the state but from the hand of God.

We dare not forget today that we are the heirs of that first revolution. Let the word go forth from this time and place, to friend and foe alike, that the torch has been passed to a new generation of Americans—born in this century, tempered by war, disciplined by a hard and bitter peace, proud of our ancient heritage—and unwilling to witness or permit the slow undoing of those human rights to which this nation has always been committed, and to which we are committed today at home and around the world.

Let every nation know, whether it wishes us well or ill, that we shall pay any price, bear any burden, meet any hardship, support any friend, oppose any foe in order to assure the survival and success of liberty.

This much we pledge—and more.

2-5. *Inaugural Address,* President Lyndon Baines Johnson *(180 words)*

My fellow countrymen, on this occasion, the oath I have taken before God is not mine alone, but ours together. We are one nation and one people. Our fate as a nation and our future as a people rest not upon one citizen, but upon all citizens.

This is the majesty and the meaning of this moment.

For every generation, there is a destiny. For some, history decides. For this generation, the choice must be our own.

Even now, a rocket moves toward Mars. It reminds us that the world will not be the same for our children, or even for ourselves in a short span of years. The next man to stand here will look out on a scene different from our own, because ours is a time of change—rapid and fantastic change bearing the secrets of nature, multiplying the nations, placing in uncertain hands new weapons for mastery and destruction, shaking old values, and uprooting old ways.

Our destiny in the midst of change will rest on the unchanged character of our people, and on their faith.

2-6. *First Inaugural Address,* President Richard Milhous Nixon *(158 words)*

The essence of freedom is that each of us shares in the shaping of his own destiny.

Until he has been part of a cause larger than himself, no man is truly whole.

The way to fulfillment is in the use of our talents; we achieve nobility in the spirit that inspires that use.

As we measure what can be done, we shall promise only what we know we can produce, but as we chart our goals we shall be lifted by our dreams.

No man can be fully free while his neighbor is not. To go forward at all is to go forward together.

This means black and white together as one nation, not two. The laws have caught up with our conscience. What remains is to give life to what is in the law; to ensure at last that as all are born equal in dignity before God, all are born equal in dignity before man.

2-7. *Inaugural Address,* President Jimmy Carter *(183 words)*

I have no new dream to set forth today, but rather urge a fresh faith in the old dream.

Ours was the first society openly to define itself in terms of both spirituality and of human liberty. It is that unique self-definition which has given us an exceptional appeal, but it also imposes on us a special obligation, to take on those moral duties which, when assumed, seem invariably to be in our own best interests.

You have given me a great responsibility—to stay close to you, to be worthy of you, and to exemplify what you are. Let us create together a new national spirit of unity and trust. Your strength can compensate for my weakness, and your wisdom can help to minimize my mistakes.

Let us learn together and laugh together and work together and pray together, confident that in the end we will triumph together in the right.

The American dream endures. We must once again have full faith in our country—and in one another. I believe America can be better. We can be even stronger than before.

2-8. *First Inaugural Address,* President Ronald Reagan *(119 words)*

Those who say that we're in a time when there are no heroes—they just don't know where to look. You can see heroes every day going in and out of factory gates. Others, a handful in number, produce enough food to feed all of us and then the world beyond.

You meet heroes across a counter—and they're on both sides of that counter. There are entrepreneurs with faith in themselves and faith in an idea who create new jobs, new wealth and opportunity.

There are individuals and families whose taxes support the Government and whose voluntary gifts support church, charity, culture, art and education. Their patriotism is quiet but deep. Their values sustain our national life.

2-9. *Inaugural Address,* President George Bush *(202 words)*

A new breeze is blowing—and a nation refreshed by freedom stands ready to push on. There's new ground to be broken and new action to be taken. There are times when the future seems thick as a fog; you sit and wait, hoping the mist will lift and reveal the right path.

But this is a time when the future seems a door you can walk right through, into a room called Tomorrow. Great nations of the world are moving toward democracy—through the door to the moral and intellectual satisfactions that only liberty allows.

We know what works: Freedom works. We know what's right: Freedom is right. We know how to secure a more just and prosperous life for man on earth: through free markets, free speech, free elections, and the exercise of free will unhampered by the state.

For the first time in this century—for the first time in perhaps all history—man does not have to invent a system by which to live. We don't have to talk late into the night about which form of government is better. We don't have to wrest justice from the kings—we only have to summon it from within ourselves.

2-10. *First Inaugural Address,* President Bill Clinton *(198 words)*

I challenge a new generation of young Americans to a season of service; to act on your idealism by helping troubled children, keeping company with those in need, reconnecting our torn communities. There is so much to be done. Enough, indeed, for millions of others who are still young in spirit to give of themselves in service, too.

In serving we recognize a simple but powerful truth: We need each other and we must care for one another. Today we do more than celebrate America, we rededicate ourselves to the very idea of America: An idea born in revolution and renewed through two centuries of challenge; an idea tempered by the knowledge that but for fate we, the fortunate and the unfortunate, might have been each other; an idea ennobled by the faith that our nation can summon from its myriad diversity the deepest measure of unity; an idea infused with the conviction that America's long heroic journey must go forever upward.

And so, my fellow Americans, as we stand at the edge of the 21st century, let us begin anew with energy and hope, with faith and discipline. And let us work until our work is done.

2-11. *Inaugural Address,* President George W. Bush *(147 words)*

We have a place, all of us, in a long story—a story we continue, but whose end we will not see. It is the story of a new world that became a friend and liberator of the old, a story of a slave-holding society that became a servant of freedom, the story of a power that went into the world to protect but not possess, to defend but not to conquer.

It is the American story—a story of flawed and fallible people, united across the generations by grand and enduring ideals. The grandest of these ideals is an unfolding American promise that everyone belongs, that everyone deserves a chance, that no insignificant person was ever born.

Americans are called to enact this promise in our lives and in our laws. And though our nation has sometimes halted, and sometimes delayed, we must follow no other course.

2-12. The Mother Tongue, Bill Bryson *(201 words)*

Whether you call a long cylindrical sandwich a hero, a submarine, a hoagy, a torpedo, a garibaldi, a poor boy, or any of at least a half a dozen other names tells us something about where you come from. Whether you call it cottage cheese, Dutch cheese, pot cheese, smearcase, clabber cheese, or curd cheese tells us something more. If you call the playground toy in which a long plank balances on a fulcrum a dandle you almost certainly come from Rhode Island. If you call a soft drink tonic, you come from Boston. If you call a small naturally occurring object a stone rather than a rock you mark yourself as a New Englander. If you have a catch rather than play catch or stand on line rather than in line clearly you are a New Yorker. Whether you call it pop or soda, bucket or pail, baby carriage or baby buggy, scat or gesundheit, the beach or the shore—all these and countless others tell us a little something about where you come from. Taken together they add up to what grammarians call your idiolect, the linguistic quirks and conventions that distinguish one group of language users from another.

2-13. Roughing It, Mark Twain *(142 words)*

The coyote is a long, slim, sick and sorry-looking skeleton, with a gray wolf-skin stretched over it, a tolerably bushy tail that forever sags down with a despairing expression of forsakeness and misery, a furtive and evil eye, and a long, sharp face, with slightly lifted lip and exposed teeth. He has a general slinking expression all over. The coyote is a living, breathing allegory of Want. He is *always* hungry. He is always poor, out of luck and friendless. The meanest creatures despise him, and even the fleas would desert him for a velocipede. He is so spiritless and cowardly that even while his exposed teeth are pretending a threat, the rest of his face is apologizing for it. And he is *so* homely!—so scrawny, and ribby, and coarse-haired, and pitiful. When he sees you he lifts his lip and lets a flash of his teeth out, and then turns a little out of the course he was pursuing, depresses his head a bit, and strikes a long, soft-footed trot through the sagebrush, glancing over his shoulder at you, from time to time, till he is about out of easy pistol range, and then he stops and takes a deliberate survey of you; he will trot fifty yards and stop again—another fifty and stop again; and finally the gray of his gliding body blends with the gray of the sagebrush, and he disappears.

2-14. Through the Looking-Glass: And What Alice Found There, Lewis Carroll *(246 words)*

"I don't know what you mean by 'glory,' " Alice said.

Humpty Dumpty smiled contemptuously, "Of course you don't—till I tell you. I meant 'there's a nice knock-down argument for you!' "

"But 'glory' doesn't mean a 'nice knock-down argument' Alice objected.

"When I use a word," Humpty Dumpty said, in rather a scornful tone, "it means just what I choose it to mean—neither more nor less."

"The question is," said Alice, "whether you *can* make words mean so many different things."

"The question is," said Humpty Dumpty, "which is to be master—that's all."

Alice was much too puzzled to say anything; so after a minute Humpty Dumpty began again. "They've a temper, some of them—particularly verbs: they're the proudest—adjectives you can do anything with, but not verbs—however, I can manage the whole lot of them! Impenetrability! That's what I say!"

"Would you tell me please," said Alice, "what that means?"

"Now you talk like a reasonable child," said Humpty Dumpty, looking very much pleased. "I meant by 'impenetrability' that we've had enough of that subject, and it would be just as well if you'd mention what you mean to do next, as I suppose you don't mean to stop here all the rest of your life."

"That's a great deal to make one word mean," Alice said in a thoughtful tone.

"When I make a word do a lot of work like that," said Humpty Dumpty, "I always pay it extra."

2-15. *Chapter Two*, Neil Simon *(95 words)*

Jennie: I am sick and tired of running from places and people and relationships. . . . And don't tell me what I want because *I'll* tell you what I want. I want a home and I want a family—and I want a career, too. And I want a dog and I want a cat and I want three goldfish. I want *everything!* There's no harm in wanting it, George, because there's not a chance in hell we're going to get it all, anyway. But if you don't *want* it, you've got even less chance than that. . . .

2-16. *The Caine Mutiny*, Herman Wouk *(123 words)*

Willie staggered out past the captain to the open wing. The wind immediately smashed him against the bridgehouse, and spray pelted him like small wet stones. He was astounded and peculiarly exhilarated to realize that in the last fifteen minutes the wind had actually become much stronger than before, and would blow him over the side if he exposed himself in a clear space. He laughed aloud, his voice thin against the gutteral "Whooeeee!" of the storm. He inched himself to the door of the radar shack, freed the dogs, and tried to pull the door open, but the wind held it tightly shut. He pounded on the wet steel with his knuckles, and kicked at it, and screamed, "Open up! Open up!"

2-17. *I Know Why the Caged Bird Sings*, Maya Angelou *(149 words)*

> "Acka Backa, Sody Cracka
> Acka Backa, Boo
> Acka Backa, Sody Cracka
> I'm in love with you."

The sounds of tag beat through the trees while the top branches waved in contrapuntal rhythms. I lay on a moment of green grass and telescoped the children's game to my vision. The girls ran about wild, now here, now there, never here, never was, they seemed to have no more direction than a splattered egg. But it was a shared if seldom voiced knowledge that all movements fitted, and worked according to a larger plan. I raised a platform for my mind's eye and marveled down on the outcome of "Acka Backa." The gay picnic dresses dashed, stopped and darted like beautiful dragonflies over a dark pool. The boys, black whips in the sunlight, popped behind the trees where their girls had fled, half hidden and throbbing in the shadows.

2-18. All I Really Need to Know, I Learned in Kindergarten, Robert Fulghum *(226 words)*

All I really need to know about how to live and what to do and how to be I learned in kindergarten. Wisdom was not at the top of the graduate-school mountain, but there in the sandpile at Sunday school. These are the things I learned:

Share everything.
Play fair.
Don't hit people.
Put things back where you found them.
Clean up your own mess.
Don't take things that aren't yours.
Say you're sorry when you hurt somebody.
Wash your hands before you eat.
Flush.
Warm cookies and cold milk are good for you.
Live a balanced life—learn some and think some and draw and paint and sing and dance and play and work every day some.
Take a nap every afternoon.
When you go out into the world, watch out for traffic, hold hands, and stick together.
Be aware of wonder. Remember the little seed in the Styrofoam cup: The roots go down and the plant goes up and nobody really knows how or why, but we are all like that.
Goldfish and hamsters and white mice and even the little seed in the Styrofoam cup—they all die. So do we. And remember the Dick-and-Jane books and the first word you learned—the biggest word of all—LOOK.

2-19. Red Sox and Bluefish, Susan Orlean *(229 words)*

As most linguists might tell you, regional accents are a lot like underpants: Everyone has them, and usually no one notices his or her own, but the world would be a very different place in their absence. This is particularly true in Boston, where we speak the kind of stunningly bizarre burr to which we, of course, pay no heed but that freezes non-New Englanders in their uninflected tracks. Quite simply, it is the Case of the Missing R. We have a number of vocalic peculiarities, but the heart of the Boston brogue is the peculiar disappearance of that very popular letter in the alphabet. With the exception of Cardiff, Wales, which for some reason has an accent nearly identical to ours, Boston is the only city in the world where the exclamation "Bob's shot!" can mean Bob either has been hit by a stray bullet or is suffering from a height deficiency.

2-20. Getting Even, Woody Allen *(87 words)*

Economic Theory: A systematic application and critical evaluation of the basic analytic concepts of economic theory, with emphasis on money and why it's good. Fixed coefficient production functions, cost and supply curves, and nonconvexity comprise the first semester, with the second semester concentrating on spending, making change, and keeping a neat wallet. The Federal Reserve System is analyzed, and advanced students are coached in the proper method of filling out a deposit slip. Other topics include: Inflation and Depression—how to dress for each. Loans, interest, welching.

2-21. "Popular Beliefs" in Brain Droppings, *George Carlin (82 words)*
Two wrongs don't' make a right. Well, it just so happens that two wrongs do make a right. Not only that, but as the number of wrongs increases, the whole thing goes up exponentially. So that while two wrongs make one right, and four wrongs make two rights, it actually takes sixteen wrongs to make three rights, and 256 wrongs to make four rights. It seems to me that anyone who is stringing together more than 256 wrongs needs counseling, not mathematics.

2-22. "College Admissions" in Dave Barry's Bad Habits, *Dave Barry. (152 words)*
College is basically a bunch of rooms where you sit for roughly two thousand hours and try to memorize things. The two thousand hours are spread out over four years; you spend the rest of the time sleeping and trying to get dates.

Basically, you learn two kinds of things in college:

- *Things you will need to know in later life (two hours).* These include how to make collect phone calls and get beer and crepe-paper stains out of your pajamas.
- *Things you will not need to know in later life (1,998 hours).* These are the things you learn in classes whose names end in -ology, -osophy, -istry, -ics, and so on. The idea is, you memorize these things, then write them down in little exam books, then forget them. If you fail to forget them, you become a professor and have to stay in college for the rest of your life.

2-23. Time Flies, Bill Cosby (426 words)
One of the compensations of getting older (and so far, I've thought of only one) is that the medicine ball in your stomach forces you to replace the athletic skills you have lost with interesting new ones. For example, you learn the challenging gymnastic arts of putting on your socks and tying your shoes. Sock putting on and shoe tying are not yet AAU events, of course, but at times they are harder for me than it was to clear a high-jump bar at six feet seven.

When a man with an excess of midsectional bloat bends to tie his shoe, his reach is not only obstructed but he may even cut off his wind and find the blood rushing to his head. It is a dangerous part of getting dressed.

"Why is Daddy taking a nap on the floor?" your son says to your wife.

"Oh, he's not taking a nap," she replies. "He passed out."

"From drinking something?"

"No, he was trying to tie his shoe and that's not easy for a man of his age. He really should go to spring training before he tries it."

"I've got a good idea, Mommy!"

"What's that?"

"Let's fix it so Daddy doesn't have to *wear* shoes and then he'll be conscious much more."

"You mean move to the beach so he can go barefoot all the time?"

"No, let's get him some *slipper* socks."

"A nice thought, honey, but he can't put those on either."

This mother has obviously seen me in the morning. There have been times when I was so out of shape that I could have used the help of a small boy in putting on my socks. Without such a boy, I was able to put on my socks only by picking up each leg with both hands and putting my heel on a chair.

Without such a boy *or* a chair, a man of my age who puts on a sock is participating in an event that requires split-second timing. As the Fernando Valenzuela of sock putting on, let me tell you how I do it. I raise my leg as high as I can; and then, for the second or two that my foot is quivering at its peak, I quickly bring the sock down over my toes. When my foot hits the floor, I finish pulling up the sock.

It is clear to me why "Miami Vice" has been so popular with men. Because millions of them watch it and dream of never again wearing socks.

Appendix A

Pronunciation List

The words in the following lists are frequently mispronounced. They're all fairly common words and, with a little practice, you should be able to pronounce them correctly. We've grouped them according to the type of mispronunciation, so we suggest you work within one type before moving on to the next. Have someone listen to you, or tape your practice session for review later.

A word about the "correct" way to pronounce words: Our language is always changing, and a pronunciation that was preferred at one time may not be so widely used today. We used the 1999 *Webster's College Dictionary* for our guide to preferred pronunciations; you may find that your dictionary shows another. If so, consult your instructor to determine which pronunciation is preferred in your area.

The IPA stress-marking system differs from the diacritical system used in dictionaries. Dictionaries place the stress mark to the upper right of the stressed syllable. The IPA system is as follows:

1. Primary stress is shown by a mark at the upper left (above and in front) of the stressed syllable. For example, that the word *children* is pronounced with primary stress on the first syllable would be indicated this way: [ˈtʃɪldrən].
2. Secondary stress is shown by a mark at the lower left (in front) of the syllable. The word *substitute* has three syllables. Primary stress is on the first syllable and secondary stress is on the third: [ˈsʌbstɪˌtut].

3. Unstressed (tertiary) syllables are not marked. The middle syllable in the word *substitute,* shown above, is unstressed and is not marked.

Reversals

The words in this section are often mispronounced because of the reversal of two sounds. For example, the word *ask,* standardly pronounced [æsk], becomes *ax* when the two consonant sounds are reversed.

Recommended Pronunciations

Word	Pronunciation	IPA*	Nonstandard
1. ask	ask	[æsk]	[æks]
2. asked	askt	[æskt]	[ækst]
3. asterisk	as′ tə risk	[ˈæstəˌrɪsk]	[ˈæstəˌrɪks]
4. children	chil′ drən	[ˈtʃɪldrən]	[ˈtʃɪldəˌn]
5. hundred	hun′ drid	[ˈhʌndrɪd]	[ˈhʌnəˌd]
6. introduction	in′ trə duk′ shən	[ˌɪntrəˈdʌkʃən]	[ˌɪntəˈdʌkʃən]
7. larynx	lar′ ingks	[ˈlærɪŋks]	[ˈlarnɪks]
8. lisp	lisp	[lɪsp]	[lɪps]
9. perform	pər fôrm′	[pɚˈfɔɚm]	[prəˈfɔɚm]
10. perspiration	pûr′ spə ra′ shən	[ˌpɚspəˈreʃən]	[ˌprɛspəˈreʃən]
11. pharynx	far′ ingks	[ˈfærɪŋks]	[ˈfarnɪks]
12. prescription	pri skrip′ shən	[priˈskrɪpʃən]	[pɚˈskrɪpʃən]
13. pretty	prit′ ē	[ˈprɪti]	[ˈpɝti]
14. professor	prə fes′ ər	[prəˈfɛsɚ]	[pɚˈfɛsɚ]
15. southern	suth′ ərn	[ˈsʌðɚn]	[ˈsʌðrən]

*IPA transcription of recommended (dictionary) pronunciation.

Omissions

The following words are often mispronounced when people omit one or more of the sounds that should be present. Say these words carefully. Make sure each sound is there that should be there.

Recommended Pronunciations

Word	Pronunciation	IPA*	Nonstandard
1. accelerate	ak sel′ ə rāt	[ækˈsɛləˌret]	[æˈsɛləˌret]
2. accessory	ak ses′ ə rē	[ækˈsɛəˌri]	[æˈsɛsəˌri]
3. antidote	an′ti dōt′	[ˈæntɪˌdot]	[ˈænəˌdot]
4. arctic	ärk′tik	[ˈɑrktɪk]	[ˈɑrtɪk]
5. basketball	bas′kit bôl′	[ˈbæskətˌbɔl]	[ˈbæskəˌbɔl]
6. candidate	kan′di dāt′	[ˈkændəˌdet]	[ˈkænəˌdet]

Recommended Pronunciations (*Continued*)

Word	Pronunciation	IPA*	Nonstandard
7. contact	kon′takt	[ˈkɑnˌtækt]	[ˈkɑnˌtæk]
8. correct	kə rekt′	[kəˈrɛkt]	[kəˈrɛk]
9. couldn't	kood′ᵊnt	[ˈkʊd nt]	[ˈkʊdn]
10. entertain	en′tər tān′	[ˌɛntɚˈten]	[ˌɛnəˈten]
11. environment	en vī′ rənmənt	[ɛnˈvɑɪrənmənt]	[ˌɛnˈvɑɪrəmənt]
12. friendly	frend′lē	[ˈfrɛndli]	[ˈfrɛnli]
13. frustrate	frus′trāt	[ˈfrʌstret]	[ˈfʌstret]
14. library	lī′brer′ē	[ˈlɑɪˌbrɛri]	[ˈlɑɪˌbɛri]
15. museum	myōō zē′əm	[ˌmjuˈziəm]	[ˌmjuˈzim]
16. orange	or′inj	[ˈɑrəndʒ]	[ˈɑˈndʒ]
17. perhaps	pər haps′	[pɚˈhæps]	[præps]
18. picture	pik′chər	[ˈpɪktʃɚ]	[ˈpɪktʃɚ]
19. pocketbook	pok′itbook′	[ˈpɑkətˌbʊk]	[ˈpɑkə bʊk]
20. poem	poəm	[ˈpoəm]	[pom]
21. probably	prob′ə blē	[ˈprɑbəbli]	[ˈprɑli]
22. professor	prə fes′ər	[prəˌfɛsɚ]	[pəˈfɛsɚ]
23. quiet	kwī′ it	[ˈkwɑɪət]	[ˈkwɑɪt]
24. recognize	rek′əg nīz′	[ˈrɛkəgˌnɑɪz]	[rɛkənɑɪz]
25. regular	reg′yə lər	[ˈrɛgjəlɚ]	[ˈrɛgələ]
26. robbery	rob′ə rē	[ˈrɑbəri]	[ˈrɑbri]
27. scrupulous	skrōō′pyə ləs	[ˈskrupjələs]	[ˈskrupələs]
28. skeptical	skep′ti kəl	[ˈskɛptɪkəl]	[ˈskɛpəkəl]
29. slept	slept	[slɛpt]	[slɛp]
30. specific	spi sif′ik	[spəˈsɪfɪk]	[pəˈsɪfɪk]
31. substitute	sub′sti tōōt′	[ˈsʌbstɪˌtut]	[ˈsʌbsəˌtut]
32. temperature	tem′pər ə chər	[ˈtɛmprətʃɚ]	[ˈtɛmpətʃɚ]
33. throw	thrō	[θrou]	[θou]
34. twenty	twen′tē	[ˈtwɛnti]	[ˈtwɛni]
35. wonderful	wun′dər fəl	[ˈwʌndɚˌful]	[ˈwʌnəˌful]
36. wouldn't	wōōd′ənt	[ˈwʊdnt]	[wʊnt]

*IPA transcription of recommended (dictionary) pronunciation.

Substitutions

These words are mispronounced by substitution of one sound for another.

Recommended Pronunciations

Word	Pronunciation	IPA*	Nonstandard
1. architect	är′ki tekt′	[ˈarkɚˌtɛkt]	[ˈartʃɚˌtɛkt]
2. asphalt	as′fôlt	[ˈæsfɔlt]	[ˈæʃfɔlt]
3. attache	at′ə shā′	[ˌætəˈʃe]	[æˈtætʃe]
4. banquet	bang′kwit	[ˈbæŋkwɪt]	[ˈbæŋkwɪt]
5. Beethoven	bā′tōv n	[ˈbeˌtovən]	[ˈbiˌθovən]
6. beige	bāzh	[beɪʒ]	[beɪdʒ]
7. brochure	brō shoor′	[broˈʃuɚ]	[broˈtʃuɚ]

(*Continued*)

Recommended Pronunciations (Continued)

Word	Pronunciation	IPA*	Nonstandard
8. charisma	kə riz′mə	[kəˈrɪzmə]	[tʃəˈrɪzmə]
9. charlatan	s͟här′lə tən	[ˈʃɑrlətən]	[ˈtʃɑrlətən]
10. chasm	kaz′əm	[ˈkæzəm]	[ˈtʃæzəm]
11. chef	s͟hef	[ʃɛf]	[tʃɛf]
12. chic	s͟hēk	[ʃik]	[tʃɪk]
13. chiropractor	ki′rə prak′tər	[ˈkɑɪrəˌpræktɚ]	[ˈtʃɑɪrəˌpræktɚ]
14. Chopin	s͟ho′pan	[ˈʃopæn]	[ˈtʃopɪn]
15. connoisseur	kon′ə sûr′	[ˌkɑnəˈsɝ]	[ˌkɑnəˈʃuɚ]
16. crux	kruks	[krʌks]	[krʊks]
17. cuisine	kwi zēn′	[kwɪˈzin]	[kjuˈzin]
18. cupola	kyoo′ pə lə	[ˈkjupələ]	[ˈkʌpjələ]
19. data	dā′tə	[ˈdetə]	[ˈdætə]
20. deluge	del′yōōj	[ˈdɛlˌjudʒ]	[ˌdɛlˈjuʒ]
21. diphthong	dif′t͟ho͟ng	[ˈdɪfθɑŋ]	[ˈdɪpθɑŋ]
22. diphtheria	dif t͟hēr′ē ə	[dɪfˈθiriə]	[dɪpˈθiriə]
23. et cetera	et set′ərə	[ɛtˈsɛtərə]	[ˌɛkˈsɛtərə]
24. faux pas	fō pä′	[ˈfo ˈpɑ]	[ˈfɔksˈpæs]
25. filet	fi lā′	[fiˈleɪ]	[ˈfɪlɪt]
26. gesture	jes′ch r	[ˈdʒɛstʃɚ]	[ˈgɛstʃɚ]
27. gist	jist	[dʒɪst]	[gɪst]
28. harbinger	här′bin jər	[ˈhɑrbɪndʒɚ]	[ˈhɑrbɪŋɚ]
29. hearth	härt͟h	[hɑrθ]	[hɝθ]
30. height	hīt	[hɑɪt]	[hɑɪθ]
31. heinous	hā′nəs	[ˈheɪnəs]	[ˈhɑɪnəs]
32. heir	âr	[ɛɚ]	[heɚ]
33. herald	her′əld	[ˈhɛrəld]	[ˈhærəld]
34. houses	hou′ziz	[ˈhaʊzɪz[	[ˈhaʊsɪz]
35. indict	in dīt′	[ɪnˈdɑɪt]	[ɪnˈdɪkt]
36. indigent	in′di jənt	[ˈɪndɪdʒənt]	[ˈɪndɪgənt]
37. Italian	i tal′yən	[ɹɪˈtæljən]	[ˌɑɪˈtæljən]
38. length	len͡gkth	[lɛŋkθ]	[lɛnθ]
39. longevity	lon jev′i tē	[lɑnˈdʒɛvɪti]	[lɔŋgɛvɪti]
40. longitude	lon′ji tōōd′	[ˈlɔndʒɪˌtud]	[ˈlɔŋgɪˌtud]
41. malingerer	mə ling′gərər	[məˈlɪŋgərɚ]	[məˈlɪndʒərɚ]
42. masochistic	mas′əkis′tik	[mæsəˈkɪstɪk]	[mæsəˈtʃɪstɪk]
43. mocha	mō′kə	[ˈmokə]	[ˈmotʃə]
44. oil	oil	[ɔɪl]	[ɝl]
45. onus	ō′nəs	[ˈounəs]	[ɑnəs]
46. orgy	ôr′jē	[ˈɔrdʒi]	[ˈɔrgi]
47. pathos	pā′t͟hos	[ˈpeθɑs]	[ˈpæθɑs]
48. pique	pēk	[pik]	[ˌpiˈke]
49. placard	plak′ärd	[ˈplækɚd]	[ˈplekɚd]
50. poignant	poin′yənt	[ˈpɔɪnjənt]	[ˈpɔɪgnənt]
51. posthumous	pos′chə məs	[ˈpɑstʃəməs]	[ˈpɑsθjuməs], [post ˈhjuməs]
52. prestige	pre stēzh′	[prɛsˈtiʒ]	[prɛsˈtidʒ]
53. regime	rə z͟hēm′	[rəˈʒim]	[rəˈdʒim]
54. salient	sāl′lēənt	[ˈseɪliənt]	[ˈsæliənt]
55. strength	stren͡gkth	[strɛŋkθ]	[strɛnθ]
56. suave	swäv	[swɑv]	[sweɪv]

Recommended Pronunciations (*Continued*)

Word	Pronunciation	IPA*	Nonstandard
57. suite	swēt	[swit]	[sut]
58. taciturn	tas′i tûrn	[ˈtæsɪˌtɚn]	[ˈtækɪˌtɚn]
59. taupe	tōp	[top]	[tɔp]
60. thyme	tīm	[taɪm]	[θaɪm]
61. tremendous	tri men′dəs	[trɪˈmɛndəs]	[trɪˈmɛndʒuəs]
62. virile	vir′əl	[ˈvɪrəl]	[ˈvaɪrəl], [ˈvɪraɪl]
63. Worcester	wo͝os′tər	[ˈwustɚ]	[ˈwɔrsɛstɚ]
64. worsted	wo͝os′tid	[ˈwustɪd]	[ˈwɚstɪd]
65. zealot	zel′ət	[ˈzɛlət]	[ˈzilat]
66. zoology	zō ol′ ə jē	[ˌzoˈɑləˌdʒi]	[ˌzuˈɑləˌdʒi]

*IPA transcription of recommended (dictionary) pronunciation.

Intrusions

The words in this list are mispronounced by addition of sounds that don't belong there.

Recommended Pronunciations

Word	Pronunciation	IPA*	Nonstandard
1. across	əkrôs′	[əˈkrɔs]	[əˈkrɔst]
2. almond	ä′mənd	[ˈamənd]	[ˈalmənd]
3. athlete	ath′lēt	[ˈæθlit]	[ˈæθəˌlit]
4. balk	bôk	[bɔk]	[bɔlk]
5. balmy	bä′mē	[ˈbami]	[ˈbalˌmi]
6. burglar	bûr′glər	[ˈbɝglɚ]	[ˈbɝgjələ]
7. business	biz′nis	[ˈbɪznɪs]	[ˈbɪzɪnɪs]
8. calm	käm	[kam]	[kalm]
9. chimney	chim′nē	[tʃɪmni]	[ˈtʃɪmbli]
10. column	kol′əm	[ˈkɑləm]	[ˈkɑljəm]
11. condominium	kon′də min′ēəm	[ˌkɑndəˈmɪniəm]	[ˌkɑmndəˈmɪniəm]
12. consonant	kon′sə nənt	[ˈkɑnsənənt]	[ˈkɑnstənənt]
13. corps	kôr	[kɔɚ]	[kɔɚps]
14. drowned	dround	[draund]	[ˈdraundəd]
15. electoral	i lek′tər əl	[ɪˈlɛktərəl]	[ɪlɛkˈtɔriəl]
16. escalator	es′kə lā′tər	[ˈɛskəletɚ]	[ˈɛskjəletɚ]
17. escape	e skāp′	[ɛsˈkep]	[ɛkˈskep]
18. evening	ēv′ning	[ˈivnɪŋ]	[ˈivənɪŋ]
19. facetious	fəsē′shəs	[fəˈsiʃəs]	[fəˈsiʃiəs]
20. film	film	[fɪlm]	[ˈfɪləm]
21. grievous	grē′vəs	[ˈgrivəs]	[ˈgriviəs]
22. momentous	mō men′təs	[moˈmɛntəs]	[moˈmɛnˌtʃuəs]
23. monstrous	mon′strəs	[ˈmɑnstrəs]	[ˈmɑnstərəs]
24. nuclear	no͞o′klē ər	[ˈnukliɚ]	[ˈnukjələ]
25. often	ô′fən	[ɔfən]	[ɔftən]

(*Continued*)

Recommended Pronunciations (*Continued*)

Word	Pronunciation	IPA*	Nonstandard
26. once	wuns	[wʌns]	[wʌnst]
27. psalm	säm	[sɑm]	[sɑlm]
28. righteous	rīc̆həs	[ˈraɪtʃəs]	[ˈraɪtʃuəs]
29. realtor	re′ətər	[ˈrɪəltɚ]	[ˈrɪələtɚ]
30. schism	siz′əm	[ˈsɪzəm]	[ˈskɪzəm]
31. soften	sô′fən	[ˈsɔfən]	[ˈsɔftən]
31. sophomore	sof′môr	[ˈsɑfmɔɚ]	[ˈsɑfəmɔɚ]
32. statistics	stə tis′tiks	[stəˈtɪstɪks]	[stəˈstɪstɪks]
33. subtle	sut′əl	[ˈsʌtl]	[ˈsʌbtl]
34. sword	sōrd	[sɔɚd]	[swɔɚd]
35. tremendous	tri men′dəs	[trɪˈmɛndəs]	[trɪˈmɛndʒəs]

*IPA transcription of recommended (dictionary) pronunciation.

Misplaced Stress

The following words are all frequently mispronounced because of misplaced syllable stress; that is, emphasis on the wrong syllable. The change in stress may also alter one or more vowel sounds.

Recommended Pronunciations

Word	Pronunciation	IPA*	Nonstandard
1. abdomen	ab′də mən	[ˈæb dəmən]	[ˌæbˈdomən]
2. absurd	ab sûrd′	[æbˈsɝd]	[ˈæbsɚd]
3. admirable	ad′mər ə bəl	[ˈædˌmərəbəl]	[ˌædˈmɑɪrəbəl]
4. applicable	ap′lə kə bəl	[ˈæpləkəbəl]	[ˌəˈplɪkəbəl]
5. bravado	brə vä′dō	[ˌbrəˈvɑdo]	[ˈbrɑvədo]
6. cement	si ment′	[sɪˈmɛnt]	[ˈsɪmɛnt]
7. chagrin	shə grin′	[ʃəˈgrɪn]	[ˈʃʌgrɪn]
8. conduit	kon′doo it	[ˈkɑnduɪt]	[kənˈduɪt]
9. delight	di līt′	[dɪˈaɪt]	[ˈdilaɪt]
10. deluge	del′yooj	[ˈdɛljudʒ]	[dəˈludʒ]
11. guitar	gi tär′	[gɪˈtɑɚ]	[ˈgɪtɑɚ]
12. impotent	im′pə tant	[ˈɪm pətənt]	[ˌɪmˈpotənt]
13. incomparable	in kom′pər ə bəl	[ɪnˈkɑmpərəbəl]	[ɪnkɑmˈpɛrəbəl]
14. incongruous	in kong′groo əs	[ɪnˈkɑŋˌgruəs]	[ɪnkənˈgruəs]
15. infamous	in′fə məs	[ˈɪn fəməs]	[ˌɪnˈfeməs]
16. inquiry	inkwiər′ē	[ɪnˈkwɑɪri]	[ˈɪnkwɑɪri]
17. irreparable	i rep′ər ə bəl	[ɪˈrɛpərəbəl]	[ˌɪriˈpɛɚəbəl]
18. maintenance	mān′tənəns	[ˈmeɪnˌtənəns]	[menˈteɪnəns]
19. mischievous	mis′chə vəs	[ˈmɪs tʃəvəs]	[mɪsˈtʃiviəs]
20. omnipotent	om nip′ə tənt	[ɑmˈnɪpətənt]	[ɑmnɪˈpotənt]
21. police	pə lēs	[pəˈlis]	[ˈpolis]
22. preclude	pri klood′	[priˈklud]	[ˈpriklud]
23. preferable	pref′ərə bəl	[ˈprɛfərəbəl]	[ˌprəˈfɛrəbəl]
24. preference	pref′ərəns	[ˈprɛfər əns]	[prəˈfɛrəns]
25. respite	res′pit	[ˈrɛspɪt]	[rəsˈpaɪt]

*IPA transcription of recommended (dictionary) pronunciation.

B Appendix B

Guide to Foreign Accents

If you learned American English as a second language, there's a good chance that you speak it with an *accent*. That is, the sounds you produce, as well as the stress and intonation patterns you use, vary noticeably from the major regional dialects of American English. The specific variations will depend on the phonemic structure of your first language and how it differs from American English. By that we mean, to what degree do the meaningful sounds of your first language match the meaningful sounds of American English?

In Chapter 4 we mentioned foreign accents, but we didn't describe typical characteristics of any accents. That's the purpose of this appendix: to familiarize you with some of the primary differences between certain foreign accents and American English.

The following charts list some significant features of the accents that usually result when American English is learned *after* certain other languages. Because the features of stress (force) and intonation (melody) are too complicated to effectively display here, we suggest you read Chapter 11, "Vocal Expressiveness," and consult with your instructor to learn more about those aspects of a particular accent.

Interference with American English Consonants According to First Language Learned

	Chinese	French	German	Italian	Japanese	Korean	Pilipino	Russian	Scandinavian	Spanish
[p]	*	*		*		*	*			*
[b]	*		*			*				*
[t]	*	*	*	*		*	*			*
[d]	*	*		*		*		*		*
[k]	*	*		*		*	*			*
[g]	*					*				*
[f]	*		*		*	*	*	*		
[v]	*		*		*		*	*		*
[θ]	*	*	*	*	*	*	*	*	*	*
[ð]	*	*	*	*	*		*	*	*	*
[s]	*		*	*		*	*	*		*
[z]	*		*			*	*		*	
[ʃ]	*		*			*	*		*	*
[ʒ]			*	*	*					
[h]	*	*	*	*						*
[w]	*		*	*		*		*	*	*
[r]		*	*	*		*		*	*	*
[j]	*			*	*					
[l]					*			*		*
[n]								*		
[ŋ]								*		*
[tʃ]	*	*	*	*		*	*	*		
[dʒ]		*	*			*	*	*	*	

356

Interference with American English Vowels According to First Language Learned

	Chinese	French	German	Italian	Japanese	Korean	Pilipino	Russian	Scandinavian	Spanish
[i]	*	*		*		*		*	*	*
[ɪ]	*	*		*	*	*	*	*	*	*
[e]										
[ɛ]	*	*							*	*
[æ]	*	*	*		*				*	*
[ɔ]	*		*			*	*		*	*
[o]								*		
[ʊ]	*			*	*	*	*	*	*	*
[u]	*		*	*	*	*		*	*	*
[ʌ]	*		*	*	*	*		*	*	*
[ə]	*	*		*	*					
[ɝ]					*	*		*	*	
[ɚ]					*	*		*		
[aʊ]									*	
[ɔɪ]									*	
[eɪ]			*	*	*				*	*
[oʊ]										*

First Language Background: Chinese

Sound	Problem	Standard		becomes	Nonstandard	Exercise
[p]	[( )]	[dip]	deep	becomes	[di]	(p. 77)
[b]	[( )]	[kæb]	cab	becomes	[kæ]	(p. 81)
[t]	[( )]	[bɛt]	bet	becomes	[bɛ]	(p. 90)
[d]	[( )]	[hæd]	had	becomes	[hæ]	(p. 98)
[k]	[( )]	[tɔk]	talk	becomes	[tɔ]	(p. 106)
[g]	[( )]	[bɪg]	big	becomes	[bɪ]	(p. 110)
[f]	[( )]	[bif]	beef	becomes	[bi]	(p. 119)
[v]	[( )]	[gɪv]	give	becomes	[gɪ]	(p. 125)
[v]	[f/]	[hæv]	have	becomes	[hæf]	(p. 118)
[v]	[w/]	[væn]	van	becomes	[wæn]	(p. 123)
[θ]	[s/]	[θɪk]	thick	becomes	[sɪk]	(p. 131)
[θ]	[f/]	[hɛlθ]	health	becomes	[hɛlf]	(p. 131)
[ð]	[d/]	[ðæt]	that	becomes	[dæt]	(p. 136)
[ð]	[v/]	[smuð]	smooth	becomes	[smuv]	(p. 138)
[s]	[( )]	[haʊs]	house	becomes	[haʊ]	(p. 144)
[z]	[s/]	[ɪz]	is	becomes	[ɪs]	(p. 155)
[z]	[( )]	[hɪz]	his	becomes	[hɪ]	(p. 144)
[ʃ]	[( )]	[fɪʃ]	fish	becomes	[fɪ]	(p. 160)
[ʃ]	[s/]	[ʃu]	shoe	becomes	[su]	(p. 160)
[r]	[l/]	[ræt]	rat	becomes	[læt]	(p. 186)
[l]	[r/]	[lɛt]	let	becomes	[rɛt]	(p. 200)
[l]	[( )]	[tɔl]	tall	becomes	[tɔ]	(p. 200)
[l]	[ə+]	[blu]	blue	becomes	[bəlu]	(p. 201)
[tʃ]	[( )]	[ɪntʃ]	inch	becomes	[ɪn]	(p. 207)
[i]	[ɪ/]	[it]	eat	becomes	[ɪt]	(p. 219)
[ɪ]	[i/]	[fɪt]	fit	becomes	[fit]	(p. 219)
[ɛ]	[e/]	[wɛt]	wet	becomes	[wet]	(p. 228)
[æ]	[e/]	[sæk]	sack	becomes	[sek]	(p. 234)
[ɔ]	[o/]	[sɔ]	saw	becomes	[so]	(p. 245)
[ʊ]	[u/]	[pʊl]	pull	becomes	[pul]	(p. 237)
[ʌ]	[ɑ/]	[nʌts]	nuts	becomes	[nɑts]	(p. 262)
[ə]	[( )]	[sofə]	sofa	becomes	[sof]	(p. 266)
[ə]	[ɑ/]	[soʊdə]	soda	becomes	[soʊdɑ]	(p. 266)

KEY: / SUBSTITUTION   ( ) OMISSION   + ADDITION

First Language Background: French

Sound	Problem	Standard		becomes	Nonstandard		Exercise
[p]	[(ʰ)]	[pʰaɪ]	pie	becomes	[p⁽ʰ⁾aɪ]	See note 1.	(p. 77)
[t]	[(ʰ)]	[tʰaɪ]	tie	becomes	[t⁽ʰ⁾aɪ]	See note 1.	(p. 87)
[t]	[̪]	[tɛn]	ten	becomes	[t̪ɛn]	See note 2.	(p. 87)
[d]	[̪]	[du]	do	becomes	[d̪u]	See note 2.	(p. 97)
[k]	[(ʰ)]	[kʰæn]	can	becomes	[k⁽ʰ⁾æn]	See note 1.	(p. 106)
[θ]	[s/]	[θɪn]	thin	becomes	[sɪn]		(p. 131)
[ð]	[z/]	[ðɪs]	this	becomes	[zɪs]		(p. 136)
[h]	[()]	[haʊs]	house	becomes	[aʊs]		(p. 167)
[r]	[ʀ/]	[reɪd]	raid	becomes	[ʀeɪd]	See note 3.	(p. 185)
[tʃ]	[ʃ/]	[wɑtʃ]	watch	becomes	[wɑʃ]		(p. 206)
[ʤ]	[ʒ/]	[ʤʌʤ]	judge	becomes	[ʒʌʒ]		(p. 210)
[i]	[ɪ/]	[il]	eel	becomes	[ɪl]		(p. 219)
[ɪ]	[i/]	[bɪt]	bit	becomes	[bit]		(p. 219)
[ɛ]	[æ/]	[lɛnd]	lend	becomes	[lænd]		(p. 232)
[æ]	[~]	[læmp]	lamp	becomes	[læ̃mp]	See note 4.	(p. 233)
[æ]	[ɑ/]	[tʃæns]	chance	becomes	[tʃɑns]		(p. 234)
[ə]	[ɔ/]	[əbaʊt]	about	becomes	[ɔbaʊt]		(p. 266)
[oʊ]	[o/]	[koʊd]	code	becomes	[kod]		(p. 242)

KEY: / SUBSTITUTION   ( ) OMISSION   ̪ DENTALIZED   ~ NASALIZED   ⁽ʰ⁾ LACKS ASPIRATION
Notes: 1. Lacks aspirated (explosive) quality of plosive sounds.
   2. Produced dentally (on the back of the teeth) instead of on the gum ridge.
   3. Uses [ʀ], a uvular-trilled substitute for the lingua-palatal glide [r].
   4. Excess nasal resonance.

First Language Background: German

Sound	Problem	Standard		becomes	Nonstandard	Exercise
[b]	[v/]	[bot]	boat	becomes	[vot]	(p. 82)
[d]	[t/]	[hæd]	had	becomes	[hæt]	(p. 87)
[v]	[f/]	[lʌv]	love	becomes	[lʌf]	(p. 118)
[θ]	[s/]	[θɪŋk]	think	becomes	[sɪŋk]	(p. 131)
[θ]	[t/]	[θru]	through	becomes	[tru]	(p. 131)
[ð]	[z/]	[ðæt]	that	becomes	[zæt]	(p. 136)
[ð]	[d]	[ðɪs]	this	becomes	[dɪs]	(p. 136)
[s[	[z/]	[si]	see	becomes	[zi]	(p. 142)
[s]	[ʃ/]	[spin]	spin	becomes	[ʃpin]	(p. 142)
[z]	[s/]	[izi]	easy	becomes	[isi]	(p. 155)
[z]	[ts/]	[zɪpɚ]	zipper	becomes	[tsɪpɚ]	(p. 154)

(Continued)

First Language Background: German (*Continued*)

Sound	Problem	Standard		becomes	Nonstandard		Exercise
[ʃ]	[tʃ/]	[ʃɪp]	ship	becomes	[tʃɪp]		(p. 160)
[w]	[v/]	[wɛst]	west	becomes	[vɛst]		(p. 182)
[r]	[ʀ/]	[graʊnd]	ground	becomes	[gʀaʊnd]	See note.	(p. 185)
[tʃ]	[ʃ/]	[tʃɝtʃ]	church	becomes	[ʃɝʃ]		(p. 206)
[ʤ]	[tʃ/]	[ʤɛlɪ[	jelly	becomes	[tʃɛlɪ]		(p. 206)
[ʤ]	[ʃ/]	[ʤæm]	jam	becomes	[ʃæm]		(p. 210)
[ae]	[ɛ/]	[pæn]	pan	becomes	[pɛn]		(p. 232)
[ʌ]	[ɑ/]	[ʌp]	up	becomes	[ɑp]		(p. 262)
[eɪ]	[e/]	[peɪ]	pay	becomes	[pe]		(p. 224)

KEY: / SUBSTITUTION
Note: Uses [ʀ], a uvular-trilled substitute for the lingua-palatal glide [r].

First Language Background: Italian

Sound	Problem	Standard		becomes	Nonstandard		Exercise
[p]	[(ʰ)]	[stɑpʰ]	stop	becomes	[stɑp⁽ʰ⁾]	See note 4.	(p. 77)
[t]	[ʰ]	[sɛnt]	sent	becomes	[sɛntʰ]		(p. 87)
[t]	[ˌ]	[tap]	top	becomes	[t̪ap]	See note 1.	(p. 87)
[d]	[ˌ]	[bæd]	bad	becomes	[bæd̪]	See note 1.	(p. 97)
[k]	[ʰ]	[bæŋk]	bank	becomes	[bæŋkʰ]		(p. 106)
[θ]	[t/]	[θæŋks]	thanks	becomes	[tæŋks]		(p. 131)
[ð]	[d/]	[ðæt]	that	becomes	[dæt]		(p. 136)
[s]	[z/]	[lɔs]	loss	becomes	[lɔz]		(p. 142)
[h]	[()]	[haʊs]	house	becomes	[aʊs]		(p. 167)
[r]	[r̆]	[rut]	root	becomes	[r̆ut]	See note 2.	(p. 185)
[n]	[ˌ]	[naɪs]	nice	becomes	[n̪aɪs]	See note 1.	(p. 173)
[i]	[ɪ/]	[fid]	feed	becomes	[fɪd]		(p. 219)
[ɪ]	[i/]	[skɪd]	skid	becomes	[skid]		(p. 219)
[ʊ]	[u/]	[pʊl]	pull	becomes	[pul]		(p. 237)
[u]	[ʊ]	[but]	boot	becomes	[bʊt]		(p. 238)
[ʌ]	[ɑ/]	[ʌp]	up	becomes	[ɑp]		(p. 262)
[ə]	[+]	[hɪt]	hit	becomes	[hɪtə]	See note 3.	(p. 266)
[ɝ]	[ɛr]	[bɝd]	bird	becomes	[bɛrd]		(p. 269)
[ɚ]	[ɛr]	[mʌðɚ]	mother	becomes	[mʌðɛr]		(p. 271)

KEY: / SUBSTITUTION   () OMISSION   + ADDITION   DENTALIZED   ʰ ASPIRATED   ⁽ʰ⁾ LACKS ASPIRATION
Notes: 1. Produced dentally (on the back of the teeth) instead of on the gum ridge.
2. Uses [r̆], a tongue-tap-trilled substitute for the lingua-alveolar glide [r].
3. Frequently added to words ending in consonants.
4. Lacks the aspirated (explosive) quality of plosive sounds.

First Language Background: Japanese

Sound	Problem	Standard		becomes	Nonstandard	Exercise
[f]	[h/]	[fon]	phone	becomes	[hon]	(p. 119)
[v]	[b/]	[vaɪn]	vine	becomes	[baɪn]	(p. 123)
[θ]	[s/]	[θɪŋk]	think	becomes	[sɪŋk]	(p. 131)
[ð]	[z/]	[ðɪs]	this	becomes	[zɪs]	(p. 136)
[ð]	[dʒ/]	[ðou]	though	becomes	[dʒou]	(p. 137)
[z]	[dʒ/]	[hæz]	has	becomes	[hædʒ]	(p. 154)
[z]	[s/]	[hæz]	has	becomes	[hæs]	(p. 155)
[r]	[l/]	[frɛnd]	friend	becomes	[flɛnd]	(p. 186)
[l]	[r/]	[let]	let	becomes	[ret]	(p. 200)
[ʒ]	[dʒ/]	[beɪʒ]	beige	becomes	[beɪdʒ]	(p. 163)
[ɪ]	[i/]	[bɪn]	bin	becomes	[bin]	(p. 219)
[æ]	[ɑ/]	[pæt]	pat	becomes	[pat]	(p. 234)
[æ]	[ɛ/]	[bæt]	bat	becomes	[bɛt]	(p. 232)
[ʊ]	[u/]	[pʊl]	pull	becomes	[pul]	(p. 237)
[ʌ]	[ɑ/]	[dʌk]	duck	becomes	[dɑk]	(p. 262)
[ɝ]	[ɑ/]	[hɝ]	her	becomes	[hɑ]	(p. 268)
[ɚ]	[ɑ/]	[fɑðɚ]	father	becomes	[fɑðɑ]	(p. 271)

KEY: / SUBSTITUTION

Note: [n] is the only consonant that may end words in Japanese. Because all other words end in vowels, many speakers of Japanese add the vowels [u] or [ə] to English words ending in consonant sounds. For example, the word *hotel* [hotɛl] may become [hotɛru] and *book* [bʊk] may become [bʊkə].

First Language Background: Korean

Sound	Problem	Standard		becomes	ᵃNonstandard		Exercise
[p]	[p̆]	[tæp]	tap	becomes	[tæp̆]	See note 1.	(p. 79)
[b]	[b̆]	[rʌb]	rub	becomes	[rʌb̆]	See note 1.	(p. 83)
[t]	[t̆]	[hæt]	hat	becomes	[hæt̆]	See note 1.	(p. 88)
[d]	[d̆]	[rɛd]	red	becomes	[rɛd̆]	See note 1.	(p. 97)
[k]	[k̆]	[pok]	poke	becomes	[pok̆]	See note 1.	(p. 106)
[g]	[ğ]	[hʌg]	hug	becomes	[hʌğ]	See note 1.	(p. 110)
[v]	[b/]	[gɪv]	give	becomes	[gɪb]		(p. 123)
[v]	[p/]	[hæv]	have	becomes	[hæp]		(p. 124)
[ð]	[dʒ]	[ðɪs]	this	becomes	[dʒɪs]		(p. 137)
[z]	[s/]	[hɪz]	his	becomes	[hɪs]		(p. 155)
[ʃ]	[s/]	[wɪʃ]	wish	becomes	[wɪs]		(p. 160)
[tʃ]	[ts]	[mætʃ]	match	becomes	[mæts]		(p. 207)
[r]	[l/]	[rɔ]	raw	becomes	[lɔ]		(p. 186)

(Continued)

First Language Background: Korean (*Continued*)

Sound	Problem	Standard			Nonstandard		Exercise
[l]	[r/]	[lɛt]	let	becomes	[rɛt]		(p. 200)
[i]	[ɪ/]	[sit]	seat	becomes	[sɪt]		(p. 219)
[ɪ]	[i/]	[sɪt]	sit	becomes	[sit]		(p. 219)
[u]	[ʊ/]	[sut]	suit	becomes	[sʊt]		(p. 238)
[ʊ]	[u/]	[sʊt]	soot	becomes	[sut]		(p. 237)
[ʌ]	[:]	[sʌn]	son	becomes		See note 2.	(p. 263)
[ɔ]	[:]	[sɔ]	saw	becomes		See note 2.	(p. 245)

KEY: / SUBSTITUTION   ~ CONFUSION   ˜ NASALIZED   : DURATION
Notes: 1. Nasalized at the ends of words.
　　　　 2. Confusion of vowel duration (length).

First Language Background: Pilipino

Sound	Problem	Standard			Nonstandard		Exercise
[p]	[(ʰ)]	[ʌpʰ]	up	becomes	[ʌp⁽ʰ⁾]	See note.	(p. 77)
[t]	[(ʰ)]	[tʰu]	too	becomes	[t⁽ʰ⁾u]	See note.	(p. 87)
[k]	[(ʰ)]	[lækʰ]	lack	becomes	[læk⁽ʰ⁾]	See note.	(p. 106)
[f]	[p/]	[kɔfɪ]	coffee	becomes	[kɔpɪ]		(p. 119)
[v]	[b/]	[vɛrɪ]	very	becomes	[bɛrɪ]		(p. 123)
[θ]	[t/]	[θri]	three	becomes	[tri]		(p. 131)
[ð]	[d/]	[ðɪs]	this	becomes	[dɪs]		(p. 136)
[z]	[s/]	[hæz]	has	becomes	[hæs]		(p. 155)
[ʃ]	[s/]	[ʃu]	shoe	becomes	[su]		(p. 160)
[tʃ]	[ts/]	[mætʃ]	match	becomes	[mæts]		(p. 207)
[ʤ]	[d/]	[ɛʤ]	edge	becomes	[ɛd]		(p. 209)
[ɪ]	[i/]	[sɪt]	sit	becomes	[sit]		(p. 219)
[ʊ]	[u/]	[pʊl]	pull	becomes	[pul]		(p. 237)
[ɔ]	[o/]	[lɔ]	law	becomes	[lo]		(p. 245)

KEY: / SUBSTITUTION   ⁽ʰ⁾ LACKS ASPIRATION
Note: [p] [t] [k] frequently lack the aspirated (explosive) quality of plosives.

First Language Background: Russian

Sound	Problem	Standard		becomes	Nonstandard		Exercise
[t]	[t̪]	[tu]	too	becomes	[t̪u]	See note 1.	(p. 87)
[d]	[t/]	[sɛd]	said	becomes	[sɛt]	See note 2.	(p. 87)
[d]	[d̪]	[ædɪŋ]	adding	becomes	[æd̪ɪŋ]	See note 1.	(p. 97)
[f]	[v/]	[kɔfi]	coffee	becomes	[kɔvi]		(p. 118)
[v]	[f/]	[hæv]	have	becomes	[hæf]		(p. 118)
[θ]	[s/]	[θɔt]	thought	becomes	[sɔt]		(p. 131)
[θ]	[t/]	[θɔt]	thought	becomes	[tɔt]		(p. 131)
[ð]	[d/]	[ðæt]	that	becomes	[dæt]		(p. 136)
[n]	[n̪]	[naʊ]	now	becomes	[n̪aʊ]	See note 1.	(p. 173)
[n]	[j+]	[fʌnɪ]	funny	becomes	[fʌnjɪ]		(p. 173)
[ŋ]	[n/]	[lʌvɪŋ]	loving	becomes	[lʌvɪn]		(p. 175)
[ŋ]	[k+]	[bæŋɪŋ]	banging	becomes	[bæŋkɪŋk]		(p. 177)
[w]	[v/]	[wæks]	wax	becomes	[væks]		(p. 182)
[r]	[ř]	[rɛst]	rest	becomes	[řɛst]	See note 3.	(p. 185)
[dʒ]	[ʒ/]	[dʒoʊk]	joke	becomes	[ʒoʊk]		(p. 209)
[dʒ]	[tʃ/]	[dʒʌmp]	jump	becomes	[tʃʌmp]		(p. 206)
[i]	[ɪ/]	[sit]	seat	becomes	[sɪt]		(p. 219)
[ɪ]	[i/]	[sɪt]	sit	becomes	[sit]		(p. 219)
[o]	[ɔ/]	[kot]	coat	becomes	[kɔt]		(p. 242)
[ʊ]	[u/]	[pʊl]	pull	becomes	[pul]		(p. 237)
[ʌ]	[a/]	[rʌʃən]	Russian	becomes	[raʃan]		(p. 263)
[ɝ]	[ɛr/]	[lɝn]	learn	becomes	[lɛrn]		(p. 269)
[ɚ]	[ɛr]	[faðɚ]	father	becomes	[faðɛr]		(p. 271)

KEY: / SUBSTITUTION   + ADDITION   ̪ DENTALIZED

Notes: 1. Produced dentally (on the back of the teeth) instead of on the gum ridge.
2. Problem occurs in word endings.
3. Uses trilled [ř] instead of lingua-palatal glide [r].

First Language Background: Scandinavian

Sound	Problem	Standard		becomes	Nonstandard		Exercise
[θ]	[t/]	[θɪn]	thin	becomes	[tɪn]		(p. 131)
[ð]	[d/]	[ðæt]	that	becomes	[dæt]		(p. 136)
[z]	[s/]	[izi]	easy	becomes	[isi]		(p. 155)
[r]	[ř]	[rɛd]	red	becomes	[řɛd]	See note 1.	(p. 185)
[w]	[v/]	[wɛst]	west	becomes	[vɛst]		(p. 182)
[ʒ]	[ʃ/]	[beɪʒ]	beige	becomes	[beɪʃ]		(p. 160)

First Language Background: Scandinavian (*Continued*)

Sound	Problem	Standard			Nonstandard		Exercise
[ʤ]	[j/]	[ʤʌmp]	jump	becomes	[jump]	See note 2.	(p. 209)
[ʤ]	[tʃ/]	[ɛʤ]	edge	becomes	[ɛtʃ]		(p. 206)
[i]	[j+]	[iɚ]	ear	becomes	[ijɚ]		(p. 215)
[ɪ]	[j+]	[wɪnd]	wind	becomes	[wɪjnd]		(p. 220)
[ɛ]	[j+]	[lɛt]	let	becomes	[lɛjt]		(p. 229)
[eɪ]	[j+]	[eɪm]	aim	becomes	[eɪjm]		(p. 225)
[æ]	[ɛ+]	[bænd]	band	becomes	[bæɛnd]		(p. 234)
[u]	[ʊ/]	[pul]	pool	becomes	[pʊl]		(p. 238)
[ɔ]	[o/]	[kɔl]	call	becomes	[kol]		(p. 245)
[aɪ]	[j+]	[aɪs]	ice	becomes	[aɪjs]		(p. 256)
[ɔɪ]	[j+]	[kɔɪn]	coin	becomes	[kɔɪjn]		(p. 250)

KEY: / SUBSTITUTION   + ADDITION

Notes: 1. Uses a trilled [ř] instead of the lingua-palatal glide [r].

2. May occur when [ʤ] is represented in written English by the letter *j*.

First Language Background: Spanish

Sound	Problem	Standard			Nonstandard		Exercise
[p]	[(ʰ)]	[pʰæn]	pan	becomes	[p⁽ʰ⁾æn]	See note 1.	(p. 77)
[t]	[(ʰ)]	[tʰæn]	tan	becomes	[t⁽ʰ⁾æn]	See note 1.	(p. 87)
[t]	[̪]	[tu]	too	becomes	[t̪u]	See note 2.	(p. 87)
[d]	[̪]	[doʊ]	dough	becomes	[d̪oʊ]	See note 2.	(p. 97)
[k]	[(ʰ)]	[kʰæn]	can	becomes	[k⁽ʰ⁾æn]	See note 1.	(p. 106)
[v]	[b/]	[ves]	vase	becomes	[bes]		(p. 123)
[θ]	[t/]	[θɪn]	thin	becomes	[tɪn]		(p. 131)
[ð]	[d/]	[ðæt]	that	becomes	[dæt]		(p. 136)
[s]	[θ/]	[æskɪŋ]	asking	becomes	[æθkɪŋ]		(p. 131)
[s]	[ɛ+]	[spænɪʃ]	Spanish	becomes	[ɛspænɪʃ]		(p. 144)
[z]	[s/]	[ɪz]	is	becomes	[ɪs]		(p. 155)
[n]	[ŋ/]	[rʌn]	run	becomes	[rʌŋ]		(p. 175)
[n]	[̪]	[noʊ]	no	becomes	[n̪oʊ]	See note 2.	(p. 173)
[w]	[v/]	[wek]	wake	becomes	[vek]		(p. 182)
[r]	[ř/]	[rɛd]	red	becomes	[řɛd]	See note 3.	(p. 185)
[ʃ]	[tʃ/]	[ʃip]	sheep	becomes	[tʃip]		(p. 160)
[ʒ]	[ʃ/]	[beɪʒ]	beige	becomes	[beɪʃ]		(p. 160)
[tʃ]	[ʃ/]	[tʃaɪm]	chime	becomes	[ʃaɪm]		(p. 206)
[j]	[ʤ/]	[jɛs]	yes	becomes	[ʤɛs]		(p. 195)

First Language Background: Spanish (*Continued*)

Sound	Problem	Standard		becomes	Nonstandard	Exercise
[i]	[ɪ/]	[sɪt]	seat	becomes	[sɪt]	(p. 219)
[ɪ]	[i/]	[ʃɪp]	ship	becomes	[ʃip]	(p. 219)
[e]	[ɛ/]	[leɪt]	late	becomes	[lɛt]	(p. 225)
[ɛ]	[eɪ/]	[tɛnɪs]	tennis	becomes	[teɪnɪs]	(p. 229)
[ɛ]	[æ/]	[sɛd]	said	becomes	[sæd]	(p. 232)
[æ]	[ɛ/]	[sæd]	sad	becomes	[sɛd]	(p. 232)
[eɪ]	[e/]	[peɪ]	pay	becomes	[pe]	(p. 224)
[ɔ]	[o/]	[kɔl]	call	becomes	[kol]	(p. 245)
[ʊ]	[u/]	[bʊk]	book	becomes	[buk]	(p. 237)
[ʌ]	[o/]	[lʌv]	love	becomes	[lov]	(p. 263)
[ʌ]	[ɑ/]	[bʌg]	bug	becomes	[bɑg]	(p. 262)
[ɝ]	[ɛr]	[wɝd]	word	becomes	[wɛrd]	(p. 269)
[u]	[ʊ/]	[ʃuz]	shoes	becomes	[ʃʊz]	(p. 238)

KEY: / SUBSTITUTION   + ADDITION   ˌ DENTALIZED   ʰ ASPIRATED   (ʰ) LACKS ASPIRATION

Notes: 1. Lacks aspirated "explosive" quality.

   2. Produced dentally (on the back of the teeth) instead of on the gum ridge.

   3. Substitutes trilled [ř] for lingua-palatal glide [r].

Appendix C

Diagnostic Materials and Speech Checklists

1. Sentences—Long List

Each of the following sentences emphasizes one sound or blend in American English. Approximate reading time: 4 1/2 minutes.

[p]	1.	Put the plastic cup on top of the pile of paper plates.
[b]	2.	The baby's bathtub was filled to the brim with bubbles.
[t]	3.	Tom took great delight in telling how fast he typed two letters.
[d]	4.	The murderer did the dreadful deed with a dirty, old dagger.
[k]	5.	Ken quit his job rather than work an extra weekend shift.
[g]	6.	Peg used to gargle vigorously after eating garlic.
[f]	7.	It's a fifty dollar fine if you don't file your tax form.
[v]	8.	"A hand of iron in a velvet glove" was his favorite saying.
[θ]	9.	Both authors used themes found in three Greek myths.
[ð]	10.	Place the leather belt with the other clothing.
[s]	11.	"Pass the syrup," said the first trombonist, "so I can play sweetly."
[z]	12.	The busiest bee wisely zeroes in on his options.
[ʃ]	13.	The magician wished he hadn't rushed to shine his shoes.
[ʒ]	14.	The explosion occurred after the collision near the garage.
[h]	15.	Perhaps it's not as humid in the western half of Ohio.

(Continued)

[ʍ]	16. Which wheel fell off when the white car hit the curb?
[w]	17. Wait until you see the new watch I was awarded.
[r]	18. Rosalie saw a red robin yesterday near her brook.
[j]	19. In my opinion, the view of that yacht is spectacular.
[l]	20. Laura left the yellow pillow in the third-floor hallway.
[m]	21. I may start writing my term paper during the summer semester.
[n]	22. Nancy was offered a chance to spend her vacation in Norway.
[ŋ]	23. Playing some guessing games requires counting on your fingers.
[tʃ]	24. Charlie had two chances to win a matching watch and chain.
[dʒ]	25. Does Virginia enjoy wearing her jeans in July?
[str]	26. The district attorney and the magistrate met near the construction barrier on the street.
[tl]	27. Littleton is a better place than Tottenville to buy
[tn]	antique bottles and buttons.
[i]	28. We were required to read *East of Eden* and also to see the movie.
[ɪ]	29. It was difficult to distinguish the pens from the pins.
[eɪ]	30. The train was delayed eight hours due to a break
[e]	in the rails.
[ɛ]	31. It doesn't make any sense to bet with your friends.
[æ]	32. Alan went to California to enhance his acting career.
[ɑ]	33. The honest guard calmly parked his car in the hot courtyard.
[ɔ]	34. Paul knocked for an awfully long time at the wrong door.
[ou]	35. "No soap, radio" is the punch line of a very old joke.
[o]	
[ʊ]	36. I couldn't find a good recipe for sugar cookies in that book.
[u]	37. It was too late to go on the cruise to Liverpool, so he flew.
[ʌ]	38. Hungry ducklings dive underwater to find their lunch.
[ə]	39. The camera-shy panda was not in the parade.
[ɝ]	40. At first, Herb only heard every third word.
[ɚ]	41. Oh brother, exclaimed the barber, I'd rather be a butcher.
[ɑɪ]	42. If I have enough time, I'll try to buy some ice cream.
[ɑu]	43. People who go around saying "How now, brown cow?" should be hounded out of town.
[ɔɪ]	44. Olive Oyl took great joy in avoiding Popeye's noisy toys.

2. Sentences—Short List

Most of the following sentences emphasize two or more sounds or blends in American English. Approximate reading time: 2 minutes.

[p] [b]	1.	The puppy bumped his paws and stopped bouncing.
[t] [d]	2.	It takes daring to be a detective in today's world.
[k] [g]	3.	The caretaker took his gardening with a grain of salt.
[f] [v]	4.	Frank sent a Valentine's gift to Vivian on February fourteenth.
[θ] [ð]	5.	Without thinking, Theo's brother bothered him for the thirtieth time.
[s] [z]	6.	Sandy was observing zebras in zoology classes last semester.
[ʃ] [ʒ]	7.	Fresh fish gives unusual pleasure when served with a measure of relish.
[h] [ð]	8.	Heather said the heat bothers her only half as much as the humidity.
[w] [ʍ]	9.	The wild whirring of the whetstone kept me awake on Wednesday night.
[r]	10.	Rockwell was too frightened to respond after he was robbed.
[l] [j]	11.	The yellow lion stretched lazily and yawned loudly.
[m] [skr]	12.	Many fans scrambled for seats near the movie screen.
[ŋ] [n]	13.	Nancy was wearing a new raincoat while singing in the rain.
[d] [t]	14.	James and Virginia won the matched set of luggage, jewelry, and Chippendale furniture.
[l] [t]	15.	Little by little, Benton analyzed the contents of the bottle.
[str]	16.	I asked why there was so much construction machinery in the street.
[ɝ] [θ]	17.	A bird in the hand is worth a great deal on earth.
[ɔɪ]	18.	Helen of Troy played it coy with the boys.
[i] [ɪ]	19.	It's easier to swallow a bitter pill if you have something sweet to drink.
[æ] [k]	20.	Allan planned to travel to California to enhance his acting career.
[ɔ] [aɪ]	21.	I ought to buy that dog from my lawyer.
[ɛ] [aʊ]	22.	For ten hours showers wet the ground and freshened the flowers.
[ʊ] [o]	23.	I looked from coast to coast for an oatmeal cookbook.
[u] [ʌ]	24.	Never do unto others what you'd rather they don't do to you.
[ə] [ʌ]	25.	The price of bananas jumped again, but bubble gum blew sky high.
[e] [ɑ]	26.	Eight o'clock is not too late in the day to honor honest responses.
[ɚ]	27.	Please pour our share here in my poor car.

3. Connected Speech

The following has been used for many years as a diagnostic and research passage. It contains all the sounds of American English in about the same proportion as they occur in everyday speech. Do *not* read the line numbers; they are for reference only. Approximate reading time: 2 minutes.

The Rainbow Passage (331 words)

1   When the sunlight strikes raindrops in the air, they act like a prism and
2   form a rainbow. The rainbow is a division of white light into many beautiful
3   colors. These take the shape of a long round arch, with its path high above,
4   and its two ends apparently beyond the horizon. There is, according to legend,
5   a boiling pot of gold at one end. People look, but no one ever finds it. When a
6   man looks for something beyond his reach, his friends say he is looking for the
7   pot of gold at the end of the rainbow.

8   Throughout the centuries men have explained the rainbow in various
9   ways. Some have accepted it as a miracle without physical explanation. To the
10   Hebrews it was a token that there would be no more universal floods. The
11   Greeks used to imagine that it was a sign from the gods to foretell war or heavy
12   rain. The Norsemen considered the rainbow as a bridge over which the gods
13   passed from earth to their home in the sky. Other men have tried to explain the
14   phenomenon physically. Aristotle thought that the rainbow was caused by
15   reflection of the sun's rays by the rain. Since then physicists have found that it
16   is not reflection, but refraction by the raindrops which causes the rainbow.
17   Many complicated ideas about the rainbow have been formed. The difference
18   in the rainbow depends considerably upon the size of the water drops, and the
19   width of the colored band increases as the size of the drops increases. The
20   actual primary rainbow observed is said to be the effect of superposition of a
21   number of bows. If the red of the second bow falls upon the green of the first,
22   the result is to give a bow with an abnormally wide yellow band, since red and
23   green lights when mixed form yellow. This is a very common type of bow, one
24   showing mainly red and yellow, with little or no green or blue.

Speech Checklist

Speaker: _____ Date: _____

Occasion: _____ Rater: _____

Articulation Evaluation Key:

Distortion = D   Substitution = S   Omission = O   Addition = A   Reversal = R

Consonants	Reading 1	Reading 2
p as in pat	____	____
b as in boat	____	____
t as in top	____	____
d as in dog	____	____
k as in key	____	____
g as in go	____	____
f as in four	____	____
v as in very	____	____
θ as in thin	____	____
ð as in the	____	____
s as in snake	____	____
z as in zoo	____	____
ʃ as in she	____	____
ʒ as in beige	____	____
h as in hot	____	____
ʍ as in where	____	____
w as in watch	____	____
r as in red	____	____
j as in yes	____	____
l as in left	____	____
m as in man	____	____
n as in no	____	____
ŋ as in sing	____	____
tʃ as in chair	____	____
dʒ as in judge	____	____

Consonant Clusters

	Reading 1	Reading 2
str as in street	____	____
skr as in scrap	____	____
tl as in little	____	____

Vowels	Reading 1	Reading 2
i as in see	____	____
ɪ as in sit	____	____
e as in ate	____	____
ɛ as in bet	____	____
æ as in pat	____	____
a as in ask	____	____
ɑ as in calm	____	____
ɔ as in awful	____	____
o as in so	____	____
ʊ as in book	____	____
u as in too	____	____
ʌ as in up	____	____
ə as in banana	____	____
ɝ-ɜ as in early	____	____
ɚ as in father	____	____

Other articulatory features:

	1	2
Consonant omissions	____	____
Consonant additions	____	____
Dentalized d, t	____	____
Intrusive r	____	____
Final unvoicing	____	____
Lisp (type)	____	____
Excess sibilance	____	____
Assimilation	____	____
Dialect (type	____	____
Other_____	____	____
_____	____	____
_____	____	____
_____	____	____

Diphthongs	Reading 1	Reading 2
ɑɪ as in ice	____	____
ɑʊ as in how	____	____
ɔɪ as in coin	____	____
eɪ as in day	____	____
oʊ as in glow	____	____
ɔɚ as in pour	____	____
ɛɚ as in air	____	____
ɑɚ as in car	____	____
ɪɚ as in peer	____	____
uɚ as in poor	____	____

Voice and Vocal Variety

Reading 1:

Pitch:	Appropriate	High	Low	Patterned	Monotonous	Other ____
Volume:	Adequate	Too loud	Weak	Uncontrolled	Monotonous	Other ____
Rate:	Appropriate	Too fast	Too slow	Hesitant	Monotonous	Other ____
Quality:	Appropriate	Nasal	Denasal	Breathy	Hoarse	Other ____

Reading 2:

Pitch:	Appropriate	High	Low	Patterned	Monotonous	Other ____
Volume:	Adequate	Too loud	Weak	Uncontrolled	Monotonous	Other ____
Rate:	Appropriate	Too fast	Too slow	Hesitant	Monotonous	Other ____
Quality:	Appropriate	Nasal	Denasal	Breathy	Hoarse	Other ____

Glossary

abdomen   The belly; contains the stomach.

abdominal breathing   A pattern of breathing that is typified by controlled movements of the abdominal muscles.

accent   (1) A pattern of pronunciation, stress, and intonation typical of the speech of a particular person, group, or geographical area. *See also* **dialect, standard speech, nonstandard speech, regionalism,** and **foreign accent.** (2) Stress given to a syllable in a word. *See also* **stress.**

acoustic   Pertaining to sound or to the qualities of a sound. See also **sound.**

acoustic noise   Unwanted sounds that may block out speech or make hearing difficult.

Adam's apple   A noticeable prominence on the front edge of the thyroid cartilage. *See also* **thyroid cartilage.**

affricate   A single consonant sound produced by following a plosive closely with a fricative. The first sound in the word *chew* is an affricate.

allophone   A variation of a phoneme. Although the variation may be noticeable, it is slight enough not to affect the meaning of a word. *See also* **phoneme.**

alveolar ridge   The gum ridge just behind the upper front teeth.

articulation   Movements of the speech organs to produce speech sounds.

articulators   The organs of speech used to produce speech sounds: tongue, lips, soft palate, hard palate, alveolar ridge, teeth, glottis.

arytenoid cartilage   Triangular-shaped cartilages in the larynx to which the vocal folds attach.

audition   The process of hearing.

back vowel   A vowel sound produced when the tongue is arched in the back part of the mouth, with the lips rounded. The vowel in the word *so* is a back vowel.

bilabial sounds   Consonants produced using both lips to block the breathstream, such as the first and last sounds in the word *pub.*

bilabial glide   A consonant sound produced with both lips moving. The first sound in *wet* is a glide.

blend   A sound that is the result of joining two sounds closely and smoothly together; for example, the first two consonants in *stall* and in *prove.*

breath control   Regulation of the exhalation rate during speech and voice production.

breathiness   An excessive loss of air while speaking. A breathy voice has a "whispery" quality.

breathing   The process of moving air in and out of the lungs for respiration.

breathstream   Air released from the lungs that is used to start vocal fold vibration and to produce consonants.

central nervous system   The part of the human nervous system composed of the brain and spinal cord.

circumflex   *See* **inflection.**

cognate sounds   Two consonant sounds that are made in the same place and the same manner. The only difference is that one is voiced and the other is voiceless. *See also* **place of production, method of articulation,** and **voiced** and **voiceless consonants.**

communication   The process by which an idea, thought, or feeling that arises in the mind of one person causes a similar idea, thought or feeling to arise in the mind of someone else.

complex tone   A sound wave having more than two frequencies. *See also* **frequency, waveform.**

consonant   A type of speech sound that is produced by completely or partially blocking the breathstream using the articulators. The first and last sounds in the word *kiss* are consonants.

cricoid cartilage   The ring-shaped cartilage at the base of the larynx.

decibel   The measurement unit of sound intensity.

denasality   Too little nasal resonance resulting in a voice that sounds as if the speaker has a stuffed nose. *See also* **nasality.**

dialect   A form of language spoken in a specific geographical area that differs from the official language of the larger area. *See also* **accent, regionalism,** and **foreign accent.**

diaphragm   The main muscle of respiration. It is located between the chest and abdominal cavities.

diction   The production of the sounds of a particular language and the selection of words of the language when speaking.

diphthong   A glide composed of two vowels, blended together, produced in a single syllable, as in the word *out.*

distortion   Defective production of a speech sound due to faulty placement, timing, pressure, direction, movement, or integration of the articulators. The sound produced resembles the desired one and can be readily identified, but it is not accurate enough to be considered standard.

duration   The length of a sound—how long it lasts.

ear training   Learning auditory discrimination between accurate and inaccurate productions of a sound.

emphasis   Stress given to a word or phrase. *See* **stress.**

environmental noise   Factors in the communication situation, such as poor lighting and distracting movements that may distort speech between the speaker and listener.

excessive nasality   A voice quality resulting from too much nasal resonance. *See also* **nasality.**

exhalation   The process of expelling air from the body during breathing.

external auditory canal   A canal leading from the external ear to the tympanic membrane (eardrum).

force   In sound production, the energy that activates a vibrator.

foreign accent   A pattern of pronunciation, stress, and intonation in a person's second language (or foreign language) that reflects the phonetic traits of the person's first language.

frequency   When referring to sound, the number of vibrations per second. The unit of frequency is Hz (Hertz).

fricative   A type of consonant sound produced when the breathstream is forced through a narrow opening between two articulators. The first sound in the word *see* is a fricative.

front vowel   A vowel sound produced with the tongue arched in the front part of the mouth, with the lips slightly spread. The vowel in the word *see* is a front vowel.

gestures   Movements of the body or extremities that accompany speech.

glide   A consonant sound produced while the articulators are in motion. The first sound in the word *wet* is a glide.

glottal fry   A rough, bubbly, crackling voice quality that usually occurs in the lower part of the pitch range.

glottis   The opening between the vocal folds.

gum ridge   *See* **alveolar ridge.**

habitual pitch   The pitch level at which a person usually begins production.

hard palate   The roof of the mouth, lying between the alveolar (gum) ridge and the soft palate.

hard glottal attack   A way of producing vowel sounds. The vocal folds are very tense, and the vowels begin abruptly. The vowels have a hard, explosive quality.

harsh voice   A rough-sounding voice that results from irregular vibration of the vocal folds.

hoarse voice   A voice that sounds both harsh and breathy. The vocal folds are not able to close completely.

Hz (hertz)   The unit of measurement of frequency, named for the physicist Heinrich Hertz.

illiteracy   The lack of ability to read or write.

inflection   Pitch changes that occur during phonation. They may be rising, falling, or circumflex (a combination of both).

inhalation   The process of taking air into the body during breathing.

innervation   The process of supplying nerve impulses to muscles.

intensity   The power of a sound.

International Phonetic Alphabet (IPA)   An alphabet that uses a special set of symbols to represent the sounds of a language. Because the IPA has one distinct symbol to represent each sound of a language, there may be little correlation with spelling using the conventional alphabet, where a symbol may represent more than one sound.

intonation   The pattern of pitch changes in connected speech; the "melody" of a language.

key   The average pitch level of a segment of connected speech. *See also* **pitch.**

kinesics   The study of body movement, posture, and facial expression as a means of communication.

labio-dental sounds   Consonant sounds produced by using the lower lip and the upper teeth. The first sound in *first* is a labio-dental consonant.

language   An agreed-upon set of symbols, written and/or spoken, used in a uniform way by a number of people in order to communicate with each other.

larynx   The structure for producing voice. Composed of cartilage and muscle, it is the uppermost part of the trachea.

lateral consonant   The first sound in *leaf.* It is produced with the gum ridge and tongue. Air is emitted at the sides of the mouth (laterally).

lateral continuant   The first sound in the word *leaf.* It is produced with the tongue on the gum ridge. Air is emitted at the sides of the mouth (laterally).

lateral emission lisp   Production of the sounds [s] and [z] with the tongue tip touching the gum ridge, as if to make the sound [l]. The result is substitution of [ʃ] for [s] and [ʒ] for [z].

lingua-alveolar consonants   Consonant sounds that are produced with the tongue touching or near the gum ridge. The first and last sounds in *sit* are lingua-alveolar consonants.

lingua-dental consonants   Consonant sounds that are produced with the tongue touching the teeth. The first sound in the word *thumb* is a lingua-dental consonant.

lingua-palatal consonants   Consonant sounds that are produced with the middle and back of the tongue raised toward the hard palate. The first sound in the word *ship* is a lingua-palatal consonant.

lingual protrusion lisp   Production of the sounds [s] and [z] with the tip of the tongue against or between the front teeth—resulting in the sounds [θ] and [ð] instead of [s] and [z].

linguistic noise   Noise caused by language misuse: faulty grammar, syntax, incorrect word choice, faulty sound production, and so on.

linguistics   The study of language, in general, or the study of the sounds and structure of a particular language.

listener-generated noise   Psychological and perceptual factors within the listener that may reduce communication effectiveness. For example, if you dislike or fear a particular person, you may not listen objectively to that person's message.

literacy   The ability to read and write.

loudness   The psychological sensation of sound intensity.

lungs   Respiratory organs located in the chest.

mandible   The lower jawbone.

mass   Thickness, when referring to a vibrating object, such as the vocal folds.

medium   A substance capable of and necessary for transmitting sound vibrations; for example, sound travels easily through both air and water.

metallic voice   A usually high-pitched voice that sounds both strident and harsh. *See also* **harsh voice** and **strident.**

method of articulation   The physical processes used to produce a consonant sound. For example, the method of articulation of the plosive that is the first sound of the word *too*—you stop the breathstream by pressing the tongue against the alveolar ridge, building up air pressure, and letting the air "explode." Other methods of articulation are fricative, glide, nasal, lateral, affricate.

mid-vowel   A vowel sound that is produced when the tongue is arched in the middle part of the mouth. The first sound in the word *up* is a mid-vowel.

misarticulation   Inaccurate or imprecise production of a phoneme.

muscle tension   The amount of contraction of the tongue muscles when producing vowel sounds. The degree of muscle tension varies with each vowel, and vowels are said to be either *tense* or *lax*.

nasal   Consonant sound produced with air emitted from the nose rather than the mouth as in *morning*. Also refers to resonance of sounds in the nasal cavities. *See also* **nasality** and **resonance**.

nasal cavity   Passageway to the pharynx from the nostrils. *See also* **pharynx**.

nasality   The quality of the voice that results from the degree of nasal resonance by the nasal cavities.

nasopharynx   The nasal portion of the pharynx. *See also* **pharynx**.

noise   A barrier to communication: unwanted sound.

nonfluencies   Repetitions, hesitations, distortions, and interjections found in everyday speech.

nonsense syllables   Sounds combined into meaningless syllables meant to be said aloud, such as *ga-ga-ga*.

nonstandard speech   Speech that is considered to be significantly different from the speech generally accepted as the "standard." *See also* **standard speech**.

nonverbal communication   All the modes and behaviors of communication, either intentional or unintentional, other than the symbolic meanings of the words themselves.

objective characteristics   Qualities that are observable and measurable with instruments and are not subject to interpretation.

omission   Failure to produce a sound where there should be one.

oral cavity   The portion of the mouth extending as far back as the pharynx. *See also* **pharynx**.

oropharynx   The point of the pharynx immediately behind the mouth, below the nasopharynx, and above the pharynx. *See also* **nasopharynx** and **pharynx**.

paralanguage   All the audible elements that accompany speech and increase or decrease the meanings of words: loudness, stress, pitch, pitch variation, rate, rhythm, and voice quality. *How* you say something, rather than *what* you say.

paralinguistic noise   Interference caused by factors other than language itself. *See also* **paralinguistics**.

paralinguistics   All the audible elements of speech other than language itself, such as loudness, rate, rhythm, pitch, and stress.

pause   A temporary stop in speech.

pausing   Using pauses at the end of thought groups or utterances to enhance meaning and to provide opportunities for inhalation. *See also* **phrasing**.

pharynx　The throat.

phonation　The production of vocal sounds using the vocal folds. *See also* **vocal folds.**

phoneme　A "family" of sounds in a language, acoustically very similar. We generally recognize the entire sound family as one sound, different from all the other phonemes of the language. The phoneme functions in a language to signal a difference in meaning.

phonemics　The study of the meaningful units of a language.

phonetics　The study of the individual sounds of a language—their production and transcription into written symbols of the International Phonetic Alphabet (IPA).

phrasing　Grouping words for better understanding or meaning; this grouping does not necessarily form a complete sentence and may not follow written pronunciation. *See also* **pausing** and **thought group.**

phonation　The production of vocal sounds using the vocal folds. *See* **vocal folds.**

pitch　The subjective perception of the highness or lowness of a sound.

pitch range　The difference between the highest and lowest pitched sounds a given individual can produce. Most people have a range of about two octaves. *See also* **pitch.**

place of articulation　The point at which the breathstream is obstructed to produce a consonant sound. The place of articulation of the first sound in the word *bee* is bilabial (both lips). Other places of articulation are labio-dental (lip-teeth), lingua-dental (dental (tongue-teeth), lingua-alveolar (tongue-gum ridge), lingua-alveolo-palatal (tongue-gum ridge-palate), lingua-palatal (tongue-palate), and glottal (vocal folds). *See also* **articulation, articulators,** and **consonant.**

place of production　The part of the tongue primarily responsible for production of a given vowel; for example, the vowel in the word *bee* is produced with the front of the tongue.

plosive　A consonant sound produced by blocking the airstream completely, building up pressure, and suddenly exploding the air. The first and last sounds in *top* are plosives.

primary stress　Application of more force to one syllable of a word than to the other syllables. The result is to make the syllable receiving primary stress noticeably the loudest in the word. *See also* **stress.**

projection　Use of enough vocal force to be heard by all your listeners or to be heard at a distance. *See also* **loudness.**

pure tone　A sound consisting of one frequency of vibration.

quality　The subjective interpretation of a sound based on its physical characteristics of frequency, intensity, phase, and so on.

rate　The number of words spoken per minute.

regional dialect   *See* **regionalism** and **accent.**

regionalism   The type of speech used and accepted in a particular area; similar to a dialect. *See* **accent.**

resonance   Amplification and modification of sound either by an air-filled chamber, such as the cavities of the vocal tract, or by another object that vibrates sympathetically.

rest breathing   Breathing when not talking. The rate and depth of inhalation and exhalation are roughly equal.

rising inflection   See **inflection.**

schwa   The neutral, unstressed mid-vowel. It is produced with the least energy of any of the vowels and is typical of unstressed syllables in spoken English. The last sound in the word *sofa* is the schwa. It is the most common vowel in English. *See also* **unstressed.**

secondary stress   Application of a degree of force (loudness) to a syllable that is greater than unstressed but less than the syllable receiving primary stress; for example, the middle syllable in the word *regional* receives a secondary stress, the first syllable receives primary stress, and the last syllable is unstressed.

sine wave   Periodic oscillation. Represented geometrically as a sine function.

sinus   A cavity or hollow in a bone. There are several sinus cavities in the face near the nose and eyes.

soft palate   The soft, muscular, moveable, rear-most portion of the roof of the mouth; also called the velum.

sound   Vibrations in a medium that stimulate the organs of hearing and produce the sensation of hearing.

speech discrimination   *See also* **ear training.**

stage fright   A combination of fear and excitement usually occurring before speaking situations.

standard speech   The way the majority of educated speakers in a large geographical area speak. The generally "correct" way of speaking.

step   An abrupt pitch change between syllables or words.

stress   Application of force to a word or syllable so that it appears to be "larger" and louder. *See* **unstressed, primary stress, tertiary stress, schwa, syllable stress, word stress.**

strident   A vocal quality that is high pitched, tense, and metallic.

subjective characteristics   Qualities that are not observable and measurable with instruments. They are subject to interpretation by the listener.

substitution   Production of one phoneme in place of another desired one.

syllable stress   *See* **stress.**

syntax The grammatical pattern or structure of words in a sentence or phrase.

tension In voice production, the act of making the edges of the vocal folds thinner and tighter to produce a higher pitched sound.

tertiary stress *See* **unstressed.**

thorax The chest.

thought group A grouping of words in a phrase or sentence that is complete in meaning and can stand by itself. A thought group is usually distinguished by pauses and is similar to a written sentence or phrases set off by punctuation. *See* **pause, pausing,** and **phrasing.**

throaty A vocal quality that seems lacking in resonance and strength; it seems to come from the back of the throat.

thyroid cartilage The largest cartilage of the larynx, shaped like a shield and forming the front wall.

tongue height The distance the tongue is moved from the floor of the mouth toward the roof in the production of vowels. For example, the vowel in the word *bee* is a *high* vowel, while the vowel in the word *on* is a *low* vowel.

trachea A tube composed mainly of cartilage, connecting the lungs with the pharynx. Commonly called the windpipe.

transcription Using the written symbols of the International Phonetic Alphabet to record speech sounds as they are heard, rather than as they are spelled. *See also* **International Phonetic Alphabet.**

unstressed Application of the least amount of force (loudness) possible to a syllable. An unstressed syllable is noticeably weaker and lower-pitched than syllables receiving primary and secondary stress. The last sound in the word *regional* is unstressed. *See* **schwa, stress, primary stress,** and **secondary stress.**

velum *See* **soft palate.**

vibrator An object that when set in vibration transmits its energy to the molecules of the medium around it, resulting in the production of sound. For example, the vocal folds are set into vibration in the process of phonation. See also **sound, medium, phonation.**

visualization Using mental images of a successful speaking situation, in advance of the actual situation, to reduce nervousness.

vocal expression The use of rate, phrasing, intonation, and stress to make speech meaningful, to gain attention, and to add interest.

vocal folds Two small bands of tissue located in the larynx. They can be made to vibrate in the airstream from the lungs and create voice.

vocal fry *See* **glottal fry.**

vocal tract The part of speech mechanism above the level of the vocal folds. It is where speech sounds generated by the vocal folds are modified and amplified. The vocal tract includes the pharynx, the oral cavity, and the nasal cavity.

voice   Vocal sound produced by the vibration of the vocal cords. *See* **phonation.**

voiced consonant   A consonant produced with voice. The first sound in *back* is voiced, the last sound is voiceless.

voiceless consonant   A consonant sound produced without voice. The first sound in *kid* is voiceless, the last sound is voiced.

waveform   A graphic representation of a sound wave showing amplitude (intensity) over a period of time.

word stress   *See* **stress.**

Permissions Acknowledgments

Index